# THE WORLD OF CONSUMPTION

For some social theorists the consumer is king. The tastes and preferences of the individual, communicated through the magic mechanism of the market, dictate what is produced and whether producers succeed or fail. For others consumption traps the individual in a fetish-like devotion to goods that can never satisfy real needs. Both positions have reached an apotheosis in the last decade, with the unequivocal arrival of the 'consumer society'.

*The World of Consumption* presents a critical analysis of the major social theories of consumption before proceeding to develop a new, more inclusive theory. The authors argue that individual commodities create their own distinct 'systems of provision', processes by which production, distribution, marketing and consumption are vertically integrated. Hence the function of marketing in the fashion industry is better explained by the function of other aspects of this industry than by comparison with marketing in the food industry. The book supports this argument with extensive case studies of the food and clothing systems.

**Ben Fine** is Professor of Economics and Director of the Centre for Economic Policy for Southern Africa at the School of Oriental and African Studies. He has served as economic adviser to the Industry and Employment Branch of the Greater London Council, to the NUM and to the ANC.

**Ellen Leopold** has been a research associate at the University of London (Birkbeck College and the Bartlett School of Architecture at University College) and has worked as an economic adviser to a variety of local and regional planning authorities, including the Greater London Council. She is currently based in Massachusetts.

# THE WORLD OF CONSUMPTION

*Ben Fine and Ellen Leopold*

London and New York

First published 1993
by Routledge
11 New Fetter Lane, London EC4P 4EE

Simultaneously published in the USA and Canada
by Routledge
29 West 35th Street, New York, NY 10001



Typeset in Garamond by
Ponting–Green Publishing Services, Chesham, Bucks
Printed in Great Britain by
Biddles Ltd, Guildford and Kings Lynn



*British Library Cataloguing in Publication Data*
A catalogue record for this book is available from
the British Library

*Library of Congress Cataloging in Publication Data*
*has been applied for*

ISBN 0–415–09588–3 (HB)
ISBN 0–415–09589–1 (PB)

# CONTENTS

## Part V Concluding perspectives

# LIST OF FIGURES

# PREFACE

The idea for this book grew out of work originally supported by the Leverhulme Trust which sponsored our researches into the world of consumption (and its connection to female labour market participation). A previous volume, by Ben Fine, *Women's Employment and the Capitalist Family*, was published by Routledge in 1992. Work on the socioeconomic patterns of consumer durable ownership, co-authored by Ben Fine, Nigel Foster, John Simister and Judith Wright, has been reported in a series of SOAS Working Papers. During the final revisions to this book, research has been funded by the ESRC for a project, 'What We Eat and Why: A Socioeconomic Study of Standard Items in Food Consumption', as part of its Research Programme, 'The Nation's Diet'. We are indebted to these funding bodies and to fellow workers for their invaluable support.

The opportunity to explore many strands of consumer theory falling loosely under the umbrella of the social sciences, revealed to us that, far from being enriched by, or benefitting from shared concerns, each discipline narrowly pursued its own theoretical interests with a shortsightedness that left much unexplained or inadequately accounted for. The failure of these theories for the most part, even to grapple with the broader questions thrown up by consumer behaviour, prompted our own interest in searching for a more constructive framework.

The solution we are proposing here – an approach to the world of consumption through systems of provision – is our response to that search. It provides an analytical framework that we hope is both sufficiently general and sufficiently sensitive to encompass the wide variety of consumption goods, their determinants and their significance. Along the way, support for the work has come in a number of ways from our friends and colleagues. We would like to thank them all and, in particular, John Mason, Sarah Smith and Lynne Walker. We are also grateful to those who have allowed the reproduction of copyright material. Last, but not least, we would like to thank each other for sustained good humour and the forbearance that is inevitably tested to the limit by a joint and transatlantic project of this kind.

# Part I

# ANALYTICAL FOUNDATIONS

# 1

# INTRODUCTION AND OVERVIEW

In our thinking, our practices and our theory, the role of consumption has been thrust into a position of prominence in a way that is historically unprecedented. Despite the fact that the vast majority of the world's population still lives on the margins of survival, the preoccupations of the First World set the terms of reference for debate over consumption. Within this framework, money is increasingly deployed by consumers, not only to house, clothe and feed themselves but increasingly to support leisure and other activities, to gratify the five senses and the seven sins, to define a lifestyle if not a *persona* itself. You are what you eat, where you live, what you drive, what you drink; the list of correspondences is as endless as the choices that confront us. The continuing categorical relevance of poverty, unemployment and class as modes of stratification has been undermined by the rise of market segmentation for classes of consumption.

How is consumption to be understood? Are we the manipulated mannequins of the advertising industry, the sovereignless victims of profit-hungry corporate capital, rational economic men and women trading off one commodity against another according to their relative prices and utilities? Or are we the continuing repositories of custom, culture and family habits, slavishly obeying the imperative to emulate the Joneses.

Such questions provide plentiful proof that both popular and more analytical explanations of consumption abound. On the whole, they tend to emphasise the gratification of deeper motives or the release of other explanatory attributes. The discipline of economics, for example, argues that consumption bestows utility; in sociology, it may well be status or social position; in psychology, it is a conditioned response to gain a level of well-being; in anthropology, it has been interpreted in terms of its symbolic role in ritual, etc. More critically, consumption can also be viewed as a passive response to the goods that manufacturers offer, with tastes manipulated to guarantee sales and profitability.

What all of these approaches have in common, whether expressed in popular or academic discourse, is what we term a 'horizontal' understanding of consumption. Whatever factors are taken to be of importance are presumed to apply generally across the economy or society as a whole. For example, members of all (but the top) social strata are presumed to emulate the tastes and habits of those occupying the next level (or more) above them; similarly 'hidden persuaders' employed by the 'tastemakers' apply equally to a very wide range of product. This type of generalisation is a direct consequence of horizontal theorising.

In fact, we know from our own experience alone how complex and varied are the factors involved in consumption. There are the economic variables of price and income, sociological variables of family and status, psychological variables of motivation and habit, cultural variables of tastes and meaning, and not least the practical variables surrounding the actual activities of shopping, preparation, disposal or even repair. It is inconceivable that any one general theory of consumption will suffice. There would simply be too much *ceteris paribus* to swallow.

None the less, the social sciences, compartmentalised into their separate disciplines, have unsurprisingly tended to construe consumption by an exclusive reliance upon their own terms of reference. Economics provides the classic example; it is notorious for its presumption that preferences (which are left unexplained) remain fixed, even across generations of the population separated by profound economic and social change (in economic studies of demand over the long run, for example). The principle of utility maximisation subject to price and income constraints is generalised across the economy as a whole to all commodities (and to all of them simultaneously).

The example of economics, whose theory of consumption has not found favour amongst other disciplines, illustrates the isolating fragmentation of consumption analysis. Each of the many horizontal approaches begins with a particular factor considered crucial to the determination of consumption and generalises from it across the economy as a whole.

The contrasting framework adopted in this book is termed a 'vertical' approach. It too is deceptively simple, characterised by the following features. First, it expects different commodities or groups of commodities to be distinctly structured by the chain or system of provision that unites a particular pattern of production with a particular pattern of consumption. Put simply, it does not search for common elements across all aspects of consumption but looks instead for differences in the way in which production and consumption are united together and the ways in which each is moderated by the connections between them. In explaining consumption, it is not sufficient to depend upon its proximate determinants – in tastes, prices or habit – nor to swing to the opposite extreme and render the system of production the sole or main determinant of what is consumed, important though it is. Production is itself variously organised, whether as mass production of uniform commodities or not. Equally important, production is connected to consumption by shifting systems of distribution, by retailing as well as by the cultural reconstruction of the meaning of what is consumed.

Different systems of provision across commodity groups then, are the consequence of distinct relationships between the various material and cultural practices comprising the production, distribution, circulation and consumption of the goods concerned.

This approach to the determinants of consumption is set out in Chapter 2. In some ways, it is by no means original. Many before have relied upon systems of provision to explain the consumption of particular goods, referring to the housing, food, energy or transport systems, etc. But such reference to systems of provision has usually been on a case-by-case basis, reflecting analytical specialisation in that commodity rather than the confining framework of an academic discipline. Consequently, the more general requirements for analysing consumption as a whole, or in constructing a theory of consumption, have understandably been overlooked. We posit an approach to consumption should always be based on the recognition of distinct systems of provision across commodities, and argue that such an approach needs to be acknowledged theoretically to emphasise the integrity of separate systems of provision and to encourage recognition of the important differences between them. Each system of provision is a species of a different genus, whose anatomy must be carefully and differentially reconstructed analytically from its constituent components. Construed in this way, consumption is placed beyond the framework offered by horizontal approaches from within a particular social science.

In pursuing our own analysis we open up two analytical avenues. One is a critical assessment of the treatment of consumption within individual disciplines of the social sciences. It is presented in Part II. In general, as already observed, these are found to rely upon horizontal analyses which begin with a particular variable, structure or process appropriate to their own discipline and generalise from it across all areas of consumption. The second avenue opens up the examination of specific consumption goods, an exercise undertaken for food and clothing in Part III.

From our perspective, horizontal theories of consumption from within particular academic disciplines necessarily entail two types of error. On the one hand, understanding the determinants and significance of particular consumption goods is misplaced since they are subject to overgeneralisation and to the absence of other crucial factors. On the other hand, the role of the particular horizontal factors involved is also misunderstood, since they are not differentiated by commodity and located relative to the systems of provision of which they form a part. These points are illustrated in Part III by reference to the food and clothing industries (as particular systems of provision) and to advertising (as a particular horizontal factor). However, even if they are not appropriately ordered analytically, the various contributions from the social sciences do perform the positive function of identifying the extremely diverse range of determinants involved. Indeed, it is possible to obtain analytical support for our approach to consumption from those very approaches that do not themselves employ it. It can be done by drawing positively upon other approaches in so far as, taken collectively, they suggest an extremely diverse range of determinants, each often associated with a horizontal approach within a particular academic discipline.

Within this framework, Part II seeks to provide a broad but *selective* survey of theories of consumption across the social sciences. Hopefully, it will provide a lead that can be taken up in greater detail and depth by others who are expert practitioners within the fields concerned (but who are prepared to acknowledge the limitations of remaining confined within their own discipline). Whatever the intellectual demands involved, this is no easy practical task. For, as will be seen, each of the academic disciplines has tended to avoid a coherent and systematic treatment of consumption, in contrast to detailed attention to production. Accordingly, whilst this neglect has often been exaggerated, especially by those who seek to redress it, the analysis of consumption as a subject in its own right has been fragmented even within the separate academic disciplines – although, apart from economics with its narrow analytical scope, marketing alone is something of an exception partly because it is driven by the primary motivation to effect a sale rather than to explain it.

A further obstacle to a comprehensive survey of thought on consumption is the absence of any substantive overlap between treatments in the various disciplines. It is not simply the co-existence of mutually exclusive explanatory factors; the definition of the subject itself differs markedly from one discipline to the next. Just as one person's meat is another's poison, so consumption is variously interpreted. For some it is a ritual, for others a means of class distinction and status, a means of satisfying utility or broader psychological impulses, etc. Within economics, consumption tends to be associated with movements of or along demand curves; in advertising and some of the work on material culture, it concerns the creation of real or imaginary lifestyles through the reconstruction of our objects of desire. As display, consumption can be the means of exercising as well as of enjoying power, revealed as much in the conspicuous consumption of the Sun King in the Palace of Versailles, as in wielding control of the beer money as the prerogative of the male head of household.

This distance between the disciplines is sharply illustrated by the state of the relatively new field of consumer behaviour which has primarily been pursued in the United States. Its aim has been to synthesise the various contributions to the understanding of consumer behaviour and to constitute itself as a separate discipline with its own independent momentum. But the goal remains elusive. The lack of any substantial consensus in basic concepts inhibits the progressive development of a truly interdisciplinary (as opposed to a multidisciplinary) approach. Consequently, as revealed in Chapter 3, the discipline of consumer behaviour finds itself to be in a self-confessed state of almost perpetual crisis, unable to constitute itself as a well-defined discipline in its own right, with its own momentum, and mostly parasitic upon its constituent social sciences as a source of innovation. It is incapable of providing stable theoretical frameworks supported by empirical regularities. In short, the theory of consumer behaviour seems to add up to less than its constituent parts, which have in practice proved primarily to be psychology, sociology and economics. This conclusion for consumer behaviour theory confirms, then, the earlier observation of the lack of overlap between the various disciplines' horizontal approaches to consumption – an issue taken up later in greater detail for the separate contributions made by psychology and economics. That they cannot be usefully combined poses a different issue, one that from our perspective is hardly surprising. Just as each discipline necessarily overgeneralises the significance and uniformity of the role played by the factors that fall within its scope, so any combination across them is inappropriate unless such interactions are sensitive to differences between the various systems of provision across commodities. It is not enough to add more variables or more disciplines. These have to be specifically oriented to the structuring of the consumption of the particular commodity (or non-commodity) concerned.

To some extent, the conundrums posed by the relationship between general theory and specific commodities are revealed by a further feature of consumer behaviour theory. Reflecting its lack of adequate roots in and across its constituent parts is its impoverished status as a 'middle-range' theory which employs more abstract concepts to situate and explain what is more concretely observed empirically. These concepts, like lifestyle or emulation, are summoned to explain the purchase and consumption of particular goods, but tend themselves to be suspended without support from any grander theory (as is generally required by proponents of middle-range theory). Consequently, explanation is simply shifted on to the more abstract concepts without any effective answer to the question of causation, apart from the informal meaning attached to the notions embodied in the middle-range abstractions.

Chapter 4 looks critically at the contribution made by economics to the understanding of consumption. An orthodox economist would probably argue that the subject, in the form of demand theory, commands one half of the discipline – with the other half taken up by supply – so that the issue has been rigorously and deeply, if not comprehensively, addressed. Nevertheless, consumer theory within economics occupies an extraordinarily narrow terrain. Although some advance has been made in the sophistication of mathematical techniques and statistical estimation, there has been little advance or shift in conceptual content since the marginalist revolution of the previous century. Prevailing theory still construes individuals as behaving rationally in maximising the production of their own utility subject to the income and price constraints they face. This is the simple conceptual basis for individual decision-making. What is specifically consumed, how much, and with what continuing effects, are essentially irrelevant to the theory – beyond their presumed contribution to generating maximum attainable utility. Everything is abstracted from quantities (of unspecified goods), prices and income – and given preferences. Moreover, the origins of individual preferences remain unexplored as if inherited at birth as part of an innate drive to seek out higher levels of goods up a (presumably predetermined) scale of gratification.

It is further argued here that from a broader perspective, economics does not effectively have a theory of *consumption*, as distinct from (its own theory of) production. For, as all students of economics know, the principles underlying the derivation of consumption are identical to those for production even if the words used are different. Each 'rational economic man' is an entrepreneur setting about the minimisation of the cost of producing a given number of utils (rather than widgets), subject to the prices of inputs (consumption goods rather than capital and labour). The mechanics of indifference curves are identical to those of isoquants.

It is not, however, simply that economics is narrow in its perception of what consumption is and of how it is determined. The theory associates itself with extracting the systematic core of 'rational' economic behaviour so that any deviations are labelled as irrational, or located outside the realm of economics altogether, or both. In short, economics provides the horizontal approach to consumption *par excellence*. It is able to furnish a system of demand across all commodities simultaneously, but only at the expense of the most egregious omission of other demonstrably crucial causal factors.

This explains the uneasy relationship between the economics and the psychology of consumption taken up in Chapter 5. It confirms that the two disciplines have very little meeting ground on which to construct a theory of consumer behaviour, and that they are otherwise mutually incompatible. Psychology itself understands consumer behaviour by relying on a much more complex and varied set of motivational and behavioural factors, some corresponding to the rational–conscious–observable–individual, others to the irrational–unconscious–unobservable–social, each of these two mixes having only a rough internal congruence. And like economics, psychology tends to discount as 'irrational' any behaviour that lies outside its (broader) realm of explanation. The latter is reduced to the behaviour patterns of individuals or to the therapeutic content of objects of consumption. Consumers are, as it were, human rats even if responding to, and with, a wider range of motives, stimuli and abilities.

Ultimately, then, the role of psychology in consumer behaviour theory can be seen as a sort of commodity fetishism in which both commodities and individuals are endowed with a variety of what are taken to be causal properties. Whilst accommodating a much broader view of rationality than that of economics, it none the less leads to a very partial and incomplete view of the *social* processes, interpreted in the broadest sense, by which consumption decisions are formed. The attributes of both consumers and consumed have to be formed before they are brought together. And how they are formed will be different for different commodity systems. Neglect of these linkages is less apparent in social psychology, which borders more closely on the field of sociology; its contribution, through emulation theory, will be taken up later.

Chapter 6 is concerned with the notion of consumer society, consumerism or the consumer revolution. These concepts are popularly used to explain, and often to condemn, the mores and practices of present-day society, with its presumed opposition between the creation and satisfaction of 'false' and 'real' needs. But as a concept with analytical content, consumer society is found to be both vague and insubstantial. First, a glance at some of the history of consumption reveals that consumer society can be traced back hundreds of years. Applied to the distant past, it has too readily been associated with bursts of consumption, often of particular, newly available items, even though this is almost inevitably a concomitant of any period of economic growth, the more noticeable in retrospect because associated with the luxury or conspicuous consumption of the wealthy, and hence more likely to have survived and to have acquired antique value in the present.

For the nineteenth and twentieth centuries, however, the analysis of the consumer revolution is inevitably richer. It has been linked to particular transmission mechanisms, such as the retail or distribution revolutions (via transport and communications). It has been seen as the counterpart to the mass production of uniform consumption goods. Advertising has been considered crucial in creating a domestic revolution around the working-class consumer, primarily represented through the purchases of the housewife – with the major exception of the male prerogative over the motor car. Paradoxically, the consumer revolution has served simultaneously to suggest increasing uniformity, even democratisation, of consumption *and* increasing differentiation as particular market segments, whether men or women, rich or poor, young or old, are cast as vanguards of demand, leading the economy forward. Critical assessment of such notions confirms the usefulness of the alternative approach proposed in Part I, based on the presumed co-existence of heterogeneous systems of provision.

Such discussions do suggest, however, that demand theory must be treated more seriously as a factor in determining economic and social change. Unfortunately, orthodox economics has not proved useful in this regard, as suggested in Chapter 7 in the context of changing approaches to the British Industrial Revolution. This is for two main reasons. First, the orthodoxy is primarily concerned with the grinding out of equilibrium on the basis of exogenously given parameters such as tastes and technology. This leaves too much of the work of explanation still to be done and the main factors in determining change left unexplored. Second, orthodox economics constructs a notion of the long run which not only is based upon equilibrium but which is also independent of the role of demand – it is assumed that long-run equilibrium is determined by full employment of resources even if the short run allows for macroeconomic deviations from it, whether for reasons of uncertainty or disequilibrium.

There are, however, radical theories which do suggest a greater role for demand. But these, especially in the monopoly capital school of Marxism associated with underconsumption (the tradition of Baran and Sweezy and Kalecki), emphasise how demand limits growth and is stagnationary. Much the same is true of Adam Smith's idea of the limitations on the division of labour imposed by the extent of the market (the source of productivity increase and, thereby, the wealth of nations). Malthus offers a more promising view emphasising the progressive role for employment played by the unproductive expenditures of the wealthy and idle.

Within economic history, then, it has proved difficult to incorporate the role of demand in explaining major changes other than on a sector-by-sector basis. Rather, economic history has tended to be a supply side subject, focusing on production and technology, entrepreneurship and work. However, there has been a counter-current which attempts to place greater stress upon demand as an alternative or complementary source of change. This is perhaps most prominent in the attempt to reinterpret the Industrial Revolution as a consumer revolution, assessed critically in Chapter 10 in the context of clothing.

The notion of an eighteenth-century consumer revolution contains some theoretical elements of more general applicability. Although not analytically profound, they may be complex in practice. Essentially, the idea is that growth and change are induced by an outward shift in demand. This is itself problematic, for how can added demand be realised for the economy as a whole in the absence of pre-existing excess capacity otherwise leading to the expansion of one sector at the expense of another? Shifts in demand can hardly be considered as autonomous from other factors. They are, however, often treated as such, most commonly conveyed through the vehicle of emulation (or trickle-down effects). Demand in this construct first arises spontaneously amongst the elite and is then diffused throughout society. Renewed differentiation at the top repeats the cycle as luxuries progressively become decencies and decencies become necessities. In this way, demand both sustains itself and spurs the continuing economic growth of supply.

It is even argued that such diffusion of tastes stimulates the emergence of a market for mass production, even though the changes in demand are associated with product differentiation and market fragmentation, traditionally seen as obstacles to the efficiency gained from scale economies. In short, there are considerable doubts surrounding the role of demand as an autonomous factor in economic and social change. Nor are these dispelled by simply complementing the theory of demand with a theory of supply. For this still leaves unexplained the underlying nature of supply and demand and the factors that alter them. At best, the result produces a structured, descriptive narrative of change. More generally, analysis of consumption, whether as cause or effect, through supply and demand, merely begs the question of what makes these what they are, and the answer must be sought differently sector by sector as a multitude of factors comes to the fore.

Discussion of consumption and growth completes Part II which is primarily concerned with theoretical issues, with reference to the occasional illustrative example. The intention is to shed light on the strengths and limitations of theories of consumption by examining them through the prism of the systems-of-provision approach. The balance between theoretical and empirical material is partially reversed in Part III, where the virtues of the alternative analysis are revealed through case studies provided by food, clothing and advertising. Those interested in these illustrations, rather than critical theoretical assessments, might skip or skim Part II.

Chapter 8, opening Part III, sets the stage for the subsequent elaboration of systems of provision in clothing and food. It highlights the continuity and long-term impact of basic distinguishing features that underpin the historical divergence between systems of provision. Chapter 9 builds upon these foundations to investigate the clothing system, with a particular focus on women's clothing in the first half of the twentieth century in the United States. The two standard approaches to this subject are rejected as inadequate. These either treat it narrowly on the demand side as a fickle product of (female) fashion or equally narrowly on the supply side as the consequence of the slow conquest of inherent technical obstacles to mass production. The analysis points instead to the evolution of the structure of provision of clothing as a whole, explaining rather than taking for granted both the pace of adoption of technical change and the relative importance of fashion. This, in turn, allows the difference between subsectors of the industry to be unravelled, not least between male and female clothing and its relation to standardised as opposed to differentiated products.

Clothing again provides the empirical basis for discussion in Chapter 10, but here set in the context of the late eighteenth century. The role of consumption in instigating economic change is taken up by exploring the putative consumer revolution of that period. Critically assessed is the view that economic growth was induced through the expansion of demand first stimulated by the wealthy and then sustained through its trickle-down to, and spread across, the lower orders – for which, supposedly, domestic servants provided a major transmission belt. The argument presented here is that the system of provision of clothing was more complex than such market-led emulation suggests, not least because servants' adoption of the habits of their employers was often just literally this. Servants depended on hand-me-downs, as part of salary-in-kind, and on the second-hand clothing market. Both of these serve, as does the servant system more generally, to *limit* rather than to enhance the market and the capacity to supply it. More broadly, it is argued that the mechanism of growth through the lead of market demand is either empirically questionable, ambiguous in its effect, or swamped by other, more fundamental factors, both quantitatively and causally, such as growing working-class incomes and urbanisation. Chapter 11 addresses the issue of trickle-down theory itself, on which the above argument is based, and points to both its broader theoretical limitations in the face of conflicting empirical evidence and its impact on the practices of other social sciences (especially economics). There are found to be hidden resonances with Reaganomics, which has been more readily assessed for its particular version of supply side economics rather than for its implications for the demand side and the virtues of supporting the elite for the benefits that they bestow on those beneath them.

Chapter 12 brings to the fore some of the special features that characterise the food industry as part of a comprehensive system. Here it is found that the critical features of food – its organic connection to its raw materials and to the human body – has skewed the development of its productive processes in distinctive ways. In other words, the pursuit of profitability has led to particular forms of preparation, preservation and packaging of food which distinguish it from those characterising other industries. The discussion is then linked to the issue of food adulteration – an offence which has been described as reaching a peak in the UK in the mid-nineteenth century. Once the particular imperatives and dynamics governing the production of food are admitted to the story, food adulteration, far from declining, can be perceived instead to have continued unabated. Repackaged and relabelled, it is now legalised in the form of allowed additives, etc., so that the problem of retaining food 'quality' over the time of production and sale can be resolved despite dependence on mass production of processed foods. The underlying imperatives guiding industrial development remain and are still crucial in determining what we eat as well as how we are led to (mis)construe what we eat.

Food remains the theme in Chapter 13, which has a number of purposes. First, it outlines the astonishing variety of what we eat and the apparent reasons we have for the choices we make. It suggests that orderly explanations of our diet cannot depend upon analysis of the proximate causes of choice alone. Where, then, does food choice originate? The standard explanation cites the trickle-down through the general population of scientific knowledge about what it is healthy to eat, although the knowledge is distorted and tempered by the advertising of those commercially involved. There is a parallel here with the analysis of clothing, where fashion is presumed to trickle down from an elite of consumers rather than from scientific professionals. But this explanation of cultural transmission is no more palatable in the context of food information than it is in the context of fashion.

This leads to a more wide-ranging assessment of theories of the determinants of food consumption across the social sciences, coupled with an examination of their application to particular foods. In general, each discipline tends to exploit food as an application of a more general theory of consumption, thereby adding very little to the understanding of food as such.

Inevitably, given the failure to create an interdisciplinary approach to consumption, the same lack of both overlap and potential synthesis across the various contributions is reproduced for food. Once again, this reflects the failure to trace the determinants of food consumption back through the systems of provision to their origins in production.

In Chapter 14 the literature on advertising is critically assessed to illustrate the limitations of what we have termed a horizontal approach, and then to open up the possibility for an alternative theoretical framework to be applied in the context of the clothing and food industries (in Chapters 15 and 16, respectively). The chapter's starting point is that there have previously been two different broad approaches to the subject, each corresponding to a different aspect of the commodity. The first is the use value approach and is primarily concerned with how the use values of commodities are subject to ideological reconstruction through advertising. This leads to various ways of reinterpreting the commodity according to the role assigned to consumption; adverts become an associated artefact of material culture. The economic content of the commodity, as opposed to the constructed source of its desirability, tends to be neglected.

The second approach focuses on exchange value and is primarily economic in content, seeking to locate advertising within the circulation of capital, as a lever of competition and as a means of manipulating demand. When this economic functioning is interpreted more broadly, and usually within a critical perspective, there is a marginal recognition of the ideological role of advertising in systemically creating a consumer society – however this might be conceived – to conform with the dictates of the era of mass production.

The performance of advertising in its economic and ideological roles is then briefly assessed. As in the overview of food choices, there is a bewildering array of factors to consider. It precludes the possibility of explaining the role of advertising by proximate influences alone – such as who advertises, how, and with what results. This serves to support the premise that each of the two approaches to advertising outlined previously, and the attempts to combine and synthesise them, leaves out of account the influence of capitalist production on the development of the commodity and, hence, on the development of advertising. The horizontal analytical perspective explores different commodities for their relation to media, culture, sexism, etc. We propose, instead, the application of a vertical perspective which views each commodity as the creation of an interdependent system of production, distribution, retailing and cultural determinants *including*, where appropriate, advertising. Recognising the special chain of linked factors that comprehensively defines a commodity makes it possible to explain the changing extent and nature of advertising rather than simply to interpret it where it does occur.

With this understanding of advertising, it becomes possible in Chapters 15 and 16 to contrast the role it plays, and the position it occupies, in the food and clothing systems. For the food system, both the sponsors of advertising and its scope have changed dramatically over time with the changing structure of production and retailing. The rise of superstores and the emergence of own-label goods competing with household names have been largely responsible for these changes. For clothing, branded advertising by garment manufacturers has until recently been much less prominent, with the exception of a few items of clothing such as jeans. The changing balance of advertising between producers, retailers and textile manufacturers has reflected the changing relations between them. Until recently, the heavy advertisers have been producers selling unbranded goods (to retailers) and textile manufacturers. The recent rise in popular design labels in women's clothing has altered this balance. The shift also highlights the different roles played by advertising in the promotion of men's and women's clothes which the chapter charts in some detail. Advertising practices now associated exclusively with women's wear are shown to have played a similar role in the development of menswear a hundred years earlier. Current differences in advertising in the two subsystems clearly reflect differences in the timing and pace of industrial development in each branch; these distinctions are lost to horizontal analyses that cut them off from their source in production and other parts of the systems of provision.

Part IV is once again primarily concerned with theoretical issues but here set in and around Marxist approaches. Chapter 17 considers what has been termed the new urban sociology, originating in Castells' notion that the city is a site of collective consumption. Crudely, for Castells, the diode factory/production has been displaced by that of city/consumption. This is taken to extremes in the work of Peter Saunders, which has been the subject of considerable debate. Saunders casts consumption as a social relation, demonstrated partly through differential access to the means of consumption, partly through the role of the state in making social provision, and partly through organised conflict over consumption. This has the effect of replacing production with consumption to yield theories in which the latter provides the potential for exploitation, defines different social strata, and serves as a starting point in the determination of other effects such as voting patterns. Whilst this view is rejected as theoretically and empirically unsatisfactory, especially where it simply substitutes consumption for production and makes consumption a crude determinant, it has, none the less, usefully raised certain problems. Though it places consumption and production in opposition to one another, it does at least focus on a relationship between them in which the former is not simply understood as a passive reflection of the latter. In addition, it brings the *social* organisation of consumption to the fore, and this necessarily raises the issue of the increasingly influential role of the state in consumption.

From our perspective, consideration of the role of the state in influencing consumption reinforces the argument for a theory based on systems of provision (a matter also taken up in the final chapter). For the role of the state is very different across the spectrum of goods; its involvement in the provision of housing, for example, diverges widely from its intervention in transport. And to a large extent, much of the new urban sociology was inspired by generalisations from housing (in a British context) which are not readily transferable to other commodities (or to non-commodity forms of provision, often characteristic of the welfare state).

Most recently, the field of cultural studies has looked at consumption more critically. Within this discipline, objects of consumption have become subjects for interpretation. In particular, cultural studies has recognised that the meaning of consumption is socially constructed, and that this is an important component in explaining what we consume and why. This is, however, not a novel insight – anthropology has long studied the significance of consumption as ritual, for example – but much greater emphasis has been placed of late on the cultural determinants and significance of consumption. As a result, Marxist theory has been targeted for criticism as too one-sided in its understanding and analysis of the commodity as use value and exchange value. Whilst this contradictory duality within the commodity has long been recognised, some have argued that undue attention has been paid to the exchange value aspect of the commodity at the expense of the socially constructed use value. The latter has also been too readily identified with its natural or physical properties alone rather than with its socially constructed characteristics.

Chapter 18 argues that Marx did not neglect either use value or consumption. The social construction of particular use values *did* lie outside the immediate scope of his political economy *unless* they were crucial to a general analysis of capital – as were money, labour power, means of production and consumption, and fixed capital. But Marx's analysis does not preclude a more detailed interpretation of particular items of consumption. It does, however, require an understanding of how commodities are produced and who affords them, before the ideology or culture with which they are accepted can itself be understood and interpreted. From our approach, the different position of commodities as items of consumption is already immanent in Marx's analysis of production, not just because they are different use values, however these are ultimately construed, but because they are produced, distributed and exchanged differently as well.

Accordingly, in Chapter 19, it is suggested that analysis of the social construction and interpretation of the use value of commodities has something to learn from Marx rather than vice versa. Commodities are socially constructed not only in their meaning but also in the material practices by which they are produced, distributed and ultimately consumed. Within cultural studies, there has been an overemphasis on teasing out the meaning of the use values of commodities at the expense of understanding the contribution to their character made by putting them together. And as the conditions under which commodities become available are transformed, not least through the imperatives imposed by the continuing pursuit of profitability, so strains are placed upon how they can be interpreted. In short, the cultural context in which an item of consumption, its use value, is reconstructed is not simply a matter of a more or less variable experience or interpretation of the object through the consumer's beliefs or desires; it is also a bridge over the gap between what the commodity actually is and how it is perceived and presented, however partially or incorrectly. Cultural theory of consumption has tended to emphasise the creation of the gap through the reconstruction of the meaning of the use value of objects of consumption. It has tended to tear this away from and neglect the creation of the objects themselves, in the sense of their production, which may affect both what they are and how they are perceived. This varies from one sector to another.

Chapter 20 is concerned with the theory of retailing. It carefully assesses the arguments of Ducatel and Blomley who make a strong case analytically for constituting retail capital as a separate fraction of (commercial) capital. Although an intuitively reasonable proposition, we reach the opposite conclusion through the elaboration of relatively minor but decisive theoretical differences. We argue that it is more appropriate to view retail capital as a heterogeneous economic category, each fraction potentially demonstrating a greater affinity with the particular commodity system to which it relates than to any other fraction of retail capital.

Finally, Chapter 21 offers some concluding remarks. It is clear from our study that consumption has not only risen in prominence as a source of study and speculation but that, in doing so, it has been endowed with an increasing range and variability of ill-defined meanings.

Why is consumption imprecise and shifting as an analytical category and ideological construct – compared to production, say? Why has this occurred recently in line with the increasing prominence of consumption? And what determines the conceptual content of consumption? Historically, a simple distinction was drawn between consumption within the production process and consumption outside and at the expense of production. In this way, the potential for accumulation could be gauged as a response to the increasing span, pressures and mechanisms of the (capitalist) market. Significantly, one of Adam Smith's definitions of unproductive expenditure was allocation to consumption as opposed to investment. This seemed to suffice in distinguishing consumption as such from production, with the removal of the former from the world of commerce. Subsequent studies of consumption have, until recently, been primarily concerned with private consumption, usually as the consequence of commodity purchases, although this has been less so for approaches derived from anthropology and cultural theory.

Today, as the world of consumption is conceptually broadened, it is increasingly being understood without a sharp division being drawn between its incidence and origins within the commercial world and its roots elsewhere, whether through state or household provision. Our lives are being interpreted in terms of the broad categories of servers and users, as producers and consumers. Whilst the language employed exhibits a degree of neutrality, the underlying model and logic is to emulate, if not to replicate, the corporate world. It is a process that treats the social and the commercial as commensurate, if not identical, the better to subject the former to the more exacting and targeted economic calculation associated with the latter. The notion of 'value for money' extracts the essence of the supposed condensing of social relations into the realm of consumption, making explicit its association with the purchase of commodities, irrespective of what explicit values are used to assess 'value' by money.

Thus, provision through the public sector has been incorporated into the understanding of consumption. Previously, it had been rarely understood as such, since it grew from different origins and was determined by different factors. Galbraith's notion of private affluence and public squalor pointed to a dissatisfaction with the relative allocation of resources but also to two different forms of provision which were hardly comparable simply as different modes of consumption. Education, health, national insurance – welfarism in short – were not to be understood as belonging to the same genus as the purchase of an ice-cream or a new item of clothing.

Today, the dividing line between the two is not so clear-cut, as argued with more detail in our concluding chapter. Public and private provision have always been intimately related to one another – not least, say, in the private ownership of motor cars and the public provision of roadways – but the rise of state expenditure has made them more overtly interdependent. While consumption theory had previously done little to recognise the distinction between the two and their mutual conditioning, it has overcompensated over the past two decades by merging the public and private forms of provision as potentially equivalent forms of (private) consumption.

We suggest that such developments in the understanding of consumption reflect a reaction to the shifting boundaries between the social and the private, and between the collective and the individual, as determined by the rhythm of late twentieth-century advanced capitalism. For, just as the rise of the welfare state in the postwar boom appeared to have set public provision aside from the ethos and practices of private consumption, so the economic crisis of the mid-1970s has brought the two into collision with one another; and where the restructuring of private and public provision has occurred, treating each as alternative modes of consumption has (conceptually) eased the adjustments involved, whether these be cuts in levels of provision and/or redivisions between public and private provision, as in privatisation of public services.

Something then has occurred more subtle than a simple reversion to the ideology of *laissez-faire* through the adoption of Reaganomics or Thatcherism, which relieves the state of responsibility for remedying unemployment, inequality and poverty as these once again become seen as matters of individual responsibility, thrift, hard work and personal (lack of) talent. All these objects of public policy and service now enter the realm of consumption, the better to minimise their being subject to collective action in practice and to analysis rooted in social relations of production in theory. In short, a more rounded understanding of both consumption itself and of its forms of conceptual packaging, to include a full account of the distinctive role of public and other non-commodity forms of provision with which commodity production interacts, depends upon an approach based on systems of provision.

This introduction has attempted to summarise the contents of the book as a whole, giving a brief outline of each chapter and the overall thrust of its argument. But an early warning is in order. The subject matter covered and the theoretical knowledge employed are extremely wide ranging. To a large extent, this reflects the complex determinants of both consumption and of the theories that have been used to explain it. Moreover, studies and theories of consumption have often been motivated by goals other than that of understanding consumption itself – for example, by efforts to create a system of social stratification, to explain economic growth, to assess the ethics and morality of society, etc. The reader interested in consumption alone may not be concerned with these broader issues within which discussion of consumption has been, often uneasily, subsumed. Consequently, each chapter has been made as self-contained as possible (at the expense of occasional repetition). The outline and the broader overview sketched above have been designed to allow the reader to pick and choose topics of interest to suit from amongst the individual chapters.

Further, the discussion carries a number of themes concurrently. It is concerned with theoretical and empirical issues, with particular commodities and particular academic disciplines, and with logical as well as historical analysis. It has not always been possible to handle each of these themes separately or exhaustively in one place. Discussions of clothing, the nineteenth century or economics, for example, appear in more than one place, although there are concentrated discussions of each in or within particular chapters. No order of presentation is ideal; we recognise that the one chosen, although the consequence of careful thought, involves a degree of experimentation.

The book has been written against an intellectual background in which the long-standing reaction against (Marxist) economic reductionism (to production or work) has increasingly been extended not only correctly to emphasise other social realities and practices but also incorrectly to autonomise them as separate arenas of both life and analysis. The understanding of consumption has suffered from this trend, perhaps more so than other topics because, as has been argued, there has been so little point of contact between previously existing analyses of consumption. Hopefully, our analysis opens up an alternative intellectual route that others will find useful to follow, through its insistence upon analysis through systems of provision. For these require an examination, both historical and social, of the connected causal links by which commodities are distinctly and materially made available, in a way that encourages more fruitful speculation about the future of consumption as well as a deeper understanding of both the present and past.

# 2

# CONSUMPTION THROUGH SYSTEMS OF PROVISION

## INTRODUCTION

On the face of it, the commodity is a very simple thing. Following classical political economy, it has become common to define it by *two* primary attributes: exchange value and use value. This division has proved the springboard for the elaboration of widely divergent economic analyses. Neoclassical economics sets up a relationship between the two properties; the ultimate (marginal) utility provided by the commodity is the explanation for its price. Marxist economics interrogates exchange and use value dialectically to flush out the concept of value – socially necessary labour time as a relationship between producers – from which is logically derived a critical understanding of capitalist commodity production. As the depository of surplus value, analytical priority is displaced from the commodity as such, and the marketplace, to the world of production, where the origins of exploitation are to be found. Keynesianism assigns paramount importance to the ability of the economic system, if not the state, to generate effective market demand, so that the potential exchange value of the commodity and its ability to command sale become central.

A further distinction flows from the dichotomy between use value and exchange value, that between purchase and sale, reflecting the two sides of a bargain. From this meeting point in the market, the life of the commodity can be traced in two directions, either forward to the buyer and an act of consumption or backward through the seller to the commodity's origins in production. For neoclassical economics, these paths may be seen as harmoniously and efficiently linked through the free play of the market mechanism. The priority assigned to individual utility, both as a determining, explanatory factor and as a desirable outcome, gives rise to the idea of consumer sovereignty. The system of production responds as a servant to the needs and wishes of consumers, subject to the availability of resources. In this sense, consumption can be traced back from the individual, through exchange, to act as a determining moment upon production – even if allowance can also be made for distortions in efficiency and competitiveness along the way.

A more radical tradition in economic thought denies the validity of consumer sovereignty, viewing the consumer more as a passive victim of the dictates of production and of producers. The line of causation between production and consumption is perceived to run primarily in the opposite direction; producers decide what is to be made, do not respond to consumers' needs or, worse, they manipulate them through advertising or through the numbness brought on by overfamiliarity with what they make available.

Keynesianism has been less concerned with the opposition between these two positions than with what determines the overall level of effective demand on the market. How well oiled are the wheels of buying? In particular, the position of money and money markets becomes crucial. Stretching a point for illustrative purposes, this can be thought of as a specific example, in this case drawn from economics, in which (aggregate) consumption is determined by an *intermediate* factor, the operation of money markets, between the two extremes of production and consumption. It has its counterpart in the idea that consumerism is driven by the ready availability of credit. But there are intermediate factors other than the ability to buy (with credit cards), which might be considered to influence the overall level and nature of consumption: marketing (of which advertising is a component) or the psychology of consumption where this is associated with emulation, 'keeping up with the Joneses', for example. In this last case, the jockeying for status assumes greater importance than what is actually consumed (or produced), which is why it can be subject to ridicule or to critical analysis – witness Veblen's theory of conspicuous consumption. Analytically, there is a common element shared between Veblen and Keynes; for one there is the passing on of demand, whilst for the other the overall level of demand is central. But, for both, the nature of that demand in terms of specific commodities is relatively unimportant (although this is historically contingent for Veblen based on items of conspicuous consumption established by the leisure class).

The details of some of these theories will be critically assessed in later chapters. Here, the intention is more to point to the extent to which they rely upon generalities across commodities. Each approach makes only a limited, or purely formal, distinction between different commodities. Some commodities may be more subject to consumer sovereignty and some less so. Emulation may be more important for some artefacts – diamonds for the rich, piano in the parlour for lesser mortals, and so on. But, in general, each theory lumps together great bundles of disparate goods which are bent collectively to follow the contours set out by that particular theory. Commodities that differ in important respects (from the point of view of consumer behaviour leaving aside how they are provided) are typically subsumed under the catch-all term, 'consumer goods'.

Each approach to consumption also tends to have difficulty reconciling or incorporating the insights offered by the others. This is a separate but not unrelated point. Even if overall demand, method of production, relative power of consumers and producers, emulation, etc. were all taken into account, integration between them might only be effectively achieved at the level of individual commodities rather than as a general theory of consumption (of all commodities). This is a conclusion to which we are drawn in this book.

Theories, then, substantially reflect dependence upon generalisation from archetypal commodities, processes or motives. Consumer sovereignty takes as its model the perfectly competitive industry, with well-informed consumers and rigidly formed or inherited preferences. Its antithesis is highly monopolised capital, with heavy dependence upon manipulative advertising and consumer ignorance. Each approach appears inadequate for two reasons. Both overgeneralise from the case in which each might be thought to have greatest purchase; both are ill placed to take account of factors associated with the other approach.

Taken together and probed further, these shortcomings are found to be even more serious. For even if, for example, we find a case in which consumer sovereignty or emulation appears to provide a satisfactory explanation for the consumption of a particular commodity, its explanatory power will be illusory. For it would still be necessary to explain why this particular commodity had not been subject, say, to monopolisation and manipulative advertising rather than to the dictates of a well-informed and 'sensible' consuming public. Sealing off individual commodities within the confines of self-contained theories denies not only the complexity of factors involved in the consumption and production of goods but also their relative weight and interaction.

Given the inadequacies of existing theories, it is reasonable to consider an alternative approach, one that is consciously sensitive to the difference between commodities, not so much as items of consumption alone, but in terms of the economic and social processes and structures by which they become such. Even where these economic and social relations are shared, the way in which they interact may well be different across commodities. All tend to be the product of wage labour, but production processes are organised differently, products develop differently, are distributed and sold differently, are consumed and disposed of differently; they serve needs that are themselves socially constructed and satisfied (or not) very differently. These separate processes are not independent of each other, nor is there a rigid one-way line of determination between them.

Consequently, this chapter and, more diffusely, this book argue that each commodity or commodity group is best understood in terms of a unity of economic and social processes which vary significantly from one commodity to another, each creating and reflecting upon what will be referred to as its own 'system of provision'. There is a sense in which this is self-evident. Compared with motor cars, food is produced, sold and consumed differently; yet both may be subject to the factory system, advertising and emulative behaviour. What is gained by emphasising their differences rather than their similarities?

First of all, re-ordering the world of commodities into systems of provision opens up the possibility for a more dynamic approach to the theory of consumer behaviour. Most of the theories reviewed in this book are revealed to be essentially static; whatever the period under investigation, whether at the time of the Industrial Revolution or in the late twentieth century, the typical 'basket' of consumer goods under review is taken as given. Though the composition of this bundle clearly varies from one historical period to the next, existing theories do not adequately explain the mechanisms that lead to the introduction of entirely new commodities, the disappearance or transformation of old ones, or the prolonged survival intact of some inveterate goods. If there is any significance to the relatively recent arrival of the motor car compared with the prehistoric availability of food and the survival of some almost prehistoric foods like bread, it will not be revealed by existing theories.

Nor do existing theories explain the consumption of particular goods in particular periods of time, or the processes by which each is made available. Rather, the goods themselves function primarily to illustrate the central argument of the theory; serving in this capacity, they often become interchangeable. Theories based on emulative (trickle-down) behaviour, for example, do not need to distinguish between the consumption of motor cars or food, housing or clothing, to make their point. Nor do they need to distinguish between the eighteenth and the twentieth century. For its purposes, consumption of any of these goods in any period will serve equally well.

The tacit presumption of such theories is that the human propensity to consume is virtually innate and, hence, of much greater importance in itself than any of the individual objects with which it interacts. It also gives primacy to activities or behaviour carried out by individuals, whether rational or irrational, rather than by social agencies, corporate or collective institutions. Such a view underpins much of the theoretical discussion within the disciplines of anthropology, semiotics, psychology and economics.

The systems-of-provision approach, by contrast, sets the role of consumer choice within a much different perspective, one that views it as determined both historically – and therefore varying over time in strength and influence – and jointly with other variables within separate systems of provision which are themselves subject to significant long-term change, achieved at different rates and with different consequences. This framework encourages the exploration of multiple perspectives, suggesting the possibility that consumer behaviour has played a more determining role in some periods of history and in some commodities than in others.

Such an approach allows theory to accommodate commonsense, which tells us that consumption over the past two hundred years has not proceeded smoothly upwards along a curve of constant slope; that the qualitative and quantitative impact of consumption during a period of labour market (and productive capacity) expansion may be greater than that of periods preceding or following it; that the domestic consumption of coal differs significantly from the consumption of nuclear energy; and so on. Moreover, analysis by systems of provision offers an antidote to what Cannadine (1984) has described as the bias of contemporary events which, in this case, has elevated the role of consumption to a more prominent if inadequately differentiated position on the agenda of most social sciences.

Part III of this book explores various aspects of the clothing and food industries. It is designed to demonstrate the benefits that flow from adopting a systems-of-provision approach to the concept of consumption. These are contrasted with reviews of both a 'horizontal' theory of consumption, namely trickle-down, and a 'horizontal' factor, namely advertising. The latter is presented as being both determined by and, in part, determining the character of the specific system of provision to which it is attached.

The development of the food and clothing industries has been governed by very different imperatives. Part III argues that the distinctive pattern of consumption prevailing in each case reflects the capacity of each industry either to overcome or to accommodate these imperatives. Discussion supporting this conclusion draws on investigation of the interconnected chains of provision linking production, distribution, marketing, advertising and consumption over an extended period of time.

## 1 LOCATING THE AESTHETIC ILLUSION

The rest of this chapter extends the theoretical groundwork for the exploration of systems of provision by returning to the earlier discussion of the two basic properties of commodities: use value and exchange value. Despite their being common to all goods, even simple and abstract analyses in the context of capitalism cut them off from one another, tending to concentrate exclusively on one property or the other. Though this produces a limited and skewed view of commodities, it can also stimulate fruitful debate. The work of Haug (1986), although far from prominent, provides a useful demonstration, bringing fresh insights to the analysis of use value and drawing on a more dialectical treatment of related issues.

Haug has focused on the way in which the imperatives of capitalist production create a tension between the changing material content of the commodity and its meaning as a purchased item of consumption. Although the scope of his analysis is too restrictive, limited to the disguise of product degradation through the endowment of commodities with a degree of sexuality, it does provide an introduction to other critical elements of analysis taken up in section 2 of this chapter.

These elements include the broad issues of periodising capitalism (into stages with corresponding structures of consumption) and the role of historical contingency (the continuing influence into the present of constructions of consumption carried over from the past). Whilst a variety of capitalist imperatives, structures and processes apply *across* the economy and society which vary between one stage of capitalism and another, their incidence and mutual interaction for particular commodities give rise to historically contingent systems of provision that differ one from another.

Subject to income and availability, individuals exercise choice over what they consume. In exploring this activity, a great deal of emphasis has been placed on those influences that lead the individual consumer to choose in a particular way. Within economics, choice is governed by the maximisation of utility, derived from given (unexamined) preferences. Psychology endows the individual with a wider variety of motivations, some of which are partially intrinsic, like appetite, while others are extrinsic or socially derived, like emulation of those in higher-income groups. This duality is mirrored on the other side of the transaction: commodities themselves also combine intrinsic, physical properties of use value (flavour, texture, etc.) with some perception of this use value which is extrinsic to the commodity itself and socially constructed. The sweetness of chocolate, for example, is both a physical and a psychological property; the latter is intricately and intimately conflated with the human characteristics of sweetness.

Consequently, choice must be seen as a relationship between the individual and the commodity. This has sometimes inappropriately been cast as a relationship between equals; in this context, either the commodity takes on human attributes or the individual is dehumanised, reduced to the status of calculating machine or animal, as in economics and psychology. But, leaving aside this reification and anthropomorphism, other pertinent questions surrounding the commodity's use value need to be addressed. Going behind immediate physical properties, how do the economic origins of a commodity affect the way in which it is perceived as a use value for consumption? This is the mirror image of the question that asks what the individual consumer brings to the act of consumption.

First, there is a relationship between the commodity's physical properties and how it is perceived. At the most basic level, this implies that given commodities are interpreted as use values within what are definite limits, although these might be remarkably elastic. A motor car cannot literally satisfy a hunger, other than metaphorically speaking. Most notably, advertising attempts to endow commodities with properties over and above their capacity to achieve them – even in the imagination. More generally, the elasticity of the meaning of commodities in consumption is tied to the changing physical content of the commodities themselves. If the origin of the commodity is traced back to production, then as production processes change, so can the nature of the products. Thus, elasticity in the meaning of commodities derives both from the changing interpretation of given physical use values and from unchanging interpretation of potentially changing use values.

An example of the latter is provided by the technical changes that have facilitated the preparation and packaging of whole meals rather than of individual foods. Eating out in a restaurant, or buying bread from the 'local' baker, creates the impression of a more personalised service than that associated with a fast-food outlet or shopping in a supermarket. Yet the restaurant may simply be concealing a growing dependence on the delivery of mass-produced or pre-prepared meals ready for their kitchen's microwave, just as the local baker may depend on the delivery of mass-produced frozen dough.

This raises a second question – how does the changing meaning of commodities in turn affect the physical content of the commodities themselves? The question goes beyond the issue of consumer sovereignty, which assumes that given preferences are satisfied by given commodities or not, but does not question the derivation or transformation of preferences themselves. Rather, it concerns the dialectic between the changing meaning of commodities and their changing content, irrespective of consumer sovereignty. To give a simple example, the recent fashion for healthy foods has led to a variety of products claiming to be 'natural', accompanied by an equally variable change of both meaning and content.

There is then a complex and shifting relation between the two aspects of the use value of a commodity – its physical content and its interpretation. Too often this complex relationship has been treated too one-sidedly. Those focusing narrowly on consumption alone tend to examine the meaning of commodities to consumers (that is, what it is sold as); little attention is paid to the tension between this image of the commodity and what it actually is. On the other hand, there are those whose concern is primarily with the quality and cost of the commodity, at the expense of how it is perceived by the consumer. Haug (1986) has made an attempt to bring these issues together. His discussion of what he calls the 'aesthetic illusion' draws the distinction between what is produced and how it is presented.

His starting point is that the need for the capitalist to guarantee sale makes it necessary to present the commodity as desirable: 'The lust for money is the reason why, under capitalist production, the commodity is presented in the image of the consumer's desires' (Haug 1986: 24). But this does not go far enough; it might also apply to non-capitalist commodity production and it also still leaves the consumer's desires undetermined. To supply a plausible source for the latter, Haug emphasises the role of sexuality in the formation of an illusory content in commodities – although sexuality also has a history that would need to be elaborated and explained. Beginning with the exchange process, Haug suggests that commodities borrow their aesthetic language from human courtship.[1] Its attributes are then universally projected on to all commodities:[2] 'It is not the sexual object which takes on the commodity form, but the tendency of all objects of use in commodity-form to assume a sexual form to some extent . . . exchange value transforms itself into sexuality' (Haug 1986: 55).

The commodity as an object of consumption may become endowed in modern parlance with the properties of a sex object, although the term is usually associated with the sexual reification of women rather than with the eroticising of objects. These properties then become desirable aspects of the commodity. Cars must appear to incorporate a sex drive, although they are not a sex drive in themselves. For Haug, the attempt to bridge the gap between what the commodity is and the preferred use value is undertaken by advertising.

No doubt the role of sexuality and of advertising are exaggerated. There are plenty of other social relations on offer to form the illusory content of commodities, and the gap between these illusions and the real thing is not only, nor necessarily predominantly, determined and filled by advertising. The media, the state and the family are, for example, primary sites for the creation, reproduction and the satisfaction of needs, although the balance between the commodity and non-commodity forms of provision has a different and shifting balance for each.[3] But, once advertising is itself recognised as a factor influencing sexuality, the structure of the analysis is compelling because it offers and draws upon a dynamic and contradictory relationship between the commodity as a use value and the commodity as an exchange value.

There is always a potential gap between the commodity's (physical) use value and its imputed use value, and this gap varies both with the product itself and its endowed sexuality. Moreover, the determining motive behind this structured gap, and its dynamic as its jaws open and close, is the wish to guarantee sale. This is a competitive process within and across the various sectors of the economy. If, for the sake of argument alone, it is presumed that the levels and nature of advertising vary with the size distribution of firms within a sector, then the aesthetic illusion (and its real effects on the commodity over time) will differ between one sector and another. More generally, the dialectic between the material and illusory content of commodities will vary from one to another, according to how the competitive process works out in practice. The endowed sexuality of each product will be as distinct as its material properties. Indeed, some, if not all, products are liable to be divided by gendering, partly as a consequence of advertising even if in conjunction with other sources of gender roles – it does not, for example, need advertising to make kitchen products primarily female.

Already the relationship between commodity, sexuality, advertising and competition in this analysis reveals that different commodities are ideologically constructed according to a logic that is not uniform across them. Cars are gendered as male. Chocolates are gendered as feminine in a way that differs from the gendering of household items employed in domestic chores. However these sex-types are constructed and assigned to commodities, capital is stretched between ensuring sale through widening the illusory gap (and getting away with the illusion) or, potentially, attempting to close it through modification of the material content of the commodity itself. Chocolate can be made sweeter, motor cars more powerful; the aesthetic illusion is not simply the commercially led misrepresentation of given use values. The latter themselves change in response to the dialectic surrounding their reconstructed and illusory properties.

Haug also locates the analysis within the realm of capitalist commodity production. He associates the movement from luxury to mass consumption with the transition from *laissez-faire* to monopoly capitalism: 'From now on it is no longer primarily expensive luxury commodities that determine big business but relatively cheap mass-produced articles' (Haug 1986: 22–3). The imperative of profitability is seen to have a number of effects in the era of monopoly capitalism. First, there is the attempt to reduce the cost of production (irrespective of the productivity increase through the use of machinery) through taking less time to bring the commodities to market, by including less labour within them and by cheapening and reducing the quantity of raw materials that are used. For Haug, since this inevitably worsens the quality of the product, it leads to a widening of the gap to be bridged by the aesthetic illusion (ibid.: 23).

Second, in order to sustain demand, there is an attempt to build obsolescence into commodities so that replacement consumption is essential. This can either come from qualitative obsolescence (as dictated by the fashion system, which makes use values irrelevant before they are physically exhausted) or it can come through quantitative obsolescence (the use of defective design with no gain in cost reduction in order to guarantee replacement demand).[4]

What is the significance of these two factors? They certainly correspond to our casual, empirical experience as consumers. Appliances, especially motor cars, do wear out unnecessarily quickly. On the other hand, consumers (and producers in turn) do become aware of this and require (at least the illusion of) longer-lasting products. Much the same is true of product quality. So, once again, the forces acting upon the aesthetic illusion are both complex and subject to a wide set of varied influences and outcomes. In the case of the American automobile, for example, the illusion of masculinity entailed not just obsolescence of the product by model change (and status by changing with it) but also the *addition* of unnecessarily heavy and dangerous bodywork to represent speed, power and strength.

In short, Haug has provided some theoretical insights for examining the dynamic, social reconstruction of use value, although his analysis is over-generalised, exaggerating certain tendencies and excluding others. But a crucial general conclusion can, none the less, be drawn. The commodity as a use value bound for consumption and as an exchange value deriving from capitalist production necessarily, across each of these facets, exhibits a potential diversity of development. How these two aspects are bound together and mutually change or support each other is the key to understanding consumption. But even at this abstract level, imperatives of profitability and of sexuality give rise to outcomes that are distinct between commodities. Consequently, even before consumption is explored more deeply through the imperative of profitability and for ideological determinants across a wider terrain than sexuality alone, it already follows that the system of provision of each commodity is potentially unique.

## 2 STAGES, STRUCTURES AND CONTINGENCY

As observed in the previous section, Haug dates the growing significance of the aesthetic illusion from the time of the transition from luxury to mass consumption, which can be alternatively identified with the transition from *laissez-faire* to monopoly capitalism. Such analysis needs to be taken further both in its depth and in its historical specificity. Within *laissez-faire* capitalism, for example, the defining characteristic is less the dominant mode of the illusory consumption of the rich as the mode of exploitation of the poor. Productivity increase is less important than the extension of the working day for men, women and children. In Marx's terms, there is greater dependence upon the production of absolute surplus value. Such extensive exploitation of labour implies that there are limits to the transformation of the production process[5] and, as a result, there are also limits on the displacement of one type of raw material by another as a consequence of changes in production methods.

The same is not necessarily true of the content of products. Because competition tends to be across fragmented, small-scale producers, intense market competition leads, on the one hand, to the imperative by producers to adulterate their products and, on the other hand, to the need for consumers to discriminate between the good, the bad and the ugly. Inevitably, competitive survival dictates that those who refuse to adulterate their products will be competitively eliminated (just as, by analogy, there is no choice but to employ child labour whatever the benevolent intentions of the employer).[6]

Further, in order to associate the aesthetic illusion with the rise of advertising, Haug neglects its place in the earlier period of capitalism, perhaps because the potential for such illusion was constrained by the very limited consumption of the poor, often bordering on the edge of physical survival. There are, for example, two competing or complementary explanations for the development of the habit of tea drinking amongst the British working class, neither of which owes much, if anything to the aesthetic illusion. One is emulation of the upper classes; the other is to create the illusion of a hot and satisfying meal when diet is otherwise confined to lumps of bread, cheese and dripping. Nevertheless, there are always some illusions around consumption, and these are not necessarily the poorer for belonging to those poor in consumption – otherwise anthropologists would long have been rendered redundant. However, as Haug suggests, under capitalism in its early stages, the preferred focus for the aesthetic illusion is to be found more in the luxury consumption of the wealthy. This itself often depends upon commodities produced by highly labour-intensive and skilled methods or through self-employed, 'unproductive' labour directly employed outside the control of capital.

The arrival of monopoly capitalism is accompanied by substantial differences which go well beyond those identified by Haug. This is the age of the factory and of large-scale machinery. First of all, competition works primarily through the cheapening of commodities, fought through productivity increase rather than through a decline in product quality. None the less, monopolisation does create the potential for formal or informal collusion (without thereby eliminating competition). Not only may this take the form of price-fixing cartels; it may also be conducive to the creation of particular norms in the aesthetic illusion surrounding the mass consumption of the working class – through, for example, an expansion in goods falling sway to the fashion system or through the failure to provide long-lasting products. The provision of high-quality goods, whether embodying extra or even lower levels of costs, may be subordinated to other non-material aspects of the commodity. For example, Haug (1986: 26) highlights the illusory status value of some commodities by pointing to the 'same' goods being sold at different prices; the higher-priced goods enjoy the illusion of higher quality (in a neat inversion of the laws of political economy, for which price is an index of cost of production). A general mechanism through which this is achieved is branding. Often, of course, created by advertising, branding works in part precisely by 'enhancing' the quality of a product merely by virtue of its name and irrespective of its content.

It would, however, be wrong to presume that there is no consumer reaction against the widening gap between the commodity and its image which the brand name is intended to fill. Consumers can be sceptical about the quality of what they buy and can initiate a counter-culture, expressed in one form as the desire for the 'real thing' or its equivalent. This has been particularly prominent in the success of unbranded goods, especially in US supermarkets or, significantly, in retailers developing their own brands, although these may be sourced from the very same producers as the branded product. It cannot be presumed that the reaction against illusion is purely the product of a restless consumer movement rather than a lever in the competitive struggle within retailing and between retailers and producers; nor that what is 'real' is not itself subject to illusion – as evidenced by the 'Real Thing' (Coca-Cola), the so-called ploughman's lunch, or by the seizure of the 'natural' or 'traditional' in foods, used as a selling point for the mass product serving the health craze.[7]

Adulteration and contamination are also transformed under the sway of monopoly capitalism. Certainly, the occasional wine is still laced with poison to preserve or to mature it. But, contemporary with the protective legislation on behalf of the working class (Marx's discussion is primarily concerned with the length of the working day), so the crudest forms of adulteration have been legally proscribed. This serves both to reduce the cost of reproducing labour power – other capitalists do not benefit from grocers selling chalk as cheese. It also diminishes the competitive position of small-scale producers, who tend to depend on the poorest quality, in product as well as labour conditions, in order to survive.

Adulteration, however, does take on a new form and new names, as revealed by Haug. It is the displacement of existing raw materials rather than their reduction (or veiled replacement). The machine age is one in which both production processes and products are revolutionised. Most notably, fresh – dare one say natural – ingredients are displaced by the artificial, perhaps most notable in the case of food. For bread, the preference for the use of white flour has been motivated by its keeping longer, holding more air and water, requiring less skill in baking, and facilitating the sale of the bran and germ extracted as animal feed (Cannon 1987). More generally, chemical additives reduce costs, add colour for presentation (so that orange flavour really does become artificial in colour), and act as preservatives. An equally important development is the rise of convenience foods. This is strongly linked to the growing labour market participation of women with children and, consequently, cannot be read off either from the needs of the economy or from the illusion of preserving whilst transforming the nature of, and need for, 'home cooking'. It is heavily determined by the changing nature of the family, following the demographic transition in the fifty years around the turn of the last century.[8]

Nor can it be presumed that the modern form of adulteration is exclusively an issue of less and different (cheaper) inputs, as has already been illustrated by the history of the American automobile. Here, the extraordinary growth in the dimensions of the models – even to the extent of their becoming grossly inefficient and unsafe – reflected in part the monopolisation of the industry in which more car could be sold by adding costly features. And cartel collusion prevented the emergence of small-scale, long-lasting alternatives. But the industry was also a reflection of the power of US imperialism with its global command of raw materials and ability to source inputs, to manufacture and to drive, these domestic 'tanks'.

This is not a simple matter of tension between the aesthetic illusion and the so-called 'adulteration' of the motor car. It depended upon a range of forces derived from twentieth-century capitalism and from the US hegemony within it at a global level, demonstrated by the subsequent decline of these monster automobile models. Whilst the consumer movement's role in undermining the market for 'gas-guzzlers' should not be underestimated, attention should also be drawn to the eventual emergence of competition from smaller-scale imports (not least the VW 'Beetle' as a Trojan horse for the Japanese) and the increasing price of oil.

Thus, there are systematic differences in the formation and the resolution of the aesthetic illusion between *laissez-faire* and monopoly capitalism arising from the different imperatives by which profitability is pursued. Such differences extend more generally to other aspects of economic organisation, not only through advertising, but also through cartelisation, finance, distribution and marketing more generally. These are all transformed between the two stages of capitalism with potential significance for the location and intensity of the aesthetic illusion. And there are also pertinent differences in the non-economic arena in the social reproduction of the workforce, the nature of the family, etc. As assessed in Chapter 6, the transition to mass production is associated with shifts in a variety of other relations, apart from that in consumption, as denoted by the transport, communications, demographic and domestic revolutions – each of which has a general and detailed impact upon the reconstruction of consumption.

As important as the differences *between* stages of capitalism in the determination of consumption are the tensions *within* a stage between its various determinants. A number of these have already been identified for monopoly capitalism, not least Haug's conflict between the material degradation of the product and its ideological enhancement, whether by sexuality or by other means. Further, monopoly capitalism also pits modern forms of adulteration against improvements in materials, production processes and products. To some extent, Haug has fallen prey to the illusion that traditional products are superior to their modern equivalents or replacements. But the vast improvements in the material quality of many products is, in fact, no mere illusion despite the occasionally deceptive use of scientific or technological wizardry as a selling point.

How are the various influences derived from production or otherwise on the formation of consumption, to be integrated? First, each contributing factor (production, etc.) may obtain across the economy as a whole or, as in the case of sexuality, across society. The imperatives associated with profitability or with disguising the commodity apply in principle to each sector embracing, for example, cars as well as food and clothing. For this reason, their use as explanatory variables will be termed 'horizontal' as they are interpreted broadly across all consumption items.

Horizontal influences should be seen as tendencies whose strength varies between one commodity and another. Variations might reflect differences in the material composition of the commodity itself, differences which will affect the potential scope for adulteration, productivity increase, etc., and will themselves be influenced by competition between capitals and the conflicts over the conditions of the factory system.

The interaction of these determinants will give rise to specific structures of provision that vary from one commodity to the next, partly because of the different strengths of the tendencies concerned and partly because their interaction can be different. Does it lead, for example, to structured degradation, obsolescence or even quality enhancement? The term 'vertical' will be used to distinguish between specific structures of provision of consumption goods that result from the interaction of horizontal factors. Consequently, vertically there is potentially a different *system of provision* associated with each commodity. Whilst the logical foundation for this approach has been provided through the elementary anatomy of the commodity, with Haug's analysis as entry point through profitability, sexuality, advertising and the aesthetic illusion, these factors neither suffice nor are necessarily the most decisive in any one system of provision.

Consequently, a system of provision (in, for example, housing, food or fashion) is taken to denote the articulation of economic and social factors that give rise both to the level and composition of consumption (quantitative aspect) and the meanings with which it is endowed (qualitative aspect). Inevitably, different authors who are engaged in this field approach their subject area with a wider or narrower analytical and historical scope. Haug describes the transport system thus: 'the private car, together with the running-down of public transport, carves up the towns no less effectively than saturation bombing, and creates distances that can no longer be crossed without a car' (Haug 1986: 54). For Ball (1983) housing is discussed in terms of a structure of provision which runs from the plot of building land, through the many aspects of the production process with its associated agencies, to the housing market itself (rather than as a system of differing forms of tenancy); Goody (1982: 37) sees food in terms of the five phases of production, distribution, preparation, consumption and disposal.

As yet, the analytical focus of academic work in the area has been predominantly upon the relation between production and consumption and between the material and ideological content of the commodity. In practice, a system of provision entails a more comprehensive chain of activities between the two extremes of production and consumption, each link of which plays a potentially significant role in the social construction of the commodity both in its material and cultural aspects. In other words, distribution, finance and marketing are all important components of provision. Advertising, after all, is only one component itself of marketing; sexuality only one component of the ideological content of commodities.

Finally, the role of historical contingency must also be acknowledged. Each structure of provision contains developmental tensions within it but these must be sufficiently compatible or articulated to enable the system to deliver the goods. They must also, for the commodity to survive, be able to accommodate change over time. How change occurs and how extensive it is will be contingent upon the extent and relative strength of persisting elements along the chain of provision and, to some degree, on the internal or external mechanisms that trigger change.

A simple example will illustrate the point. It is well known, as documented by Noble (1985), that the needs of the military have been highly important in accelerating the development of some consumer goods through the transfer from the military to the civilian arena of technology, production, innovative organisations of work, and the products themselves. Historically, the supply of military uniforms acted as a stimulus to the mass production of civilian clothing just as government provision of biscuits and canned goods hastened the pace of innovation in the preservation of foods.[9] The first system of standardised clothing sizes, for example, was introduced in the American Civil War in response to the sudden large-scale demand for soldiers' uniforms. After the war, the ready availability of standard sizes gave a spur to the mechanised development of men's clothing, particularly men's work clothes. This stimulus was not transferable to the production of women's clothing which continued to lag behind that of men's well into the twentieth century.

Some war-triggered innovations fail to have a lasting effect; witness the postwar displacement of women workers from factories, the corresponding disappearance of full-time workplace nurseries, and the closure of subsidised restaurants serving nutritionally balanced meals at cost. Other innovations, however, did take hold; workplace canteens became commonplace, as did the provision of school meals. The survival of some government-sponsored interventions but not others points to the multiplicity of often competing factors at work that determine, at the end of a long chain, the goods and services available at any one time.

In another sector, the history of sugar offers a different illustration of the impact of historical contingency on the pattern of consumption. The fact that Britain still maintains one of the highest per capita consumptions of sugar in the world testifies to the enduring effects of its imperial past (Mintz 1985); the patterns of Britain's cultural and economic domination remain visible in the British diet today. The reality of slavery is lost in an illusion of sweetness (much as a diamond is forever if not the apartheid system that produced it). Historically, sugar served as a luxury item of consumption – as a medicine, a decoration or a spice (accompanying 'all things nice'). With colonisation and the proletarianisation of the British workforce, it became a cheap source of energy in the hot meal provided by a cup of tea. In the modern period, its association with dental decay and heart disease has led to a drop in the consumption of sugar direct from the bowl. But the level of two pounds per head per week has been maintained, much to the advantage of capital's productive capacity, through the increasing use of sugar as an additive to preserve and sweeten manufactured foods. As such, it has the added advantage of being a 'natural' ingredient for advertising purposes.[10] In this way, the earlier dependence upon sugar as a part of the British diet has been preserved in line with the interests of the sugar industry.

Even so, sugar's structured continuity with its past has been subject to erosion. The British refining industry has been associated with cane sugar, predominantly from the Commonwealth, whereas its new ties are with the European Economic Community, which has depended exclusively on home-grown sugar beet. Sugar is also vulnerable to overproduction and the rise of the artificial sweetener. In these and other respects, the consumption of sugar bears the markings of influences not shared by the consumption of other foods like cheese and milk. Yet these distinctions tend to disappear in discussions of food advertising, for example, where the meaning of a product as presented is divorced from the meaning derived from its origins so that the cases of both sugar and cheese may inappropriately be used as generalisable examples to support broader cultural or economic arguments.

Differentiating and identifying those critical factors that have profoundly influenced the character of consumption (public sector purchasing and imperialism in the cases of clothing and sugar cited above) emphasises the heterogeneity of factors at work, and opens up the possibility of a much richer discussion of consumption. The vertical approach applied here, concerned with the linkages along the chain from production to consumption, does not refute the presence and importance of horizontal factors that may be common to more than one system of provision. But it suggests that these are liable to play a different role within each system of provision. This is true both of cultural and material factors; products are advertised *and* produced differently, and these differences apply equally to distribution, marketing and consumption itself. But there must also be some overall coherence in how these elements are integrated and developed, even if subject to contradictory forces.

Such is the subject of Part III, where the approach based on systems of provision is illustrated by analyses of retailing, advertising, food, clothing and the role of consumption in the Industrial Revolution. Their content is far from comprehensive, even within their selected vertical and horizontal areas of focus. Hopefully, they serve to demonstrate what can and needs to be done in understanding consumption and in moving beyond those half-serious maxims of consumerism – 'When the going gets tough, the tough go shopping'; 'I shop, therefore I am' – which have informed the latest fashions in the study of material culture.

# Part II

# THEORIES OF CONSUMPTION

# 3

# DISARRAY IN THE THEORY OF CONSUMER BEHAVIOUR

## INTRODUCTION

This chapter addresses the problems confronting the construction of a theory of consumption through examining the relatively new field of the theory of consumer behaviour. First, a review of its literature reveals the commonly held view amongst its leading practitioners that the new-born discipline has failed to find its feet and has not matured past its infancy. Rather it remains in a state of perpetual, self-confessed crisis, dependent on its parents amongst the social sciences – particularly, in order of importance, on psychology, sociology and economics. The problem has essentially been the failure of the new field to move beyond a multidisciplinary to an interdisciplinary approach, a failure which itself sheds light on the lack of substantive overlap across the disciplines analysing consumption.

Both the lack of overlap and the inability of the social sciences to integrate their treatment of consumption reflects the tendency of each individual discipline to adopt a horizontal approach. This has involved two closely related limitations. First, a particular explanatory factor, appropriate to the discipline, is considered in isolation from other factors, especially those from other disciplines. Second, the resulting theory is generalised too readily across different commodities or items of consumption. Consequently, when the attempt is made to combine the analyses, the outcome is a vertical stack of non-intersecting horizontal layers which, according to the vertical approach based on systems of provision adopted in this book, is bound to be unsatisfactory.

These matters are taken up, especially with reference to economics and psychology, in the next two chapters. Here, following the literature review, the crisis of the theory of consumer behaviour is revealed as a particularly weak version of what is known as middle-range theory, in which consumption is understood on the basis of intermediate, explanatory concepts, which are left suspended without any connection to any grander or deeper theory.

To a large extent, the literature and discipline of the theory of consumer behaviour have been neglected by other social scientists. There are a number of reasons for this. First, it has the stigma attached of being associated with the less intellectually demanding, more commercially oriented fields of advertising and marketing. Second, where it is confronted from the perspectives of other disciplines, such prejudices are almost inevitably confirmed by the multidisciplinary content of the theory of consumer behaviour, which is perceived to be shallow as far as any constituent discipline is concerned. Third, and most important, as will be argued, the fledgling discipline has failed to develop its own momentum and a genuinely interdisciplinary content. This failure is despite the genuine attempt of its academics to achieve the goal of elevating their chosen discipline to the same levels of status and rigour as that of other disciplines.

It would be all too easy to dismiss these attempts as the consequence of the limited capabilities of the intellectuals drawn to the discipline of the theory of consumer behaviour – as if the field could attract only those, like in advertising, accounting, marketing, business studies, etc., with restricted potential and ambition for intellectual development. A more revealing explanation for the failure of the theory of consumer behaviour is that it has set itself an impossible task, beyond the capabilities of any practitioner of whatever merit. For, given the validity of our argument, that consumption can only be explained by analysis of differentiated systems of provision, then the search for a general theory of consumption across the social sciences, combining the horizontal variables that are their concern, is doomed to failure.

## A NEW DISCIPLINE EMERGES – INTO THE DOLDRUMS

Consumer behaviour is generally recognised to have emerged as a separate academic discipline in the 1960s.[1] Its rationale is to provide a more circumspect and less practical, might one say less manipulative, approach to the influences on, and significance of, consumer behaviour than is normally found in journals devoted to marketing and advertising. Some, such as Rossiter (1989), have found the divorce that has occurred between marketing science and the theory of consumer behaviour to be disturbing, especially where this has led the latter to neglect simple empirical regularities (such as how many will try a new supermarket product or what its maximum take-up will be). Others, like Holbrook (1985), welcome the separation of consumer behaviour theory from marketing science and view its incorporation into academia as a desirable deterrent to the usurpation of the discipline's scientific enquiry by commercial consultancy.

Despite its relatively recent vintage, consumer behaviour theory has rarely been entirely free of the charge, even from its own practitioners, of being in a state of crisis: 'To lament that the field of consumer behaviour suffers from shortage of good theories has long become a popular claim within our discipline' (Kassarjian 1982a: 20). While, for Sheth: 'After a spectacular rise in the last two decades, the discipline of consumer behaviour has matured and seems to be in search of some new excitement and new directions. The discipline seems to be experiencing midlife crisis' (Sheth 1985: 1).

It is often difficult to distinguish between what are taken to be the symptoms of this crisis and what are taken to be its causes. Engel (1981: 12) characterises work in the field as a 'theory of the month club' and 'a fishing expedition throughout the social sciences'. Belk (1986a) demands, 'What should consumer research be when it grows up?' Jacoby (1978) complains of the lack of use of theory in empirical investigation, wide arrays of definitions for the same object,[2] and trivial subject matter, all within the context of a booming research output. Simon (1984: 259) takes a generally dismal view of its achievements, observing that marketing science and, by implication, consumer research, 'has to cope with this dilemma between practical relevance and scientific methodology'.

A closely related but separate issue for consumer research theory is its identity and existence as a discipline. There is no intention here to explore what are the criteria by which a body of research or an area of intellectual endeavour justifies the nomenclature of a separate academic discipline. Clearly, this depends upon the theory and techniques that it employs, its objects of research, its relations with other disciplines, and even institutional factors – whether there are separate academic departments and journals, etc. But for consumer research, even more readily recognised than its chronic state of crisis is its dependence upon a range of other academic disciplines – a dependence that leaves its own independent pedigree in permanent doubt. Here there are three separate issues.

First, is consumer research truly *inter*disciplinary rather than simply *multi*disciplinary? That it depends and draws upon a host of disciplines is well recognised and uncontroversial. Holbrook (1987), for example, lists macroeconomics, microeconomics, psychology, sociology, anthropology, philosophy and the humanities as the parent disciplines.[3] Kassarjian suggests: 'Although the term "interdisciplinary" has often been applied to the field of consumer behavior, it is in fact not always interdisciplinary, and perhaps a better term would be "fragmented"' (Kassarjian 1982b; 642). Uusitalo and Uusitalo (1981) distinguish between the multi- and the interdisciplinary possibilities, suggesting that consumer research has relied primarily on the former in practice.

They point to the number of essentially separate traditions within consumer research corresponding to the different parent disciplines, such as the psychological and the neoclassical economic traditions, and that these have seldom been welded together.[4] Because consumer research in this view reflects separate applications of the individual disciplines to a loosely defined common problem, it operates simultaneously within a number of separate Kuhnian paradigms, since the nature as well as the explanation of consumer behaviour is understood differently by the various disciplines.[5]

A second issue in the identity crisis of consumer research is the extent to which it is simply parasitical upon the parent disciplines. Here it is a matter of whether an analytical shift in another discipline is simply translated into a further application to consumer behaviour. This would tend to deny consumer research its status as a separate discipline. On the other hand, if developments in consumer research did lead, as a result of its objects of enquiry, to substantive independent advances in its theoretical or empirical content, then it would tend to become a discipline in its own right, even if confined to a multidisciplinary approach.[6]

The evidence for the parasitical nature of consumer research is strong, as is suggested by the preface to volume VIII of *Advances in Consumer Research* (Uusitalo and Uusitalo 1981:vi): 'We have become skilled at *borrowing* theories from other disciplines and *applying* them to our problems. . . . Our discipline applies borrowed theory, but does relatively little to *develop* theory.' Kassarjian (1986) observes how the counter-cognitive revolution in psychology, following upon the cognitive revolution in the social sciences, has been taken up by consumer research. The crisis of methodology in the social sciences, especially around the status of positivism, has been reproduced at a later date in the consumer research literature.[7] A further example has been the flush of publications that has arisen out of the incorporation of semiotics into consumer research.[8] But perhaps the most revealing, even if marginal, example is provided by Dholakia (1982), who deplores the absence of radical theory in the area. He suggests that this is anomalous because each of the constituent disciplines has its own radical tradition which the fledgling discipline should be able to draw upon. But, in practice, it has proved no more capable of doing so with a radical orientation than with an orthodox foundation.

Finally, a third question in the identity crisis of consumer behaviour is whether the sum of the separate parts of the discipline make up a whole that surpasses them. This Bagozzi (1984) claims they do, based on his attempts to unite a particular philosophy of science with statistical methods to provide a holistic construal. The result, however, seems to be an extremely complex diagram combining a variety of concepts, observations, measurements and inferences, all joined together by arrows connecting the boxes that contain them. All this has quite a striking similarity to many other, equally complex diagrams that abound in consumer behaviour theory which seek to combine a multitude of influences, motives and attributes in a sequential and structural explanation of individual behaviour. It has to be doubted whether this does lead to anything other than more of the same, within a *multi*disciplinary context.[9]

In reality, even claims for multidisciplinary study are not borne out in practice. Consumer behaviour has, in fact, drawn very little from economics. Zielinski and Robertson (1982) found, in a survey of the subject matter of articles in the *Journal of Consumer Research*, that almost 40 per cent were devoted to psychological theory and over 20 per cent were concerned with methodology (including problems of modelling and measurement), whilst well less than 10 per cent involved economic theory and related experiments. Sociology was more important than economics as a source of articles, accounting for almost twice the number of articles which focused on the provision of social explanatory variables – such as the family, culture and class.[10]

In short, the theory of consumer behaviour has a number of problems – of identity, of theoretical crisis, of its own internal innovativeness, and in its relation to other disciplines. The reasons for this are explored in the next two chapters by reference to economics and psychology. The rest of this chapter examines the discipline as a middle-range theory.

## CONSUMER BEHAVIOUR AS MIDDLE-RANGE THEORY

One way in which the ambiguous status of the theory of consumer behaviour has been recognised has been to characterise it as a 'middle-range' theory, located within three tiers of concepts, with grand theory and immediate outcomes at the two extremes. In the middle range are situated intermediate concepts whose connection to grand theory is often left implicit or ambiguous. For the theory of consumer behaviour, this vagueness has been taken too far, to the extent that the grand theory has been absent altogether. Consequently, the theory becomes a simple translation of the details of consumer behaviour into the language of other, more abstract, but unrooted concepts – clothing choice is explained by lifestyle, the love of chocolate by gratification, etc. With no grand theory lying behind these intermediate concepts, it is hardly surprising that they too cannot be instrumental in forging an interdisciplinary approach to consumer behaviour.

First used in this context by Robertson and Ward (1973),[11] the idea of middle-range theory harks back to a methodology proposed by Merton (1968, originally published 1949). His intent was to construct theories which lay between the grand world view and the more mundane propositions culled from empirical observation:

> Theories that lie between the minor but necessary working hypotheses that evolve in abundance during day-to-day research and the all-inclusive systematic efforts to develop a unified theory that will explain all the observed uniformities of social behaviour, social organisation and social change.
>
> (Merton 1968: 39)

Merton was in part motivated by the belief that sociology was not yet ready for a unified and comprehensive theory. In addition, each of those grand theories that were available[12] might well be compatible with the lower-level, middle-range investigations, which would serve to clarify available knowledge where possible and identify social mechanisms at work: 'A given theory of the middle-range, which has a measure of empirical confirmation, can often be subsumed under comprehensive theories which are themselves discrepant in certain respects' (ibid.: 43). Whilst Robertson and Ward (1973) consider Merton's method to be highly appropriate for consumer behaviour, they overlook the integrity of this theory, appearing to leave aside as irrelevant the 'grand' theories for which sociology was as yet unprepared. This is hardly surprising given the lack of any grander theory above the middle range in the theory of consumer behaviour other than the bundling together of an ever larger range of influences and mechanisms. In other words, it is not quite clear what is on either side of the middle range as defined for consumer behaviour. By contrast, whatever its merits as a methodology, Merton perceives middle-range theory to be intermediate – since he considers particular examples may be nested within competing 'grand' theories, as previously mentioned.

This weakening of the original intent of middle-range theory is brought out by comparison with another application. Many sociologists have welcomed middle-range theory as appropriate in the study of segmented labour markets.[13] For this purpose, what is required is the empirical identification of particular labour market segments – defined by sex, race, industrial sector or location, for example – with what may be competing theories of the economy or labour markets; each relies on a distinct theoretical framework to explain the potential structural division of the labour force into segments.

This linking of the middle range to a higher-level theory may often be implicit, as with the use of patriarchy, for example, to explain sexual segregation and discrimination in the labour market. But for the theory of consumer behaviour, it is less implicit than absent. The consequence is that the middle-range theory not only generates the middle-range spread associated with the theory of the month, it does so by a very close identification between the theory and what it seeks to explain. Thus, whatever its depth in conceptual content, the use of the concept of lifestyle to explain consumption patterns borders on the tautologous in so far as the latter is a major part of the former. What is already a considerable danger, even for the more sophisticated versions of the middle range which are embedded in a grander theory, becomes almost inevitable for the theory of consumer behaviour. Empirical observation is readily translated into a range of custom-built, middle-level concepts that are used only too transparently to explain the very observations from which they have been derived.

It might be thought that this discussion of middle-range theory is marginal to the critique of the theory of consumer behaviour, since the middle range has rarely been called upon to justify the discipline. But this is only because the methodology of consumer behaviour theory has rarely been broached at all by its practitioners and, when it has, the focus has usually been drawn from debates in the other social sciences rather than from the theoretical practice of consumer behaviour itself. Once it is squarely addressed, the theoretical poverty at the centre becomes visible. This is not a result as such of the intellectual poverty of the practitioners of consumer behaviour theory. Rather, it reflects the vain attempt to construct a general theory of consumption from a series of horizontal factors that are necessarily insensitive to the differences between systems of provision across the commodities that account for the vast majority of consumption.

# 4

# ECONOMIC AND CONSUMER BEHAVIOUR

## INTRODUCTION

This chapter begins with a conceptual critique of the contribution that economics has made to the understanding of consumer behaviour. Overall, demand theory within economics has changed very little over time and so has not been a source for innovative thinking: first, economics has been confined to a narrow behavioural and motivational calculus – individual utility maximisation; second, in formal theoretical terms, and contrary to immediate impressions, economics does not effectively have a distinct theory of consumption – either to confront the specific nature of what is consumed or to distinguish consumption from production. In short, economics is the most extreme version of a horizontal theory of consumption. It takes a simple and single idea, utility maximisation, and generalises it across all commodities simultaneously, whilst keeping all other factors constant, not least unchanging preferences and products.

Of course, this account is confined to mainstream economics. By way of exception, there are occasionally contributions that break with the normal rigid assumptions. Preferences may be endogenised, if habit-forming consumption is allowed, for example. Or, as expressed in the relative income hypothesis associated with Duesenberry, consumption may be made dependent on relative social status. These exceptions, however, are rare and never integrated into an alternative and sustained theoretical framework. This is because the whole edifice of the orthodoxy would collapse if preferences become endogenised. There are problems with multiple equilibria. And the interpretation of competitive equilibrium as a standard – from which market imperfections yield welfare reducing divergence – no longer pertains. Indeed, the positive association of welfare with utility, which is so fundamental to orthodox economics, is no longer sustainable. Orthodox economics cannot be amended to incorporate a richer theory of consumption. It would have to be discarded altogether. No wonder then that economics has entertained only sporadic heresies in this area.

An inevitable corollary of this rigidity is that the economics of consumer behaviour suffers from severe conceptual poverty. To some extent this is compensated for (some might say camouflaged) by mathematical and statistical techniques which are extremely sophisticated relative to the other social sciences and a source of intimidation to the uninitiated. But these characteristics isolate economics from other social sciences and render it incapable of finding a partner for an interdisciplinary marriage, as will be seen in the next chapter which explores its relationship to psychology.

## THE UNCHANGING ECONOMICS OF DEMAND THEORY

Consumer theory within economics has remained essentially unchanged since the last century; the marginalist revolution of the 1870s displaced the labour theory of value of classical political economy and came to focus instead on the atomised behaviour of individual economic agencies. Today's students of economics are still required to match relative marginal utilities to relative prices in a way that would be recognisable to the students of Alfred Marshall.

Economics has been built upon the central notion of the rational economic individual,[1] who optimises subject to constraints. For the firm, there is given technology and, in conditions of perfect competition, given prices for both inputs and outputs. The object is to maximise profits, and those firms that fail to do so are eliminated by competition. For the individual consumer, there are given tastes or preferences and the individual's motivation is to extract as much utility as possible from the given income available. They do so by choosing between a mix of goods whose enduring ability to satisfy utility is tempered by the price that each commands.[2] In this presentation, consumer theory has been reduced to demand theory with no substantive adjustments to allow for the limitations of treating the behaviour of the individual consumer, as optimiser, as analogous with the behaviour of the firm, a matter to which we will return.

The mathematical presentation of these results and the econometrics for estimating their implications empirically have increased significantly in sophistication.[3] But the idea that consumption is predominantly determined by the maximisation of utility subject to the prevailing budget and price constraints has been the undeviating focus throughout. The conceptual poverty of this approach has been noticed from early on, if habitually confined to the margins of the discipline, like the twitching of an unwanted but unavoidable guilty conscience. Kryk observed this narrow-mindedness, criticising 'economists adopting utilitarianism even as it is being rejected by other social scientists' (Kryk 1923: 138). In an introduction to a survey article, Brown and Deaton assert:

> In particular we are interested in the effects (on consumption) of changes in real income per head, the structure of relative prices and the distribution of income, and we should like to have a means of allowing for the introduction of new commodities and changes in taste.
>
> (Brown and Deaton 1972: 1150)

Scitovsky (1976: xii) has been more blunt in reflecting the state of the art: 'People's tastes, the way they spend their money and arrange their lives, are matters economists have always regarded as something they should observe, but must not poke their noses into.' While for Waller (1988), the role of 'habit' in economics is found to fall outside orthodox economics, essentially because of its departure from purposeful, reflective behaviour and the inconvenience it creates for models of general equilibrium theory.[4]

Consequently, partly because economics has tended to be sealed off from other social sciences, those economists that do criticise demand theory have usually had some other axe to grind, having found the orthodoxy too blunt a tool for their particular purpose. Scitovsky, for example, was concerned with what appears a simple enough problem – why people did not seem to be happier with increased affluence. To raise such problems and others like them, especially in the context of non-economic factors and theory, is to court the label of idiosyncrasy as far as economics is concerned – both by stepping outside economics to embrace the considerations of other disciplines and by breaching the conventional assumptions within economics.

Conceptually, the economic approach to consumer behaviour is justified on the grounds that it extracts the rational and systematic part of the determinants of demand, thereby separating them from and discarding other motives or behavioural characteristics. The latter, then, are presumed to be of secondary importance and, more in hope than expectation, to cancel each other out when aggregating over all individuals to obtain total demand. Economics considers all other aspects of consumer behaviour to be the subject matter of other, external disciplines, despite occasional concern with the origins of initial preferences or with breaches from 'rational' behaviour. On the extremely rare occasions when these appear in the literature, they are treated as deviations from standard optimising behaviour – in this sense, the 'irrational' or 'non-rational' being determined by the previously conceived 'rational'.[5] By homogenising and setting aside all non-utility maximising behaviour as 'irrational', economics effectively eliminates itself from the possible development of an *interdisciplinary* theory of consumer behaviour and heavily discourages even a *multidisciplinary* approach.

In addition, the economic theory of consumer behaviour focuses attention away from individual acts of exchange. These become of no interest in their own right, since each is meaningless in isolation from the others. Only 'bundles' of commodities give utility, so that the individual acts of obtaining and enjoying individual purchases become irrelevant. This results in a form of reification around the act of consumption. For it is now the commodities rather than individuals that take on the attributes of commanding pleasure. This is formally made clear by expressing underlying preferences as relations between the goods. As Deaton and Muellbauer (1980: 27) point out, 'we write $q_1 \sim q_2$ and say "$q_1$ is indifferent to $q_2$"', where the qs are different bundles of goods over which *individuals* have preferences.

Leaving aside these polemics around commodity fetishism, demand theory concerns itself with the interdependent totality of sales and purchases undertaken by the individual. In theory, this would include all acts of sale and purchase over a lifetime – incorporating initial assets, not least ability to labour or human capital, and intertemporal discounting of present as against future consumption (plus account of the disutility of labour and the utility of leisure).[6] Aside from these factors and acknowledging the role of transactions costs and imperfect information, little attention is paid to the necessity for consumer behaviour to take place over time, combining together a number of discrete activities, not least the carrying out of purchases and their consumption, as well as the process of decision-making itself. On these issues, economic theory tends to be silent.

Instead, existing theory constructs a self-contained and narrow notion of consumer behaviour, both in terms of its objects of analysis and in terms of its associated causal factors. It has been concerned with regular empirical laws, theoretical regularities derived from demand systems, and the connection between these two.[7] For example, empirically, Engel's Law hypothesises that the poorer a family, the greater the proportion of income spent on food; theoretically there is the fixed requirement that the substitution effect of good i for good j must equal that of good j for good i. In recent times, axiomatic consistency through mathematical modelling has been used to give rise to powerful parametric constraints that prove important in estimating demand curves or, more exactly, demand systems, and this serves the supportive function of linking the theory to empirical enquiry. For Blundell: 'Perhaps the most appealing feature of economic research into consumer behaviour is the close relationship between theoretical specification and appropriate estimation technique' (Blundell 1988: 16). This allows Deaton and Muellbauer (1980: 80) to reject casual reliance upon, and neglect of, theory and to call for: 'careful theoretical analysis . . . The real challenge is one of intellectual honesty; we must construct models that are fundamentally credible as representations of the behaviour and phenomenon we are trying to understand.'

Yet by theory, they mean mathematical consistency in obtaining parametric constraints from neoclassical demand analysis. This might be considered careful only along a very narrow and well-worn path, with no account taken of what economists tend to dismiss as irrational or outside their compass – they ignore behaviour other than individual utility maximisation and they refuse to explore the origins of (changing) preferences. Their only concession to violation of rationality in consumer behaviour is to consider the possibility of money-illusion (under which individuals falsely feel themselves to be better off because they have more money but do not take sufficient account of higher prices).

Moreover, the idea that consumers make decisions independently of one another is so deeply ingrained that the aggregation problem in demand theory (the relation between the collection of individual demands and of overall demand) takes on an almost perverse logic. Initially, a single consumer was taken as representative of society as a whole as if society were a single rational consumer. This has been found to be excessively restrictive, both theoretically and empirically, for even if each individual (household) has the same preferences, aggregation over them is not simple given the impact of differing distributions of income. Accordingly, Blundell argues:

> The most persuasive level of analysis must be at the individual consumer or household level . . . and some form of aggregation prior to empirical analysis is often inevitable. . . . The clear attraction of individual level data is that they avoid aggregation bias. Such bias can result both because of the complex interactions between individual characteristics and price/income effects and also because of nonlinearities in consumption behaviour due to non-linear Engel curves, corner solutions, rationing, non-linear taxation and imperfect credit markets.
>
> (Blundell 1988: 18)

Though this quotation points to some specialised economic concepts, most important to note is the theoretical and empirical detail that is embraced in respecting the independence of individual consumers. No account is taken of social factors that might lead consumers to behave in similar or even identical ways. Though to do so would not in itself resolve the aggregation problem, the absence reflects the way in which this problem is conceived – and the treatment of consumption more generally – exposing the refusal to acknowledge anything other than the narrowest of determinants.[8]

It is precisely the narrowness of this approach to consumer behaviour by economics that sets the points of departure for contributions to consumer behaviour from the other social sciences. These are concerned with the formation of preferences, with information processing by the individual, the activity of purchase, the activity of consumption, and the feedback mechanisms between these – although no particular structure and sequential division of these processes is sacrosanct.

In pinpointing this non-intersecting duality between the approach of economics and that of other disciplines to consumer behaviour, it is crucial to recognise that they all tend to have one central factor in common, the focus on the individual in and around the act of exchange. Within economics, this is usually taken as a focus for criticism by radical theories, with their emphasis on social relations and behaviour, such as class and conflict. In response, neoclassical theory, especially in contrasting itself favourably with classical political economy or Marxism, prides itself on having provided a theory of demand to complement the theory of supply.

Even this is misleading in anything other than a formal sense. True, the theory of utility maximisation subject to a budget constraint does lead to the derivation of demand curves in which the relative marginal utilities are equated to relative prices. But, significantly, this is completely independent of the specific use values of the consumption goods concerned. It is crucial that the goods be distinguishable from each other in their capacity to enhance utility, but the specific reasons for their differences are quite irrelevant. Hence, the nomenclature in the simplest textbook case of the existence of just two goods labelled as $x_1$ and $x_2$ in order that indifference curves can be drawn to illustrate substitution between them. The goods might be labelled bread and cheese to add some readership interest. But the economic theory that prides itself on incorporating demand does not in effect do so, since the nature, causes and motivation of that demand remain absent – except in the broadest sense of satisfying utility.[9]

This is as true for broad categories of consumption, such as food and clothing, as it is for specific items. Paradoxically, this is brought out most sharply in the particular functional form for utility associated with Geary-Stone.[10] For this, there is hypothesised a minimum standard of living necessary to obtain positive utility, signifying some concession to physical and even social survival. But even this can be specified abstractly as an undefined vector of goods, $(g_1, g_2, \ldots g_n)$. Indeed, the exact nature of the consumption goods under consideration is only specified once empirical studies are broached. This leads to speculations like Engel's Law which, once formulated, are then translated back into what must have been an appropriate form of the utility function in the first place. The causal content of such theory is extremely limited, since it essentially seeks merely to discover those utility functions that would generate the empirically revealed expenditure patterns – and under a set of assumptions that are far from realistic. There is also the assumption that given preferences extend not only across populations but also across time.

In short, neoclassical consumer theory is not only self-contained relative to other social sciences, it is also akin to a sealed unit within economics itself. It is partly for this reason that there has been negligible advance in the economics of consumer behaviour over the past century. The poverty of the economic theory of consumption is, however, not simply confined to its inability to deal with the nature of the goods consumed. There is also a deficiency in conceptually distinguishing the theory of consumption (treated as demand) from the theory of production (treated as supply). For between the two, there is an exact parallel; the demand theory is essentially identical to the axiomatic theory of supply. The maximisation of utility subject to price and income constraints creates an identical mathematical problem to the minimisation of cost subject to output constraints and factor input prices. Conceptually, individual consumers can be interpreted as if they were entrepreneurs producing utility, rather than output, as efficiently as possible. The strict parallel highlights the extent to which neoclassical economics lacks a distinct theory of consumption – for the equality of marginal rates of substitution with relative prices applies indiscriminately both to ratios of marginal productivities and to ratios of marginal utilities.[11] The duality theory associated with cost functions, which applies equally to supply (production) and to demand (utility), is an explicit acknowledgement of theoretical duality/identity between production and consumption.[12]

Interestingly, the traditional radical critique of neoclassical economics is that it does not have a distinct theory of production – by which is meant that it cannot explain the source of a surplus through some form of exploitation and/or that it treats the production process in narrow technical terms alone rather than as a relation of conflict between workers and bosses at the factory. On the other hand, radical theories have been charged with the reverse weakness, that of failing to offer their own theory of demand, depending upon cost of production alone. Putting radical theories on the defensive over demand has allowed the poverty of neoclassical economics' own demand theory to go largely unnoticed. The exception has been the critique of the concept of consumer sovereignty and all that this entails in pointing to the powerful role of producers in determining, first, what our preferences are and, second, what the goods are that are made available to satisfy them.[13]

The manipulation of preferences returns analysis to the traditional concerns of non-economic consumer behaviour theory, like those concerned with investigating the impact of advertising. Significantly, as will be discussed in Chapter 14, advertising in economics is more at home within the field of industrial economics, as part of the theory of the firm or industry rather than that of the consumer. This is indicative of the greater depth and variety of economic analysis around issues of supply as opposed to demand. Within orthodox economics, control over supply concerns the exercise, for example, of monopoly power, for which the theory of supply does have a richer and more changing content than the theory of demand. The poverty of the latter follows from the passive role played by consumers as the depositories of the utility that is ultimately created by the economic system. Central to this is the concept of competitive equilibrium in which, for example, a size structure of industry is ground out that is endogenous to the system (although it depends upon the parameters of supply that determine least average cost of production). So the number of firms is analytically determined, unlike the number of consumers which is given as a datum. In economics, there are competitive mechanisms at work that can transform the system of production. The same is not true of the system of consumption.

The divergence between the analytical content devoted to supply and demand does not, however, rest there. For the notion of competitive equilibrium forms a key concept from which potential divergencies are identified. Almost inevitably, these divergencies focus upon the conditions of supply, although externalities and monopolisation are equally possible, in principle, for both supply and demand. The simplest example is provided by the model of pure monopoly. But the incorporation of other causal factors or behavioural assumptions, around oligopoly theory and managerial motivation, has led to a rich set of models within the economics of supply, even though these tend to be limited by the continuing assumption of exogenously given technology.[14]

## THE ISOLATION OF ECONOMICS

The preceding discussion has laid out some of the causes for the limited contribution made by the discipline of economics to the theory of consumer behaviour. First, its notion of rationality excludes the concerns of other social sciences. Second, it does not have a specific theory of what is consumed, with utility created in the abstract through optimisation like any other 'production' process (cost minimisation for a given level of utility/output). And, third, developments within economics tend to focus upon supply and are, thereby, removed from a concern with consumption.[15]

Matters are not, however, quite so simple. For, within economics, developments in the theory of supply have been highly relevant to the determination of consumption. In the case of the economics of advertising, for example, there have been two strands.[16] The first links it to industrial economics and sees advertising expenditure as part of, or akin to, an accumulated fixed cost. This can act as a potential barrier to entry. Assessing the effects of advertising in this context has been primarily carried out within the discipline of marketing, or economics itself, as distinct from the discipline of consumer behaviour. For it has been closely linked to modification of demand curves (through the addition of an advertising variable) and their interaction with supply, with emphasis on econometrics and the associated problems of modelling, sampling and statistical techniques.[17]

The second focus for the economic theory of advertising has been in the role played by information.[18] Recently, this has gained in prominence within economics more generally, especially in view of the 'rational expectations' revolution, but it has also occurred through the development of microeconomics on a number of separate fronts. Models have been concerned with principal-agent problems, moral hazard and adverse selection. But these have had little point of contact with the informational models that make up consumer behaviour theory outside economics, which are based more upon the variety of responses to information than to 'rational' behaviour in the light of asymmetry in the availability of information.[19]

In short, advances in economics relevant to consumer behaviour tend to be confined within and adapted to the needs of the parent discipline without broadening its own field of enquiry. Theoretical advances within economics have not found independent application within the theory of consumer behaviour even in the parasitical sense discussed previously as a parent to this new discipline. This is partly because the ideas involved, such as differential access to information, have already been present, although emphasis outside economics tends to be more upon generating or passively receiving information than upon obtaining it. But it also reflects a difference in approach. Whilst the economics of information is built upon the microfoundations of individual behaviour, its significance lies in the implications for the economic system as a whole (or for some part of it). This is illustrated by the 'market for lemons', where asymmetry of information between buyers and sellers can even lead to the absence of a desirable market.[20]

By contrast, consumer behaviour theory, let alone economics, has rarely had such systemic concerns, especially where the linking of the effects of supply to demand are concerned. Rather, where social factors do occur, they arise through their role in bestowing socially determined characteristics upon individual consumers (or items of consumption).[21] Typically, the standard textbook for consumer behaviour theory, such as Mahatoo (1985), starts out with the simplest model of attributes and motivations as far as the individual is concerned. This is then built up into a more complex model which ultimately allows society to have an effect in the final pages of the text. Through sociology, variables such as the family, class, status and lifestyle enter into the explanation. More on the research than the textbook agenda, anthropology provides a ritualistic account of consumption, and semiotics deals with its symbolic content.

Significantly, what is missing from the theory of consumer behaviour is any determination of consumption through the influence of the system of production. Economics does not make up this deficiency since production is primarily the passive, if at times distorted, servant of demand. Exceptions tend to be treated as idiosyncratic[22] or are liable to be retained within their parent discipline. Consequently, whilst the role of economics for the theory of consumer behaviour has been to provide an increasingly irrelevant core of rational, optimising behaviour, the role of other disciplines, psychology in particular, is to provide a broader core of more relevant behaviour. Thus, the social sciences other than economics contribute a reservoir of causal factors – whether these be drawn from the environment external to the individual, from the intrinsic nature of the individual, from the article of consumption, or through some combination of them all.[23] It is to this that attention now turns.

# 5

# CONSUMER BEHAVIOUR AND PSYCHOLOGY

## INTRODUCTION

This chapter provides a cursory overview of the relationship between psychology and the theory of consumer behaviour. It argues that economics and psychology are, for the most part, incompatible disciplines sharing little common ground on which to construct a theory of consumer behaviour. Apart from their subject matter, economics and psychology also represent opposite extremes in their respective approaches. Neoclassical economics single-mindedly focuses on one essential principle – maximisation of utility subject to price and income constraints. Psychology rushes to the opposite extreme, embracing as many motivational factors (and constraints) as it can muster to explain the diversity of consumer behaviour.

Psychology understands consumer behaviour by conjuring up a complex of motivational and behavioural factors, some corresponding to the rational–conscious–observable–individual, others to the irrational–unconscious–unobservable–social, with each of these two mixes having only a rough internal congruence. Ultimately, then, the role of psychology in consumer behaviour theory can be seen as a sort of commodity fetishism. In short, commodities and individuals are endowed with a variety of properties which motivate or trigger a consumption relation between them. This necessarily represents a very partial and incomplete view of the social processes by which consumption decisions are taken, let alone brought about.

## CONSUMPTION ON THE COUCH?

In many respects, psychology's contribution to the understanding of consumer behaviour can be seen to be analogous to, but more general than, that of economics. It too takes the role of the individual as central but broadens attention to a wider set of human characteristics than simply maximising utility. Thus, psychology moves beyond the simple parameters of the rational economic individual to encompass, in principle, almost any physiological or emotional need, impulse, motivation or behavioural hypothesis.

In contrast, then, to its position or treatment within economics, psychology sees consumer behaviour as much more than a conceptually simple optimising process. In this way, especially as it is employed within marketing both as a discipline and as a business activity, the psychology of consumer behaviour becomes multidimensional – an exchange motivated by any of the causal factors behind behaviour to be found either from within the individual or as derived from across the various social sciences. Utility maximisation is just one amongst many possible motives behind consumption. An economist might view a transaction merely as the purchase of a utility-enhancing commodity. In reality, a whole bundle of social interactions, intangibles and symbolic aspects are involved. The market is a social institution and not just an enabling mechanism. Accordingly, the full range of human behaviour is to be found there and potentially to have a causative impact on consumption.

Analytically, this can be dealt with in one of two ways. The more common approach has been to project the social aspects of consumption on to individual commodities or consumers and then to examine acts of purchase as correspondingly more complex. For example, does a commodity offer the purchaser the quality of a particular lifestyle through its consumption? Less common is to examine the social relations themselves as something prior to, even if represented by, the commodity. This is to engage an even broader perspective that more properly belongs to anthropology or sociology. The broadened scope of consumer behaviour opened up by psychology is not simply a matter of adding more motivations. There are other extensions involved. First, in economics, consumer behaviour is identified with decision-making alone. Decisions are automatically translated into purchasing and consuming behaviour. The act of going out to buy commodities and the act of consuming them are essentially missing. Whilst Belk (1987) draws attention to the neglect of consumption itself in consumer behaviour theory (with the primary focus having been on what makes people buy), it is also important to examine what causes people to buy, how they do it, and how they experience consumption.

Psychology concerns itself with these issues. The focus is upon how individuals seek, receive, calculate with, and respond to, the information available on commodities. In the simplest attitude–attribute model associated with Fishbein and Azjen, consumers' individual attitudes interact with the commodities' specific attributes. Nicosia (1966) has a model, described by Mason (1984: 26) as one: 'which explores the process of product or brand choice and which identifies four "fields" of activity – consumer attitude formation, information search and evaluation, the act of purchase and finally post-consumption feedback.'

This has given way to the model of Engel *et al.* (1968), described thus by Mason: 'Whilst Nicosia saw attitude, motivation and experience as the key elements, the Engel–Kollat–Blackwell model takes a broader view, and identifies the major input variables as perception, values and attributes, personality and past experience.' (Mason 1984: 27). But Howard and Sheth (1969) is, according to Mason:

> regarded by many as producing perhaps the most satisfactory explanation of consumer decision processes .... The model comprises four major elements – namely, input (stimulus) variables, hypothetical constructs (concerned with perception and learning) and a set of exogenous variables (importance of purchase, personality traits, financial status, time pressure, social and organisational setting, social class and structure). Hypothetical constructs, as intervening variables, connect the input and output variables within the model.
>
> (Mason 1984: 29)

Each successive model involves an analytically finer (re)division of the structure of consumer behaviour, leading to a potentially explosive growth of associated causal factors. What these turn out to be is, in part, determined by individual studies of the consumption good concerned and, in part, determined by the stimulus parasitically drawn from other social sciences. In the first case, different factors are drawn from psychology, for example, according to whether the good concerned is a humdrum (brand) repetitive purchase or an infrequently purchased durable. In each case, most recent attention has been drawn to the role of 'affect' in consumer behaviour, or how people *feel* about the goods they purchase (or adverts concerning them).[1] This, no doubt, reflects an increasing interest by psychology (and by society at large in the age of therapy) in the role of feelings. As will be seen shortly, this is only one amongst a multitude of causal factors which can be employed.

Interestingly, Mason's succinct account of the standard models of consumer behaviour is intended to discover what light such theories can shed upon 'conspicuous consumption', which is, in a sense, perceived to be deviant from normal consumer behaviour by way of a form of excess and/or display. He argues that existing theories are unable to confront such 'exceptional behaviour' since, 'while both rational (economic) and "irrational" (social) elements will both often influence particular purchase decisions, the rational element must be considered dominant' (ibid.: 31). Thus, 'the treatment of exceptional consumer behaviour remains neglected because of this failure to move away from theoretical structures which are based on assumptions of rational behaviour' (ibid.: 35).

Implicit here is the view that consumer behaviour can be divided into the exceptional and the (more weighty) unexceptional, and that the latter can be explained adequately by the various theories based on rationality. Mason's complaint is that the exceptional then necessarily falls outside the scope of prevailing theories. As such, it illustrates that the dichotomy between rationality and irrationality, as corresponding to a division between economics and the other social sciences, must be a misconstrual or at least an oversimplification. For, within psychology, exactly the same division has been forced between rational and irrational behaviour with the former corresponding to a set of activities as a consequence of systematic information processing. This is brought out by Tuck, who begins by pointing to the speculative element in the orthodox theories, complaining of, 'untestability and lack of specificity of variables. They offer models of what consumer choice behaviour *might* be like, but offer no evidence that it is in fact like their theories' (Tuck 1976: 37). Tuck observes that the consumer is thought of as having a fragmented mind, which leads to conscious and unconscious consumer behaviour, the first of which (and, presumably, some automatic part of the second) is open to explanation:

> The consumer is thought of as having two parts to his mind; a conscious or rationalising part which can answer survey questions and an 'unconscious' or 'autistic' part which can only be reached by projective techniques, drawings and acting out. It is held that it is the 'unconscious' inaccessible motives which are the influential ones.
>
> (Tuck 1976: 45)

In parallel, then, with the economist's notion of the consumer as a rational maximiser of utility, there is the notion of the consumer as rational processor of, and actor upon, information (although this should be interpreted broadly to include stimuli of various sorts that are not strictly confined to information as such). Thus, rational behaviour is perceived as leading to an act of purchase on the basis of appropriate information gathering and processing, even if this is within a broader perspective than utility maximisation and, indeed, may be taking place unconsciously. By this means, the economist's narrow motivational perspective but broad range of calculation across the totality of prices and income is inverted, producing a narrow focus on individual goods associated with a wide range of mixed motivation and behaviour. Irrational behaviour, best exemplified perhaps by impulse buying, becomes identified with deviation from the theoretically preferred or identified outcome norms. However you define rationality, it seems that consumers will be prepared to revolt against it.[2]

In short, rationality tends to become linked with what can be explained or with what has been encompassed within theory and, as such, tends to become more inclusive over time. The incorporation of affect, for example, allows the role of feeling in purchasing to become a part of rational behaviour. This illustrates the extent to which the theory of consumer behaviour attempts to create an ever-widening core of systematic behaviour, which may well be labelled rational, whilst experimentation and observation in consumer research increasingly expands the frontier of factors into the periphery that has previously been excluded (as will be seen below). The result is an eclectic agglomeration of hypotheses that straddle the border between the core and the periphery, creating and investigating causal factors and corresponding concepts that are almost as numerous as the number of goods available for purchase. Casual collection of these variables yields the following, by no means comprehensive, list recalling the 'theory of the month' club for the theory of consumer behaviour as discussed in Chapter 3:

> High or low involvement, arousal, attitude, affect, attributes, intention, reaction, learning, satisfaction, expectation, atmospherics, environment, context, convenience, memory, familiarity, judgement, choice, impulse, generics, cues, status, brand, impression, class, time, age, inference, endorsement, stereotyes, community, socialisation, norms, knowledge, lifestyle, enthusiasm, materialism, culture, self-perception, routinisation, stimulus, sentiment, role-playing, psychographics, mood, encoding, focus, situation, adaptivity, opinion, leadership, imagination, variety, scripts, vividness, disconfirmation, precipitation, persuasion, reinforcement, reminder, seduction, aesthetics, humour, etc.

In the psychology of consumer behaviour, there are potentially as many explanatory variables are there are acts of consumption to explain. There is a simple projection of individual acts of consumption on to appropriate psychologically determined variables.

## THE DIVIDE BETWEEN PSYCHOLOGY AND ECONOMICS

When an economist places a consumer in front of a mirror, reflected back is the image of an entrepreneur purposefully optimising the production of utility subject to the constraints of price and income. The psychologist sees a more complex, splintered reflection, one signifying a broader range of motives and activities, but is also determined to look through the looking glass to hidden influences on the human psyche. Clearly, these two approaches can meet only on the surface of the mirror and their point of contact is analytically flat. This is illustrated by the discipline of economic psychology around which practitioners gather from the margins of each of its constituent parts and for which, 'consumer behaviour is certainly the most intensively investigated part' (van Raaij *et al.* 1988: 250). This perhaps reflects the more limited extent to which psychology is prepared to challenge the single principle of business behaviour to be found within economics, namely profit maximisation, although various managerial theories of the firm, for example, have been popularised. For economic psychology, the starting point is the widening of behavioural factors:

> To psychologists who know a little about economic theory the concept of the economic man often raises an insurmountable wall between economics and psychology; the psychologist tends to think that a science based on such simplified notions about humans must necessarily be wrong.
>
> (Warneryd 1988: 4)

Economists must concede on this since, 'Tastes and preferences are "given" within traditional microeconomic theory. In a consumer's life, however, they have to be learned along the lines of . . . learning principles; instrumental, cognitive and social' (van Veldhoven 1988: 68). Then, explanatory scope will be widened to encompass the 'irrational': 'Economic behaviour as economists study it, is modelled with cognitive factors. Psychology could bring in affect to increase the value of models of economic behaviour. Affect may contribute to the explanation of "irrational" behaviour' (Pieters and van Raaij 1988: 138). But there is no movement in economic psychology from the focus of economists upon the allocation of scarce resources to competing ends, even if a broader notion of means and motivation is proposed: 'Economic psychology encompasses the study of human behaviour and experience in connection with how scarce resources in terms of money, time and effort are handled so as to satisfy needs' (Warneryd 1988: 9).[3] In short, there is not much scope for a fertile marriage between economics and psychology in the plane of consumer behaviour, despite what is a growing minority interest in the field of economic psychology. This is illustrated by the paradoxes to be found in Kassarjian's (1982b) thirty-page review of consumer psychology. He observes in his opening sentence that 'Few areas in consumer psychology can claim the persistence and longevity of economic psychology.' Thus, the attempt to marry the two disciplines around consumer behaviour is far from new. Yet, over the page, Kassarjian's closing sentence on the matter concludes that 'The future for research in economic psychology is bright, at least in Europe.' It seems unlikely that what has failed to blossom in the past will now bloom in the future. For once the barriers posed to the study of consumer behaviour by economics are assaulted by psychology, the core role of economic rationality is simply swamped – as illustrated by the formidable range of factors listed above.[4] Utility maximisation with parameters set by prices and income becomes theoretically marginalised, although there is a place, for example, for perceptions about the relationship between price and quality and what constitutes a credible price, whether high or low. Consequently, the axiomatic strength of the economics approach, in constructing a complete demand system across the totality of an individual's exchanges, is lost. It is replaced by a more or less complete system of the possible influences upon the demand for a particular good or set of goods – with many purchases of different goods associated with, for example, some sort of lifestyle analysis, and repeat purchases of the same good corresponding to the theories of brand (dis)loyalty.

Upon reflection, these multifarious approaches to consumer behaviour by psychology can be summed up in two words – commodity fetishism. It is apparent that commodities are increasingly perceived to be taking on the attributes that are ascribed to them by individual attitudes. Put the commodity rather than the consumer in front of the mirror and what stares back is a lifestyle or some other such flavour of the month. But commodities as things do not have lifestyles or feelings, even if they are uncritically presumed to provide them. Now let the consumer join the consumed in front of the mirror. The relations between them, in or behind the mirror, are but a pale reflection of the economic and social system that allows them both to stand there. Consequently, the nature of commodity relations as a social system needs to be fully explored before consumer behaviour can be appropriately examined. This is taken up in subsequent chapters by examining, for example, the way in which commodities are produced and distributed, and their historical significance.

# 6

# WHAT IS CONSUMER SOCIETY?

## INTRODUCTION

In the modern world, it has become a cliché to suggest that we inhabit, are even victims of, a 'consumer society'; that 'consumerism'[1] is rampant; that we are dominated by 'consumer culture', having passed through a 'consumer revolution'. Such a focus on the consumption associated with affluence is remarkably blinkered, not only for its neglect of those who live on the margins of advanced capitalist economies, but also more strikingly for those in the Third World for whom consumption remains a matter of life or death – whether through starvation, disease or homelessness. No doubt, it is the general relief from such hardship in the developed world, some would say at the expense of the Third World, and also the recent historical origins of such affluence, that renders possible a preoccupation with levels and patterns of popular consumption beyond the mere minimum.

But what precisely is it that makes up consumer society? A flood of images immediately suggests itself; the opulent megastores that occupy the centres, and increasingly the fringes, of our cities, the rows of houses packed with both consumer durables and the more immediate items of gratification to the five senses. Whether the sixth sense of inner well-being is any more satisfied, however, remains a moot point, to which critical reference is often made.

In short, the notion of consumer society has a powerful hold; it releases an array of ideas and associations as wide as the range of possessions to which they correspond. Yet it lacks a coherent analytical content by which is meant a reasonably precise definition with an associated explanatory role, whether in terms of cause or effect. In fact, precise and meaningful definitions of consumer society are extremely hard to come by; they are as rare as the use of the term is common.

One reason for this is that consumption itself has played a minor role in the social sciences, i.e., with the notable exception of economics, where it occupies an important position but remains conceptually underdeveloped for any purpose other than statistical estimation. Rather, it is production which is most likely to be used as an analytical starting point with a corresponding neglect or subordination of consumption. Again and again, it has been argued within each particular social science, particularly by those that react against the orthodoxy of supply side dominance, that consumption has been set aside or is simply perceived to be a passive reflection of production.

As other chapters here demonstrate, this view is not entirely correct. The various social sciences have been shown to have much to say about consumption. A fairer criticism is that theories of consumption have been less systematic than for production and less easily co-ordinated across the social sciences. No doubt this reflects the relative lack of uniformity in consumption as compared to production relations – there appears to be a wide choice of what to consume, less on whether to work or not and how. Consequently, the notion of consumer society has served as an umbrella, indeed a middle-range concept, under which consumption has been examined. This has been done by drawing selectively upon what is presumed, but is not demonstrated, to be a coherent set of analytical insights, most of which have an immediate empirical derivation.

In this light, section 1 of this chapter presents a selective review of various uses of the term 'consumer society'. This is followed by some criticisms of the concept and a proposal for an alternative method of examining it through a systems-of-provision approach.

## 1 IN SEARCH OF CONSUMER SOCIETY

It is impossible to provide a satisfactory review of the literature on consumer society for two related reasons. First, it is a concept so widely used that searching out a comprehensive overview would be an endless task. The problem is aggravated by the common use of consumer society in a supporting role rather in a centre-stage role – the background against which some other theme is played out, such as the mores or the manipulated possessiveness of modern society. Second, where the term is used, its meaning and significance are often taken for granted. There is very little literature spotlighting the consumer society as such.

Here an attempt is made to isolate and explore certain themes that have been employed in the notion of consumer society. An obvious starting point is that of timing. When did the consumer society arrive historically? McCracken (1987) provides a useful survey of literature on the history of consumption. In doing so, he freely uses the term 'consumer society' without ever explaining what he means by it. However, one condition does appear to be irreducibly necessary – that consumption should be served by exchange through market forces. There may have been certain systems of production which were well provided for by self-sufficiency and which enabled the few to lead luxurious lives at the expense of the many. But this would not fall under the rubric of consumerism, even allowing that the variety of what could be consumed would be constrained by the absence of commodity exchange.

Given this basic ground-rule of provision through the market, consumerism has historically been allowed a free range, subject to the empirical identification of the growth in the market for one or more consumption goods. Stretching a point, Stuard (1985), in reporting upon a collection of studies by medieval historians, traces the effects of consumption on the economy back to the thirteenth century. More specifically, Mukerji (1983) identifies consumerism with the rise of capitalism and with the innovations that it is able to provide in consumption goods in response to a materialist world of thought (so that reproduced maps become a popular item of display, depicting and reflecting colonial discovery and conquest). Thirsk's (1978) book *Economic Policy and Projects* carries the subtitle *The Development of a Consumer Society in Early Modern England* to connote the growth of consumer goods in the seventeenth century; some of the goods remain familiar today, such as pins, vinegar, tobacco and starch (now disappearing), while others are now less familiar or unknown, such as woad, aulnage, hand-knitted stockings and copperas.

Weatherill focuses on the growth of the pottery trade in the period before 1780: 'The mechanics of the trade – the business, the travellers, the shops – bound producers, traders and consumers together into a composite whole. A consumer society would not have been possible without them' (Weatherill 1986a: 72).

Equally, she argues that, 'Increasing demand for a wide range of goods and clothing was as important in industrialisation as the invention of new methods of production' (Weatherill 1988: 2).

For Lemire, the period 1750–1800 witnessed the development of consumerism in the ready-made clothing industry. She concludes: 'Consumerism had developed apace under the combined influence of popularised fashions, a growing British cotton industry and a small but impressive trade in ready-made clothes' (Lemire 1984: 41).

Breen extends the influence of early British consumerism to colonial American imitators: 'this consumer revolution affected the lives of all Americans' (Breen 1986: 487), with the result that, 'without too much exaggeration, Staffordshire pottery might be seen as the Coca-Cola of the eighteenth century' (ibid.: 496). Interestingly, whilst elsewhere Breen argues again that, 'the eighteenth century witnessed the birth of an Anglo-American "consumer society"' (Breen 1988: 77), this 'vast consumer society' is then seen as reacting against the consumption of British goods as a form of protest during the War of Independence, following events in Boston.

Clearly these studies, and many more like them, do not merely reduce the historical versions of the consumer society to a simple growth in the consumption of marketed goods. Each links it to particular causal factors whether they be ideological, distributional, technological or based on marketing. Such studies reach their limits, both analytically and, to a large extent, historically, in the work of McKendrick *et al.* (1982). The authors of this work bring together a complex range of formative influences on the development of consumption which is deemed to operate favourably for the economy. Locating their study around the end of the eighteenth century, they present its consumerism as not simply analogous to the present day's but as providing its foundation or birth (whereas other studies of earlier periods see it as, at best, an abortive model).[2] In this way, the consumer revolution of the eighteenth century is considered as complementary and equal to the supply side transformations of the Industrial Revolution.

The work of McKendrick and his colleagues is critically assessed in Chapters 9, 10 and 11. It provides a benchmark for studies dealing with later periods, since these are generally situated in (or beyond) the era of consumerism in which mass production is presumed to have taken hold. Here then, there is a sense of history in defining the consumer society – it is defined as the modern period of mass consumption, based on mass production, and thereby sets itself apart from the past. Consequently, the analysis of consumer society tends to have a greater economic content. Indeed, production tends to be restored as the key causal factor, diverging from most of the historical analysis of earlier periods which argues against the predominance of supply/production over demand/consumption.

Put most simply, consumer society is perceived to be the consequence of mass production (of uniform goods through the factory system, particularly during the twentieth century). Thus, Westley and Westley link the creation of working-class norms of consumption – 'there is a tendency for everyone to want the same things and even to buy the same things' (Westley and Westley 1971: 14) – with factory production in 'the age of automation and mass consumption' (ibid.: 43). For Alt, the interwar period

> is precisely the period of the transition from competitive to monopoly capitalism, from limited production to planned mass production, from the occupational communities of the early industrial working class to the consumer leisure of the mass industrial laborer. . . .
>
> The transition to monopoly capitalist society tends to shift the source of social relations, culture and ideology from a class culture of work to a mass culture of consumption.
>
> (Alt 1976: 72, 80)

Most significant in perceiving consumer society as deriving from production is Hudson's (1983) *Archaeology of the Consumer Society: The Second Industrial Revolution in Britain*. Like many other studies, the evolution of consumer society is transformed into the history of mass production. An appendix, for example, lists one hundred or more key inventions or innovations, all of which are to do with the technology of production (even if this has been directed to the creation of new consumer goods).

If the notion of consumerism that informs studies dealing with the period of the nineteenth century onwards is firmly based on the centrality of mass production, a diversity of approach is still made possible through distinguishing the *mechanism* by which mass production is translated into mass consumption. This mechanism can then be taken to be an important causal factor which can itself influence the timing of the arrival of the consumer revolution.

The earliest candidates, put forward to undermine the primacy of production in this way, are retailing and distribution. Logically, and to a large extent historically, a wedge can be driven between mass production and mass consumption. For the latter can exist without the former, with standardised goods being sourced from a fragmented industrial structure and serving a widely dispersed market. Mass consumption then precedes and paves the way for mass production through the distribution and marketing system (see Fraser 1981). Further, through display forms of retailing, demand for consumption goods can itself be stimulated. As and when sufficient mass markets are created, then mass production can displace fragmented production.[3] In this way, the development of retailing takes on a prominent role in transforming mass consumption into mass production and in forging a continuing link between the two.[4] Consequently, the transition to a consumer society is one charting the rise of mass and multiple retailing and its subsequent subordination of retailers to producers and their branded goods (see Jefferys 1954).

Advertising is a related but chronologically later mechanism which has also been put forward as translating mass production into mass consumption. It is argued that the arrival of mass production in the United States, typified by Ford, required producers to create markets for their goods by breaking down traditional working-class consumption habits. This is deemed to have occurred during the interwar period in the US, concurrent with the rise of the advertising industry. The most prominent exponent of this view is Ewen (1976) who points to the need to manufacture consumers as well as products.[5] The argument rests on the questionable presumption that, prior to the introduction of widespread advertising after the First World War, the American working class had somehow resisted the invasion of capitalist products into their working and domestic lives. Nevertheless, the attention devoted analytically to Fordism as a mode of production is complemented by its necessary significance as a manufactured mode of consumption.

In many ways, in identifying the interwar years as the period which witnessed the manufacturing of consent to consumerism through advertising, Ewen's contribution brought to a close what might be termed the psychological approach to understanding consumer society. Before him, there had been a generation of social commentators arguing that American society had been employing advertising, or depending upon psychological influences more generally, to create false or undesirable needs. These were only to be satisfied by a process that reproduced them at a higher level. Vance Packard (1957) refers to the eight hidden needs preyed upon by advertising – emotional security, reassurance of worth, ego-gratification, creative outlets, love objects, sense of power, a sense of roots, and immortality. For him, advertising is less about selling products and more about buying customers. Similar sentiments were to be popularised by Galbraith (1962; 1969; 1973) and Lefebvre:

> Needs are seen as clearly defined gaps, neatly outlined hollows to be stopped up or filled in by consumption and the consumer until satiety is achieved, when the need is promptly solicited by devices identical to those that led to satiety; needs are thus incessantly re-stimulated by well-tried methods until they begin to become rentable once again.
>
> (Lefebvre 1971: 79)

In this light, consumer society becomes one dominated by the imperatives of profitability which, in pursuit of markets through psychological manipulations, creates and serves false needs without necessarily generating greater happiness, satisfaction or harmony. In addition, such critical stances (the guilty conscience of affluence), whilst tied to an economic analysis, were also concerned with the ethics of consumer society, with its vulgar materialism and possessiveness – summarised by Marcuse in his work *One Dimensional Man*. Marcuse acknowledged his intellectual debt to Vance Packard whilst also distinguishing between true and false needs and the general failure to recognise the disease of 'toil, aggressiveness, misery and injustice' (Marcuse 1964: 4–5).

Such analyses tend to have a close affinity with those that understand consumerism by reference to the idealised ethics of an earlier age and its corresponding way of life. It borders on what has been the most commonly used context for the idea of a consumer society, a moral critique of the lifestyles and ethics of modern capitalism. Of course, throughout history, consumption has always fallen between being condemned and being pursued:[6]

> The definition of consumption as a social problem is an old story and not an exclusively American one. Concern about the moral consequences of new patterns of consumption has persisted with remarkable tenacity from early in our history. . . . By the late 1600s in the Anglo-American world there emerged the ideological origins of an economic theory emphasising the beneficial effects upon production of a free market, acquisitive instincts, and a rising standard of living. . . . Materialistic and individualistic ideologies found legitimisation. . . . From 1880 through 1920 the shift from a producer to a consumer culture gained new momentum. . . . This change from the sanctions of religion to those of personality involved the increasing identification of happiness with pleasure.
>
> (Horowitz 1985: xvii–xxvii)

Since the mid-1970s, however, and coinciding with the end of the postwar boom, the theory of real and false needs has been legitimately brought into disrepute. Beyond the bare minimum of physical survival,[7] all needs are socially determined and it is arbitrary to divide them into those that are genuine and those that are not. Interestingly, more recent literature concerning deprivation has recognised this by defining it in terms of a capacity to participate in society, which immediately construes needs in terms of access to socially agreed norms of consumption.[8]

The move away from the notion of consumer society as a psychology of spiralling and artificial needs has led to much more emphasis being placed on consumption itself rather than its being treated as a confined response to the imperatives of mass production. This has given rise to the new urban sociology in which consumption is seen as a major factor in creating rather than simply reflecting social stratification. It is perceived as bringing into question the idea that work and production, as opposed to consumption, are the crucial existential spheres (see Moorhouse 1988).

This view is assessed in more detail in Chapter 17. Shifting the site of analysis in response to consumerism has not been entirely novel. The analytical amalgam of Fordism as motive force and advertising as transmission belt moved the locus of attention away from the factory into the pages of magazines and on to (the intervals between) the programmes of radio and television. But, most importantly, an interest developed in the home, expressed in two ways. First, the consumer revolution is identified with a domestic revolution, in the making of the modern home:

> The change, for example, from the laundry to the washing machine is no less profound than the change from the hand loom to the power loom; that the change from pumping water to turning on a faucet is no less destructive of traditional habits than the change from manual to electric calculating.
>
> (Cowan 1982: 223)

Not only is self-sufficiency eroded within the home as commodities are bought in place of home-made goods, but also the home itself becomes a temple to consumer society. Filled, and surrounded, by the artefacts of mass production, if rarely itself such a product, the home and activities within it become transformed (see Hardyment 1988; Hayden 1982). Out go servants and in come mechanical devices, intensifying and extending the housework to be done and creating the modern nuclear family with the dedicated housewife at its centre. The discovery of the 'household germ' goes hand in hand with the standardisation, if not fixedness, of kitchen, bedrooms, living rooms and bathrooms: 'The bathroom evolved more quickly than any other room of the house; its standardised form was accomplished in just over a decade (the 1920s in the United States)' (Cowan 1982: 227).

Second, then, the analytical focus (and material direct responsibility) for consumption fell upon the housewife (although by no means the chief beneficiary of expanding levels of consumption). With the major exception of the motor car, consumerism has always been heavily associated with the female, particularly in its early forms when tied to luxury, display and distinction. The gendering of consumerism has also occurred in the modern period but, for quite the opposite reason, i.e., because of the close identification of women in the household, serving as mundane and unobserved providers (and purchasers).[9] This is certainly true of the interwar period in which the housewife was no longer to be perceived as a cook but as a can-opener (Ewen (1976: 171), quoting C. Frederick, *Selling Mrs. Consumer*, New York, 1929). From the same source, Hayden quotes, 'Consumptionism . . . the greatest idea that America has to give to the world; the idea that the workman and the masses be looked upon not simply as workers or producers, but as consumers' (Hayden 1982: 280).

It is important, however, not to exaggerate the extent to which notions of consumer society have been constructed on the basis of divisions between men and women. More significant have been the divisions between rich and poor (although the focus for consumerism has at times also shifted to those of different age groups). Historically, consumerism has inevitably been associated with the expenditure of the wealthy, for it is only recently that the majority of the population, at least in advanced countries, has had a sufficiently weighty level of expenditure to be included in what has previously been a highly exclusive society. Walton (1986), for example, argues that bourgeois women in mid-nineteenth-century Paris had a decisive influence on industrial development through their taste for hand-made items. On the other hand, Rostow (1967), characterises his fifth stage of economic growth as the age of high mass consumption with the emphasis on the new middle class, a suburbanised population, durables, and higher grades of manufactured food and drink – all from the 1920s onwards in the United States.

Initially, then, consumerism is associated with the elite. The patterns that they set are then emulated through time and with the growing income of the lower orders, giving rise to a 'democratisation' of consumption (Boorstin 1973) – a sort of universal franchise to consume.[10] In this way, the notion of consumer society is necessarily moved away from the privileges of the few, at least within advanced countries. With or without trickle-down effects, it is mass consumption of mass-produced commodities by the mass of the population which comes to the fore. Recognition of this is best illustrated by the work of Katona (1964). He understands *The Mass Consumption Society* as unique in the general degree of affluence and the high share of consumer expenditure in national income. Consequently, mass consumer psychology is able to influence the course of the economy through the availability of, and fluctuations in, general discretionary spending power.

No sooner has this theoretical state of affairs been reached than its presuppositions are thrown into doubt. First, there is in the theory of post-Fordism, the notion that mass production can potentially be displaced by co-operating firms, using small-scale but flexible production processes and serving market niches.[11] Second, mass consumption is perceived to have attained its limits as consumers have become satiated with standardised goods. Third, and following upon the rejection of the distinction between real and false needs, all products are endowed with a highly variable content in terms of what they represent or signify (what they mean to those who consume them). Fourth, advertising does not merely act to endow products with false attributes; it becomes part and parcel of a more general articulation of the economy together with the media, communications and culture. In short, consumption becomes one, if not *the*, leading activity within postmodernist society. Far from clarifying our understanding, these more recent considerations unleash a conceptual chaos.

Jameson, a leading exponent of postmodernism in an article entitled 'Postmodernism and Consumer Society', points to:

> a periodizing concept whose function is to correlate the emergence of new formal features in culture with the emergence of a new type of social life and a new economic order – what is often called modernization, postindustrial or consumer society, the society of the media or the spectacle, or multinational capital. This new moment of capital can be dated from the postwar boom in the United States in the late 1940s and early '50s or, in France, from the establishment of the Fifth Republic in 1958. The 1960s are in many ways the key transitional period, a period in which the new international order (neocolonialism, the Green Revolution, computerisation and electronic information) is at one and the same time set in place and is swept and shaken by its own internal contradictions and by external resistance.
>
> (Jameson 1985: 112–13)

So far, this is a disorganised and unweighted bundle of the many features that make up contemporary capitalism and its history. However, it continues as follows:

> I want here to sketch a few of the ways in which the new postmodernism expresses the inner truth of that newly emergent social order of late capitalism, but will have to limit the description to only two of its significant features, which I will call pastiche and schizophrenia: they will give us a chance to sense the specificity of the postmodernist experience of space and time respectively.
>
> (ibid.)

One can but speculate that the second quotation is but a schizophrenic pastiche of the first; it adds little order to our understanding of consumer society (whilst saying much about the concept of postmodernism – at least in this area of application!).[12]

## 2 TOWARDS A CRITICAL ALTERNATIVE

In a review of McKendrick *et al.* (1982), Rosalind Williams (1984: 337) asks, 'How valid is the concept "consumer society"?' The previous section has provided some considerable support in favour of posing this question. By briefly re-examining the reasons for this, a rather different and, hopefully, more analytically rigorous approach will be suggested to explain the significance and sources of changing patterns of consumption.

First, consumer society has problems dealing with historical specificity. Under its rubric, the affinities between any two acts of consumption are forced to be accommodated, even in as diverse episodes in history as the expanding consumption of luxuries in the thirteenth century and the mass consumption associated with contemporary advanced societies. Scientific enquiry does prosper by discovering regularities across apparently diverse phenomena, but the uniformities here are both superficial and questionable. Once account is taken of wider economic and social factors, acts of consumption cannot be legitimately identified as different species of the same genus. Consequently, consumption is not to be understood by reference to itself, alone, in isolation from anything other than its proximate causes and accompaniments (such as what is consumed and by whom).

Production is the most obvious factor to link with consumption even if, in the context of consumer society, this has often been shunned because of the belief that the supply side has already commanded too great an analytical attention. The major exception is in notions of consumer society which draw upon the determining role played by mass production. From this there follows, almost automatically, the predominance of mass consumption, with its accompanying relishes of manipulative advertising, unsatiated appetites, and a generalised individualistic and materialistic ethic.

But, on close examination, the simple and general linkage between mass production and consumption founders on its narrowness; it provides at best only a partial model of what is consumed. Even today, more than half a century after the classic development phase of mass production, many other models of production/consumption abound; many commodities fall outside the framework of the classic model. This is especially so of the increasingly important service sector and of housing – paradoxically so for the latter, which has been perceived as the primary site of mass consumption.

In short, accepting the centrality of mass production as the leading edge of industrial society does not provide an adequate explanation of what is consumed and why. There are differences in the methods of development of mass production across different commodities and across different countries (despite some trends towards the globalisation of both production processes and products). There is sufficient diversity in production itself, through technology and design, labour processes, etc., to allow for diversity in consumption even if it were the passive reflection of production.

But, of course, consumption is not simply a passive reflection of production even if one were to embrace fully the heaviest criticisms of the notion of consumer sovereignty. Whilst an interest in consumption alone might focus on the slip twixt cup and lip, there is equally a wide variety of slippage between the factory and the cup and its contents. The link between production and consumption is not a simple unity of opposites – as often presented both in a simplistic Marxist model of contradictions between exchange value and use value and in the simultaneous model of supply and demand in the orthodoxy of neoclassical economics. Before production can be translated into consumption, income has to be generated and distributed across different socioeconomic groups, their preferences and habits have to be formed and (re)acted upon, and products have to be packaged, distributed and marketed. These chains in the link between production and consumption confirm the problems of defining a single model, either for the dependence of consumption upon production (what has been termed here a vertical approach) or for the suggestion of the uniform significance of factors (such as advertising or emulation) on consumption across a range of diverse commodities (what has been termed a horizontal approach).

Briefly summarising, the analysis of consumption should not seek to deny the pervasive influence of the characteristics that have been associated with consumer society, revolution or culture. Nor must it neglect the immanence of trends acting indirectly upon consumption – through mass production and modes of retailing and distribution. But the impact of these factors must be studied in relation to each other in anticipation of diverse outcomes for particular commodities or groups of commodities, according to their specific interaction in combining different economic and non-economic factors. In other words, a systems-of-provision approach (as developed in Chapter 2) opens up the possibilities for a much richer discussion. Its advantages will be brought out in specific sector studies in the next part. The distinct set of imperatives governing different sets of commodities is implicit in the use of terms that describe them – viz., the food system, the energy system, the housing system, the fashion system, the transport system, etc. The use of the term 'system' signifies the idea that certain structures and dynamics have been set in place for each separate group of commodities. Whilst these are not cast in stone, or without affinities at least in part across commodity groups (sharing technical, marketing or other features), the presumption must be that there is a stronger vertical link in the process from production to consumption within each of the systems of provision than there is between them.

# 7

# CONSUMPTION AND GROWTH

## INTRODUCTION

Chapter 7 addresses the putative usefulness of consumption demand as an agent of significant economic and social change. Although the arguments supporting a prominent if not always primary role for demand are of general applicability, here they are applied within the context of the British Industrial Revolution. Discussing theoretical issues in the context of a specific period allows them to be more succinctly illustrated. It also reveals the limited usefulness of consumption (and its implied impact on the economy through market demand) viewed in isolation from other economic and social factors and treated monolithically, i.e., undifferentiated by industrial or economic sector.

More specifically, there is a school of thought, led by McKendrick (McKendrick *et al.* 1982), that sets demand on an equal footing with supply as an instigator of the Industrial Revolution. The great changes associated with this period, whose timing, scope, character and impact are still disputed, are recast as the consequences of a contemporaneous consumer revolution. This treatment of demand is at odds with the more common theoretical approach which places it in a subordinate position to supply, abetting or constraining it through the pressures of overheated, insufficient or fragmented markets. The intuition of demand-led growth, let alone revolution, seems to follow from the informal extrapolation to the economy as a whole of a particular sector within it.

Some of the empirical evidence thrown up by this argument, found to be misleading and superficial, is taken up in Chapter 10, where McKendrick's discussion of demand for fashion in eighteenth-century clothes is investigated in some detail. This chapter investigates instead the more general theoretical and empirical questions raised by such an approach.

It also examines the theoretical role of demand as it interacts with supply. A more balanced view would appear to give each of them equal weighting in the simultaneous determination of outcomes. In this context, to emphasise one or the other side is to err in the extreme, cutting analytically with only one blade of the scissors. This view, however, is also inadequate: at best it can only *describe* market outcomes as determined by supply and demand; it still cannot *explain* them. Supply and demand are themselves the structured consequences of dynamic economic and social relations and processes; they cannot simply be reduced to shifts in a set of curves as the dismal science of economics so lifelessly portrays them.

## IS THERE A SUPPLY AND DEMAND FOR INDUSTRIAL REVOLUTION?

Within economics there has always been an uneasy dichotomy between the long run and the short run. It has usually been accommodated by focusing attention exclusively on either one or the other at any particular time. In the era of Keynesianism, the short-run movement of the economy has been central, with macroeconomics occupying its leading edge. Whilst microeconomics has grown in both sophistication and scope, especially in serving the theory of general equilibrium, the subject has advanced conceptually little beyond the partial equilibrium foundations provided by Alfred Marshall – which were designed to explain the behaviour of the individual consumer and firm. Aggregating these individual units into the economy as a whole yields macroeconomics when the market co-ordination of supply and demand are potentially imperfect in the short run. In the long run, such market imperfections tend to be set aside, so that aggregation leads to a focus upon the changing contours of supply and technology. This leads in economic history to the increasingly familiar measurement of growth and total factor productivity, necessarily calculated, in principle, on the basis of full employment.[1]

Over the past decade or so, the balance between macro and micro has been disturbed. Keynesianism has given way somewhat to a revival of monetarism in the form of the new classical economics.[2] There has also been greater attention to the 'supply side' in the light of policies designed to strengthen market forces (privatisation and deregulation) and individual incentives (tax cuts). None the less, there remains an uneasy compromise between the short and the long run. Whilst Say's Law, the idea that supply creates its own demand, is rejected in the short run which is predominantly demand side determined, the long run is still primarily perceived as given by unexamined supply side conditions. Thus, in statistical work, the long run is usually netted out as the supply side trend around which short-run, demand side fluctuations are to be estimated and explained.[3]

Not surprisingly, economic history has reproduced this analytical division between the short and long runs and between demand and supply, respectively, particularly as cliométrics has brought it analytically closer to the theoretical framework of orthodox economics. Different economic periods have been designated by reference to modes of supply, and especially to technology – as captured in the ages of steam, of the railway, and of the automobile. Traditional historiography, in other words, has been dominated by an interest in supply side questions which have clearly claimed the high ground in the study of the British Industrial Revolution. How could so much that was new and different have been produced over such a short period? Inevitably, the sheer scale of the changes that took place has created a logical asymmetry between awareness of, and interest in, supply and demand.

The latter has lagged far behind. Not surprisingly, the imbalance in historical analysis has been redressed by a revisionist school which seeks to place emphasis on long-term change as the consequence of demand as well as of supply. Gilboy is frequently cited as an early exception to supply side hegemony, arguing that, 'in the field of economic history as well as that of economic theory there has been a tendency to overemphasize the factor of supply' (Gilboy 1932). Later historians have reiterated Gilboy's lament, bringing the role of demand into greater prominence.[4]

McKendrick argues most forcibly that the birth of the Industrial Revolution owes as much to demand or, more exactly, to consumption as it does to supply. What is more, demand may even have been the midwife of the shift in supply. With respect to consumption, he talks of a 'revolution' (McKendrick 1982: 1); changes 'of lifestyle' (ibid.: 3); 'consumer boom', 'men, and in particular women, bought as never before' (ibid.: 9); so that 'the first of the world's consumer societies had unmistakably emerged by 1800 . . . (if not) *all* the features of modern consumer society' (ibid.: 13). In sum, 'the consumer revolution was the necessary analogue to the industrial revolution, the necessary convulsion on the demand side of the equation to match the convulsion on the supply side' (ibid.: 9).

For orthodox historians, especially those leaning to the right across the intellectual spectrum, this demand side approach has certain attractions. First, it is an open invitation for detailed study of the changing patterns of consumption. As these expand, they are perceived as the motive force of economic progress – neatly combining the welfare theorems of static *laissez-faire* economics with consumer satisfaction as the source of growth. Second, as consumption is increasingly confined to those with direct or indirect access to income, so economic progress is associated with the history of the rich or *nouveau riche*. Accordingly, for McKendrick, an important ideological accompaniment of the consumer revolution of the eighteenth century is the overcoming of the puritan ethic against consumption. Unfortunately, this development has been seen too readily as a reaction against a blanket ban on all consumption or enjoyment rather than against the moral outrage at its unequal distribution.

Third, the preoccupation with consumption diverts attention away from supply, production and work, which all too readily carry a connotation of Marxist and class analysis. Consumption, by contrast, is primarily a private affair for the individual concerned.

Finally, and paradoxically, there are resonances between this approach and the revival of contemporary monetarism. Those that have reacted against

Keynesian policy-making eschew state intervention to manipulate effective demand and, instead, rely upon supply side factors to provide full employment in the short run. In doing so, they tend to embrace the role of demand in the long run. And that demand will be sustained by activities from the *nouveaux riche* of the 1980s, driving consumption which becomes a kind of *de*industrialised revolution.

## ECONOMIC THEORY AND THE CONSUMERIST APPROACH

Such are the attractions, especially to those on the right, of stressing the long run role of demand. Analytically, however, these leanings are far from being theoretically rigorous and fully developed. Can economic theory provide a sound foundation for the role of demand in major long-run change such as that occurring during the period of the Industrial Revolution? In particular, can a consumerist revolution be a decisive factor?

The theoretical content of the consumerists is problematic. The simplest economic model they rely upon is the notion that increases in demand represent a shift out of the demand curve and more output at a higher intersection with a given supply curve. This is entirely unacceptable. If this occurs within a particular sector of the economy, then the shifting demand curve must be compensated for by an equivalent but negative shift in some other sector.[5] If the shift concerns the economy as a whole, then we enter Keynesian territory in which increases in output can only follow upon excess capacity for, otherwise, inflation is the commonly perceived outcome.

In economic theory, a common, if not mainstream, model for long-run growth in the context of excess capacity is that associated with Kaldor-Pasinetti and the widow's cruse, a goblet from which the liquid that is drunk is always replenished. Here, Kaldor put forward the dictum that workers spend what they earn and capitalists earn what they spend. The latter proposition follows in the joint presence of excess capacity and deficient demand, for what one capitalist spends creates demand and hence profits for the class as a whole. The simple Keynesian multiplier applies to the profit economy alone; the lower the saving rate of capitalists, the more profits they have to earn in order to attain the level of investment and other autonomous expenditure. In short, demand (out of profits) creates its own supply.[6]

There are a number of disturbing features of this model as far as the consumerist approach is concerned. First, apart from depending upon excess capacity, any increases in profitability on the supply side have the effect of depressing the economy, since necessary savings are achieved at lower levels of economic activity. This means that the complementary supply side industrial revolution would have been self-defeating. Second, the model takes the growth rate as given, and determines that the level of saving should adjust to the level of investment by compensating changes in the distribution of income should one or other class change its saving behaviour. In other words, if capitalists spend more, then the distribution of income will adjust in their favour and the saving and growth rates will remain as before.

More generally, those that argue that a shift in demand gives rise to an industrial revolution rarely specify what the latter means, even in a narrow economic sense. After all, the theoretical apparatus involved is identical to the partial analysis of a single market, say, for umbrellas, experiencing a demand shift in view of a damp summer. To pursue the analogy, shifts in the climate do not usually lead in such models to a higher growth rate in the use and manufacture of umbrellas but to a higher equilibrium level of output and price. To return to the industrial revolution, the consumerist approach has neglected to specify whether increased demand should lead to a once-and-for-all shift in the level of output or, as seems less likely from such a shift but reasonably required of a revolution, a once-and-for-all shift in the level of the rate of growth of output.

Lastly, the demand-led model of growth has been put to use in conjunction with a supply side analysis in the model of monopolistic stagnation, derived from the economics of Kalecki.[7] This suggests that monopolies invest too little in order to sustain prices and to restrict output, whilst workers' wages are forced down to sustain profitability and at too low a level to sustain demand. Obviously, this Marxist genre of underconsumptionism is far removed from the intentions of the consumerist school. But it does serve to illustrate the difficulty of sustaining the school theoretically on the basis of aggregate demand shifts.

Much more fruitful is the idea that shifts in demand effect shifts of the supply curve itself rather than shifts along it. Whether for individual sectors or for the economy as a whole, the idea depends upon the role of the extent of the market, a type of argument predominantly associated with Adam Smith's focus on the potential for the growing division of labour. Crudely, the larger the market, the greater is the scope for economies of scale with existing technology. In addition, larger markets will provide greater inducements to innovate, since the potential returns will be so much greater.[8]

Such an approach appears to be the most favoured explanation of those who seriously consider the matter of the effect of demand in the long term.[9] It is a sort of infant industry argument, only to be applied in the absence of any grown-ups. But the effect of protection, or larger and more certain demand, is subject to dispute – does it lead to featherbedding and higher prices or to dynamic accrual of scale economies? Quite clearly, this cannot be answered by reference to demand alone. Which of these two responses occurs depends upon other conditions for which the structure of supply is most important, as well as the level and distribution of income.

Probing this further reveals problems for the consumerist approach. For, to put it in extreme form, the idea of firms straining to revolutionise supply but held back by deficient demand presupposes either a monopoly having mopped up the available markets, or a fragmented industrial structure operating in the absence of competition. Otherwise firms would compete with each other for the available demand and rationalise where scale economies warranted it. All of this appears highly improbable for the period of the Industrial Revolution, where large numbers of small firms in competition with each other seem to have been more the order of the day for at least a century. Of course, greater demand would help any firm or industry but whether this leads to cushioning or to innovation is conditioned by factors surrounding supply – availability of finance, for example, or market restrictions – most of which are studiously ignored by those relying upon the direct or indirect impact of demand upon supply.

Interestingly, McKendrick implicitly rejects the demand-led theory of transforming supply. His emphasis, for pottery and clothing and fashion more generally, concerns the entrepreneurial and social creation of a differentiated demand in conformity with status enhancement. Accordingly, limitations upon demand, especially where they affect economies of scale, are irrelevant since capital itself is fragmenting demand as a marketing strategy – changing the design, colours and articles of the pottery manufactured to serve and to sustain changing fashion.

McKendrick's analysis of the pottery industry, with its focus on the entrepreneurial activities of Josiah Wedgwood, has not escaped criticism, especially from Weatherill (1986b). She argues that Wedgwood was neither a typical representative of the industry, nor its leader, so that he cannot be taken to be the exemplar of its specific success; nor can the potteries exemplify the economy as a whole. And, even *within* this one industry, different sectors need to be acknowledged based on differences both in quality of raw materials employed and of markets served. It is far from clear, for example, why a decorative piece of Wedgwood display should give rise to a functional demand for coarse tea-drinking ware. In any case, even after a period of rapid expansion, the sector still employed only 1 per cent of all industrial workers and just half of 1 per cent of all workers (Weatherill 1986b: 299). This cuts the impact of the Wedgwood enterprise down to size.

But even if this is set aside, and Wedgwood is granted the status of leading entrepreneur, does the type of role he played in the creation of demand necessarily lead to an industrial revolution through a consumer revolution? The answer is ambiguous. For the Wedgwood characteristics that McKendrick describes are ones that are usually associated with inefficiency, even within orthodox economic analysis. By employing fashion to charge a high price on a new piece and then dropping the price to reach a wider market, Wedgwood is essentially operating as a discriminating monopolist for 'he had accomplished, in fact, the most spectacular example of a successful policy of product differentiation in the history of British pottery'.[10] Nor is charging prices well above marginal cost to give goods a snob value a recipe for economic efficiency. Indeed, modern consumerist society is more accustomed to the introduction of goods at lower prices initially in order to gain acceptance for mass-produced goods.

These factors point to static inefficiencies in Wedgwood's activities which would have had the further effect of fragmenting the market for pottery, thereby potentially *delaying*, not hastening, the availability of the demand for, and the supply of, a less fashionable but cheaper and more generally available product to serve more of the 'lower orders'. It is at least as plausible to see the luxury market of the eighteenth century as an obstacle to the development of mass production for the lower classes in the nineteenth century, as it is to view it as a stimulus to emulation from below.

In short, on theoretical grounds, the argument that demand as such can play a significant role in long-run economic change is extremely weak, and the theoretical analysis presented here suggests that the conditions under which it could play a role are not typical of the period of the Industrial Revolution. The consumerist approach tends to presume that if the consumption of the lower classes chronologically follows that of the upper classes, then this is evidence of trickle-down (and of a sort of multiplier demand effect from a higher-level stimulus). There is a simple fallacy in this. Without necessarily presuming that the growth of consumption habits is naturally determined or that it is uniform across a population, exactly the same sort of observations could occur even if there were no emulative effects. This is so if consumption is simply expanding across the population in line with rising incomes – you eat beef once you can afford it!

The substantial increase in the domestic consumption of coal illustrates this process. Flinn (1984: 252) estimates it rose from between 1 and 2 million tons in 1700 to over 5 million tons in 1800. Distribution and marketing of the coal required the development of a highly sophisticated and complex set of activities, especially in the run from the mines of Newcastle down to the hearths of London.[11] And different grades of coal, in terms of both burning capacity and associated toxins, influenced consumption in the domestic and the industrial markets. Indeed, Weatherill (1986b: 384) observes that Wedgwood used at least five different grades of coal.

Not surprisingly, growth of domestic consumption has tended to be overshadowed by the dramatic rise in the use of coal for the production of iron from the last quarter of the century onwards and for its presumed role as an energy source in the Industrial Revolution. As far as domestic consumption is concerned, however, there are considerable parallels with the economics of the pottery industry – even if the Wedgwoods of coal do not readily present themselves. Yet it would be far-fetched to view the rise in coal consumption as originating out of the emulative behaviour of the lower classes (with fashion emanating from London as the major domestic market). More important was the availability and cost of transport, the price of coal, its potential substitutes, and the levels of income, together with overall population size and housing conditions (given the weather).

Two further differences between coal and pottery are relevant here. First, coal was more important in quantitative terms, contributing about 60,000 to total employment in 1800 (Flinn 1984: 365), roughly six times the level of employment in the potteries (Weatherill 1986b: 453). Second, its ability to expand demand had been heavily circumscribed both by monopoly and by taxation. Though the effects of monopoly control on final prices may have been small, taxation may have raised them to a level at least twice the costs of production, especially in the London market (Hausmann 1984a; 1984b). This is evidence of the driving force of income even in the context of *restricted* demand.

The arguments around pottery and coal concern individual sectors of the economy. They also concentrate on the expansion of existing markets rather than on the chronologically earlier creation of these markets. Study of the earlier period involves a closer look at the displacement of earlier forms of production and consumption, thereby siting the development of the market economy within a specific historical framework and identifying it as just one of many forms of economic life.

## IS EMPHASIS ON DEMAND *AND* SUPPLY THE ANSWER?

Do these arguments against the consumerist approach lead then to the restoration of the orthodox dichotomy in which Say's Law appears to rule in the long run and effective demand appears to rule in the short run? The answer is, 'not necessarily' – first of all because the orthodoxy is no longer quite so simplistic. It recognises that the industrial revolution is the product of a complex multiplicity of factors. Only the impassioned researcher in a highly restricted academic field will tend to produce a self-interested, monocausal explanation. Moreover, demand is and has always been taken into account, even if in a subsidiary capacity. This is certainly true of attempts to assess the impact of growing exports as opposed to the domestic market[12] (although serving the world market would be unable to explain, of itself, why one country rather than another should experience industrial revolution). And, as cliometrics renders more analytically rigorous the orthodox economic analysis underlying historical change, demand factors are a logical requirement. For Cole, 'a substantial literature has begun to appear on the subject, and the growth of demand is now widely regarded as one of the essential elements in the transformation of the economy' (Cole 1981: 36). For Crafts,

> In the short run supply does not create its own demand . . . the level of output depends on the level of aggregate demand, which may not be that which achieves full employment in the short run. Levels of demand that push the economy towards full employment in the short run might elicit greater investment and productivity increase, thereby enhancing the growth rate of the productive potential.
>
> (Crafts 1981: 131)

Even McCloskey (1981: 120–2), who generally denies the role of demand for the economy as a whole, makes three exceptions – in case of foreign trade, high unemployment and demand-induced technical progress – all of which he dismisses on empirical grounds.

However, the orthodoxy not only takes account of demand; embracing it within a multicausal explanation is taken one distinct step further by incorporating the variety of explanatory factors into a system of demand and supply. Crafts continues:

> Levels of demand that push the economy towards full employment in the short run might elicit greater investment and productivity increase, thereby enhancing the growth rate of the productive potential. . . . The long-run rate is made up of a large number of these short-run spells, and so the economy's rate of growth will depend on levels of demand. The majority of recent English economic historians of the eighteenth century have (*possibly unconsciously*) written in this vein.
>
> (Crafts 1981: 131 (emphasis added))

This probably exaggerates the extent to which long-run models have been worked out with a strong component of effective demand in attendance, and with the long run constructed as a sequence of short-run (unemployment) equilibria. As previously observed, orthodox economics has considerable difficulties relating the long run to the short run in this way. More accurately, Crafts is describing an analytical procedure whereby the variables that are considered important to short-run macroeconomic analysis – such as demand created by exports, autonomous expenditure in the simplest multiplier model – are incorporated into explanations of the long term. What is equally significant is the implicit appeal to a stark synthesis in which both demand and supply interact to yield economic change. Even those who do not intend to do this are interpreted as having no choice, inadvertently contributing to the analysis of the level of demand and/or the level of supply.

In other words, there is a sort of analytical reductionism in operation, in which all authors and their suggested causal factors contribute to the specification of the shifting supply and demand curves. Individual causal factors can be examined in this context by reference to their effect on such curves. Because the framework accommodates this, it is hardly surprising that, whilst there has been muted praise for the consumerist approach, criticism has rarely reached beyond the level of questioning the empirical emphasis. Paradoxically, opposition is more likely to come from those such as McCloskey, whose rigour in orthodox economic analysis and prior commitment to Say's Law in the long term led him to tend to reject the long-term role of demand. Otherwise, the supply and demand framework gives rise to an appealing commitment to a multicausal explanation for the Industrial Revolution but one that depends upon the simplest of causal analytical structures that is essentially eclectic.

This discussion raises a number of further problems. First, is it appropriate to treat major historical events such as the Industrial Revolution in the same analytical and empirical framework as is used for an individual sector over a shorter and less dramatic period? The likely answer is that the more extensive the degree of change, if of a qualitative nature, the more variables must be included in order that the source of shifts in demand and supply are isolated and the *ceteris paribus* type assumptions are justified or, more exactly, adjusted. In principle, almost any variable could enter as a factor in supply and demand. This can be taken to extremes; a counterpart in the ideological realm is to be found in Campbell (1987), who argues – to parody – that just as the Protestant ethic shifted out the supply curve, so the romantic ethic shifted out the demand curve. No wonder the economy boomed!

Second, though, a sequential relaxation of the boundaries of *ceteris paribus* leads to a hierarchical ordering of the causal factors between those in the short run, which are always included, and those in the long run which, for the shorter period, act as parameters. In narrow economic terms, employment and output tend to be treated as variable in the short run and the capital stock as variable in the long run. Technical progress tends to endure a schizophrenic existence. At some times it is incorporated continuously into the economy; at other times, it has to be positively sought over the longer term. As Musson observes of the growth models that are still standard,

> the scientific and technical achievements of the past two centuries are so overwhelmingly obvious in their transformation of economic and social life that it seems almost incredible that, until very recently, most modern economists, building 'growth models', left them entirely out of account. (Musson 1972: 1).

Third, the causal model involved is one of simultaneous determination, in parallel with, if not always formally equivalent to, the mathematical sense of the term. Supply and demand are equalised by whatever underlying causal factors are taken to influence them. These factors, as mentioned in the previous point, are structured chronologically rather than causally. There is a tendency to look first at the elements making up the measurement of growth and total factor productivity, then to move to explain a second level of variables, such as exports, and, finally, to incorporate a third level of qualitative factors usually associated with socio-economic change, like entrepreneurship, skills and business culture.

Doubts have to be raised about the explanatory content of such an approach. Though it does provide a powerful, if at times obscure econometric means by which to structure the presentation of empirical material, there is a profound absence of theoretical content, even if the underlying approach is the soon-forgotten optimising behaviour of individuals. McCloskey (1981) reminds us of this by referring to the isolated, closed and atomised economy of Robinson Crusoe when arguing that aggregate demand cannot shift output.

Indeed, it is far from clear how supply and demand analysis can do anything other than chart the change in economic and social relations (and the relation between the two) when discussing the Industrial Revolution or other such sustained periods of economic and social change.

This is not then simply nor predominantly to press for a richer set of variables to be considered as influencing supply and demand – an attractive option for those who wish to take account of class conflict, redistribution of income, work intensity, i.e., for those who wish to reject the undoubtedly restrictive and conservative variables that are the common fare of the neo-Keynesian approach. Rather, a structured theory of economic and social change is essential, one that relates underlying tendencies and tensions to more specific developments and resolutions. This is, of course, easier to propose than to elaborate, and nothing more than hints can be offered within the confines of this chapter. The analytical point of departure is the focus upon underlying historical and social forces that give rise to supply and demand but which are not reducible to them. The classic example is given by Marxist theory, in which the specification of a capitalist mode of production and its tendential laws of production give rise to abstract propositions from which more complex categories and the historical process are derived and analysed. That such a method is not confined to Marxism can be illustrated by reference to classical economists, even those who are generally considered to be supportive of the consumerist approach.

Adam Smith, for example, perceived the stage of commerce as an articulation between the growing division of labour and the limited extent of the market, which in turn reflected more fundamental historical forces determining the ethical balance between altruism and the wish for self-regard, on the one hand, and self-interest in conjunction with the natural propensity to truck, barter and exchange, on the other.[13] For Smith, the Industrial Revolution as transition to the commercial stage of society required breaking down feudal barriers to the market so that the division of labour could develop; a similar view underpins the contemporary ideology of the 'Single Market' for the European Community of 1992.

In contrast, Malthus as praised by Keynes, stressed the progressive role played by landlords' unproductive expenditure in maintaining demand. This too, however, was linked to an underlying conflict between the virtuous pursuit of happiness and its potential for generating excesses (most notably in population growth in the lower orders). For Malthus,

> treated all universal passions, impulses and wants, when considered abstractly or generally as being natural or good. . . . The danger to happiness lay not in these impulses but in the 'fatal extravagances' to which they gave rise.
>
> (Winch 1987: 38–9)

Accordingly, Winch (1987: 76) quotes from Malthus, 'the science of political economy bears a nearer resemblance to the science of morals and politics than to that of mathematics'.

Just as references to Smith and Malthus (and, most notably, Marx) exemplify the error of reducing all economics to matters of supply and demand,[14] so this conclusion is reinforced by broadening the scope of the analysis. Population growth, for example, crucial to the Industrial Revolution, reveals the analytical limitations of an approach based on supply and demand. For the orthodoxy, demand is ultimately determined by optimal family formation, and supply by employment opportunities and rewards. To generate change, however, requires breaking out of a tautology. For the supply of labour is, once demanded, the source of the supply of output which is, in turn, through wages, the demand for goods whose consumption is the supply of the next generation of labourers. This is a closed loop whose dimensions can be changed only by external intervention. Consequently, Lee and Schofield (1981: 35) conclude that population growth in the Industrial Revolution was part endogenous and part exogenous. In other words, to put it a little more sharply, whatever the model cannot itself explain will be left to be externally accommodated, i.e., taken as exogenous and hence unexplained.[15]

In short, whether dealing in grand theory or analysing a single sector over a shorter period, the use of supply and demand provides an unsatisfactory approach. These curves – and the functions they serve – are themselves the product of a structure of economic and social forces that have to be identified. Whilst primarily intending to set aside the consumerist emphasis on demand as an independent agent of economic progress, a much more general critique has been offered here of the approach to economic history that operates as a more or less complex interaction of supply and demand. The consumerist approach does not then involve a fundamental break with the orthodoxy's dependence upon supply and demand, but merely lies at one extreme – in contrast to the more balanced approach of Crafts, say, or in contrast to the other extreme, represented by McCloskey (1981) and Mokyr (1977), for whom supply conditions are paramount in the long run.

However, the emphasis on demand does serve to shift attention away from changes in technology to changes in 'taste'. The mainstream emphasis on supply has an informal literature supportive of its models and statistics addressing the transformation of production – as when considering entrepreneurship. The consumerist approach, in the general absence of formal models, relies almost exclusively on informal discussion of the historical transformation of preferences which are perceived intuitively to shift out the demand curve. The drawbacks of this approach are set out in detail in the review of McKendrick's work on fashion in Chapter 10.

# Part III

# SYSTEMS OF PROVISION IN FOOD AND CLOTHING

# 8

# INTRODUCTION TO AN ALTERNATIVE FRAMEWORK

The chapters in this part of the book begin to open up discussion of the food and clothing industries as systems of provision with the aim of illuminating the distinct patterns of consumption associated with each. However, any attempt to demonstrate the analytical framework set up in Chapter 2 faces an immediate deterrent; that is, the necessity to adopt a much more inclusive approach to the empirical evidence. Not only must linkages be made between areas that have traditionally constituted separate fields of study pursued by disciplines with different objectives and different analytical tools (the rise of retailing and department stores, of power looms and synthetic fabrics, of markets and volumes of production, etc.); these linkages must also be reconstituted and re-examined for different historical periods.

This is a daunting task, one that these chapters, alas, cannot realistically accomplish in full. More modestly, what follows below seeks to demonstrate the potential value of the systems-of-provision approach by applying it to particular segments of, or 'problems' associated with, each industry at particular points of their historical development. The useful by-products of this approach are various and surprising; they explain how men's clothing has escaped the theoretical scrutiny of those concerned with the derivation and function of fashion. They also explain the persistence of food adulteration in the late twentieth century. Though no single, coherent picture of either industry emerges from these studies, they none the less revise received wisdom in each case by offering fresh perspectives. These emerge from an application of the analytical tools made available through the systems-of-provision approach.

## NAKED AND HUNGRY INTO THE WORLD: EARLY SYSTEMS OF PROVISION

Like food, clothing has always been a necessity as well as a luxury. For several centuries it has, at one extreme, provided basic covering to protect the human body against the elements and the improprieties of nakedness and, at the other, decorated the costume of elites, however these may be defined (i.e., whether privileged through the possession of property, magical powers, physical attributes, etc.). The long-term co-existence of utilitarian and ornamental clothing finds an easy parallel in the contrast in diets that have been available concurrently during any historical period (gruel at one extreme, lark's tongue pie at the other).

Both involve the provision, on the one hand, of basic goods to meet the needs of the vast majority of the population with the minimum of expense and effort and, on the other, of highly elaborated, individually tailored goods produced at exceptional expense for an economically insignificant but powerful fraction of the population. Each has historically depended on separate sources of supply and distribution, catering simultaneously to separate income groups. In both clothing and food, a 'bespoke' form of distribution has always co-existed with a variety of mass markets. In food, specialist grocers in the nineteenth century were skilled craftsmen in many respects; in selecting and blending teas, grinding and mixing spices and sugars, they were carrying out many of the functions of manufacturers as well as those of retailers (Jefferys 1954: 127). The majority of consumers who could not afford the luxury of the private grocer's personal service were forced to buy food in weekly markets peddling cheap goods of unknown quality and provenance.

The bespoke tailor also combined making and selling roles, but in this case the craft skills exercised the determining influence and control over the development of distribution; retailing followed production. In the food business by contrast, the distribution functions were paramount and, as the next hundred years would demonstrate, more readily detachable from the specialist back-up services they required of the provider. It is perhaps for this reason that the direct involvement of the trader in the preparation and packaging of supplies in the food trades passed much earlier to the realm of manufacturing. There was no contradiction in food, as there was in clothing, between the control of production which involved a complex labour-intensive process of assembly co-ordinated by the master tailor (often carried out on the retail premises themselves) and the requirements of a growing market which, ultimately, could afford neither the cost nor the time involved in the bespoke tailoring process.

The very occasional nature of consumption in the clothing markets made the resolution of these conflicts between supply and distribution less critical than they would have been in the provision of food, where the requirements of daily consumption (and on the other side, the guarantee of steady custom) would increase the incentive to rationalise supply. Markets in food had to deal much earlier with the inescapable contradiction between the rural and often remote location of agricultural production and the location of consumers, concentrated in increasing numbers in urban centres.

In food, the two ends of the market could, paradoxically, be integrated earlier by being separated earlier. At the turn of the century, grocery firms operating multiple branches distributed throughout Britain began to manufacture their own goods, which included sauces, preserves and cooked meats, based on technologies developed independently of the distribution network. Firms selling tea often placed contracts with tea growers; occasionally they owned plantations themselves (Jefferys 1954: 145). Distinctions between luxury and basic food markets began to disappear as national firms continued to expand their range of products which they delivered to shops more frequently and ready packaged in smaller quantities.

As the two ends of the market conflated, the personalised service that had characterised food shopping among the better-off also began to disappear, leading ultimately to the ready acceptance of self-service food shopping. Pre-packaging of messy goods (like jams and honey), blended goods (like teas) and small packages of perishables (like milk and butter) rendered superfluous much of the specialised knowledge, mixing and preparation skills of the retail trader. The establishment of reliable brand recognition, although it did not at first automatically guarantee a standardised product, none the less reduced the shopper's dependence on the provider for basic information and reassurance. At the same time, branding removed responsibility for quality from the trader, to whom the customer could complain directly, to a much less accessible and impersonal agency in the chain of provision, that is, the manufacturer. This distance between consumer and supplier would be exploited subsequently in the development of product labelling.

Set against this change-over to self-service in the food business is the persistence to this day of sales assistance in clothing shops; this is itself a mark of the distinctive histories of food and clothing provision.[1] It highlights both the powerful role played by information in cheapening the provision of food (through branding, which eliminated some of the intermediate costs involved in bringing products to final sale) and the correspondingly weak role played by information in the many branches of the clothing industry which, until very recently, failed to use either branding or advertising as a major element in its cost-cutting strategies.

This characteristic of market segmentation in both food and clothing, catering simultaneously throughout history to widely divergent needs, tastes and incomes, has to some extent confounded historical investigations of both. Economic history has tended to concentrate on supply side explanations associated with the most utilitarian end of the spectrum while sociology and related disciplines have focused more on the other extreme, where discussion has been dominated by the role and nature of differentiated demand. Substantial empirical evidence documenting both patterns of consumption has made it possible to sustain parallel if contradictory explanations of the industrial development associated with each type of consumer good rather than encouraging a more fruitful analysis of the links between them and the way in which these have been strengthened or attenuated over time.

In fact, the concurrent provision of clothing for the rich and clothing for the poor through history has had continuing consequences for the development of consumption in the twentieth century. Clear differences in the organisation of supply and in the establishment of markets for the two groups of consumers have sometimes been sharpened, advantaging one group at the expense of the other. But equally, technical and social change over the past century has also tended to overcome some of the more persistent contradictions in the provision of basic and luxury clothing, leading gradually to the creation of some kind of industrial coherence. Disentangling the relative contributions made by these opposing tendencies to the current pattern of consumption is neither straightforward nor simple. But it is necessary to reveal the unique features of the industry's system of provision.

The need to trace the histories of both luxury and mass markets in food and clothing does not complicate the discussion of consumer goods of relatively recent origin. Automobiles and radios, for example, which first appeared early in the twentieth century, were new products which entered the market as luxury goods; their gradual transformation into necessities was the result of active marketing and distribution strategies set in train by manufacturers. Markets for these goods had to be created from scratch but all depended more or less on a technological base driven by similar imperatives – the drive to improve and cheapen basic goods to achieve high-volume standardised production. Though market segmentation has now, of course, become a marked feature of the car and electronics industries, it does not carry with it the traces of competing or contradictory technologies which still cling to the clothing industry and influence its current aspects of consumption.

To the extent that it is possible to generalise about the direction taken by the clothing industry over the past two hundred years, it may be described as having transformed the consumption of goods from the occasional major purchase of essential items of dress designed to last a generation if not a lifetime, to that of multiple purchases of a much broader range of cheaply produced garments intended to be discarded or replaced at frequent intervals. In this respect, it has come to mimic the food industry with goods marketed more like perishables, 'like milk that spoils and citrus fruits that decay' (Meiklejohn 1938: 325). However, over the same period, the driving dynamic governing development of the food industry has been to move in the opposite direction, precisely to overcome the constraints imposed by the perishability of its raw materials and products. While the clothing industry has sought to reduce the 'shelf-life' of its products, both in shops and in the home, the food industry has striven to extend it.

Paradoxically, one of the many factors contributing to the capacity of the clothing industry to behave like the food industry has been its relatively greater freedom from the constraints imposed by nature. The manifest benefits of clothing do not depend upon any demonstrable connection with organic raw materials, as do those connected with food. On the contrary, the early industrial development of textiles presents the classic case for the advantages to be gained through the use of mechanical processes to overcome the inherent constraints imposed by nature. Raw materials were literally transformed beyond recognition to become fungible 'inputs' in the production process.

By contrast, the development of food has always been constrained by the need to preserve, even to enhance or restore, recognition of the raw materials (fruits, vegetables, etc.) provided by nature. This has meant that a substantial proportion of industrial research has been devoted to limiting the possibly damaging effects of unpredictable weather, animal diseases, organic toxins, etc., any one of which can violate patterns of recognition acceptable at any one time (in terms of the shape, size or colour of any food presented to the buyer in the shop and the taste and texture experienced when consuming it at home). The many chemical and/or mechanical processes that may be applied to an apple between the time it leaves the tree and its arrival on the table are designed to minimise and often to disguise the consequences of severing the crucial link with nature. They are intended to suppress the effects of time and distance, to make the transition appear as an instantaneous one – 'fresh from the field to your table'.

This very basic distinction has dictated the terms in which technology has been applied in the two industries. Though it is true that the earliest development of cloth depended upon sheep farming for its supply of wool fibres, by the eighteenth century it was no longer dominated by a raw material whose production was vulnerable to all capricious disturbances that nature could exhibit. Technical innovations turned out to be better suited to exploiting the potential of cotton, a plant that could be grown cheaply and widely and could be transported over great distances without loss of quality. The arrival and widespread adoption of synthetic fabrics in the twentieth century further distanced the textile industry from any dependence on organic materials.

But if clothing has been more successful than food in bypassing nature, it has been less successful, in some important respects, in overcoming technical constraints. Unlike the food industry, it has had to meet the additional demands of naturally segmented markets, however basic: infants, children and adults are not the same size; men and women are not the same shape or size; women often change shape (particularly during childbearing years). This segmentation has simply complicated what has traditionally been a much longer and more complex chain of production and processing, from fibre production through spinning, weaving or knitting to the sewing or manufacture of the final product. Historically, all these stages along the path of production required the acquisition and application of different types of skills; loom operators and tailors were not easily interchangeable. The concentration of clothing workers in urban workshops, rather than dispersed over wide areas like the farm labourer, encouraged the development of craft-based skills and organisation which reinforced the differentiation of clothing manufacture from textile production.

While textile machinery very quickly outstripped the capacity of the skilled worker and offered the potential for production on an unprecedented scale, clothing manufacture moved from a dependence on hand-sewing skills to a dependence on the individually operated sewing machine. Neither technique offered the possibilities for high-volume output to match those made available by power looms, yet both play an integral role in the overall system of provision that constitutes the clothing industry. Each is driven by a different set of productive imperatives and marketing strategies that are forced into contact with one another in the process of preparing goods for final markets. The resulting contradictions and tensions this has created are unique to the clothing industry and have had a profound influence on the pattern of consumption.

A part of this story is set out in greater detail below to demonstrate the complexity of the issues involved. It focuses on the development of the fashion system because this has traditionally mixed up several components of the clothing system in a way that has obscured rather than enlightened the history of the industry. This particular retelling of the story attempts to unpick some of the tangled skeins with a view to enhancing our understanding of the pattern of consumption that has evolved.

# 9

# THE MANUFACTURE OF THE FASHION SYSTEM

## INTRODUCTION

Study of the fashion system is a hybrid subject. Loosely defined as the interrelationship between highly fragmented forms of production and equally diverse and often volatile patterns of demand, the subject incorporates dual concepts of fashion: as a cultural phenomenon and as an aspect of manufacturing with the accent on production technology. The first aspect traces the rise and fall of fashion trends (e.g., the wearing of wigs by men, the wearing of trousers by women) and attempts to explain the origins of each by reference to a stage of development of the particular society involved. Attention focuses on the fashionable object as the embodiment of cultural and social values prevailing at a specified time and place.

The second aspect of the fashion system – its manufacturing side – grapples with broader categories of industrial history – the organisation of labour, availability of raw materials, the supply of capital, the growth of disposable incomes – to shape some explanation of the drive towards mass production and mass markets. It is concerned with the underlying dynamics of the production process, the shifting combinations of factor inputs, rather than with questions about the changing character or significance of the goods that emerge at a particular place at the end of the line.

This dual aspect of the fashion system has made it a difficult subject to accommodate within a tradition of economic history in which the histories of consumption and production plough largely separate and parallel furrows. The typical approach has been to treat each aspect separately, producing discrete histories of the evolution of tastes, demand and patterns of consumption, on the one hand, and of technical innovation and the emergence of factory production, on the other. Though the traditions make reference to each other and draw on common pools of raw material, inclusion of the other is, in each case, highly selective and determined by almost non-overlapping objectives. At one extreme sits the wholly descriptive tradition of costume history, which typically charts in minute detail over the course of several centuries the addition or deletion of every flounce, pleat, button or bow, worn by every class on every occasion.[1]

Attempts to identify the source of this phenomenal richness and turnover in styles have produced a literature of their own which draws on the academic disciplines of sociology, anthropology, psychology and, more recently, semiotics.[2] These move one step away from the descriptive catalogues of fashion change to the human motivation that abets and welcomes it, considering the emotional needs that might be satisfied by the constant turnover in products. There is no shortage of hypotheses in this area; the fickleness of fashion has been explained variously as 'a manic defence against ageing and death', an attempt to keep sexual attraction alive through the use of 'a constantly shifting erogenous zone', a reflection of the 'turbulent world of motion, speed and change' associated with modernity, etc.[3]

Like the catalogues of costume, this area of discourse also fails to address the capacity of industry to organise production in the context of the instability and short-run planning which rapid turnover implies. The flexibility of industrial production is transmuted into a discussion of the changeability and unpredictability of the consumer, particularly of the female consumer. If the animating spirit driving the dynamics of fashion resides in the realm of the subconscious, then production simply becomes a passive, unequal partner in fashion history, pandering to deep-seated longings of the female psyche.

Such a view implicitly reinforces the determining role of demand in the history of the fashion system, implying that 'it is fashion that makes the industry rather than the industry that makes fashion'.[4] It concentrates interest on the visible results of change, failing to ask either why or how production has been organised to allow for the apparently continuous differentiation of goods. The most recent manifestations of this trend in the literature have been discussions of the broader influence of culture and ideology on the nature of fashion change.[5]

At the other extreme of the literature on women's clothing is the history of supply.[6] Charting the history of technical innovations that have made the manufacture of clothing possible; it concentrates on the measurable rise in productivity, the associated growth and organisation of labour, and the central role played by various immigrant groups. Though the literature has incorporated demand for clothing, it is viewed primarily as a consequence of the rise of disposable incomes created by factory employment. The specific pattern of demand that characterises women's clothing and its role within a unique configuration of distribution and supply have rarely been addressed. In short, the history of clothing production has made little contribution to an understanding of 'fashion'; it leaves unexplained the causes of rapid turnover in product and the proliferation of styles.

The sheer scale of the task represented by either a demand- or supply-led view of history is in itself a powerful deterrent to alternative methodologies and imposes its own discipline on the available historical evidence. But this is achieved at considerable cost. The late-twentieth-century vantage point, with its presumption of universal mass production for mass markets, tends to flatten out retrospective differences in the paths taken by individual industries in their development. While some differences between industries do level out in the long run, others may not; important differences in the timing of technical innovation or in the accumulation of capital, for example, may have long-lasting effects on the character of overall development.

In the history of women's clothing, timing is critical. In the 1920s, the industry was still operating at a fairly primitive level of development compared with that of other domestic consumer industries (like radios and cars). The latter were poised to exploit recent innovations in transport and infrastructure which enabled them to consolidate national markets for their mass-produced goods, enhancing the market power of increasingly concentrated enterprises. Since contemporary women's clothing manufacturers were too small and too fragmented to make use of this opportunity, the potential gains offered by improved infrastructure were seized more by those controlling distribution in the industry than by those in charge of production.

A late-twentieth-century 'post-industrial' vantage point also begs the important question of whether the women's clothing industry ever achieved mass production, a question that can be answered only by reference to its history of supply. This chapter suggests that it did not, and that the evolution of the fashion system represented an accommodation with this failure, supplying a complex range of compensating mechanisms in response to its particular form of economic development. More specifically, it argues that the seemingly anarchic and rapidly changing proliferation of style in women's clothes, a feature that distinguishes it not just from other industries but from other branches of the clothing industry as well, served as a substitute for technical innovation, arising not in response to a rise in incomes or to changes in consumer preferences or to the exhaustion of possibilities arising from early mass production but rather from the industry's failure ever fully to embrace mass production.

This explanation is offered as a more plausible alternative to those which treat fashion as an emanation from the innate drive of all women to consume conspicuously. The mutual exclusiveness and incompatibility of these views are succinctly illustrated by the belief that 'categorically, man is always the producer . . . woman the consumer' espoused at a time when four-fifths of the producers of women's apparel were themselves women, working in dangerous conditions at extremely low wages. The starkness of the contradiction between the world of high fashion and that of the sweatshop reveals the weakness of a framework which, in denying any link between consumption and production, dismisses any historical consideration of the class relations that have determined them and their relationship to one another.

The implied preference in the literature for either a demand side or a supply side explanation has the critical effect of diverting interest away from the changing history of the relationship *between* them. The divergent paths taken by different industries may ultimately owe as much to the emergence of agencies mediating supply and demand (like distribution networks in the clothing industry) as to the development of either set of forces on its own. It is not just the character of these intermediate structures that have been influential, but also their timing (e.g., whether they first appeared during the *laissez-faire* or monopoly stage of capitalism), their endurance and their influence on subsequent changes in the development of consumption or production.

Giving greater prominence to the dynamics of the linkages between all agencies participating in industrial development argues, in effect, that each industry (and in the case of clothing, each subsector) has developed a distinct system of provision which displays an internal coherence of its own. Taking up such a view makes it possible, for example, to give greater weight to the consolidation of the role of the jobber or stock house in the US women's apparel industry at the close of the First World War. Operating as a middleman, the jobber first appeared in the 1880s, supplying fabric and dress designs to be made up by small manufacturers on a contract basis (hence the use of the term 'contractors') and selling the finished products.

Though used originally to cope with short bursts of excess demand which could not be met by the so-called 'inside' manufacturers, the jobbing function grew in the immediate postwar period to become the rule rather than the exception. In 1910, almost 90 per cent of women's ready-made apparel in the United States was produced by manufacturers operating independently of jobbers; by 1924, this had declined to less than 20 per cent of total output.[7] Concentrated during the short period between 1919 and 1924, the jobber gained control over the entire dressmaking sector, enlarging the operating scale and scope of the individual stock house at the expense of the manufacturer, whose opportunities for increasing economies of scale were correspondingly thwarted.

A proper explanation of the jobber's meteoric rise to dominance requires reference to the history of clothing supply. Once established in the early 1920s, the jobber's centralised authority then went on to play a critical role in the subsequent development of what has become the fashion system, particularly its unusual structure of demand. A full-bodied discussion of the sector's industrial development, therefore, requires a discussion interweaving the roles of supply and demand with the connective tissue between them. This is pursued in more detail below within a historical framework which views industrial development as a matrix of agencies with a shifting balance of power between them that has, over time, determined its specific character.

## PRECONDITIONS FOR TWENTIETH CENTURY CHANGE: THE SEPARATE DEVELOPMENT OF MEN'S AND WOMEN'S CLOTHING

The story of women's clothing is the focus of this chapter because it has been almost exclusively linked with the development of the fashion system.

Because men's clothing in the United States, has, at least until recently, escaped this association, men have been less implicated in the attempts by sociologists, behavioural psychologists and others to explain the origin of the fashion 'impulse'. But many historical factors can be summoned to relieve women of this burden by identifying some of the sources of divergence in the development of men's and women's clothing. This also establishes from the outset an awareness of long-term dissimilarities in the provision of goods that can separately define two sectors of the same industry.

Demographic factors play an important part. Primary among them is the differing roles played by cities and rural areas in facilitating or constraining the development of an indigenous industry. Throughout the eighteenth and for much of the nineteenth century, American merchants carried out a thriving trade importing fashionable clothing (for both men and women) from London and Paris. Americans travelling abroad were loaded up with commissions from friends and relatives for the latest fashionable goods and fashion news.[8] In this way, European habits of dress continued to exert an appreciable influence on patterns of dress in American cities.

Eastern cities were also the ports of entry and first residence of millions of immigrants from Europe. Among them were many skilled artisans (largely male) who re-established in the United States the craft-based traditions of their homelands. The early dominance of transplanted skilled workers in the needle trades in US cities guaranteed the continued production of relatively complicated garments that copied European styles and tastes as it reproduced their methods of manufacture.

But settlers living beyond the immediate reach of European culture constituted the great majority of the American population. As late as 1900, just one-third of all Americans lived in places with 8,000 or more people.[9] In the vast hinterlands beyond the reach of the great cities, the new settlers required less refined and more rugged garments better suited to the demands of pioneer, i.e., distinctly non-metropolitan, life. In the newer, more sparsely developed settlements, the scarcity of skilled tailors combined with the demand from population growth put a premium on technical change that could both transform the nature of garments and increase their availability. Given these stimuli, it is perhaps not surprising that technical innovation appeared first in rural rather than urban areas.

The use of rivets as fabric fasteners and materials borrowed from other uses (like the tent fabric used in the first jeans) was motivated by the need to make cheap and simple garments that could stand up to hard wear. The trappings of the American cowboy – unknown and faintly ridiculous to the city gent – illustrate the link between the new clothes and the new patterns of work:

> His wide-brimmed hat protected his eyes and head from the merciless heat and glare of the sun; in rain it served as an umbrella; at a waterhole it substituted for a bucket. The bandanna around his neck was really a

> mask to shield his mouth and nose from the clouds of dust kicked up by cattle on the move; the 'chaps' or leather leggings protected him against the stings and thorns of the sagebrush and cactus.
>
> (Degler 1977: 58)

The cattle industry needed the cowboy to drive herds of Texas longhorns across the Great Plains to northern markets near railheads where cowboys bought made-up clothing imported from larger towns.[10] The era of the long cattle drives coincided with the construction of the first transcontinental railway. The appearance of new clothes for these jobs – first chaps and waistcoats, jeans and overalls, then pants and work shirts – reflects the very large numbers of men caught up in the process of early industrialisation.

In the nineteeth century, this work depended on backbreaking human exertion. As late as 1850, manual labour still supplied more power than machines.[11] When the Central Pacific Railway was built through the Sierra Nevada mountains, no machine-driven tools existed to carry out the necessary cutting, tunnelling and bridging.[12] The construction of basic infrastructure required rugged yet comfortable clothes which had to be worn for long hours (sometimes days) at a stretch in mines and quarries, railways, shipyards, etc. These were worn by men organised into large and transient workgangs, often located at great distances not only from cities where tailors could be found but, equally important, from their homes where clothing would normally be cleaned, repaired or replaced by women.

The tools and materials adopted for the heavy engineering tasks on which men were engaged would inevitably, in the absence of more traditional means of production, lend themselves to the new task of making clothes – hence the use of rivets to replace the hand-sewn seam and the acceptance of clothes that were strictly utilitarian; the clothes, like the men themselves, were interchangeable parts of the production process. They increased the productivity of their wearers and extended their working lives by offering some protection from the dangers of extreme exposure (to heat, cold, wind, dust, cuts, lacerations, sprains, etc.).

Though in some sense, markets existed for these goods, individual consumers did not. The client was often either the procurement agency of the state itself (as in the case of military uniforms) or subsidised by the state (to supply clothing to men constructing the railways). Even where private funds were involved (plantation owners buying clothes for slaves, employers buying clothes for indentured or domestic servants), transactions did not hinge on the exercise of individual consumer preferences! As a spur to industrialisation, the relevant attributes of these early markets were precisely their uniformity and their size, both of which facilitated changes in the organisation of production. After the Union blockade of the South in the Civil War, the Confederacy had to create its own supply of uniforms for its troops. Factories in the South sprang up 'almost like magic' to churn out 10,000 garments a week.[13] These

*Figure 1* Group portrait of nineteenth-century cattle men in Kansas. The picture illustrates the adoption of work 'uniforms' which underpinned the later development of mass production.
*Source*: Kansas State Historical Society.

markets were the creation of public spending driven by the need for high-volume outputs of standardised goods.

The new nineteenth-century waterways and railways pushing westward from the East coast opened up enormous distribution channels for domestically produced clothing which was still manufactured almost exclusively in Eastern cities (especially New York, Boston and Philadelphia). Increasing demand for men's clothing emanating from the South and the West was met, in the first instance, not by the establishment of local manufacturing but by the emergence of large-scale wholesalers sent by eastern clothing firms to key regional transport exchanges (St Louis, Chicago, New Orleans). These merchants found it easy to sell large quantities of eastern-made goods; in fact, when demand rose suddenly – as it did during the Gold Rush of 1849 – most clothing had already been sold at auction by the time it arrived in California.

The steadily rising demand of an expanding workforce helped to stimulate the development of large-scale clothing manufacture, manifested first in the production of men's shirts. As early as the mid-1850s, a firm in New Haven, Connecticut, was producing an average of 100 dozen shirts daily, employing 300 people inside its factory and a further 3,700 outside it (Feldman 1960: 33). In this branch of the industry, then, systematic factory organisation preceded the process of mechanisation that followed the later introduction of the sewing machine. The prior existence of large-scale manufacture must certainly have influenced the pace at which machinery was adopted and the specific ways in which it was incorporated into production. In this, as in so many aspects of its historical development, menswear contrasts strongly with many branches of women's wear; the latter has typically been associated with small production units, relatively low levels of mechanisation, and low volume output.

The Civil War helped to remove another obstacle to the evolution of large-scale ready-to-wear markets for men's clothings. It produced the first system of standardised sizing for military uniforms. Tabulations of chest and height measurements taken from recruits were put to use in the manufacture of civilian clothes after the war. Though still relatively crude, their widespread adoption reduced the risks of advance production for the ready-made market by improving 'product specification', refining the definition of 'fit', and increasing a general understanding of its distribution within the male population.

The advantages conferred by such innovation in menswear were not easily transferable to women. The earliest ready-to-wear clothes for them came later and responded to different needs. Factory-produced 'wash' dresses for women did appear in large numbers well before the end of the nineteenth century but they were intended primarily to be worn to work either in enclosed factories or inside and around the home; in any case, their performance specifications were less stringent because the wearer was assumed to be capable of making whatever alterations or repairs might be necessary herself.

For women's clothes, the same early prerequisites for change were lacking: their conditions at work were not so extreme nor were their numbers in the workforce so great; moreover, unlike men, women carried with them into rural isolation the sewing skills that helped keep alive traditional modes of production. In other words, alternative and competing productive tendencies were weaker in women's clothing than in men's and this left it more vulnerable to the entrenched practices concentrated in cities from which the American fashion system emerged.

## THE WOMEN'S DRESSMAKING SECTOR: AN ALTERNATIVE FRAMEWORK

Karl Marx predicted that the arrival of the 'decisively revolutionary sewing machine' would, in combination with other progressive forces, help to do away with 'the murderous, meaningless caprices of fashion' while 'the development of ocean navigation and of the means of communication generally' would sweep away the 'technical basis on which season work was really supported'.[14] Over a century later, despite many far-reaching changes in the clothing industry and in transport and communications, both of these brakes on large-scale mass production remain, particularly in branches of the women's apparel industry. This is in itself a good indication of the limited extent to which the revolutionary changes which transformed other industries and led to the dominance of the Fordist production line bypassed the clothing industry.

The apparel industry is composed of several wholly separate branches, each with its own pattern of historical development. For statistical purposes, the Standard Industrial Classification used by the US Bureau of the Census recognises eighteen separate segments of the industry, including children's wear. For each segment, a distinction has to be drawn between the development of ready-to-wear and factory-made clothing. The former grew out of bespoke tailoring (Beazley 1973: 56), which allowed for the build-up of stock dresses during seasonal periods of slack but which did not imply any changes in the methods, organisation or location of manufacturing. English guild records and stock inventories indicate that making clothes in advance of purchase was well established by the sixteenth century. Factory production, which came later, implies the investment in, and co-ordination of, labour and machines in a dedicated workplace for the purpose of increasing the productivity – and profitability – of manufacturing. The earlier spread of many ready-to-wear garments (particularly those which were loose-fitting and simply cut) means that in a limited sense, mass markets preceded mass production.

As outlined above, in the United States, both ready-to-wear and factory-made clothes for men appeared first, encouraged at least partly by demand for clothing for sailors (with only 24-hour turnarounds in port), by demand for clothing for slaves in the South whose time was more productively employed in the fields, and by demand for military uniforms at the time of the Civil War. The earlier demand for standardised work clothes for men (particularly shirts) which coincided with their earlier mass participation in paid labour, contributed to the earlier development of large-scale markets in some of these goods.[15]

Women's factory-made clothes did not begin to appear until the beginning of the twentieth century, corresponding to (though not entirely the consequence of) their later entry into the labour market. Yet even at the close of the First World War, the industrial development of women's clothing continued to lag behind men's, displaying characteristics increasingly at odds with those conducive to the spread of mass production.

Dressmaking, in particular, failed to conform to the orthodox pattern. It was also the branch of the clothing industry most closely associated with the evolution of 'fashion', i.e., with the rise of the role of demand as an active and transforming agent on its own. The link between these two attributes is revealed most clearly in the history of dressmaking in the United States in the decade immediately following the end of the First World War: this is the period commonly cited as triggering off the fashion phenomenon in its twentieth-century mode.[16]

## Beginnings of industrial development

Primary among the distinguishing characteristics of clothing in the twentieth century was its continuing dependence on the individually operated sewing machine. Introduced in the middle of the nineteenth century, it remained at the core of factory production a century later. The central dynamic at work in most incipient mass production industries (viz., the progressive subordination of the worker to the machine and his or her eventual displacement by large-scale capital equipment) simply did not occur in the clothing industry at a comparable stage of development. Instead, the enormous variety of attachments that had developed by the 1880s made the sewing machine the tool of flexible specialisation *par excellence*. By 1882, 68 different machine stitches were in use, all readily available to the individual operator whose tailoring skills were now greatly enhanced. Mechanisation in this case served to reinforce rather than undermine the craft basis of production.

Nevertheless, the sewing machine did stimulate factory production of clothing; however, the increases in productivity it made available were exploited more by manufacturers of men's clothing than by women's wear producers. As early as the 1860s, the sewing machine made it possible to produce eleven men's shirts in the time formerly required to make one shirt by hand (Fite 1910: 89). Calico dresses that took six and a half hours to stitch by hand took less than one hour to put together on the new machine (Cooper 1968: 58). But as the sewing machine streamlined production in menswear branches of the industry, it simultaneously contributed to a further stalling of development in women's wear, driving an additional wedge between them.

The extension of home dressmaking facilitated by the sewing machine also strengthened the association of a single operator with the full range of tasks required to create a finished product, a link which the factory system tended to break down. It introduced a new trade-off between gains in productivity and increases in complexity. Though advertised as a labour-saving device, the sewing machine served rather to increase expectations of dress (and hence of the dressmaker), leading to the production of ever more elaborate clothing, requiring more seams, trimmings, drapes and ruffles[17] and enabling 'her to put a hundred tucks where once she put three'.[18] The tendency towards increasing complexity of dress made possible by the new machine exemplifies the more general contradiction between the avowed labour-saving attributes of mechanised forms of housework and the countervailing rise in labour-consuming expectations which such equipment brings in its train.

Home dressmaking on the sewing machine was given a further spur by the commercial development of paper patterns in the second half of the nineteenth century. By the 1880s, the American firm of Buttericks had, outside their headquarters in New York, 2,500 agencies in the US and 300–400 in the United Kingdom.[19] The inexpensive packaging of full-size diagrams on paper – which included all necessary panels of a complicated dress together with instructions for their assembly – brought serious dressmaking within the reach of a much greater number of women. While the widespread use of paper patterns served in this way to perpetuate dressmaking as a domestic industry, at the same time, it stimulated the factory production of textiles. Textiles, at this stage of the development of women's clothing, were sold directly to the consumer as finished or semi-finished goods rather than as the intermediate goods to manufacturers which they subsequently became. Their manufacture was already highly mechanised and concentrated in large-scale factories. The contrast between the highly capitalised production of materials and the pre-capitalist mode of final production made prospects for establishing productive linkages between the two systems of provision extremely problematical.

Linkages set up at the point of distribution were to prove more fruitful. Drapers were responsible for the stocking and selling of both patterns and fabrics. This placed them in a position that could be exploited to advantage, since they would have their pulse on changes in the nature and volume of demand for particular fabrics and patterns whether purchased by women sewing in the home or by seamstresses and tailors. The move to supply ready-made goods by exploiting some of their trade experience would be an easy one, one that tailors and dressmakers could also undertake. The critical positioning of the wholesaler/distributor between the supplier of raw materials and the supplier of skills needed to work these raw materials up into finished products foreshadows the powerful influence of the middleman contractor/jobber in the twentieth century (taken up below).

Technical progress in other industries was radically different. In the first decade of the twentieth century, the development of heavier and more rigid tools in the automobile industry for example – particularly the universal grinding machine – made it possible to guarantee the production of interchangeable parts and so to reduce dependence on the highly skilled work of the precision engineer.[20] This set the long process of industrial deskilling and technological unemployment in motion. By contrast, the development of machinery in the clothing industry neither displaced labour on the same scale nor stripped it completely of its skills. Such transformation as did occur from the hand-sewing to the manufacturing of clothing was based on the mechanisation of tailoring practices rather than on the wholesale transfer of the production process to machinery.

Based in New York City, the entry point for literally millions of skilled and unskilled immigrants from Europe, the fledging clothing industry faced none of the skilled labour shortages that would act as a spur to earlier innovation in Detroit and elsewhere. Until the advent of immigration restrictions in 1923, labour was so plentiful and competition for jobs so cut-throat that employers could often pass on some of their overheads to the workforce, insisting, on occasion, that workers supply their own machines and thread. Despite technical innovations that occurred before the mid-1920s, technological unemployment remained low as aggregate demand for clothing continued to rise.[21] Nevertheless, while the incentive to replace labour altogether was much attenuated, the drive to reduce the skill content of sewing jobs was clearly in evidence.

In the move towards mechanisation, the multiple skilled tasks formerly provided by a single skilled worker (tailor or seamstress) were broken down into separate processes. Nevertheless, most tasks still required the individual handling of a single garment (or piece of garment) by an individual operator. However simplified the task, the worker remained a machine operator rather than a machine minder.

Early innovations that reinforced this relationship while increasing mechanisation include an automatic button-holing machine invented in 1862 and a button sewer patented in 1875.[22] These were followed by blind-stitching machines, introduced first in 1900 and which allowed for invisible stitching that passed only halfway through the thickness of the material; overedgers, that could wrap thread around the edge of a fabric in order to produce a finished appearance; and new pressing machines and irons that could generate live steam directly. These inventions all sped up the pace at which the tailoring tasks could be carried out[23] but they did not increase the number of garment pieces that could be worked on simultaneously.

An early exception to this one-to-one link between the individual garment or segment of a garment and the individual operator was the introduction in the 1870s of the steam-powered cutting machine, followed in the 1890s by a portable and electrically powered rotary knife. These enabled an individual worker to cut up to twenty-four layers of cloth at one time.[24] Offering clear advantages in accuracy, efficiency and ease of manœuvring over hand tools, the new machines rendered obsolete the use of the short-bladed knife and scissors. With the loss of the hand-tooled craft came the rise of a clearly demarcated, highly productive, and hence lucrative source of employment. Women who had been cutters alongside men up to this point, rapidly disappeared from the newly enhanced trade (Levine 1924: 11).

All clothing workers in the apparel trades shared the problem of dealing with soft and shapeless raw materials which therefore required – and still require – a great deal of individual handling before being submitted to machinery. As quoted in Alderfer and Michl (1957: 36) (from the US Bureau of Labor Statistics, *Productivity of Labor in the Cotton Garment Industry, Bulletin*, no. 662, 1939: 36):

> It takes but a few seconds to make a seam, so far as the actual stitching is concerned; but it takes a great deal more time to pick up the parts, put them together properly, place them under the needle, bring down the attachment which holds the work in place, start the machine, and then to repeat the process for the next seam. It is estimated . . . that the actual sewing takes only from 15 to 33 per cent of the time taken by the workers to make the garments, depending on the length of the seam and

> the complexity of the operation. From 67 to 85 per cent of the time is spent in handling and manipulating the garment. It becomes clear, therefore, that the effect of improvement in machinery upon the time required for an operation is sharply limited because of the comparatively low ratio of operating time to handling time.

As recently as the 1970s, a survey estimated that only 20 per cent of a sewer's time was spent in actually sewing, with the rest spent in garment handling (Lamphere 1979). So industrial development which adds an increasing assortment of specialist operators – and machines – to an increasingly subdivided sequence of production must inevitably generate additional dead time between operations which might or might not be offset by the increased productivity of the operations themselves.

Solutions to the problems of assembly in the clothing industry in the first quarter of the twentieth century more closely resembled the workings of Adam Smith's eighteenth-century pin factory than the twentieth-century production line at Ford's. New machinery gradually paved the way for an extension in the type of specialist operators, which included fellers, basters, snappers, folders, gaugers, etc. These technical innovations encouraged the adoption of the 'section' system in which each machine operator, rather than carrying out all the sewing operations to complete a single garment (the 'whole-garment' system) performed instead one or a limited number of operations (pocket or collar making, sleeve seaming, etc.) on a number of identical pieces delivered to her in a bundle.

The change in the sequencing of production brought only modest gains in productivity. On the one hand, it encouraged increased standardisation and larger production runs and made possible intra-process inspection to which the 'whole-garment' system did not easily lend itself. On the other hand, the growing subdivision of labour increased the overall time lost to handling by a growing number of participants, each working on one piece at a time. It also created further problems in co-ordinating the pace of each operation and the transfer of garment segments between one work station and the next.

'Section' work did not find easy acceptance within dressmaking firms. It did not offer the flexibility in production achieved by the 'whole-garment' system that made it possible to respond immediately and frequently to changes in style. With a premium on fast turnaround, a whole-garment shop could turn an order around in three to four days compared with a much more sluggish three weeks required by a section workshop. Such an imperative naturally encourages those productive forms that have the capacity to exploit this competitive edge. Of all the main branches of the women's clothing industry, dressmaking, based on the simplest sequence of operations, lent itself most easily to the whole-garment system. With the entire dress under the control of one operator, changes in style could be implemented instantly. Once set in train, this short cycle of demand and supply would be hard to break.[25]

Branches of the industry that did achieve uniform production of popular garments (like work shirts and jeans) took the section system one step further, subdividing machine operations so that an operator performed only one simplified task before passing the piece on to the next operator. Though still dependent on operators working one piece at a time, this system ('line-production') eliminated hand-sewing entirely. Buttons were riveted rather than sewn and rivets were used, rather than tacking, to reinforce seams. Garments like jeans made from denim could also be compressed into compact bales rather than ironed and packed in boxes, further reducing the required range of separate operations.

The dressmaking branch did not follow this path but instead remained one of the least mechanised of all industries. In 1913, at least a third of the 25,000 workers in the waist and dress industry were still engaged in hand operations and a similar proportion of operators in the coat and suit section of the industry were finishing garments by hand as late as 1921 (Waldinger 1985). In 1923, the average horsepower per plant across all industries was 169.0; for men's clothing the corresponding figure was just 11.4 but this was still almost three times the level of power achieved in the women's clothing industry, namely 4.0.[26]

But even this very modest consumption of power is in a sense misleading. Most of it was used to support an increasing number of individually operated machines. Though these increased in sophistication and speed of operation, they essentially propped up an unchanging production system still firmly based on tailoring, i.e., on individual operators carrying out all the separate, specialist tasks needed to put together an entire garment. Though the manufacturing process had been subdivided into several basic crafts – cutting, operating, finishing and pressing – the skilled operator remained at the heart of what was a largely unspecialised division of labour (Belfer 1954: 188). Under this system, every garment produced was essentially unique.

## CHANGES AFTER THE FIRST WORLD WAR

The postwar rise in industrial employment, together with the growth in the population, lifted the level of disposable incomes (and hence effective demand) to new heights. National transportation and distribution networks began to emerge after the First World War and helped to smooth the way for new patterns of consumption.

Although the apparel industry did not play a central role in raising the scale or pace of postwar markets for consumer goods, it was none the less caught up in its consequences. Unprepared for the sudden expansion in demand in the immediate postwar period, the dressmaking branch remained undercapitalised and undeveloped, made up of a large shifting mass of intensely competitive firms too small to wield market power or to reap the economies of scale arising from increasing concentration of capital. In 1929, 96.5 per cent of clothing firms were still single-unit establishments (Meiklejohn 1938: 327). The great majority of them were very small and this made large production runs of standardised products impossible.

Given these conditions, the coming together of the underdeveloped dressmaking sector with the newly emergent retail and distribution channels was bound to become more a confrontation between unequal partners than a mutually reinforcing spur to development. The accommodation that ensued retarded the further development of the apparel industry.

## The rise of the jobber

The response of the dressmaking industry in the first decade after the 1914–18 war centred on the rise and consolidation of the power of the jobber, a middleman who first appeared at the end of the nineteenth century when manufacturers first began to farm out some of their excess production to outside firms. It was the jobber who organised newly arrived immigrant labour for contract work. By the 1920s, he had transformed this middleman role into a much more powerful position, one that widened the gap between the production of women's wear and its marketing. The jobber now took over from the manufacturer all decisions about what was to be produced, how much and when, designing garments and supplying raw materials and later selling the finished products to retailers but subcontracting manufacture to outside firms.

The jobber, freed from technical and labour problems arising in the factory, was able to concentrate his attention on styles and sales. The capacity to commandeer and direct production from a multiplicity of sources enabled him to sell to retailers from an exceptionally wide range of stock which could quickly adapt to changes in demand. The emergence of jobbing activity was to some extent a mark of the increasing leverage of retailers who now insisted both on delaying the placing of orders until the last possible moment and on minimising the length of time any merchandise took up prime selling space in their shops.

The consequences of this change for the production of clothing, particularly women's clothing, were almost entirely negative. The new 'hand-to-mouth' buying practice adopted by retailers led to the rapid decline of advance orders on which manufacturers had previously depended to help them plan and smooth out production over a longer period. With increased uncertainty and decreasing production runs, manufacturers (now contractors) could only survive by underbidding each other, through lowering the quality of work, lowering wages, or both. Not surprisingly, there was a very high turnover of firms. Of 2,000 dress manufacturers in existence in 1929, 709 were new entrants and 478 went out of business. In 1931, a further 621 new firms entered the fray while 504 abandoned it (Meiklejohn 1938: 324).

With so little capital required for entry into the dressmaking business, it was almost as easy to enter the industry as to withdraw from it. Strong family connections in many clothing shops allowed family members to pool savings to elevate one of them up to contractor status, only to see him return the next year to the shop floor. The composition of, and boundaries between, participating firms were constantly shifting; winners in one year's round of activity might be forced in the next 'to sell off equipment to last year's losers. Under these circumstances, every employee could become a subcontractor, every subcontractor a manufacturer, every manufacturer, an employee'.[27] In effect, dresses were really financed more by the lost savings of contractors, unpaid indebtedness to workers, and many defaults to landlords and power companies than by any kind of planned or dynamic accumulation (Meiklejohn 1938: 351).

The rise of the jobbing system represented an increasing fragmentation of industrial production at a time when other industries and other branches of the clothing industry were moving rapidly towards increasing integration and concentration. The loss of direct control over markets, product design and levels of output deprived producers of important stimulants to technical change, contributing instead to delays in further development.

The fact that dressmaking became vulnerable to this form of reorganisation is itself a mark of the limits to growth inherent in the preceding generations of technical change. Conditions had not been conducive to the amalgamation of smaller firms into larger operating units, nor to heavy investment in dedicated machinery to produce high-volume output of staple goods. Dressmaking took instead what appears as a retrograde step, highlighting the continuing co-existence of variable modes of production within an economy moving increasingly towards mass production technologies.

The ascendancy of the jobber did not significantly alter or undermine existing methods of production. Rather, it took them as fixed. Stripping away from manufacturers the remnants of decision-making powers, the jobbing house removed from the productive sphere most incentives to technical change. In assuming control over the dressmaking sector, the stock house relocated the site of dynamic change within the sphere of distribution and relied upon the primary mechanisms by which it had risen to power – marketing, design and product differentiation – to secure and consolidate its position.

During this same period, trends in the menswear branches of the industry displayed a dynamic which ran completely counter to that emerging in women's wear. Just as jobbers (and distribution agencies) were gaining the upper hand in the system of provision governing the dressmaking branch of the industry, they began to disappear altogether from branches of menswear. Menswear manufacturers not only retained their dominance but extended it. Large-scale producers of men's clothing (like Hart, Shaffner & Marx) were selling their goods through retail outlets which they owned themselves, as well as supplying their goods to other retailers (a practice known as dual distribution).[28]

The direct link between producer and seller was strengthened by the mushrooming of the made-to-measure suit trade where individual customer measurements and requirements taken in the shop were relayed directly to the factory and the finished suit dispatched back to the shop again without the need for any of the intermediate services provided by the jobber. The linkage was even more direct in other menswear branches (like shirts and work clothes) where production was already highly mechanised and brands established. Even the need to extend credit to retailers, a function still carried out today by jobbers (factors) in the women's wear sectors, was assumed by the increasingly large-scale producers in menswear. The jobber fell away, leaving the way clear for the imperatives of large-scale mass production to set the pace and direction of industrial development.

The timing of this marked divergence in the paths of development taken by women's and men's clothing was crucial for their continuing development. An industry like menswear, already organised around the mass production of standard goods, would exploit the development of new transport networks and mass media to consolidate its markets through the advertising of already established brands. The dressmaking branch of the clothing industry, which had attained neither the same of level of standardisation nor the market power and geographical reach which sustain it, was affected very differently by the arrival of mass communications. And the particular accommodations that it made in the interwar period locked it into and aggravated its pre-existing eccentricities. These became more entrenched and more pronounced as determinants within its system of provision.

The use of design was intensified, applied not only to fabric and dress styles but also to the composition of the market itself, introducing new products (walking, tennis, cocktail dresses, etc.). In this, it was materially aided by the concomitant rise of the mass media. The spread of both national magazines (carrying fashion advertising) and movies (projecting fantasies which the fashion system could bring to life) sped up the diffusion process and potentially deepened the market penetration of any particular style or trend. The opening of new interstate road networks made it possible for the promotion of new fashions through the media to be quickly followed up by the arrival of these advertised goods in the shops. Current fashions could now reach semi-rural and small town communities with a much shorter time-lag than had hitherto been possible. This made it increasingly difficult to extend the 'shelf-life' of any one fashion trend by off-loading on to customers from the less sophisticated hinterlands those styles that had already peaked in the metropolis or that had never 'taken off' there at all.

In this way, advances in mass communications, while encouraging the growth of mass demand, simultaneously inhibited the corresponding rise of mass production. The creation of mass demand was based on a levelling up of expectations, but by the time this occurred, those expectations were no longer simple nor stable; paradoxically, the now uniform expectation, fed continuously by the fashion system, was for unceasing diversity. Caught at a particular moment in time, the universal expectation of product turnover and diversity became the norm in the dressmaking sector. This had the effect of legitimising the system by which these expectations could be fulfilled. The chaotic lack of planning that characterised the relationship between producer and distributor now became accepted as standard business practice, and the expectation of continuous turnover in fashion became institutionalised.

The subsequent though slow spread of this pattern of demand was moderated in other industries by the dominance of mass production technologies which retained the upper hand. The gradual acceptance of dynamic obsolescence in other industries (though fiercely resisted at first by some like Henry Ford) served to bestow a retrospective legitimacy on unregulated product differentiation in the dressmaking industry, and, by implication, on its associated mode of production.

## The high fashion house

The specific path that mechanisation took in the dressmaking industry preserved the possibility and hence embodied a preference for the traditional made-to-measure product over a machine-made one. This led to a potentially open-ended system of product differentiation. As a strategy to widen markets, it could not be more different from the market-widening consequences of mass production, which were based on very large-scale output of a very limited number of products. The women's clothing industry could not achieve these economies of scale and so pursued a form of market fragmentation as a means of increasing the volume of sales. The high fashion house played a key role in achieving this goal.

The *haute couture* end of the market producing the most expensive dresses depended for its survival on the notion of exclusivity, i.e., on the preservation of the privileged relationship between a bespoke tailor and his or her client. In this, it represented a pattern of consumption of exceptionally long lineage, recalling the luxury habits of the European court. *Haute couture* dresses were presented as one-off style 'creations' that enhanced the originality and individuality of the consumer in a world of increasingly mass-produced goods.

The survival of this pre-industrial, service relationship kept its desirability alive; it had a profound impact on the imagery of advertising, which sought to play down if not to conceal entirely the contribution of machinery to the production of clothing while emphasising the individuality of the product. At a time when the superiority of factory over hand-made goods had been decisively established for many other garments purchased by women (stockings, corsets, brassieres, etc.), a lingering preference for the designer original dress was propped up and encouraged by the fashion houses.

*Figure 2* From the fashion runway to the food counter.
*Source*: Peter Sickles/Stock Boston

In France, the home of *haute couture*, the image of the hand-sewn designer dress was almost literally true. In many fashion establishments, the only machinery ever used was the simple sewing machine, and this was used for only 2 or 3 per cent of the work.[29] Yet many firms grew to an astonishing size. The House of Chanel employed over 2,000 people in twenty-six workrooms, each presided over by its own 'première', in charge of the sewing of his or her own staff.[30] The House of Dior reached a similar size. In effect, these firms pushed the co-ordination of craftwork to its limits, mimicking the growing concentration occurring in factory production but without achieving any of its economies of scale or increases in productivity. They were modern only by virtue of their scale and marketing sophistication; the increased visibility gained from these attributes conferred a renewed legitimacy on the mode of production which they employed.

Paradoxically, it was interwar improvements in air transport and mass communications (giving such a boost to other consumer industries) that enabled French couture (and the attitudes it embodied) to be transplanted in the United States. The practice of presenting the latest Paris and Italian fashions to American buyers was introduced on an experimental basis in the 1930s and had become an established promotional device ten years later (Roshco 1963: 153).

The monopoly profits that could be reaped through the sale of expensive dresses required tight control over output, which was threatened by style piracy. The process of copying and cheapening an expensive dress (i.e., the natural action of competition) shortened the sales life for the original producer who did the bulk of his or her business through frequent re-ordering in very small batches (Baran 1937: 72). But no matter how carefully designers tried to cloak their creations in secrecy, once sketches and photos were formally released, there was no way to prevent mass copying.

Fighting a losing battle, the French houses decided to institutionalise what they could not stop. Their arrival in the US coincided with the introduction of 'line-for-line' copies,[31] i.e., designer models sold to department store buyers for the explicit purpose of copying. They were reproduced for sale in large numbers at a fraction of their couturier price. In this way, couturier fashion has had a profound effect on both the demand for and the supply of dresses. It forces the dressmaking industry to adapt hand-sewn garments to machine production, to mimic the very techniques of manufacture it was designed to replace.[32] This inhibits the reverse process, in which the capacity of machinery is pushed to the limits to open up possibilities for technical innovation. The dominance of couturier design, therefore, can be viewed as perpetuating a retrograde orientation in production which trickled down through all layers of dressmaking.

## WIDENING DIFFERENTIATION

The basic sewing machine used in industrial production – throughout the interwar period and beyond – remained similar to the domestic machine, distinguished primarily by its capacity to achieve a higher rate of sewing speed. Running parallel with this correspondence between industrial and domestic technology was a correspondence between the factory made and the home-grown product; distinctions between manufactured and hand-sewn dresses remained small. The sustained continuity in both technique and product between domestic and factory modes of production compares strikingly with the radical discontinuities in both achieved by other consumer industries (like those supplying automobiles and radios where the gap opened up by mass production was virtually unbridgeable).

The general tendency toward product differentiation in clothing became more marked during the postwar period, taking new forms which were quickly adopted as standard features. A few of these are briefly described below: large-scale, made-to-measure outlets, special order firms, price lines, and the substitution of 'little ticket' items (separates) for 'big ticket' items (like suits and evening wear). Almost all of them left the basic productive techniques unchallenged and unchanged. The persistence of static and inefficient production methods was to some extent disguised by significant cost reductions that were achieved during the same period in the manufacture of women's clothes, particularly dresses. These were attributable more to exogenous factors, like the introduction of versatile yet cheap new fabrics, than to any changes in the production process itself.

## The dominance of the made-to-measure ethos

In the 1920s, the jobbing/contracting system placed a premium on the rapid and repeated turnover of stock, reinforcing a demand that was increasingly fragmented and less and less tied to traditional seasonal buying habits. With increasing decentralisation of production under the thumb of an increasingly centralised marketing network, it became both possible and necessary to extend markets by massive differentiation of the garments on offer. The organisation of the industry, with its proliferation of specialist operators, each perpetuating a single tailoring skill, made this approach still feasible.

It is hard to overestimate the extent to which manufacturers attempted during this period to minimise risks by extending their markets at the margin of production. A study of waste in industrial production carried out just after the First World War described one firm that:[33]

> In a recent season offered its customers 29 stock-models of sack-suits and also made up suits in 14 special models designed by certain customers. Each of these was offered in 3 styles of lining construction, 3 combinations of lining material and in nearly 1,100 varieties of cloth. Thus each purchaser had a free choice among 278,000 combinations.

The annual output of this firm was 400,000 suits a year in lots which averaged twelve garments each and rarely exceeded twenty. Astonishingly, many lots were as small as three or four. Although over 90 per cent of sales were based on just eleven basic models, fear of losing ground to competitors prompted the manufacturer to 'conduct a ready-to-wear business almost on a made-to-measure basis'.[34] Essentially, the strategy pursued was to make up suits only in response to orders, what was then called a 'sell-then-make' policy (a phrase almost identical to the one used much more recently by Benetton to describe its own marketing strategy). One men's tailoring firm pushed to the limit the apparent contradiction between open access to a mass market and the bespoke character of the goods on offer; it restricted the sale of some lines to only one suit in one pattern in one city (Morris 1926: 39).[35] As a marketing ploy, this was designed to preserve the image of exclusivity which the very large scale of the firm's operations would otherwise belie.

In fact, the limited economies of scale achieved by these giant 'tailors to the trade' derived from organisational and marketing advantages of size rather than from any technical benefits. Their growth and persistence had a

BY THE TIME YOU FINISH READING THIS AD

*You may hate the place where you bought your last suit.*

Hate, did we say?

That's certainly a strong emotion. And how emotional can a person get over a suit?

We think very. More than just a piece of clothing, a suit is a reflection of yourself.

And perhaps you haven't realized it, but those suits hanging in your closet weren't made with you in mind.

Most likely, they were glued together in another country, and shipped to a store that knows nothing more about clothing than how to sell it.

We think that's a mistake.

At Saint Laurie, we can sell you the perfect suit because we do what no other New York clothing store does. We make them ourselves. Right upstairs, in the very same building where you buy them.

Would you like a Super 100's wool suit, in single-breasted instead of double?

A three-buttoned style in a size 46 long instead of a 40 regular?

Or do you need a model with a 34-inch trouser waist, to go with your 44-inch shoulders?

No problem. If you don't find what you want from our selection of 10,000 ready-made suits, we will make it for you. At no additional cost.

And we create each suit by hand, with needle and thread. Which makes them, at $395 to $695 with free alterations, better crafted than designer labels at twice the price.

So forget the animosity you may now feel toward the place where you bought your last suit. And visit the place where you're going to purchase your next.

SAINT LAURIE NEW YORK CITY

SAINT LAURIE Merchant Tailors

FOR MORE INFORMATION CALL 1-800-221-8660

Saint Laurie Ltd. 897 Broadway at 20th St. New York City 10003 (212) 473-0100

Mon-Sat 9:30 to 6 (Thursday till 7:30) Sun 12 to 5

*Figure 3* Saint Laurie advertisement from the *New York Times*, 1991. This illustrates the persistence of the made-to-measure tradition in men's tailoring – 'If you don't find what you want from our selection of 10,000 ready-made suits, we will make it for you.'

*Source*: Kirshenbaum and Bond

predictably inhibiting effect on attempts to introduce – and sustain – rational production processes or long-range planning. The organisation of production – which still required from 80 to 150 separate operations in making a sack coat – continued to be dominated by an implied preference for the made-to-measure over the mass-produced garment. The constant switching of styles and fabrics (to which the flexible sewing machine readily lent itself) created havoc on the shop floor with some types of operators absurdly overworked and others kept idle or waiting for their next piece of work.

Because markets for clothing were also fragmented by seasonal and cyclical variations, it is impossible to separate out and quantify the effects of differentiation on efficiency and plant utilisation. A survey of plants carried out after the First World War estimated that average plant utilisation over a period of three years was only 69 per cent of a possible maximum.[36] Disaggregating the average figure also reveals very sharp local fluctuations in the numbers of workers employed as bunched production alternated with long periods of slack. Established practices persisted. A generation later, with standardised products still a long way off, and capital start-up costs extremely low, the industry remained small and fiercely competitive. As *Fortune Magazine* put it in 1939: 'with $2,500, a few customers and a colossal amount of nerve, almost anyone can go into the dress business'.[37]

In addition to the lure of low start-up costs, the scale and fluidity of the dressmaking business did offer the possibility of considerable profits. Dress firms, on average, turned over their capital seven or eight times a year (Helfgott 1959: 31). Occasionally a firm offering a particularly 'hot' style could reap windfall profits over a very short period. But investment remained pitched to the short term; capital was almost universally financed by credit rather than by retained earnings. Under these conditions, long-term planning was impossible.

## Price lines and the emergence of little ticket items

Another important strategy for diffusing risk was the introduction of price lines. Widely adopted in the dressmaking branch of the industry, it segmented the market for dresses into rigid price categories which allowed for a varying proportion of skilled labour to be applied to similar styles and fabrics, according to circumstances. In the interwar period, dresses were typically distributed in six separate price categories which were recognised by manufacturers and retailers alike.[38]

'Price lining' led to a reversal of the usual relationship between cost and price in which the former, under conditions of competition, determined the latter. Under 'price lining', dresses could be 'built' up or down by manufacturers to given price categories, thereby squeezing the gross margin of retailers. Retailers meanwhile benefited from price lines because it allowed them to carry smaller stocks in each category which could be turned over faster. However, while serving to limit risk to both manufacturer and retailer, the practice acted as a further disincentive to both cheapening and standardising production.

Another change which encouraged a higher rate of turnover in apparel stocks was the gradual emergence of 'separates'. Ready-made suits and dresses had traditionally been thought of as major purchases, like many other consumer durables. They involved considerable outlay and were expected to be used over several seasons, if not years. The 1920s eroded this approach to clothing, encouraging the idea of obsolescence in fashion and design. Manufacturers had been left with unused capacity in a depression which followed a sudden surge in demand in the immediate postwar period.

They turned to the production of separates, promoting the substitution of jackets and slacks for suits, and that of sweaters and skirts for dresses. Each of these so-called 'little ticket' items was cheaper to produce – and to buy – than the 'big ticket' item which it replaced. Wardrobes could be infinitely extended by the incremental addition or substitution of relatively inexpensive individual garments. Items which quickly became unfashionable could be discarded without guilt. Small-scale clothing purchases could be made continuously.

By this means, clothing was transformed from a consumer durable to a non-durable good. The change-over was accompanied by yet another form of differentiation, an emphasis on the versatility of separates. An article in the *Atlantic Monthly* (1953) cites their ability to provide 'a greater variety of effects for a given outlay. For instance, three skirts and three blouses, waists or sweaters are capable of nine different combinations, whereas three dresses are still only three dresses'.[39] Between 1929 and 1950, the number of dresses as a proportion of the total production of women's 'outwear' garments declined from 86.9 to 53.1 per cent while the share of blouses and skirts over the same period rose from 2.7 to 37.9 per cent.[40] The switch to co-ordinates pushed up the total volume of purchases at the expense of individual profit margins which declined. It also to some extent facilitated further deskilling as the subdivision of outfits into their separate components led to a subdivision of the tasks involved in their manufacture. It did not, however, generate any significant changes in production techniques.

## The introduction of new fabrics

The failure to adopt mass production techniques in dressmaking was masked to some extent by significant advances in the production of textiles, the raw materials of clothing. In the strongest possible contrast to the apparel industry, textiles – having got off to an early start – showed all the classic features of mass production. It was heavily capitalised, highly concentrated and operated large-scale production units. By the end of the First World War, it was surpassed only by the iron and steel industry in the total volume of capital invested.[41]

Particularly important for the dressmaking trade was the emergence and rapid diffusion of synthetic materials, especially rayon. Introduced in England at the end of the nineteenth century, rayon was first known and worked as 'artificial silk'. By 1940, the consumption of rayon was twelve times higher than it had been two decades earlier, and its price had plummeted.

The take-up of rayon allowed the dressmaking industry to achieve considerable reductions in the prices of finished products without having to undergo any changes in technology or organisation. Furthermore, the much higher quality of the fabric allowed for widening of the market for the cheapest grade of dress; those styles traditionally made in small batches of more expensive fabrics could now be made much more widely available. Since the greatest scope for standardisation already lay at the bottom end of the market where skilled labour and design costs were minimised (in the so-called 'dozen-priced' dress category), the introduction of rayon in effect facilitated a quantum leap in the production of mass-produced garments.

Between 1929 and 1939, the proportion of the total number of dresses produced that wholesaled at under $2.00 rose from a third of the total to more than half (Drake and Glasser 1942: 81). The corresponding share of the total wholesale *value* of dresses rose from just 6 per cent attributable to dresses under $2.00 in 1929 to 17.4 per cent in 1939.

The rise of the cheap dress corresponds with, and was in large measure responsible for, triggering the decline of the specialised industrial district that was the New York City garment centre. The increasing substitution of unskilled for skilled machine operators which accompanied the spread of synthetic fibres and the development of improved freight transport enabled manufacturers to relocate outside of New York City, in areas of cheap labour, beyond the grip of the City's high wages and closed shops.

The nub of the industry left behind continued to depend upon the same organisation and technical base established generations earlier. It made a virtue of necessity by concentrating on the margin of markets, increasing differentiation of products as it decreased their volume of production. Rather than cheapening its products, it has turned more to the custom-made end of the spectrum, relying more heavily on those aspects of design that increase the cost differentials between its own products and those mass-produced in the hinterlands. It has then exploited this reputation by using its top-of-the-line activity (which is largely unprofitable for most firms) as a loss leader for designer brand, ready-to-wear price lines pitched to lower-income groups.[42] The discussion of advertising in clothing in Chapter 15 goes into these practices in greater detail.

Taking the long view, it is clear that differentiation in apparel has been incontrovertibly – and almost uninterruptedly – the norm, from the days when all clothing was hand-made. The mechanisation of tailoring skills did not replace this attribute of clothing with an alternative idea of apparel as a consumer durable designed to be worn until literally worn out. Instead, it preserved the possibility for a high turnover of an unlimited elaboration of styles. Outdated replaced outworn as the primary stimulus to change. Constant renewal of designs substituted for high levels of output. The industrial organisation that emerged in the dressmaking sector exploited this open-endedness: first, by continuously maintaining a large and constantly shifting pool of compliant and competing small-scale contractors; second, by rooting transactions and market strategies exclusively in the short term. In this way, dresses came to be marketed more like perishables.

Finally, this active strategy for survival was recast as a passive response to changes in consumer demand. The fickle consumer, and by extension, the retailer, were charged with responsibility for encouraging the increased differentiation and turnover in fashion goods. Set against this tradition, the longevity of truly popular garments like Levi 501 jeans bedevils the industry – and contradicts the classic 'consumptionist' explanations from Veblen onwards – because it suggests an underlying receptivity to genuinely mass-produced clothing that contradicts what has been accepted as orthodox behaviour.

But outside the dressmaking sector, it is possible to discern a clear lineage in the mass production of clothing growing out of ready-to-wear markets for simple goods selling at modest prices. Levi 501s embody the dynamics of this opposing tradition which is based on a widening of markets through a trickling *up* of demand for garments, exploiting the distinct capacities of machine production. This contradicts the tradition discussed here of a fashion system that takes the hand-sewn product as the ideal form and which tolerates the sewing machine because it allows the original to trickle *down* in cheapened form into more profitable volume production.

The two types of goods – basic jeans at one extreme and the *haute couture* outfit at the other – represent the end products of two separate systems of provision in clothing, of equal antiquity and significance. Though each has been profoundly influenced by the shifting dynamics of the other, sometimes accommodating and sometimes rejecting the other's changing habits, the visibility of the separate strands remains – and enlightens our understanding of the industry overall. The two traditions have responded differently to the possibilities and limitations of the sewing machine, to the secular rise in disposable incomes, to technological change in textiles and infrastructure, and to the perception of demand for fashion.

Adding a further level of complexity has been the co-existence of many subsystems woven around each of the primary strands of which those based on gender are perhaps the easiest to identify – and the most discussed here. Again, there has been considerable interweaving and cross-fertilisation between the men's and women's branches of the industry, however, differences in the staging of their development that run parallel to historical differences in the economic and social roles of men and women have left indelible marks on contemporary patterns of consumption. These distinguishing characteristics are more vividly brought to light by viewing them as linked components in their own systems of provision.

# 10

# CLOTHING

## Industrial or consumer revolution?

J.H. Clapham wrote that 'Even if . . . the history of "the" Industrial Revolution is a "thrice squeezed orange", there remains an astonishing amount of juice in it.'[1] The period is so rich in economic and social change and so much new empirical evidence has emerged that there is still room at the table for new and competing assessments, some adding a degree of analytical novelty. One such view which has appeared recently suggests that the eighteenth century be (re)interpreted as a consumer revolution. The 'consumerist approach' (exemplified by the work of McKendrick and his collaborators) has been understood – and embraced – as a reaction against the current orthodoxy in economic history, which has increasingly come to rely upon cliometrics. Revisionism occurs, partly as a switch of emphasis from supply to demand with a corresponding shift in narrative from production to consumption, and partly as a means of retaining or opening up explanatory factors beyond those within the narrowing confines of orthodox economic analysis.

The mainstream literature on the Industrial Revolution has tended to limit its scope to core issues concerning the pace of growth of output, population and their compositions. A consequence of this approach has been to create an artificial separation between the economy, on the one hand, and urbanisation, the class structure, local and central government and the simultaneous revolutions in the arts, politics and religion, on the other. It is as if all of these are the effects of the Industrial Revolution rather than part and parcel of it.

Although a further narrowing or shift of focus to the demand side might appear to be a recipe for an even greater degree of economic reductionism, it appears to have the opposite effect in practice. The association of demand with culture, fashion, lifestyle, etc., which serve as analytical counterparts to technological change, give the demand side approach a potentially wider compass than the orthodoxy. Students of history may find these topics considerably more appealing than the government statistics that form the centrepiece of many articles on supply side subjects. The preference for an approach with a seemingly immediate contemporary relevance no doubt contributes to its popularity.

Nevertheless, by comparison with the systems-of-provision approach described in earlier chapters, the consumerist approach is found to be highly restrictive. The very narrow parameters of demand which frame discussion, and the dismissal from consideration of most other factors intersecting with demand, produce arguments that are excessively one-sided and easily challenged. Yet, paradoxically, it is precisely the narrowness of the terms of reference employed in the consumerist approach which enhances its appeal. The self-containment of the argument, characteristic of all horizontal theories, imparts a misleading sense of integrity to the discourse, achieved at the expense of richer interpretations which require an admission of uncertainty, contradiction and conflict.

The inadequacies of this approach are particularly striking in McKendrick's discussion of the role of fashion in clothing in the second half of the eighteenth century; this was exactly the period when the textile industry at the other end of the same chain of provision was undergoing a radical transformation, brought on by an unprecedented sequence of technical innovations, following one another in quick succession. From the vantage point established by McKendrick, these extraordinary events – and their consequences (the emergence of wage labour and mass-produced goods, the breakdown of domestic production and the proletarianisation of the household) – remain almost totally hidden from view. The McKendrick argument suffers irreparably from their absence, underlining instead the need to relate the causes and course of shifts in demand to a more structured and dynamic explanation of the Industrial Revolution as a whole.

## THE DEMAND FOR FASHION IN CLOTHES

In McKendrick's article on the 'Commercialization of Fashion' (in *The Birth of a Consumer Society* (McKendrick *et al.* 1982) social emulation, class competition and emulative spending in the second half of the eighteenth century become the prime movers behind the development of mass-based consumer demand fifty years later. Demand emerges as a necessary precondition and stimulant to the subsequent growth of mass production. In particular, the 'trickle-down' effects of the demand for luxury goods, i.e., the gradual percolation and diffusion of upper-class tastes through all strata of society, anticipate and expedite the arrival of mass markets. According to McKendrick, once the pursuit of luxury 'was made possible for an ever-widening proportion of the population, then its potential was released and it became an engine for growth, a motive power for mass production' (ibid.: 66).

Demand, in this scheme, becomes an active transforming agent on its own, viewed independently of production. McKendrick's writing manages to attach a kind of dynamism to the force of demand by documenting the frenetic pace and manifestations of changes in taste. In the rapid displacement of one style, one colour, one eighteenth-century flavour-of-the-month by another, the course of fashion begins to acquire a self-sustained momentum of its own.

For McKendrick, this progressive emulation is manifested by the dress of the domestic servant which, in the second half of the eighteenth century, is often almost indistinguishable from that of the employer. Foreign fascination for the apparent blurring of social distinction that this implied is much quoted; the historian Von Archenolz 'complained that he could "not distinguish between guests and servants" when he visited the Duke of Newcastle, and was particularly thrown by the fact that the butler dressed like his master' (ibid.: 58).

How this mirroring of costume between upper and lower classes came about is not addressed by McKendrick. For him, the transmission of taste, like that of demand, is a disembodied process, not explicable by reference to prevailing social or economic relations. There is no attempt to link the surge in demand in the late eighteenth century with the production and distribution of goods, nor is there any reference to the source and distribution of consumers' incomes unless it be by a minimal lip-service paid to the supply side of the extraordinary world of late-eighteenth-century fashion. But his clear lack of interest in its dynamics leads him to make casual and misleading references to 'the sales of mass-produced cheap clothes' in an eighteenth-century context (ibid.: 53). It may not be apparent to all his readers that few mass markets for cheap clothes existed (except for the most basic garments and for fabrics and accessories) until almost a hundred years later, well after the arrival of the sewing machine in 1851. Even the systematic use of measuring tapes in the manufacture of clothes by size did not influence the cutting of fabric until the nineteenth century (Tozer and Levitt 1983).

Giving the impression that the supply underpinning mass markets already lay in readiness and simply awaited the catalyst of demand for luxury goods to spring into action is highly misleading. First of all, it conflates the idea of differentiation operating at the luxury end of the market with the standardisation of goods that is the hallmark of mass production. The emphasis on the expansion of markets through rapid and continuous change in the products themselves cannot be used to explain the process by which goods are homogenised to meet the requirements of large-scale volume production. In fact, the former can be viewed as obstructing or at least delaying the arrival of the latter.

Having resolutely turned his back on both the producers and distributors to give centre stage to the role of demand, McKendrick is left without any means to explain the transformation of a bespoke market in luxuries to a mass market of essential goods. It is simply observed, almost by a natural progression, in that 'luxuries' become 'decencies', and 'decencies' become 'necessities', (McKendrick *et al.* 1982: 1). At some stage, the frenzied proliferation and pace of fashion change just burns out, leaving 'a greater social uniformity . . . which of course suited those producing and selling fashion'. He argues that 'demand could be controlled to suit their needs' but without postulating any mechanisms by which this might have been achieved (ibid.: 56). The madness of compulsive differentiation in the consumption of hand-made luxury goods is presented as simply petering out, through some unexplained shift in the *Zeitgeist*, transforming itself into a more even-keeled and sensible uniformity which could then be exploited by producers to consolidate and generalise the emerging features of modern-day consumer society.

## MISSING MARKETS

One of the central flaws embedded in McKendrick's argument is his assumption that the expansion and broadening of interest in fashionable clothing during the second half of the eighteenth century in itself signified an expansion and broadening of the market demand for these goods. This is to confound consumption of goods with their exchange, i.e., to assume that the diffusion of fashion within society, from mistress to maidservant, demonstrated a progressive broadening of purchasing power. Social emulation, it is assumed, in itself begets emulative spending.

The argument is really a recasting of the optimist's position in the debate over changes in the standard of living brought on by the Industrial Revolution. In the absence of any reliable information on the distribution of incomes during the period, the hypothesis of a closely stratified society which encouraged the idea of social mobility between groups would allow for the progressive redistribution of income as of fashion from the top down.

More specifically, McKendrick argues that 'the expansion in the market, revealed in the literary evidence, occurred first among the domestic-servant class, then among the industrial workers and finally among the agricultural workers' (ibid.: 60). Though the argument depends on emulative behaviour triggering emulative spending, it offers neither documentary evidence chronicling such behaviour nor any discussion of the social relations that might have influenced it.

In fact, neither spending nor any act of exchange appears in McKendrick's scheme of things at all. In the discussion of clothing at least, the market remains an altogether shadowy not to say invisible figure. The acquisition of goods – as opposed to their display – is never addressed. Who purchases what, from whom, and for what prices? What are the incomes or wealth of those making such purchases and what is their source? To answer these queries would be to detract too much from McKendrick's central concern which rests squarely, if narrowly, with the growth of consumer demand induced by luxury consumption. In an earlier article, McKendrick does attempt to address these issues, hypothesising that the marked increase in the second half of the eighteenth century in the participation of women and children in wage labour explains the sudden surge in money wages that led to an expansion of demand (McKendrick 1974). Curiously, no mention is made here of the role played by social emulation and emulative spending. Women and children as industrial wage-earners are seen as contributing directly to an increased demand for household necessities rather than for luxuries and particularly for those goods formerly made by the women themselves. It is their wage income that pushes demand.

This at least grapples with the sources of income that are translated into effective demand for consumer goods. It also suggests that the process of transformation in demand and production occurred together over a much longer period than is suggested by McKendrick's later work. Moreover, it points to the contradiction between the entry of significant numbers of women and children into the labour force and the growth of unproductive domestic servants in the eighteenth and nineteenth centuries. On the other hand, it takes a positive view of this transition, arguing that the shift of women into wage labour represented a liberation from the oppression of 'cottage' industry, rather than the coercive deprivation of the means of home livelihood.

In short, there are problems of consistency across McKendrick's work. Either he sets aside the source of the income that provides for growing demand, simply relying upon the filtering-down of tastes from the wealthy to the lower classes. Or, in a sideshow, wage income is generated by the proletarianisation of women and children. Here, however, he would need to enter a much grander canvas of economic and social change over a longer period. Arguably, the destruction of domestic industry involves causal factors and associated effects whose own direct influence on demand is liable to be greater, through the wage income generated, than the indirect effect of the impact of fashion.

McKendrick's later article emphasises the key role played by the unproductive domestic servant as a carrier rather than an active consumer of fashion – transmitting changes in taste both from the upper to working classes and from London to the provinces. It makes no reference to the dampening role played by the servant class as a whole on the evolution of wage labour and its limiting effect on the extent of the market – of so much concern to Adam Smith. The perpetuation of almost feudal relations between servant and served could not be dismissed as insignificant when the number of men and women so employed was estimated at almost a million in 1806 – 800,000 female and 110,000 male, equivalent to about one in every eleven in the population at large (Hecht 1956: 34).

Servants are withdrawn from other potentially productive activity and are paid a variable combination of wages, tips and goods-in-kind. Their exclusion from wage labour must have had an inhibiting effect on the development of both large-scale demand and mass markets, both key features of modern consumer society. In addition, their absorption into households other than their own held down demand for all those consumer goods which depended on the growth of individual households (everything from housing itself to sets of furniture and pottery) as well as on the growth of cash wages. In other words, the perpetuation of this relationship and its later extension to the middle classes can in itself be seen as moderating the growth of industrial capitalism.

Nowhere in McKendrick's article is the huge disparity in income between master and servant ever commented upon. Yet the annual income of most housemaids in the second half of the eighteenth century would have been insufficient to pay for the material alone for a single dress made up for her mistress (Barbara Johnson in the 1760s paid £7 15s 9d in material for a day dress, a 'negligee', at a time when her housemaid was probably earning a basic annual salary of about 7 guineas) (see Hecht 1956 and Johnson 1987). Clearly, domestic servants were not in a position to purchase newly made clothes in imitation of their employers. On their incomes, they could not possibly contribute to any growth in the effective demand for new fashion goods. Emulative spending emanating from below stairs appears highly improbable.

Those clothes worn by servants which echoed upper-class rather than working-class tastes came to them, for the most part, directly from their employers, unmediated by markets of any kind. No money changed hands. Most were simply handed down from mistress to maid with increasing frequency as the turnover in fashion tastes increased (in an early demonstration of dynamic obsolescence). Extending the lifespan of still serviceable, though slightly outmoded garments could widen the general currency for fashion dress by raising its visibility and extending its use. In this, it functioned as a form of advertising. However, no discerning exercise of taste on the part of domestic servants was required.

In fact, the strength of emulation as a transforming mechanism can be even more comprehensively questioned. Employers often selected and purchased clothes for their servants to wear, in pursuit of a kind of 'vicarious consumption' which McKendrick mentions in connection with exotically dressed black page boys who adorned some eighteenth-century households. (There is much evidence of this practice, from Parson Woodforde to Anne Lister.) Lavish dress provided by the employer which cut across accepted social distinctions reflected his or her taste and not that of the servant. Furthermore, clothes purchased in this way often remained the property of the employer.

Extravagant dress for female servants in lieu of uniforms served as a kind of livery comparable to the more formal outfits worn by coachmen. Though male servants wore livery from an early date, uniforms were not adopted for female servants until the second half of the nineteenth century. Until then, their dress had always echoed the style and taste of their mistresses. For both male and female servants, clothes were a highly visible sign of their employers' wealth and status – much more so than their living quarters or diets, which remained completely hidden from the visitor's gaze and hence were less extravagantly catered for (Hecht 1956: 120).

The more exposed the servant to the public life of the house, the more he or she contributed to setting the overall social tone of the establishment, forming an integral part of the domestic display. Upstairs maids were clearly better dressed than those working exclusively below stairs. The coachman's livery was often the most elaborate of all because he carried the employer's reputation directly into the public realm. Even when servants purchased their own wardrobe, its contents would be carefully vetted by an existing or potential employer to guarantee that it was in acceptable taste. In this respect, emulation – whether reflecting genuine preference or not – might be perceived as enhancing job prospects.

Many servants were also bequeathed dresses upon the death of their mistresses. For instance, Sarah, Duchess of Marlborough stipulated in her will that her wardrobe be divided between her lady's maid and two other maidservants (Hecht 1956: 116). The acceptance of the bequest in no way signified a preference for whatever fashion might be reflected in the clothes passed on. As an alternative to extending a housemaid's own wardrobe, inherited dresses might be sold on to the second-hand clothing market, a substantial and lucrative trade in the eighteenth century. So established was the market in used, reconditioned or repaired clothes that many servants were granted the rights to their masters' cast-offs as an agreed condition of their contract of employment. The preference for cash (from selling hand-me-downs) over the pleasures to be had from keeping and wearing the master's old clothes suggests a definite limit to the allure of emulation.

The persistence of a strong second-hand market does lend weight to the influence of trickle-down effects of fashion. But equally powerful would be the attraction of slightly used goods set at low prices, relative to their cost when new. If cost is the primary factor in making such a choice – as it must be where a pair of boots could account for more than a month's wage – the contribution made by fashion or style is liable to be negligible.

Perhaps the clearest evidence of the servant's apparel as an accoutrement of the household is in their wearing of mourning dress upon the death of an employer's relative. Clothes for this purpose were supplied by the employer. Following the death of her uncle in 1817, Anne Lister noted in her diary:

> The mantua-maker came & bombasines & stuffs were sent over from Milne's & bombasines from Butters. Chose mourning for the 2 women servants from the former place, & from the latter, 50 yds (a whole piece) bombasine at 4/9 for ourselves. The servants had each 8 yds, 6/8 wide twilled stuff at 2/4, and 3½ yards of the same for a petticoat.
>
> (Lister 1988)

It is interesting to note that material for the servants' mourning dress was half the price of that worn by the mistress.

Servants had no choice in the matter any more than would children in the household. They were required to assume – literally – the mantle of a grief which they were unlikely to feel, particularly since mourning dress was worn

**"CHACUN POUR SOI."**

*Lady's-Maid.* "I BEG PARDON, MA'AM, BUT YOUR DRESS IS TRAILING—HADN'T I BETTER LOOP IT UP BEFORE YOU GO OUT?"

*Lady.* "NO, THANKS, PARKER, I PREFER LETTING IT TRAIL, AS IT'S THE FASHION JUST NOW——"

*Lady's-Maid.* "YES, MA'AM—BUT AS THE DRESS IS TO BE *MINE* SOME DAY, I THINK *I* OUGHT TO HAVE SOME SAY IN THE MATTER!"

*Figure 4* Nineteenth-century *Punch* carton used on the cover of *Social History*, vol. 15, no. 2, May, 1990.
*Source*: *Punch*.

in memory of relatives outside the immediate household as well as of those within it.[2] Mourning dress is simply the sharpest example of the control exercised by the employer over a servant's attire. None of the other means by which servants acquired their masters' or mistresses' clothes – through loans for the duration of service, hand-me-downs, bequests – demonstrates any preference for their employers' taste. The element of choice or preference expressed through monetary or any other form of exchange simply does not come into it.

McKendrick concentrates on the surge in demand for fashionable clothing in the late eighteenth century, i.e., before the advent of significant advances in the technology of clothes production (all clothing remained hand-made). This allows him to raise the importance of demand as a precondition of, and catalyst for, the revolution in production that was presumed to follow. But, as suggested above, the omission of any evidence relating to the development, source or exercise of purchasing power weakens credibility in this concept of demand, and the emulation on which it is founded is also unproven. Moreover, by the time capitalist production of clothing, as opposed to fabric, is finally under way – in the second half of the nineteenth century – the structure of purchasing power is very different from that prevailing fifty years earlier. By the middle of the nineteenth century, a distinct pattern of demand emerges reflecting the rising income, and numbers, of industrial workers.

This coincides with a significant shift of population growth away from the South to the Midlands and the North, where the new centres of industry were located. While in 1801 only five towns in England boasted populations of more than 50,000 (Liverpool, Manchester, Bristol, Birmingham and Leeds), by 1851, their number had risen to 24. The same period showed the proportion of the labour force engaged in manufacturing, mining and industry rising from 29.7 per cent to 42.9 per cent. This considerable growth in cash wages as a source of demand was, therefore, based on a completely different pattern of social relations governing consumption (as well as those governing production). The influence of London fashion and the importance of domestic servants were both much weaker in the industrial hinterlands and largely contained within the squirearchy maintaining active links with the capital. There is something more than a little absurd in reducing these regional patterns of, and stimuli to, industrialisation to the dictates of London fashion emanating from the London upper classes.

It seems highly probable that the emergence of demand and of consumption norms amongst the industrial working class took place outside McKendrick's social nexus altogether, i.e., that the influence of the dynamic he describes was both self-contained and historically specific. McKendrick has no way of bridging the gap between the luxury trade and the evolution of mass markets, just as he supplies no connecting thread to link the bespoke fashion trade with the evolution of the machine-based clothing industry.

One of several more plausible explanations for the change in taste is the spread of the protestant ethic in dress (Ribeiro 1984). This emphasised modesty and conformity in the place of worldly showiness and individuality and was indisputably a middle-class phenomenon. The growth of the professions also contributed to the increasing sobriety in middle-class dress – clergymen, doctors, lawyers, all donned working clothes that were uniformly black and unadorned. The gradual adoption of these habits by the aristocracy is in part a reflection of the decline in the influence of the court within the economic and social life of the country and a reflection too of the rise in the secular culture of work. Emulation *upwards* signifies the court's (and the aristocracy's) decline as an arbiter of taste and style. The wearing of court dress, with its expensive and impractical finery, became increasingly rare, limited to gala royal occasions and grand social events. As the influence of the rising bourgeoisie grew, so their taste and emphasis on working dress began to take hold across a wider spectrum of society.

Equally overlooked by McKendrick was a more naked emulation by the upper classes of the dress of labourers. The introduction of the workman's frock-coat into the higher reaches of society is a clear example of this countervailing trend (repeated in the twentieth century by the fashion history of jeans). According to the Cunningtons' history of costume, the 'frock' had become the common wear of the urban working man by 1700. Designed for comfort (and therefore loose-fitting) from cheap materials, its distinguishing characteristic was a flat, turned-down collar. By the middle of the eighteenth century, the 'gentleman' had taken it up as a comfortable alternative to his traditional heavy stiff coat. In the following decades, it became established ordinary wear for gentlemen. By the end of the century it annexed the classier word 'coat' becoming the 'frock-coat', 'with a long career ahead as a symbol of Class; a truly remarkable garment to have climbed the whole social scale from the farmyard to the Royal Enclosure' (Cunnington and Cunnington 1972: 18). Nor were those who took up the wearing of the frock-coat unmindful of its political implications. With its reputation as a more 'democratic' mode of dress, it became popular during the period of the French Revolution among those wishing to show their opposition to the *ancien régime* (Tozer and Levitt 1983: 55).

Both the examples of the frock-coat and that of the puritan ethic suggest that the trend towards equality in dress emanated from below, pushing its way upwards towards the wealthier classes, as well as from above and trickling down. This two-way influence, however, deprives luxury spending of its progressive attributes. The lower orders are no longer simply passive beneficiaries and transforming multipliers of consuming habits imposed from above. Moreover, spending by the upper classes is no longer required to serve as a catalyst in the transformation of goods from luxuries into basic necessities. The diffusion of the frock-coat represents an opposing tendency – the mutation of a humble garment into an essential component of the upper-class wardrobe. It also demonstrates that emulation need not necessarily lead to a cheapening of the final product through either increases in productivity or cheapening of materials. In other words, the widening of demand, on its own, cannot provide an impetus for progressive technical change.

## PRODUCTION OF CLOTHING

Conspicuous consumption of clothing in the eighteenth century (as also in the nineteenth) depended on the provision of goods by labour-intensive means. It was the display of tailor-made goods on the body designed to reflect the individual's personal taste – and measurements – that conveyed some measure of wealth. Increased demand for these goods did not reflect any change in their price, any cheapening in the process by which they were made nor any change in their utility. Nor did it necessarily imply any significant growth in the numbers of people who could afford to make such purchases. Instead, increased consumption was a response to the quickened turnover in style which overrode all considerations of usefulness and availability of income.

Increased demand for luxury goods simply extended the use of hand production techniques. Until the arrival of the sewing machine in the middle of the nineteenth century, all clothing was hand-made. Though there had been considerable changes in the relationship of producers to distributors and retailers, which allowed for the development of some ready-to-wear goods, the persistence of a highly labour-intensive method of production kept prices up. The fashionable world of eighteenth-century London demanded an ever-growing number of tailors, seamstresses, milliners and haberdashers to accommodate the sudden expansion in demand for bespoke garments. The incomes of these artisans rose as a group because of a surge in their numbers in response to demand for their services rather than through any increase in their individual productivities.

Looking more closely at the way clothes were actually made in the eighteenth century – particularly women's dresses – it becomes easier to understand how they lent themselves to the rapid changes in taste that fashion demanded. The most important and most expensive element in a woman's dress was its fabric. Because a fashionable dress could require more than 20 yards of material, the contribution of the fabric to the total cost of a dress remained remarkably high, swamping both the labour costs involved in its manufacture and the costs of trimmings. By mid-century, the cost of labour involved in the making-up of material into a completed outfit could still be as low as 5 per cent of the cost of fabric (Ribeiro 1984: 53). The central role played by the fabric was in part reflected by the greater status and wealth of the mercer who supplied it, relative to the mantua-maker or tailor who worked on it. Such economics dictated a long life in use for any particular piece of quality dress fabric which would be passed on from one generation to the next.[3] The much-cited Parson Woodforde in 1790 gave his niece a green silk damask gown that had belonged to an aunt who had died in 1771 (Tozer and Levitt 1983: 45).

The use of large running stitches combined with a minimum of complicated cutting in eighteenth-century dressmaking allowed the same piece of fabric to be altered and restyled several times without seriously damaging it. In the absence of fixed sizes, dress styles were achieved by the pleating and draping of basic shapes rather than by close tailoring to the body in tight and small stitches. This enabled dresses to be fairly easily unpicked and rearranged and, with the addition of new relatively cheap trimmings, to re-emerge in a new guise with a minimum of fuss and expense, particularly if the work was carried out by the woman herself (Tozer and Levitt 1983: 45). The stimulus of changing fashions therefore, intensified and perhaps prolonged home-based and non-marketed dressmaking while encouraging a greater production and consumption of the small but essential newly manufactured trimmings (buckles, ribbons, stays, lace, etc.) (Eversley 1967: 239).

It was these latter, essentially superficial goods, that facilitated the necessary differentiation in fashion. If emulative spending did occur, it is most likely to have been in the market for these trinkets which would have been more easily within the reach of modest incomes. Dress fabric, by comparison, appears to have served more as a consumer durable. For men, the greatcoat, passed down from one generation to the next, played a similar role. The value placed on these garments is revealed by the frequency with which advertisements for the recovery of stolen clothing appeared in eighteenth-century newspapers.

The persistence of the second-hand market in clothes (facilitated by the lack of fixed sizes and the loose cuts in women's dress) also underlines the durability of clothes – and their expense relative to income. In the 1780s, a female domestic worker, earning as little as 3s per week, might be asked to pay over 6s for a common second-hand gown and 4s 6d for a second-hand linsey-woolsey petticoat (Ribeiro 1984: 64). The second-hand market at least enabled such clothes to be recycled, to outlive their role as fashion goods, and to pass into the world of basic necessities without impinging on the realm of production.

At the same time, the proliferation of bizarre and often excessive fashion trimmings and accessories (mouse-skin eyebrows, muffs for the wrists, artificial nosegays), which so transfixed foreign visitors, may itself have masked the slow pace at which genuine advances in the production of clothes (as opposed to fabric) proceeded. Dress fabric worn by the wealthy remained a luxury good. The flurry and intensity of interest in fashion and its increasing diffusion throughout society were not accompanied by any substantial growth in the markets for new clothes construed as necessities. Those at the bottom end of the market remained as dependent as ever on hand-sewing of inferior and sometimes reconstituted fabrics (like shoddy).

While the peripatetic Scotch pedlars in the provinces would not sell finished ladies' dresses, they could and did carry out a roaring trade in the small change of fashion, as McKendrick demonstrates. This could be the link between the world of fashion centred in London and its diffusion throughout the country.

When clothes could be transformed through the minimum application of effort and at minimum cost, it becomes more credible to consider the transmission of taste across income groups. But taste, in this context, remains grounded in the world of decoration and surfaces; it does not engineer more profound changes in production and society.

## THE SEPARATE DEVELOPMENT OF LUXURY AND MASS PRODUCTION IN CLOTHING

It should be clear from the detailed criticisms above that the credibility of McKendrick's argument depends upon the reader's willingness to be charmed by the tidiness of a single idea, attractively packaged. It stands alone, denying any links between the transmission of cultural values and the material conditions with which they interact. This leaves it highly vulnerable to conflicting empirical evidence from any of the many other factors contributing to the density of historical experience. Not only does it fail to connect with the other elements of its own system of provision (attending to the production or distribution of luxury clothing itself); it fails to admit the possibility of other systems of provision operating concurrently within the clothing sector with which the luxury trade might interact or conflict.

That other clothing systems existed is undeniable. A more explicit acknowledgement of their operation, scale and overlapping histories offers a deeper understanding of the long-term development of the clothing industry. It certainly drives a wedge between the consumption of luxury goods and the evolution of mass-produced clothes. As late as the second half of the nineteenth century and even into the twentieth century, the production of luxury goods remained untouched by the revolutionary changes in machine-made clothing. Well after the adoption of the sewing machine, it was not unusual for men and women to continue to have a great deal of their wardrobe hand-made. (The demand for the bespoke product continues in the late twentieth century in the market for machine-made goods which are designed to look hand-made.)

A department store like the Bon Marché took pains to emphasise the individual craftsmanship of the clothing they sold. The arrival of these large-scale emporia in fact extended the market for the hand-made production of clothes and related goods. In 1880, Lewis's department store in Liverpool, with 300 working tailors, claimed to operate the largest tailoring establishment in England (Briggs 1958: 130). In 1890, Bon Marché had more than 600 men and women workers employed in ateliers within the store to work on hand-made or made-to-measure items like men's shirts, trousseaus, baby clothes and white goods. (Because they were not in factories, sweatshops in stores also escaped state supervision by health and safety inspectors). Specialised workshops which supplied hand finishing to a wide variety of products catered to the demand for differentiation in consumer goods. In the machine age, the snob value of 'custom made' grew apace. Cards advertising Bon Marché showed 'pictures of skilled artisans working at their trades . . . on the reverse side, the history of the craft . . . the Industrial Revolution, apparently, had never been heard of' (Miller 1981: 218).

Evidence from the Industrial Revolution, however, when recognised and pursued, points to the development of distinctly working-class consumption as an important stimulus to industrial development. The mechanisation of the production of cotton played an extremely important role in this process. Despite a variety of prohibitions on the use of other fabrics designed to protect the domestic woollen industry (including the requirement to bury the dead in wool shrouds), innovations designed to promote its development were much more successfully applied to cotton. The advantages offered by cotton were largely technical; the material also lent itself to the production of a greater variety of finished fabrics (from chintz to corduroy). All these benefits helped transform cotton into a readily available, cheap alternative to the more expensive woollens, linens and silks.

The attributes of woven cotton also contributed to its popularity. It was lightweight, which made it easier to work up into a greater variety of goods. It was washable, which made it desirable for many occupations requiring hard-wearing material; corduroy, for example, began to replace leather in breeches.

The early technical innovations which triggered mechanisation and expanded cotton production all appeared during the last quarter of the eighteenth century (Hargreaves' spinning jenny, Arkwright's water frame, Crompton's mule, Cartwright's power loom). Between 1770 and 1800, the consumption of cotton increased twelve-fold. Tailors, milliners and mercers who continued to provide their clients with hand-sewn bespoke clothing were now also able to stock a supply of ready-made cotton caps, aprons, pockets and handkerchiefs (Lemire 1984: 34). These could be made up during periods of slack, available for sale at any time. This capacity for advance production was in part made possible by the relatively small outlay required. Unlike tailored goods, which were produced on credit, cotton goods were sold for cash, thus speeding up turnover and the replacement of stock. The ready-to-wear trade also depended on the growing acceptance of standard goods for which demand was stable and predictable.

It was also related to a tendency towards increasing uniformity in tastes across class lines, spreading upwards from the broad base of society rather than down from its apex, as McKendrick argues. Cheaply produced cottons extended large-scale advance production from the periphery of clothing markets in accessory goods to its centre with the arrival of women's shifts and gowns. Their success reflected the broadening of markets made possible both by the reduction in prices achieved by technical innovations and by the growth of cash wages as more and more workers entered the labour market, exerting their influence through high levels of aggregate demand.

The early introduction of cotton shifts by the East India Company provides a good illustration of the opportunities these changes began to suggest to entrepreneurs. Concern about the impact on prices of a possible oversupply of Indian cottons led Josiah Child of the East India Company to arrange for calicoes 'to be strongly and substantially sewed for poor people's wear', i.e., to be made up into simple shifts (Lemire 1984: 32). In an attempt to encourage product substitution of cotton for linen, Child specified the manufacture of 200,000 shifts for sale in Britain and other parts of northern Europe. This was manufacture on a large scale, predicated on both the widespread acceptance of a very basic garment and the purchasing power to demonstrate it.

Printed calicoes were cheap and immensely popular. In 1786 Robert Peel (director of a family firm that combined factory spinning with weaving and printing) remarked that '3 parts of 4 of printed goods are consumed by the lower classes of people' (Mukerji 1983: 235). The earliest recorded orders for cotton gowns in 1767 show a price of 9 shillings per gown (Lemire 1984: 36). It was only later with refinements in production techniques driven in part by the large market demand for cheaper goods that cotton could be made into fine quality muslins which would appeal to middle- and upper-income purchasers.

The consumption by working-class women of cheap printed calicoes for themselves by 1818 constituted almost the entire home market for printed cottons (Forty 1986: 73). The wearing of ginghams, woven and printed, was also largely confined to the working class. These expressed preferences are themselves signs of the growth of incomes and markets which are so conspicuously absent in McKendrick's tale of eighteenth-century London. Half a century later, those ready-to-wear markets that stimulated the development of mass production were unequivocally if critically linked to lower-income groups. A leading English designer, Henry Wampen, wrote in 1863:

> Ready-made articles of apparel . . . find their admittance only among the vulgar, or those devoid of taste. . . . [Only] in countries where people are sunk below the standard of taste, or have perhaps never reached it . . . ready-made clothes establishments are to be found; and that in the same degree that people advance in culture of taste order [i.e., bespoke] trades increase, and those of the opposite kind decrease.
>
> (Feldman 1960: 75)

## THE IDEOLOGICAL UNDERPINNINGS OF THE CONSUMERIST APPROACH

The discussion of fashion above is an attempt to respond to McKendrick on his own ground. Like McKendrick, it marshals empirical evidence and contemporary commentary to create historical narrative that clings fairly closely to the period under consideration. But even operating within these limits, it is possible to undermine the credibility of the transforming role of demand simply by fleshing out some of McKendrick's hypothesised links in the chain of transmission (looking, for example, at relative incomes between master and servant, at their social relations and prevailing conditions of employment). Bringing in evidence to remind the reader of the existence of other classes between those at the top and those at the bottom (the professions, commercial and trade interests), each contributing their own tastes and habits to changes in the dress code, reveals the extraordinary narrowness of McKendrick's field of interest, for all the exuberant detail of fashion he puts on parade.

The concept of emulation (source of the trickle-down effect discussed in detail in Chapter 11) serves an important function here. It establishes a progressive role for the upper classes in the creation of consumer society. They are seen as the ultimate source of demand, introducing ideas for consumption goods which are passed down through all other strata in society, transformed as they go from luxuries to decencies to basic necessities. There is an implication that the state of idleness made possible by unearned incomes may be warranted by the inventiveness of those so underoccupied in dreaming up demands for new luxury goods (a kind of leisure-class R&D hothouse!). This view reaches its peak in Plumb's contribution where, for example, the impact of Empire shows through more in the discovery and breeding of exotic species from the New Worlds for sport and for pets than for their potential economic use and exploitation (Plumb 1982).

The belief that wealth produces 'breeding', which is itself the source of taste and refinement, is therefore used to justify the existence of the social pyramid. But the inequalities of that pyramid are entirely glossed over. Nor is there any mention of either the changing sources and diffusion of income, nor of changes in the overall pattern of its distribution. In their absence, there is neither getting nor spending. So the radical transformations in both brought about by the Industrial Revolution disappear from view.

In their place is substituted a cashless and almost arcadian view of early capitalist society in which harmonious relations do away with gross inequalities and replace class-based antagonism. What safer example to draw upon than the relation between master/mistress and servant, a relationship which remained largely untouched by the development of wage labour in factories and which depended on the maintenance of personal, quasi-familial relations between employer and employee. In this context, emulation of the mistress by the maidservant could be seen as proof of continuous harmony running right through the social hierarchy, from top to bottom, casting a whiff of 'happy families' over British society as a whole.

In this story, not only could those at the bottom benefit directly and almost immediately from the superior tastes of their employers (by taking on their outmoded clothes), but in so doing they were also contributing to economic progress by whipping up consumer demand. But because this demand prefigures the Industrial Revolution, it can emerge within a pattern of social relations which are untainted by the conflicts that grew out of factory employment. The closely stratified nature of British society (by comparison with other European countries) is presented as a measure of the higher level of democracy in Britain. It allowed fashion to percolate down with greater speed and effect just as it fostered (at least the illusion) of greater social mobility. In other words, society, in its patterns of consumption, though based on inequality, was not only benign; it was also progressive.

To create the image of a forward-moving society fuelled by demand from above, consumerists have to jettison the interests and contributions of at least three-quarters of its members. The incomes and consumption habits of the labouring and middle classes are left out of the picture altogether, obviating the need to measure the relative impact of luxury spending on the economy as a whole. This is just one indication of the general absence of the economy and its transactions; there is no production and no exchange. The state also falls away, allowing the reader to forget its role in promoting or enhancing the interests of some in society at the expense of others, whether through direct intervention to increase or reduce inequality or through passive acquiescence in the status quo. The picture of apparently harmonious social relations exemplified by the master/servant relationship gives the impression that corrective state action would in any case be superfluous.

Notions of conspicuous consumption, dynamic obsolescence, product differentiation, etc., all lurk in the background of McKendrick's eighteenth-century society. The retrospective application of contemporary habits of consumption and marketing – which was carried out to excellent effect in McKendrick's studies on the entrepreneurial genius of Josiah Wedgwood – cannot be so easily accommodated in a broader picture of society at large. The sheer complexity of factors determining economic activity in any particular period preclude this wholesale transfer. None the less, McKendrick has achieved an ideological *tour de force*, both in transforming the categories of consumerism into progressive causal factors and in identifying the eighteenth century with consumer society, itself identified with contemporary capitalism.[4]

For the latter, the almost exclusive concern with female fashion which has dominated much of postwar consumerism in this century is not so appropriate for the eighteenth-century context, where the market might well have been dominated by men and where women's participation and economic leverage was more restricted. This is a curious oversight of McKendrick, since his work on women's and children's employment in the early factory system is one of the few early attempts by a male historian to bring women's contribution into sharper relief (McKendrick 1974).[5] The shift is partly explained by the withdrawal of explicitly economic variables from the later work, which concentrates on a more idealised view of the world of fashion and is more concerned with the transmission of cultural values than with the transmission of economic power.

The two are not seen as directly linked. This makes it possible to view the upper classes as the repositories of what have come to be seen as 'superior' rather than simply 'dominant' cultural values. Rather like the British Museum or other institutions which have selectively appropriated culture from a wide range of sources and recast them in a British mould, so the fashions of the British upper classes, also drawn from elsewhere (Europe, the Far East, etc.), have been repackaged and reintroduced as British. In both cases, the results of such refining eclecticism acquire a certain inviolability because of the significance assigned to those who espouse them. They appear as unchallenged and hence universally approved sources of cultural definition and renewal rather than as choices of a particular social group granted certain privileges at a particular time in history. Since this assigns them an essential role at the top of the social order, they are the bearers of modernity. The proper mechanism for the dispersal of the values they embody throughout society remains the trickle-down from above, or emulation from below. In this spirit, Plumb provides the final word in the McKendrick volume, by way of a non-Communist manifesto for demand that parallels Rostow's stages theory for supply: 'As Marx realized, the revolutionaries in 1800 were the bourgeoisie and most of these believed, as they had to, in modernity. No consumer society can exist or expand without such a belief' (Plumb 1982: 344). To the extent that the past is viewed through the prism of current concerns and prejudices,[6] the consumerists bear the responsibility for reflecting the contemporary belief that modernity in the eighteenth century, as today, flows from the cosseted, if not corseted, body and minds of the bourgeoisie.

There is, nevertheless, something that is positive about the consumerist approach. It attempts both to conceal and to compensate for the poor service provided by economic theory in finding a place for demand in the long run and in significant economic and social change. Rather than do this through a more or less formalistic model of shifting supply and demand curves, it focuses on the latter alone through the supposedly dynamic impact of changing patterns of (luxury) consumption. The discussion of clothing in this chapter reveals the necessity of breaking out of the confines of such narrowly conceived notions of the Industrial *Revolution*. The transformation in the mode of work, in the mode of organisation of society more broadly (institutional, regional, rural and urban, etc.), in the family – all have to be considered in locating and structuring the role of the changing mode of consumption, with the latter both as cause and effect, and as impediment and stimulus to the birth of modern capitalism.

# 11

# TRICKLE-DOWN THEORIES

The previous chapter provided a demonstration of the pitfalls of a 'horizontal' theory of consumption, even if apparently reasonably applied as a factor in explaining the Industrial Revolution. This chapter looks more closely at the pedigree of the theory of trickle-down which makes an appearance in almost all discussions of clothing. It briefly traces its course over the past eighty years and its transfer from one academic discipline to another. Reference to material in both the earlier chapters on clothing help to place this theory in a healthier perspective.

The theory in its original form has been attributed to Simmel (1904), whose ideas on fashion first appeared in 1904. It provides a dynamic for the diffusion of tastes and styles throughout society; this is based on the presumed propensity to emulate, expressed as a drive towards upward social mobility. Each of the stratified layers between the top and bottom of the social pyramid emulate the tastes of those occupying the next layer up while at the same time rejecting the tastes associated with the group directly below it. The combined effect of these two forces – emulation pushing up from below and differentiation pushing down from above – in a process described by McCracken (1988: 94) as 'chase and flight' – propels the diffusion of fashion. Pressure to consume 'upwards' allows tastes to trickle 'down'.

According to the theory, those at the very top are just as active in protecting their privileged status as those in any stratum below. Motivated by the continuing need to differentiate themselves from imitators snapping at their heels, they are constantly pushed to invent new fashions that set them apart and redefine status at the summit. As Simmel put it:

> Just as soon as the lower classes begin to copy their style, thereby crossing the line of demarcation the upper classes have drawn . . . the upper classes turn away from this style and adopt a new one, which in its turn differentiates them from the masses; and thus the game goes merrily on.
>
> (Simmel 1904: 135)

Those at the top call the tune; their greater access to money enables them to participate more extensively and more often in the process of exchange. It is their relationship to exchange which interests Simmel. For him, the entire economy is grounded in exchange, 'it is just as productive and value-creating as production itself'; production is simply viewed as 'an exchange with nature' (Frisby 1984: 98). By dismissing both the social and technical relations of production to concentrate on 'what really happens in the mind of each economic subject', Simmel in effect severs the linkages in what has been described in earlier chapters as a continuous chain of provision; here, half of the process is denied or at best subordinated to the other half. The focus on an abstract concept of exchange also strips away relevant distinctions between, for example, subsistence and market economies, the purchase of land and the purchase of commodities, etc. What remains is an ahistorical theory of social formations with more relevance for sociology than for economics.

Within this exchange-based paradigm, Simmel explains the quickening pace of fashion change as a consequence of the rise to power of the middle classes:

> Classes and individuals who demand constant change, because the rapidity of their development gives them the advantage over others, find in fashion something that keeps pace with their own soul-movements. Social advance, above all is favourable to the rapid change of fashion, for it capacitates lower classes so much for imitation of upper ones, and thus the process . . . according to which every higher set throws aside a fashion the moment a lower set adopts it, has acquired a breadth and activity never dreamed of before.
>
> (Simmel 1904: 151)

Following on from this, the increasing animation of the middle classes applies pressure on the forces of production to cheapen fashion goods so that the upper classes will be able to afford to continue playing their role as catalyst to mass consumption. In this conceit, the 'breadth' and 'activity' of 'social advance' possess motive properties that most economists would attribute, at least in part, to the rapid rise in disposable incomes made available through the rise in mass factory employment. Simmel's theory instead gives primacy to the dynamics of social change viewed not as a consequence of economic change but as a transforming agent on its own, pulling production behind it. The theory casts the upper class arbiter in a leading role; his or her arbitrary adoption of new fashions in luxury goods sets in train a process that transforms them into mass-produced commodities, conjuring them up from the unseen netherworld of production, in the style, volume and materials required to clear the markets at the right price.

The performance of this role (a manifestation of *noblesse oblige*) shields the upper class from accusations of parasitism and awards them instead the rather more progressive role of stimulating the creation of consumer society. Their styles of dress, their tastes in food, their amusements – in other words, all their primary occupations – carry weight because of the status they enjoy at the top of the social pyramid. As their tastes are emulated by those in the ever-widening layers of society beneath them, demand grows apace, culminating in the creation of mass markets for goods which the trickle-down process transforms *en route* from luxuries into basic necessities.[1]

The theory, as originally formulated, has no historical specificity. Simmel applied it equally to the rise of the third estate in late-eighteenth-century France as to culture in late-nineteenth-century Germany. Over the first half of the twentieth century, neither the emergence of factory-based mass production as the dominant mode of industrial organisation nor the concurrent spread of national markets and distribution networks seems to have dislodged faith in the disproportionately influential role of a small social group sitting at the top of the social pyramid. Demand emanating from those at the apex of this triangle is still deemed to determine the character, volume and turnover of final products within a wide range of consumer goods industries. This constancy in the face of historical and social upheavals lends weight to the belief in universal and innate drives powering demand, in this case the drives to emulate and/or differentiate.

But evidence cited in the discussion of clothing above undermines the credibility of such a monolithic point of view. First, the theory does not allow for a distinction to be made between goods which enter the market through different systems of provision either as necessities (work clothes) or as luxuries (fur coats). A discussion of the contrasting mechanisms by which necessities and luxuries are altered to extend their market reach falls beyond the scope of trickle-down, which offers only an explanation for the latter. Even this fails to acknowledge the presence of real constraints in the transformation of luxury goods (e.g., the very limited availability and very great expense of clothing that depends on supplies of rare, live animals like mink). Clothing that moves against the tide, of humble origins rising up through the social strata (like the eighteenth-century frock-coat or, more recently, jeans),[2] are often propelled in that direction by qualities more commonly associated with basic necessities than with luxury goods (e.g., comfortable, loose fitting, durable, easily washed or replaced, cheap). These are also attributes of the earliest mass-marketed and mass-produced goods. Since they are not often linked with the provision of bespoke luxury clothes, their contribution to the widening of clothing markets tends to be neglected. Theories of the trickle-down reinforce this neglect because of their emphasis on the relatively short-term fashion cycle at the expense of longer-term and often more significant secular change.

In the context of the hugely successful designer jeans market, the significance for the history of clothing production of its more modest yet more enduring predecessor is completely set aside. Until virtually the mid-1960s, the market for blue jeans remained untouched by the transforming hand of fashion. In the late 1940s, Levi's still sold to its market of largely blue-collar workers just one style of blue jeans which it mass produced in forty-six different sizings (Finlayson 1990: 46). Yet for the apparel industry at the time, the $20 million market which Levi's operated was big business indeed, outstripping annual revenues for most women's fashion houses.

The summary overview of the development of the clothing industry at the end of the nineteenth century in the United States also emphasises the co-existence of several strands of demand, each linked to its own system of supply. Yet only one strand concerns Simmel and other proponents of trickle-down: namely, the one associated historically with cosmopolitan markets supplying hand-made luxury garments to an economically negligible segment of the national population. In particular, the behaviour of women has come to dominate discussion of this consumer group. However, for the future development of mass production, much more significant sources of demand were those originating in the hinterlands, beyond the reach of city tailors, home-sewing services or European imports and concerned primarily with clothing men.

The demand for industrial clothing to protect men engaged on building the nation's infrastructure, for military uniforms, for slaves on plantations in the South, all involved large-scale production of a very limited range of very basic garments. There was hardly any overlap between either the fabrics or styles of these clothes and those worn by the privileged elites. But their requirements were well suited to the potential capacities of factory production, and the mass production of basic work clothes precedes that associated with forms of urban dress. In fact, techniques developed for the manufacture of work shirts to supply rural workers were eventually imported back into the cities for the manufacture of office and dress shirts.

This fleshing out of the clothing story depends on the recognition of empirical evidence contributing to patterns of both supply and demand in a specified historical period. Not only do the results contradict the theory of trickle-down but the method itself violates the approach adopted by Simmel, who applied his theory horizontally across all periods and places as well as across all items of consumption within any given period.

More recent versions of trickle-down still pay lip-service to the assumption of an abstract governing concept which remains universally and continuously valid. Half a century after Simmel's work, Barber and Lobel (1952) provide a re-statement of trickle-down which retains the spirit of the original:[3]

> The 'trickle' system is perpetuated because the American class system makes some women continually seek for symbols of their difference from those just below them in the class system and at the same time makes other women continually seek for symbols of their equality with those just above them in the class system.

How the productive system facilitates or thwarts trickle-down is not addressed. The argument simply implies that production must somehow follow suit – 'As the "fashion" trickles down, fabrics become cheaper and mass production necessary. . . . When a general style has "trickled down" through all levels, the "fashion" must change' (Barber and Lobel 1952: 327). Even within the terms of its own argument, the actual productive and distributive agencies responding to demand are wholly absent. Writing a decade later, Robinson (1961: 376) reproduces the conviction that higher socioeconomic groups adopt new fashions first: 'new fashions tend to filter down by stages through the levels of affluence'.

McKendrick's retrospective application of trickle-down to late-eighteenth-century consumer society (examined in the previous chapter) follows closely in the same tradition, with similar disregard for all evidence outside trickle-down's own narrow terms of reference. Some have challenged the relevance of trickle-down in the face of the 'levelling influences' and increasing prosperity that (at least in American society) have blurred formerly distinct class boundaries and altered the roles played by different strata in the social hierarchy. King (1964) points to the incompatibility of the trickle-down theory with the actual mechanics of fashion merchandising, and demonstrates (as does the McKendrick example cited above) the essential weakness of trickle-down when empirically tested. Field (1970) argues that, in the world of women's clothing, the time factor effectively impedes the vertical flow of fashion demand: styles for all social strata (i.e., all price lines) are introduced simultaneously and differences between them are not primarily differences of design but rather of quality (using less expensive fabric, trimmings, etc.). This makes it hard to claim an avant garde role for those buying at the top.

The persistence of the original theory despite its untenable hypothesis suggests that its real purpose is to justify a particular view of society rather than to offer a serious explanation of economic activity. Since the relationship between the organisation of society and the organisation of the economy is never raised, the theory can have little relevance to a proper explanation of consumer behaviour which must acknowledge both. The dynamics of trickle-down do not, after all, ever disturb the underlying presumption of a pyramidal structure; they lend it the appearance of dynamism through periodic but superficial internal upheavals without ever questioning the economic basis on which it might initially have been established or preserved. What remains is a view of society driven solely by the tastes and preferences of individuals identifying with the goals of the social groupings to which they belong; the provision of goods to meet these demands simply follows automatically without the transforming intervention of investment, production, competition or crisis of any kind.

## VARIATIONS ON THE ORIGINAL THEORY

Interest in the trickle-down theory amongst marketers and sociologists is driven by their attempts to pin down an explanation for the diffusion of fashion, i.e., to establish a fashion adoption theory with predictive powers. To this end, the original theory has been altered to accommodate emulation that moves horizontally or upwards from below: Blumberg (1974) argues that the long hair, beads and head bands of the 1960s counter-culture percolated up through society as an expression of the breakdown of social cohesion arising from the anti-war movement and student unrest.[4] In this section, we sample such improvisations prior to an elaboration (in the next section) of the use of the theory to bolster the supply side economics of Reaganomics.

Bell, for example, offers a more comprehensive statement of the dynamics of trickle-down which does allow for shifts in the direction of emulation (like that proposed by Blumberg) in response to historical changes:

> Fashionable dress is tied to the competition between classes, in the first place the emulation of the aristocracy by the bourgeoisie and then the more extended competition which results from the ability of the proletariat to compete with the middle classes.
>
> (Bell 1976: 155)

Yet there is still no indication of the forces at work translating this sartorial ideology into clothes on bodies. Class struggle is perceived through its impact on culture and society, suppressing any view of the conflicts over the control of economic resources with which they are bound up but not in ways that can be read off superficially from changes in fashion trends. The danger of making too simplistic a correspondence between surface signs and underlying phenomena is revealed forcefully by Harrington:

> Clothes make the poor invisible too: America has the best-dressed poverty the world has ever known. . . . It is much easier in the United States to be decently dressed than it is to be decently housed, fed, or doctored. . . . Even people with terribly depressed incomes can look prosperous.
>
> (Harrington 1962: 5)

In the absence of an explicit link between the social and economic spheres, struggles over stratification taken up by proponents of trickle-down are couched as issues of 'status' rather than of class.[5]

Other narrower variations on the original trickle-down theory substitute elites based on class by those based on income, attitudes or gender. McCracken (1985) seeks to strengthen the predictive power of Simmel's original argument by adding a theory of clothing symbolism to provide a credible motivation for emulation. He uses this to explain the executive dress of businesswomen which, in emulating that of men, hopes to throw off the symbolic liabilities associated with more traditionally female modes of attire.

The original trickle-down theory allied 'fashion' power with economic power, arguing that the former directed the latter in a productive way. By implication, variants of the theory which hypothesise a trickle effect moving up or across rather than down suggest a link between these more recent expressions of demand and more democratic or at least decentralised catalysts for economic activity. In other words, though never explicitly stated, these acknowledged shifts in the directionality of the trickle effect or in the composition of significant social groups imply a relatively greater openness or classlessness within American society and an economic framework that is responsive to these social changes.

These variations, then, share the basic belief of the original theory in the pre-eminent power of demand. The emphasis in all of them is squarely on (wo)man the consumer; production has been banished. One of the consequences of this is to elevate the historical significance of demand so that it becomes the constant centre of a world in a state of flux. This creates the impression that patterns of demand in themselves have determined the character of industries. If, for example, the demand for women's clothing had more closely resembled that for cars or radios rather than being driven by fixed emotional imperatives – whether down from above or up from below – then its productive history would have followed suit, i.e., it would have led to a steady and predictable demand for standardised clothing, mass produced by increasingly concentrated, large-scale operations. It is hoped that reviewing such an idea within the broader framework made available by the systems-of-provision approach exposes the narrowness and limited explanatory power made available by this (and other) form(s) of ahistorical determinism.

## Supply side economics

The arrival of 'supply side' economics in the 1980s, most closely associated with the presidency of Ronald Reagan, represents the most recent infiltration of trickle-down into the realm of economic theory and practice. Here, it has been disguised and repackaged with more damaging consequences.

Supply side theories rest upon the motivation and economic behaviour of *individuals*, particularly those constituting wealthy elites at the top of the social pyramid. Sometimes this is made explicit; at other times, it is hidden behind the more general appeal to the added incentives associated with tax and government expenditure cuts which inevitably disproportionately advantage the highest earners. Whether overtly or not, the upper classes are deemed by advocates of supply side theory to act as 'the cutting edge of the economy'[6] in much the same way that the eighteenth-century aristocracy was credited by McKendrick with acting as a catalyst in the development of the clothing industry. According to one of its proselytisers, 'leadership is supply and public opinion is demand'.[7] In the supply side framework, the upper classes perform this function through the disposal of their incomes which must be left unencumbered by high taxes and particularly by high marginal tax rates which are presumed to act as a disincentive to their skilled labour and entrepreneurial talents and investment. Tax cuts for the rich become, therefore, justified as the policy of (their) free choice, neatly complementing the ideology of *laissez-*

*faire* and purportedly designed to generate and liberate additional output through increased entrepreneurship and investment – thereby benevolently bestowing employment and income opportunities for those dependent on the initiatives of the economic elite.

The use of the term 'supply side' to describe this presumed chain of events is based more on wishful thinking than on rigorous analysis, unless there is absolute faith in the perfect workings of the market. In addition, the term 'supply side' has been stripped of any complexity, particularly when set against the context of this book where it has been used to describe technical and social, rather than individual, determinants of production. The use of 'supply side' by the apostles of Reaganomics is intended to forge a dynamic link between the atomised private decisions of wealthy individuals and the operation of the national economy. It involves a leap of faith comparable to that taken by McKendrick in arriving at mass production from a consideration of the exotic spending habits of eighteenth-century aristocrats. It adds force to our observation that his account implicitly serves as a rationale for a particular view of twentieth-century capitalism in which the elite serve as the fount of economic and social progress.

At the crudest level, supply side economics assumes the operation of a single, global system of provision across the economy as a whole, dispensing at a stroke with the myriad constraints, regulations and incentives determining the nature and level of provision in each and every industry. Blurring the distinctions between public and private sector systems of provision, it treats the effects of tax cuts on individuals as events of the same magnitude and character as the effects of cuts in government spending. In fact, it is not a theory of investment at all but rather a smokescreen through which to defend and promote inequalities in patterns of consumption and to erode wages and conditions of working people. Hence it has a place in this discussion of trickle-down, since its associated theory of demand is often overlooked by those more intent on critically assessing only the supply side of supply side economics.

An *Atlantic Monthly* article of 1981, charting the progressive disillusionment of Reagan's budget director, David Stockman, provides a useful illustration of the way in which theory may be perverted to disguise the ideological underpinnings of consumption. Stockman confesses that the original supply side tax proposal which brought down income tax rates in all brackets 'was always a Trojan horse to bring down the top rate'. He conceded:

> what the liberal Keynesian critics had argued from the outset – the supply-side theory was not a new economic theory at all but only new language and argument to conceal a hoary old Republican doctrine: give the tax cuts to the top brackets, the wealthiest individuals and largest enterprises, and let the good effects 'trickle down' through the economy to reach everyone else.... 'It's kind of hard to sell "trickle down"

*Figure 5* Dan Wasserman cartoon of 1981.
*Source*: Dan Wasserman, *The Boston Globe*

> [Stockman] explained, 'so the supply-side formula was the only way to get a tax policy that was really "trickle down". Supply-side is "trickle down" theory.'[8]

The public espousal of trickle-down theory with its concomitant redistribution of wealth away from the poor and towards the rich, would, of course, be untenable in a country publicly devoted to equality of opportunity. It would also expose the real aim of policy measures which are concerned more with liberating individual consumption than with promoting collective economic welfare through investment. The nakedness and inadequacies of this theory when transferred from the relatively insignificant and enclosed world of social theory to the hard world of economic reality and subjected to the glare of media publicity, has been something of a public embarrassment, much parodied in the press. But at least it provides a clear demonstration of the analytical and practical pitfalls of a globally applied horizontal theory.

# 12

# THE FOOD SYSTEM

## INTRODUCTION

This chapter begins by acknowledging that the idea of a food system has been popularly accepted in much of the literature. Section 1 identifies the components of the food system by sampling this literature. One of its distinguishing features is the extent of its dependence on organic material. This is of significance at both ends of the food chain, in both its origins in agriculture and its destination in the human body. This subjects it to the particular constraints and requirements associated with natural growth and development cycles. In section 2, the 'natural' content of food is seen as having a continuing impact upon the evolving structure of the food system, limiting the extent of industrialisation and inducing a shifting divide between the sectors of agriculture and industry at the former's expense.

As discussed in section 4, these features of the food system impose certain imperatives on preservation and quality in the manufacture of food which may constrain those of profitability. How they are dealt with, both historically and across different products, distinguishes the features and history of the various systems of food provision.

Historically, one response to the added expenses arising from the use of organic materials has been to adulterate. This is considered in section 3. In the UK, adulteration is presumed to have peaked in the middle of the nineteenth century, after which legislation supported by analytical chemistry is thought to have tipped the balance against poisonous or ersatz substances. The view taken here, while seeing legislative intervention as a part of a general move towards the protection of the working classes, does not accept that adulteration declined, rather that it was transformed through the legalised use of additives and its scope enlarged by the acceleration of mass production in food. As a consequence, whether and how food is adulterated is viewed as the outcome of a complex conflict between the imperatives of profitability (in the context of organic products bound for the human stomach) and the enhancement, or preservation, of standards of consumption. This is examined in section 4 in terms of the relationship between the manufacturing of food, changing products and eating habits.

## 1 THE FOOD SYSTEM

To suggest that the determinants of food consumption should be based on an analysis of a system of provision is to push against a door that is already wide open. Perhaps more than for any other commodity, the systemic nature of food supply has been recognised. Why this should have happened is an interesting question. The answer is in part a consequence of the special features of the food system itself. For a variety of reasons, the vertical links along the system of provision generate interest. The interaction of environmental with consumer concerns has been of significance, these partially displacing and partially complementing concern with the exploitation of the Third World as exporter of primary commodities and subject to endemic poverty and starvation. This reflects a feature distinguishing the food system from other systems of provision, the preoccupation with the content of what we eat, whether it be nutritional, toxic and/or ecologically sound. This generates impetus for an investigation of food's origins which is ultimately traced back to agriculture.

In looking at the motor car, our argument would still be that it is important that the origins of its inputs be as thoroughly examined as those of the food industry. Yet, it is understandable that there be less general concern over the *origins* of the motor car's inputs except in so far as they affect the quality of the final product. In the case of food, the quality and origins of the inputs generate considerable concern, given the organic origins of food, the vulnerability of the human digestive system, and the dangerous passage over distance and through time, from one to the other. The intimacy between food and the body requires absolute trust in the probity of supplies and suppliers. This trust is often threatened by the growing awareness of deliberate intervention designed to deceive the consumer (artificial flavours and colours, for example). Those charged with the caretaking of the young are now faced with more complex responsibilities carried over much longer periods of anxiety.

Such risks do not attach to the consumption of clothing except, again, where the body is directly affected, as with the absorption through the skin of possibly harmful ingredients in dyes or in laundry detergents and conveyed through clothes. These immediate and personal concerns must at least in part explain the exceptional interest in the food chain. But it may also bias that interest towards aspects of food provision whose consequences are most immediately linked with consumer concerns.

Many writers have attempted to address perceived deficiencies in the literature on food. 'Food activists' Lang and Wiggins argue that:

> The dynamics of the food system . . . cast doubts upon the value of

> describing the catering and food distribution sectors as service industries. It is more valuable . . . to see them as links in a food chain which goes from production to consumption. In so doing, it is possible to highlight how capital intervenes at as many points as possible between production and consumption in order to maximise opportunities for profit and control.
>
> (Lang and Wiggins 1985: 53)

Wardle (1990), in introducing a collection on the sociology of consumption, suggests that sociology search for a way to integrate the cycle of production and consumption to give rise to an explanation of the food chain, itself a popular concept in many food studies. Wardle points to 'the process of production or provision, the conditions of access, the manner of delivery and the environment of enjoyment' (ibid.: 3).

For Goody (1982), food provision covers the four main areas of growing, allocating/storing, cooking and eating. Each of these has a corresponding phase of production, distribution, preparation and consumption and a corresponding locus of farm, granary/market, kitchen and table. He adds a further triple in clearing up, disposal and scullery. This whole structure is situated in the widest possible social context:

> My own discussion of cooking takes place not so much in terms of the dichotomously based structures of gustemes, lexemes or even technemes, but of the more diversified structures of household and class. Food and sex must both be related to the central human process of production and reproduction. Since the former is linked to the mode of production of material goods, the analysis of cooking has to be related to the distribution of power and authority in the economic sphere, that is, to the system of class or stratification and to its political ramifications.
>
> (Goody 1982: 37)

On the other hand, McKenzie (1980: 91), drawing upon Yudkin, divides the food system into three broad categories with their own subcategories – physical (containing geography, season, economics and other), social (religion and social custom, social class, education in nutrition, advertising and other) and physiological (heredity, allergy, therapeutic diets, acceptability and needs). In uncovering the anatomy of the humble lettuce industry, Friedland *et al.* (1981: 22) argue that, 'agriculture must be conceptualised as a system of social organisation that includes, among other factors, production and exchange'. And for Thomas (1989: 17), the food industry is conceived of as a series of overlapping and superimposed stages of historical development comprising, first, the satisfaction of hunger, second, the pursuit of pleasure, modified, third, by the criterion of nutrition, fourth, by the criterion of healthy foods, and, fifth, by the trend towards more exotic foods.

In terms of explaining food consumption, these approaches acknowledge influences over and above those that are suggested by an exclusive or primary focus on the act of consumption. Instead, they locate it within a structure of provision. That the architecture of this structure is differently construed by different authors reflects both different theoretical stances, differences empirically or historically in the particular structures of provision under scrutiny, and different emphases along the system of provision. These differences, in turn, reflect the forms of vertical and horizontal integration in the various activities comprising food provision. The result in the literature is the useful identification, both theoretically and empirically, of a variety of components of the food system.

How these components relate to each other and materialise in practice is not predetermined. What can be identified are a number of conflicting tendencies, for example, between First and Third World interests. Consider, for example, the simple matter of what actual crop varieties are available. As Barrau recognises, there are fewer than 1 per cent of species used for economic purposes.[1] There has been:

> a growing homogenization and specialization of the world's cultivated flora. As an example, seven crops (wheat, rice, maize, potato, barley, cassava and sorghum) provide the bulk of the world's food supply. In the course of the same process . . . the numbers of cultivars (except in the case of ornamentals) has spectacularly decreased, particularly during the last thirty years.
>
> (Barrau 1989: 402)

This, of course, leads to considerable vulnerability to crop failure, especially in the Third World because of:[2]

> An indiscriminate imposition in many parts of the world of standardized agrotechnic and agroeconomic models conceived in the ecological and historical contexts of advanced countries. This has been an active factor in the erosion of not only the diversity of the cultivated flora but also of local and often efficient systems of knowledge and practices concerning resources and their uses.
>
> (Barrau 1989: 402)

O'Beirne makes similar points with regard to livestock:

> Up to now, however, the objectives of breeding and husbandry have mainly been high productivity, evenness of maturity, suitability for processing, storeability, expression of scientific attributes demanded by consumers, minimising levels of natural toxicants, etc. Nutritional value has been a significant consideration in only a few crops.
>
> (O'Beirne 1987: 223)

In LeMay (1988: 8), it is recognised that biotechnologies are increasingly



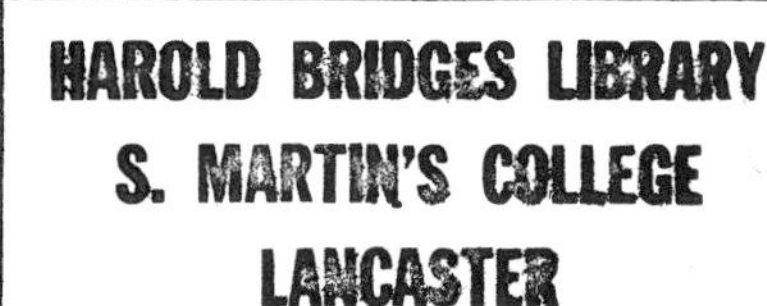

being funded privately rather than publicly, so that they encourage factory-like production and increased linkage between seed varieties and chemical use for large-scale capitalist farming. This is again to the disadvantage of small-scale Third World producers.

But capitalism also has the capacity to breed variety even as it compels uniformity. Historically, this arose out of the adoption and adaptation, through cross-breeding, of species from the New Worlds.[3] As Mason (1936) observes, five-sevenths of the world's agricultural crops originated with the American Indians. The current situation for innovation is rather different, since the new world of biotechnology opens up the vista of specially bred species in the laboratory rather than the conservatory.

In freeing or loosening itself from the constraints imposed by dependence upon agriculturally produced raw materials, the food system has made an increasing use of chemicals in farming. Chemical intervention has the goals of altering taste, enhancing appearance and of shortening growing period. O'Beirne (1987: 234) reports that the world market for pesticides in 1984 was $13.8 billion (of which 43 per cent went on herbicides, 32 per cent on insecticides and 18 per cent on fungicides). Nineteen per cent of this was applied in Western Europe and, in the UK, the expenditures were £168 million, £31 million and £90 million on herbicides, insecticides and fungicides, respectively, this having risen by 50 per cent between 1980 and 1984. Fertilizer added a further £250 million per annum in the UK, and additives £235 million.

At one end of the scale, then, there are, as is described in LeMay (1988: 8), 25,000 superfarms in the United States with annual sales of $500,000 or more, accounting for almost two-thirds of total net farm income. At the other end, in the final purchase price of bread, the farmer's share of revenue has fallen to a mere 8 per cent. So, between farmer and consumer, there lies a range of economic and social activity. Apart from distribution and retailing, for example, there is processing, one important aspect of which is mechanisation which intervenes even before the product has matured. Morris describes cane fruit harvesting:

> Horizontal beaters positioned vertically on each side of the row agitate the fruit attached to the canes. The range of 100–150 strokes/min at a ground speed of 1.6 km/hr (1 mph) is adequate to harvest only the ripe fruit, leaving the unripe fruit for later harvesting. This frequency of stroke also provides a complete shaking throughout the hedgerow. . . . Air-blast cleaners remove leaves and foreign matter as the berries drop and are deposited in crates. This machine, with one operator and four field graders, can do the work of 80–85 hand pickers.
>
> (Morris 1990: 97)

In this case, but not in all, mechanical harvesting can lead to higher quality and more uniform produce. For sweet corn, a harvester replaces 10–15 hand pickers and has the advantage of being operable in the cooler, quality-enhancing, night-time conditions (ibid.: 99). Larger fruits, such as apples, pears and peaches, tend to suffer bruising and premature harvesting from the shaking of trees to remove them mechanically.

However, as Friedland *et al.* (1981) observe, the relative benefits of mechanical harvesting are dependent upon the cost of labour and, consequently, upon its degree of organisation and militancy. They argue that mechanisation had proceeded further for tomatoes, as compared to lettuce, because of the employers' response to the formation of trade unions. More generally, Morris (1990: 97) points, as a great stimulus to mechanisation, to the termination in December 1964 of the Bracero programme, whereby thousands of Mexican workers had been admitted into the United States for agricultural work. No doubt the direction of causation could run in the opposite direction, with migrant labour being restricted once mechanisation has been introduced.

The losers through mechanisation in the case of meats have been the animals as much as the labour force. For the UK, there has been a dramatic increase in poultry consumption over the past forty years. Between 1956 and 1965, UK consumption per capita increased seven times as nominal price fell by 30 per cent. In the next twenty-five years, consumption per capita doubled again as prices rose five times (but beef prices rose nine times). All this followed from the ability to mechanise chicken manufacture through battery farming.[4]

Clearly, then, the relationship between methods of production, food variety and labour relations is a complex one. Whilst Woodrof (1990: 94) reports that there have been more improvements over the past fifty years in the freezing of fruits and vegetables than in any other processing method, this has, in consumption, been mainly at the expense of canned products. The consumption of fresh produce has been enhanced by transport and by the greater availability of varieties from around the world at many more times of the year, so that seasonality has been less restricting. The availability of fresh produce, in turn, has depended upon improved transport and chilling but equally upon the selective choice of species for uniform and simultaneous early cropping for ripening after picking – often undertaken at the expense of taste and quality.

This selective dip into the literature on the food system suggests three conclusions. First, there is a variety of systems of provision which corresponds to different groups of commodities. Even use of broad categories, such as meats, grains, fruits, vegetables and dairy produce, is not sufficiently sensitive to variations in the ways that foods are grown, cropped, processed, packaged, sold and consumed. Second, many of the features highlighted in the discussion of the food system are not unique to it: mechanisation, conflict between capital and labour, concentration of corporate power, etc., are common across most economic activities. Third, as an item of consumption, food is also subject to social (re)construction as a use value. Food is, after all, one of the most heavily advertised commodities, and a focus for ritualised domestic and social activity.

## 2 DYNAMIC APPROACHES TO SUPPLY

Goodman and Redclift (1991) and Goodman *et al.* (1987) perceive the dynamic development of the food system as being conditioned by two underlying processes and their interaction: 'appropriationism' and 'substitutionism'. Appropriationism refers to the industrialisation of discrete elements within agriculture. Historically, they trace a series of innovations, such as the manufacture of ploughs, the harnessing of energy (as horses and oxen are displaced by tractors and their accessories), increasing use of chemical fertilisers, and the development of new seeds more amenable to industrialised farming, as in mechanical cropping. Because the pace of agricultural production is heavily dictated by a natural rhythm, it is not easily nor generally industrialised across all its aspects. Consequently, appropriationism has proceeded in a piecemeal, fragmented and uncoordinated fashion, through time and across the food sector. This explains why agriculture remains a less concentrated economic activity than others and leads Goodman *et al.* (1987: 6) to point to the 'historical inability of industrial capital to transform the agro-food system, from agricultural production to final consumption, as a unified whole'.

Given the limits to appropriationism, Goodman *et al.* argue that it is complemented by substitutionism in which the manufacture of food is increasingly relocated away from its agricultural origins and absorbed into the industrial system: 'Not only does industrial activity account for a steadily rising proportion of value added but the agricultural product, after first being reduced to an industrial input, increasingly suffers replacement by non-agricultural components' (ibid.: 2). Thus, capital has a twofold dynamic effect on the structure of the food system: first, shifting the boundary between agriculture and industry and, second, industrialising and minimising the impact of natural processes and components on both sides of the boundary. Ultimately, through the use of biotechnology, the food system continues to articulate appropriationism and substitutionism. For genetically manufactured seeds or species will sustain the industrialisation of agriculture and reduce it to the role of supplier of food components. Its products can potentially be broken down and reconstituted into foods along with, and increasingly indistinguishable from, non-organic components (or organic components that have been industrially grown).

The arguments of Goodman and others are compelling. They help to explain both the specificity of the food system, as opposed to other systems, and the frequently observed, but inadequately explained, tendencies for foods both to be stripped of their nutritional content (as in white bread) and to be supplemented by chemical additives (such as colourings and flavourings). Too often, these are seen almost as a conspiracy on the part of corporate capital to increase its share of value added in final price at the expense of the farmer and consumer. But such arguments have to be treated with caution, and their specific place in relation to the food system more carefully located.

For the possibility of manufacturing commodities with unnecessary, and even dysfunctional, components is not unique to food. It has also been observed of the car and of the clothing industries. It is endemic to style and fashioning. If demand for specific products with such 'extras' can be sustained, individual capitalists do have an incentive to promote and make a profit on these unnecessary inputs to the output. But other capitalists equally have an incentive to compete by producing the commodities without these extras, thereby selling them more cheaply and/or at an extra profit. Thus, such reasons for increasing proportion of value added in food by manufacturers is not specific to it as a system of provision, nor is it a systematic source of permanent degradation of the product without counter-influences. Rather, substitutionism as a strategy of freeing the food system from its organic roots is a source of increasing share of value added within the manufacture of food, irrespective of nutritional content. If manufacturers were concerned simply to sell more value, they would have an easier time by adding more wholesome, organic ingredients than unwholesome or inorganic ones. Having made this point, however, it may well follow as a corollary that the incentives and opportunities to add unnecessary ingredients are greater than for other systems of provision, given the continuing process of substitutionism.

Not surprisingly, Goodman's work has focused most heavily on agriculture and technology and how the two interact, along with the changing economic and social organisation of the food system. Less attention has been paid to the demand side, reflecting an antipathy to the exaggeration of analysing food by way of interpretation of its meaning:

> Too much attention has been devoted to the 'signifying' aspects of food and diet, the semiology of food consumption, by sociologists and anthropologists, to the detriment of a wider understanding of the social transformation implied by the economic and technological changes in the food system.
>
> (Goodman and Redclift 1991: 241–2)

A further, related issue is the changing role of women in the food system, which is in part a consequence of the changing division of labour in and out of the household and around the food system itself. In this context, there is also criticism of Charles and Kerr (1988) for placing too much stress on the meaning and distribution of food within the household at the expense of consideration of the changing nature of the foods made available. These issues will be taken up in Chapter 13. The meaning and distribution of food within the household are what have been termed horizontal factors. They should not be treated in isolation as explanatory factors. But nor should they be set aside.

The next two sections of this chapter address the food system as a system of supply. They employ and develop the framework suggested by Goodman and others by examining food adulteration and manufacture. Agriculture is not further discussed here, partly because it is already covered by a voluminous literature.

## 3 ADULTERATION

In the present day, there is much consumer concern over food additives. Given the dynamics of substitutionism described in the previous section, this is understandable. Chemical additives to food enable a number of processes and ingredients to be displaced from agriculture to industry. Clearly, additives change the nature of food; as such, their use is not so different from the earlier most sinister-sounding process – adulteration. Accordingly, this section examines adulteration, not only as a particularly sharp example of substitutionism, but also to locate the latter in the broader historical, economic and social contexts that make up the shifting food system. The point is not so much to forge a polemical analogy between adulteration and additives as to demonstrate analytically how each is a particular reflection of the practices and structures of the food system.

It is generally recognised that adulteration of food reached its peak in Britain in the middle of the nineteenth century. According to Filby:

> The history of adulteration seems to fall roughly into three periods. The first, lasting from the earliest times to about 1820, was a time when there was but little, and very slow, development in either adulteration or its detection. There followed a period of nearly a century when both adulteration and its detection came very much to the fore. Perhaps we may, none too confidently, affirm that we are now in the third period when the grosser forms of adulteration have been completely abolished and the lesser ones held severely in check.
>
> (Filby 1934: 17)

Two factors are summoned to explain this chronology.[5] First, the rise of analytical chemistry created a poacher–gamekeeper spiral in which science served both to generate new substances with which to adulterate and new methods by which to detect them. Increasing ingenuity on one side only upped the ante on the other side. Second, the spread of literature made readily available the sources of knowledge necessary to pursue these activities.

There are a number of problems with this account and its simple presumed ordering of events with first the crime and then the detection gaining the upper hand. Apart from its superficiality, it remains oblivious to the neat coincidence of this high period of adulteration with the transition to the era of mass production. For, along with other forms of welfare legislation and provision, measures against the adulteration of food from the end of the nineteenth century onwards can be seen to be part of a more general process of enacting policies on behalf of the working class. In classical Marxist terms, the era of the crudest exploitation of the working class had been dependent upon long hours of work and low standards of living. This gave way to the factory system in which productivity increase both enabled and induced a prolonged working life (even if a shorter working day) and a higher standard of living, thereby increasing the profitability that a wage labourer could contribute over a lifetime. Establishing quality controls and standards has the effect of undermining the most blatant forms of adulteration, those most likely to be associated in production, distribution or sale with the weaker small-scale capitals (although the advantages of adulteration may be even greater for large-scale capital). Thus, controls over the quality of food are not simply a matter of representing the interests of consumers, they also have an impact on levels of profitability for the system as a whole (the immediate advantage of cheaper adulterated wage goods has to be set against the ultimately higher costs of reproducing a workforce). It also affects the competition between different capitals both within and between sectors of the economy (as regulations have uneven effects in the competition between capitals).

Partly because of its gregarious effects, adulteration has always seemed to be clear-cut, both in principle and historically. Burnett, following the work of Accam, the nineteenth-century campaigner against adulteration, offers a typical catalogue of offences:

> Publicans resorted to sulphuric acid to 'harden' new beer. . . . Those who preferred to drink tea were hardly more fortunate. Large quantities were manufactured from native English hedgerows, the leaves of ash, sloe, and elder being curled and coloured on copper plates: an official report . . . estimated that 4,000,000 lb of this rubbish were annually faked and sold, compared with only 6,000,000 lb of genuine tea imported by the East India Tea Company . . . the poisonous pickles which owed their green colour to copper, the 'nutty' flavour in wines produced by bitter almonds, the rind of Gloucester cheese coloured with vermilion and red lead, and the pepper adulterated with the sweepings of the warehouse floor.
>
> (Burnett 1989: 89)

Moreover, 'there existed at least eight factories in London in the 1840s expressly for the purpose of drying used tea-leaves and reselling them to fraudulent dealers' (ibid.: 91).

On closer examination, however, adulteration is much more than the simple accumulation of abuses. At one level, it is the substitution of one set of ingredients for others – most alarming when the substitutes are not only unrelated to the genuine requirements but have repulsive connotations and even harmful effects. At another level, adulteration is defined by law either in general terms, as in, for example, a trade description act, or by specification of required or excluded ingredients.

But false ingredients are inevitably concealed, leading to the presentation of the commodity as something other than it is. Yet it is clear that this is something common to many commodities, especially in the context of advertising. On the other hand, the evolution and implementation of the law is itself socially determined, so that the definition of adulteration, even in principle, becomes historically specific.

In this light, a rather different view is taken here from that proposed by Filby. While he presumes that adulteration peaked in the mid-nineteenth century as the gamekeeper eventually tamed the poacher in the diffusion and application of analytical chemistry, an alternative interpretation is of gamekeeper turned poacher. Subsequent legislation and practice is perhaps better seen as the legislation *for* adulteration rather than as its erosion. True, transgressing the law has apparently declined, but the law has itself laid down the terms and conditions under which one substance may displace another in the manufacture of particular commodities. In short, in parallel with enlightened criminology, there is no right or wrong as such, only what is laid down by the law which is socially determined. The same applies to 'good' and 'bad' substances, those allowed and those proscribed. But, equally, like the law and concepts of justice, the parameters are not randomly determined. They have a definite history, partly contingent and partly the consequence of underlying imperatives.

Historically and analytically, these remarks can be substantiated by consideration of the development of the food industry itself during the middle of the nineteenth century when adulteration rose to its peak. The rise of manufacturing processes at that time were met with suspicion, partly because of their affinity with adulteration – in what must have appeared to be 'unnatural' treatment of food in order to allow for both mass production and delayed consumption, thereby requiring some kind of preservation:

> In the history of food preservation, there is a turning point at about 1860. Before this date, preserved foods were costly, luxury items, used by the rich and by the naval and other expeditions . . . and thus hardly able to help to feed the urban poor. After 1860, preserved foods began to be produced where the raw material was cheap and plentiful – in Australia and South America – for export to Europe. The introduction of mass-production techniques from the 1860s onwards effected a rapid reduction in the costs of preserved foods. At about the same time, microbiological causes of food deterioration began to be appreciated and the empirical processes of food technology began to be based on a sound scientific understanding.
>
> (Thorne 1986: 18)

In particular, there were problems with canning: 'Putrid food and inability to examine canned food which, as processed, carried stigma of potential adulteration' (ibid.: 61). Thus, it became necessary to legislate against adulteration, not only to beat out the competition and harmful effects of small-scale, dishonest producers and traders, but also to make manufacturing of food acceptable.

The history of margarine illustrates more general influences upon the evolution of consumption patterns. Invented by a French chemist, Hippolyte Még Mourié, and patented in 1869, the product margarine was a response to a prize offered at the Paris World Exhibition of 1866 for the development of a substitute for butter, perceived to be necessary in view of its rising price and the need to feed labourers and troops as cheaply as possible.[6]

In the United States, margarine production began in 1875 but was immediately confronted with a hostility which, understandably, had its origins in dairy interests. Although no firm evidence seems to have been presented that margarine was harmful, it was initially prohibited in Missouri in 1881. As Ball and Lilly report:

> New York State banned margarine in 1884 in model legislation adopted almost exactly by Maine, Minnesota, Ohio (with exceptions), Pennsylvania and Michigan in 1884. These laws forbade the manufacture, sale, or possession of margarine with intent to sell.... The Supreme Court declared the New York State law an unconstitutional attempt to suppress a wholesome product.... Yet the following year, the same court upheld an almost identical Pennsylvania law on grounds that the legislature had officially declared: (1) that oleomargarine was unquestionably harmful; and (2) that oleomargarine manufacturing was inherently fraudulent.
>
> (Ball and Lilly 1982: 489)

Subsequently, a total of twenty-four states passed restrictive laws and pressed for economic sanctions against margarine, which resulted in a sales tax and an annual licence fee for manufacturers, wholesalers and retailers. The parallels in treatment with alcohol are striking, if not stretching to illegal stills and total prohibition, and in this case reveal the extent to which vested interests presented themselves as guarding against adulteration of butter. This is brought out clearly by Ball and Lilly:

> Anti-margarine forces began to concentrate on additional legislation to regulate the colour of the substance. New Jersey outlawed yellow margarine in 1886, and 34 states accounting for nearly 80 per cent of the population of the United States followed by 1900 – five of them going so far as to require that margarine be coloured pink.... Massachusetts legislation outlawing yellow margarine was upheld by the United States Supreme Court, which ignored the fact that butter was also artificially coloured throughout most of the year.
>
> (Ball and Lilly 1982: 489)

Eventually, coloured margarine was taxed at a higher rate than uncoloured and the need for a licence was extended to those establishments serving it with meals.

Despite these restrictions, consumption of margarine rose rapidly during both world wars as dairy products became scarce and expensive (and an object of patriotic war-sacrifice); however, only after the Second World War was its growth sustained with the removal of obstructive legislation from the late 1940s onwards. Paradoxically, as we are all now aware, the status of margarine, especially when high in polyunsaturates, has been enhanced following the linking in the 1970s of butter to heart disease through increased cholesterol levels. Ideologically, it has been less necessary, and even disadvantageous, to present margarine as an alternative to butter. Less fanfare has attended the advantages of margarine's very long shelf-life, the consequence of minimising its organic ingredients.

The case of margarine in the United States, then, illustrates the way in which adulteration is socially and legally determined – not least through the heavy influence of dairy interests – even though margarine could presumably have prospered as a substitute for butter without pretending to be (as good as) butter and even though it was not demonstrably harmful. A rather different example is provided by meat products. Here there are clearer examples of legalised adulteration, enhanced by modern factory methods. In the case of British pork sausages, they are required to contain 65 per cent 'meat', but of this only a third needs to be 'lean' meat. But as Walker and Cannon observe:

> Put into plain numbers, 32.5 per cent (one third) of the weight of a pork sausage *must* be lean meat; the next 32.5 per cent could also be lean meat, but it could equally well be fat, or a delectable mixture of gristle, sinew, diaphragm, rind and pancreas. . . . [But] when Public Analysts . . . do the chemical analysis for lean meat, they assume that the 32.5 per cent lean may actually have a *further* 10 per cent fat 'naturally associated' with the lean meat! So the regulations mean in reality that a pork sausage can get away with being only 29 per cent lean meat.
>
> (Walker and Cannon 1985: 133)

Another way of limiting the use of meat is to dilute the product with water. For bacon, a label must declare the proportion of water added if it is more than 10 per cent. This, in turn, may be supplemented by a further 5 per cent of the contents that make up the curing solution, a major part of which will be salt (with polyphosphates E450 used to ensure that the meat holds the water and gives us the texture which, we are told, we crave as consumers).[7]

In the two cases of margarine and meat, 'adulteration' has taken the form of incorporating cheaper and less desirable raw materials. In each instance, the pace, rhythm and extent of adulteration is in part determined by legal standards, although these in turn are not simply, nor predomiantly, the consequence of dietary needs which are themselves subject to change (as in the preference for margarine over butter). Thus, while there may be imperatives derived from production, these are not realised in the form of consumption uncontaminated by other considerations. Included in these are changes in the relationships between the scale of private capital invested in food chemistry and the capacity – and willingness – of government scientific agencies to evaluate and regulate the products of research. The influence of consumers is not negligible, but nor is it as decisive as proponents of consumer sovereignty would have us believe. Their influence is most marked when their interests are collectively represented (and, hence, have been formed in some way other than through the market), most notably but not exclusively through the state, which will equally be subject to producer interests (as illustrated in the case of margarine).

Thus, the Committee on Technological Options to Improve the Nutritional Attributes of Animal Products (CTO) argues that:

> Despite demonstrated general consumer interest in less fat in food products, the national food supply continues to show annual increases in total fat content. Market forces based more on consumer preference for convenience and taste than on nutritional merit continue to dominate the food system.
>
> (CTO 1988: 99)

On the other hand, 'A principal finding of the committee is that public policies influence consumer choice.' Yet, completing the circle of influences and effects, it is suggested that there have been breeding shifts in response to consumer concerns around diet and health: 'The animal products industry has been remarkably responsive to consumer demand . . . [since previously] "high quality" has historically been associated with high fat content' (ibid.: 98).

The Committee observes that a simple solution in the short term would be for fat to be removed on the slaughterhouse floor. But, as is easily recognised, this would lead to 'waste' of the fat which it is more profitable to sell as meat. Moreover, this fatted calf is itself the result of standardised product, processes and animal varieties, leading Sanderson (1986) to coin the phrase 'world steer' to describe the system that grows cattle in Mexico but processes them in the United States which itself feeds the vast majority of its grain harvests to cattle – whilst much of the rest of the world's population suffers shortage of grains to eat.

Yet another example of adulteration is provided by baby food and, in particular, by formula milk which is designed not to cheapen/lower the quality of the commodity consumed but to displace the non-commodity form of production altogether as supplied by mothers' milk (leaving aside the economic role of wet-nurses). Before this century there was little alternative to mothers' milk, and alternatives made little impact until the Second World War. Subsequently, in the UK for example, in the hands of large-scale agribusinesses and pharmaceutical companies, babies were increasingly fed on artificial formulas based on cows' milk. This was reversed in the 1970s despite nutritional improvements in the formulas which were, however, unable to match complex immunological properties of human milk.[8] Decline in markets in advanced capitalist countries were met by an onslaught upon Third World markets, where extensive advertising and monopolised conditions of supply induced prices and habits that could be ill afforded by those already impoverished and susceptible to disease through malnutrition. Here, however, the worst excesses of producer interests have been held at bay by pressure groups and international agencies (as discussed in Chetley 1986), bringing to the fore the greater desirability of mothers' milk for the health of babies and for development policy.

The degree of success in campaigning against formula milk in place of breast-feeding is a particularly sharp example of the circumstances in which producer interests may be mitigated. For, in this case, diet and a single high-profile product can be easily identified and are more or less synonymous with each other, given the simplicity of a baby's nutritional intake. More generally, where a single item can be identified as hazardous or undesirable (rightly or not), either as a consumption good (or group) or as an ingredient, then it is much easier to campaign for its more limited production and consumption and, equally, this is most vigorously resisted by producer interests. This is illustrated, in different circumstances and with mixed outcomes, by the examples of tobacco, alcohol and food additives. Occasionally, of course, foods are sold for their dietary virtues, as with slimming products, and even have the image of a healthy lifestyle associated with them. But, whatever their actual content, they cannot determine what else is consumed along with them – and may even encourage unhealthy practices in other consumption items by way of compensation for such virtue – a form of behaviour exploited in the advertising slogan 'Naughty but Nice', to encourage purchase of cakes with fresh cream.[9]

## 4 FOOD MANUFACTURING

In many ways, the food industry resembles other manufacturing operations. It is highly concentrated and is dominated in particular subsectors by multinational corporations that are familiar to all – firms such as Nestlé, Cadbury-Schweppes, Unilever (with its many constituent companies such as Walls), etc. As an industry, it has grown through acquisitions and mergers typical of the more general restructuring of capital that accompanies its accumulation.[10] As Meyer reports for 1988/9, partly in anticipation of 1992, 'the global giants are gobbling up mid-size companies in Europe as well as in the US' (Meyer 1989: 57). The EEC reports that:

> The last ten years have been a remarkable period for the world food industry. From 1976 to 1986, over a hundred mergers of $50 million or more took place in the food industry. Moreover, the pace of merger activity seems to be quickening. From 1984 to 1986, nine acquisitions of over $1 billion occurred.
>
> (EEC 1988: 38)

Nestlé has been most prominent with a 1988 expenditure of $6 billion on acquisitions which compares with its market capitalisation of £6 billion. In the United States there has been a strategy of nation-wide brand promotion rather than multi-product retailing on a regional basis. This, in a sense, contrasts with the European Community, where relatively few firms have a presence in many countries. It is anticipated that this will change with 1992.

Like many other manufacturing industries, food has experienced increasing capital intensity of production, increased plant size and declining levels of employment. Between the 1950s and the 1980s, employment in the UK has fallen from 696,000 to 524,000 along with an even sharper fall in the number of plants from 8,253 to 6,250. Whilst consumers' expenditure on food as a proportion of total consumer expenditure has fallen from 30 to 15 per cent, the share of the food industry in manufacturing capital expenditure has risen from 7.9 to 12.4 per cent and the share of net in gross output (signifying more 'value added' rather than materials processed) has also grown from 24.8 to 32.0 per cent.[11] Holmes (1988) provides a stunning example of what can be achieved, referring to Cadbury's chocolate egg plant, which cost £14 million and is able to manufacture 300 million eggs per annum (1,100 per minute).

Are there, however, any features that set the food industry apart from others? In the discussion of adulteration, it has been suggested that the imperative of profitability has had effects on what is processed and how it is processed. Also the discussion of advertising in Chapter 16 points to the rise of giant retailers, who are presumed to have gained the upper hand over manufacturers in the structuring of supply and demand. But these two aspects of the industry are far from unique to it. In the case of furniture, for example, both the adulteration of materials (use of mass-produced chipboards and artificial veneers) and the dominance of retailers have also occurred. Where the food industry is different is in the organic destination (human consumption) of its products and in the equally organic origins of many of its ingredients (its dependence upon agricultural products). Food has to be digested, and whilst the same is true of medicines, the latter do not in general derive from plant material. Otherwise, food processing does have an increasingly close affinity to the pharmaceutical industry.

The organic nature of food means that time is of the essence. In some cases, as in the maturing of wine or cheese, time is required before final production is achieved. In order to hasten the turnover of capital, ingredients are often added to imitate the effect of maturation or to expedite it. For bread, the Chorley Wood process, initiated in 1961, managed to dispense with much of the standing time necessary for the dough to rise through the action of yeast. In conjunction with intense mechanical mixing, this has allowed a saving of time of about 60 per cent (together with the ability to add more air and water to the final product) (Davis 1987: 20).

More generally, it is necessary to avoid the action of time upon ingredients and products since it brings a deterioration of quality. Consequently, apart from the preparation and packaging common to most products, food production also involves preservation. These three ps – preservation, preparation and packaging – are not always easily separable in practice. Consider, for example, the following techniques employed in food processing, few of which are confined to one of the ps alone:[12]

> Cleaning, sorting (for quality, size, colour and weight), peeling, size reduction (by compression, impact or cutting), mixing and shaping, separating, fermentation (and other enzyme actions), irradiation, heating (blanching, pasteurisation, sterilisation and evaporation), extrusion (combining two or more of mixing, cooking, kneading, shearing, shaping and forming), dehydration, baking, roasting, frying, microwave and infrared cooking, chilling, freezing (including drying and concentrating), coating, filling and sealing.

In many instances, the imperative of food preservation has been closely associated with sustaining nutritional quality, if not necessarily matching fresh produce. This has been borne out by technological developments in food processing. Amongst what are considered to be the top ten food science innovations of the past fifty years are included aseptic processing and packaging, minimum safe canning processes for vegetables, frozen concentrated citrus juices, controlled atmospheric packaging, freeze-drying, frozen meals, understanding of water activity in foods, and ultra-high-temperature (UHT) processing.[13]

However, these innovations have been selected by representatives of the industry with an eye to their impact on nutrition. It does not follow that the development of preservation techniques is unambiguously associated with improved nutrition. This is brought out most clearly in the related role of additives, which are used for many purposes; less than a hundred additives have been developed as preservatives in the UK whereas there are nearer 4,000 additives in use for the purposes of cosmetic preparation of foods (especially for flavouring).[14] In short, preservation will be applied both to good and to bad food and does not determine the greater availability of the former. Consider American potato chips (crisps in the UK). Almost twenty years ago, Gutcho (1973) was able to devote 50 pages to the variety of ways in which these could be made: 27 pages based on manufacture from raw potato slices; 6 pages from a dough base containing fresh potato puree; and 16 pages from a dough base containing dried potato products. The ability to preserve ingredients means that the fresh can be displaced by the pureed or dried as much as by the adulterated, and potato chips can be sealed in airtight packages however and with whatever they are made. In general, it is easier and cheaper to preserve and to use non-organic ingredients and to incorporate these into the nature of the product as flavouring, texture or colour.

Food processing techniques, then, are driven by the need to reduce costs and to increase sales rather than, except as a by-product of these, by the need to bring out the intrinsic quality of the product. A further distinguishing feature of the food system – constraints on sales – is imposed by the overall level of demand associated, in high-income countries, with low population growth rates and the tendency of food expenditure per capita to rise much less than in proportion to income. There are limits to the capacity of the stomach. Consequently, there are strong competitive pressures to sustain sales, and this is associated with particular sorts of product development.

Apart from the wide variety of cosmetic additives that have arisen, there is an increasing variety of products – each with a longer or shorter lifetime. Key Note (1987) reports the emergence in the UK of 2,000 new products in 1986. These have to compete for a limited budget and a limited appetite. Preservation means that the time of manufacture can be divorced from the time of sale and also that the time of sale can be divorced from the time of consumption. Consequently, foods have been developed to be consumed at any time and to be sold as such. Snack foods have been one result with an impact on eating habits. Key Note (1989b) reports that in the UK, 75 per cent of adults and 91 per cent of children consume a snack food at least once per day between, or even instead of, a meal. Such habits are no longer predominantly a consequence of impulse purchase, since over a half of all snack purchases are in multipacks, presumably for future consumption. With higher levels of consumption amongst the young and for those families with children present, it appears as if the snack habit will continue to grow. Two-thirds of those between the ages of 15 and 24 buy crisps once a week but this falls to one in five for those over 65.

The growth of snack foods (at about 8 per cent per annum in the UK between 1983 and 1988) has led to what has been termed 'grazing' in eating habits. Food is eaten more frequently but in smaller quantities.[15] As a result, there is a tendency to skip regular meals. Key Note (1989c) estimates that Britons on average eat 6.5 times per day (and eat out of the home three times per week). Sloan *et al.* (1986: 64) report that 72 per cent of families at times skip at least one meal – 62.5 per cent go without breakfast, 25.5 per cent without lunch and 7 per cent without dinner. None the less, set meals, and especially dinner, have remained an important part of consumption habits. While breakfast has become a predominantly self-service meal, based on cereals for half of the population (Insight Research 1988: 12), the desire for a main course of meat and two vegetables persists, even though dessert has now become an optional extra. However, the main course has itself been open to the displacement of fresh by frozen vegetables, especially peas, and there has been a limited development of what are termed convenience joints and also of complete frozen meals.

Convenience foods more generally, i.e., those that require limited preparation and can be stored in the home, fall into a number of different types.[16] There are those that are canned, vacuum packed, frozen or dehydrated; those that form part of a meal, a whole meal or a snack; those to be grilled, baked, boiled or microwaved; and there is the more recent innovation of chilled foods. But, as has been seen, there is a complex relation between these foods and patterns of consumption. Products can themselves be directed at grazing or at specific meals, thereby undermining or reinforcing existing routines. Even where specific meals are the target, there is a tendency to reduce the time necessary for preparation of any one part or for the whole of the meal. These changes themselves interact with changes in more general family routines – as women go out to work and seek to spend less time in cooking, and as meal times themselves become more flexible. There is equally an interaction with other factors such as the availability and use of durables, most notably fridges, freezers and microwaves, and the availability and use of methods of eating out of the home – whether through public or private provision.

Thus, to some extent, the role of hamburgers in the United States has corresponded to that of fish and chips in the United Kingdom. For both, frozen potatoes in the form of chips (french fries) have been important, but frozen fish and fish fingers have been much more important in the UK. However, as a fast-food outlet, the fish and chip shop is in relative decline as 'ethnic' takeaways, such as Indian and Chinese, have expanded and as franchised chains, most notably McDonalds, have aimed at global expansion.[17]

For reasons of historical differences in eating habits, then, the trend towards convenience foods cannot simply be read off as a combination of conveniences to producer, distributor, retailer and consumer – although, properly interpreted, these are of considerable importance. This view is reinforced when account is taken of the historical origins of innovations in convenience foods. For the preparation of full meals, for example, the motivation lay in providing for the displacement of labour in large-scale canteens (see NEDO 1971). For the more recent chilled foods, on the other hand, there has been a targeting of market niches, and success for this in the UK has depended upon the special reputation that Marks and Spencer has possessed for high-quality, own-label products. In the United States, frozen meals were first marketed in 1953 as an emergency and as a TV dinner, and the association with low quality has been carried over into their subsequent role as a staple source of food.[18]

Thus, changing food products and eating habits are not the simple consequence of manufacturers' intentions nor of the competitive pressures upon them. Equally, however, nor are they the exercise of consumer sovereignty, in which changing lifestyles around work and home are the independent origin of the convenience and other qualities slavishly supplied by the food system.

# 13

# FOOD FOR THOUGHT

## INTRODUCTION

A popular approach to consumption is to perceive it as responding to or even defining characteristics of the individual. The consumer is endowed with attributes of the commodity as if these were themselves human. Language allows these projections to proceed smoothly, with adjectives such as strong, tender and sweet serving to conflate the physical use value of the commodity with the emotional goals of the individual. For food, this is summarised in the catch phrase, 'You are what you eat', just as you are what you wear, what you drive, where you holiday, and where you live. For Finkelstein (1989: 7), in studying the significance of dining/eating out, the observation is to be extended from what one eats to where and how one eats. *Dining* out is a special occasion, signifying extravagance, intimacy or an expense account. *Eating* out, if at McDonalds, is the opposite – to be one of the crowd, with guaranteed uniformity in product and experience. And from eating to drinking. For the Advertising Director of Pepsi-Cola, 'what you drank said something about who you were' (quoted in Levenstein 1988: ix).

What, where and how we eat, and how much or how little, is socially determined. Of course, what many animals eat is also socially determined, given their increasing role as both inputs and outputs in the mass production of food. But they have very little influence over their own diet, serving more as machines to convert one form of feed, such as grain, into another, namely animal protein. Whilst human consumers are conceived by some to be manufactured by advertisers directly, or by the power of corporations indirectly in determining what is placed on the market, suspicion of consumer sovereignty does not necessarily entail a belief in the consumer's total loss of volition. There is choice over foods and it is exercised. The issue is how, why and with what effects.

Section 1 of this chapter looks informally at some of the proximate influences on food choice and at some food choices. It reveals a bewildering array of factors. These include physiological needs (what the body wants) and nutritional knowledge, however well informed (what the calculating mind wants), but these are not decisive in and of themselves. In any case, even if these two aspects could be seen as independent of each other, knowledge about what is good to eat is itself socially constructed and a terrain of conflict reflecting different interests. As is illustrated by the campaign around Coca-Cola, consumer pressure to retain 'the real thing' can take on the most alien logic in relation to any function of nutrition or taste.

Food is also distinguished by its special organic properties, both in the way in which it is produced, in its dependence upon agriculture, and in the way in which it is consumed, in being eaten or drunk. There is necessarily individual and social concern over the content of food – as a result of its impact on health and standard of life – as well as in guaranteeing survival itself, in case of poisoning. Consequently, choice over food is much more heavily influenced by the information system around it, whether originating in the media and in advertising, via government health campaigns, or informally transmitted by family, friends or daily experience. Section 2 critically assesses the way in which the relations between the food and information systems have been structured and understood. Too often it is presumed that 'good' knowledge trickles down from the scientific community leading to 'better' food choice and consumption, much as it is assumed that habits in consumption more generally are themselves passed along – a view criticised in the context of trickle-down in Chapter 10. This is, however, to misunderstand the way in which these processes operate in general and to overlook decisive determinants of the creation and transmission of awareness about food.

Despite the apparent embarrassment of choice in variables that can be summoned to explain diet, their specific application to the consumption of food has been far from satisfactory. Section 3 exposes this lack of coherence in the theory of food choice: hardly surprising in view of the diversity involved. The most expedient response to such variety of behaviour is to treat the theory of food choice as an application, rather than as an extension, of existing theory. Certain foods are available, usually unexamined as such, and choice between them verifies a pre-existing analytical scheme. A consequence of this is to fail to deal with the specificity of food even if it is served up as ritual, status, socialisation or emotional gratifier. Other goods could, and do, perform these functions equally well for the academic (or for the punter). Food does, however, have the advantage of being consumed by all and of being sufficiently varied that it provides the raw material to illustrate an equally varied range of theoretical propositions.

On the other hand, there have been theories that focus more on the availability of choice rather than on the choice of what is available, reflecting the extent to which food has been recognised as belonging to a system of provision. These theories tend to belong to economic history, given its concern with the long-term patterns of supply, and to anthropology which has sought to unravel the relationship between material and cultural practices, including those surrounding food. Do primitive societies adopt rituals to legitimise their most favourable sources of food, or do their rituals and customs prescribe foods which are permissible? Whatever the answer, the relevance of such an approach to modern capitalism is questionable; the variety and level of food choice moves it well beyond the realms of subsistence for many, if not a majority, of human feeders around the world.

A synthesis of these approaches and determinants is not possible without some further organising principle. This is supplied by treating food choice and consumption as one element in a system of provision. A number of writers already adopt this framework, whether consciously or not, particularly those who point to the powers of the producers, the retailers and government in determining what we consume, and who seek to track back from the kitchen table to the source and exercise of that power. Similarly, those who show an interest in the nutritional content of what we eat are liable to follow the same route in discovering what foods are grown and what happens to them *en route* to the cooking pot, microwave or ready-to-eat product.

## 1 CHOICE FOODS

Frequently, a starting point for examining food consumption is the recognition that (human) food is not fodder; humans do not feed. Consequently, foods are chosen for their perceived content, which may go far beyond a matter of ingredients. Certain foods signify particular attributes: steak, for example, is perceived as bestowing strength (reflected in the idea of 'beefy'); fish as bestowing intelligence. For Kittler and Sucher,

> The correlation between what people eat, how others perceive them, and how they characterize themselves is striking. In one study, researchers listed foods typical of five diets: vegetarian (broccoli quiche, brown rice, avocado and bean sprout sandwich); gourmet (oysters, caviar, French-roast coffee); health food (protein shake, wheat germ and yogurt); fast food (Kentucky fried chicken, Big Mac, pizza); and synthetic food (Carnation Instant Breakfast, Cheez Whiz), it was found that each category was associated with a certain personality type. Vegetarians were considered to be pacifists, drug users, and likely to drive foreign cars. Gourmets were also thought to be drug users, liberal, and sophisticated. Health-food fans were described as drug users, anti-nuclear activists, and Democrats. Fast-food and synthetic-food eaters were believed to be religious, conservative, and wearers of polyester clothing. These stereotypes were confirmed by self-description and personality tests completed by persons whose diet fell within each of the five categories.
>
> (Kittler and Sucher 1989: 4–5)

If valid, such conclusions would prove the presence of an awful lot of drug users and a boon to those seeking to target consumers through advertising. Camporesi provides a comparable example of becoming what you eat at the bottom end of the market in early modern Europe:

> Sorghum . . . passed from pig to man, and if there was none, it was bran that became 'good fodder for men', soaked in hot water and formed into a bran mash for 'pig men' . . . so reduced to wallowing as to resembling snuffling animals.
>
> (Camporesi 1989: 37)

Once it is accepted as central that you are what you eat, any number of influences come into play in determining consumption patterns. There are traditional variables, such as price, income, nutrition and preferences together with other factors, such as ritual, taboo, folklore, culture, energetics, emulation, differentiation, ecology, habit, aversion, craving, intimacy, security, love, deprivation, religion, status, control, palatability, veneration, etc.[1]

The determination of consumption patterns, then, is addressed in a number of different ways across the social sciences. For economics, it is a matter of supply and demand, although the focus is primarily upon the latter. Propositions such as Engel's Law, which suggests that the share of expenditure on food ultimately declines with growing income, are incapable of explaining either why this should be so or what exactly is consumed. Indeed, Engel's Law is equivalently interpreted as predicting that the share of expenditure on non-food rises with income, so far removed is it from a concern with specific foods. Theoretically, there is also an uncomfortable dependence upon constant preferences as an unexamined diet passes from one generation to the next.

Such immutability might be justified by a demonstration of the cultural or physiological determinants of taste; both do exist and can be important. After all, why do the British drink so much tea and consume so much sugar (the latter also linked to the preference for rum in the Caribbean as an inheritance of the slave trade)?[2] The trouble, however, with relying upon stable cultural, historical or habitual determinants is that rapid, or even slow, divergence from them leaves the analysis floundering. It is necessary to know when and why these customs are broken, as well as when and why they are respected.

The problem with physiological determinants is rather different. It is known, for example, that there is a predilection for sweetness in human taste as well as in other species. But, whilst there are innate physiological bases for some food preferences, and response in the mouth is more important than response in the stomach, long-term tastes for specific foods appear to be acquired (Lyman 1989: 32). More food altogether tends to be eaten when there is a variety from which to choose ('there is always room for sweet' syndrome) (Gilbert 1986: 171–8). More generally, nutritional deficiencies often do lead to cravings for foods that may meet the need involved.[3] However, it is apparent that what is consumed is not obviously determined by physiological or biological needs. Psychological needs also play a role; foods used to reward children tend to become even more preferred. If the reward is for a food that is disliked, but 'good for you', this strengthens the dislike (Bennett 1988: 50). The more we eat a food, even if spitting it out, the more it tends to be liked (ibid.: 55), even if is not addictive as such.

Even at the level of physical subsistence, consumers can be finicky. They may even prefer to go without rather than eat the unfamiliar:[4]

> Indeed, it has often happened in the history of the potato that not even famine conditions were sufficient to overcome the inertia, or allay the prejudice, peasant or artisan. Such was the case in Naples; about the year 1770 a cargo of potatoes was sent there to relieve a famine, but the people refused to touch them.
>
> (Salaman 1949: 446)

No wonder that children have such powerful resistance to eating what is deemed to be good for them. They are in the company of adults! In more recent and 'civilised' times, American prisoners in the Korean war died rather than stomach an unfamiliar, but adequately nutritional, local cuisine (Levenstein 1988: ix).

On the other hand, following the siege of Paris by the Prussian army in 1871, Harris points out that: 'Pricked by necessity, Parisians ate every horse they could lay their hands on – sixty thousand to seventy thousand of them. . . . They also ate the animals in the zoo as well' (Harris 1985: 101). Consumption of horse subsequently remained a tradition within French cuisine; it is abhorrent to the sensitive, but less sophisticated British palate with its preference for beef. In short, the balance between physiological and psychological needs in determining food choice seems capable of swinging to extremes in either direction. We are all fascinated by, and even accepting of, the ultimate taboo – the cannibalism of castaways and the stranded;[5] but humans will also starve rather than breach deeply ingrained notions of what is fit to eat, whether edible or not.

Differences in (the reasons for) what is consumed are multiple once subsistence is guaranteed. If consumption were purely or predominantly motivated by need, nutrition or biological or physiological determinants, it would appear to be impossible to explain the causes of hunger itself, especially amongst those who have already been fed well enough. Compulsive eating is a response to emotional needs or turmoils, as is anorexia. Thus, apart from feeding the stomach, it is generally recognised that appetite for food responds to a variety of emotionally and socially determined needs displaced on to feelings of hunger. These needs are not and cannot be straightforward, as is illustrated by the extent to which the desirable image of thinner women has accompanied and been intensified by the increasing weight of actual women (Gilbert 1986). A further index of collective angst is the swelling popularity of both cookbooks and dieting books.

These considerations must deflate the importance of inherent tastes, needs or knowledge which become, at most, just one amongst many determinants of diet. As Ruf observes in assessing how ready we were for ready-to-serve-foods: 'The majority of these (nutritional or eating) habits are not subject to the free will of the individual. They are already programmed by biopsychic, political, legal, economic, technical as well as sociocultural factors' (Ruf 1978: 15). Or, in more technical terms, quoting Garrow (1980): 'In man, control of food intake is complex, and the primitive hypothalamic reflexes are so buried under so many layers of conditioning, cognitive and social factors that they are barely discernible' (James *et al.* 1980: 3).

As soon as conscious (or even unconscious) choice intervenes between plate and palate, then knowledge of, and attitudes towards, food and nutrition become important. It is not simply that foods satisfy needs; it is a matter of how it is known what those needs are and why they are satisfied by (particular) foods. This then raises the issue of the origins of nutritional knowledge and how it is acted upon or, as Gormley (1987: 10) puts it, who is it that determines CHNT (current human nutrition thinking)? Downey takes the problem one stage further:

> Most of the general public are poorly informed on nutritional matters and even amongst those who are well or adequately informed, there is little or no connection between the possession of nutritional knowledge and its application when shopping.
>
> (Downey 1987: 150)

Consequently, whatever the influences upon CHNT, they do not simply translate into corresponding eating habits. This is hardly surprising given the sources of knowledge of nutrition, for they are heavily tempered by other sources and types of knowledge:[6] 'The main sources of information on healthy eating in the UK were television (including advertisements), magazines, and popular books' (O'Beirne 1987: 216).

For advertising in particular, as is the case with other products, notice of availability is integrated into a representation of the commodity as something other than it is, but this does not mean that the messages are believed nor that they lead to purchases when they are. O'Beirne (1987: 216) reports that claims for food products have levels of credibility less than 20 per cent. Of course, many advertisements are based upon the health-giving properties of particular foods, for which there is contrary, no or, at best, disputed scientific evidence (Campbell and O'Connor 1988). None the less, advertising plays a crucial and increasing part in the provision of food, at least in the minds of those who produce and sell it. In the United States, its share in manufacturing advertising has risen from 27 per cent in 1963 to 34 per cent in 1984 (when it stood at $8.5 billion plus another $2.9 billion devoted to the peddling of tobacco) (Connor 1988). In the case of the UK, whilst the food industry spent over £300 million on advertising in 1985, the then Health

Education Council had less than £1 million with which to advertise healthy eating habits (London Food Commission 1988: 21). Yet, particularly in the last few decades, the lobby for healthier food has been both prominent and demonstrably successful.

To some extent this has depended upon government support and regulation, serving to moderate the clash of what are represented as the competing interests of consumers and producers. One example is provided by the dispute over food package labelling, which raises the issue of whether and how much consumers should know about what they are digesting:[7]

> There is considerable controversy over exactly what nutrients should be labelled and a wide range of formats have been suggested. There are two main opinions: the food industry favours labelling calories, total fat, protein and carbohydrate on a grammes per 100 grammes or per serving basis. The health food lobby broadly favours calories, total fat broken down into saturated and polyunsaturated fatty acids, added sugar, salt and fibre.
>
> (Luba 1985: iv)

Here is an example of conflict over what nutritional knowledge is made available – with manufacturers more or less reluctantly complying with regulations that are perceived to reveal the poverty or health risks of their products. Such revelations add to their costs, though the capacity to add the label 'healthy' may be warmly embraced where it can become competitively advantageous. Or there can be claims for 'natural' products which, none the less, can often mislead about health, as in the case of products *without additives* but *with* high sugar content. A more fundamental conflict concerns the definition of CHNT itself. Who gets to say what is and what is not healthy? In the case of Britain, it is often the representatives of producers who are active not only in advertising the health of their products but also in defining what is healthy, through the sponsorship of research and through predominance on governmental or non-governmental organisations nominally concerned with health.

Sugar provides a particularly good example of how the provision of information becomes a terrain of conflict. Its significance for the world food industry is indicated by its global annual production, which has grown from 0.25 million tonnes in 1800 to over 100 million tonnes in 1982 (three times the level for 1950 and half as much again as in 1970) (Yudkin 1986). It now provides 10 per cent of the world's calories (Heasman 1987: 18). Before the mid-nineteenth century, however, it was primarily a luxury.[8] But, as Mintz (1985) argues, from that time on it became a major source of calories, often rendering palatable, but less nutritious, sufficient energy intake for long hours of work. For the UK, sugar was the single leading import for every year from 1701 to 1814 (Mahler 1986: 150), and this has proved a tooth that has gone from sweet to sweeter. Over the century from 1870 to 1970, annual sugar intake per head has risen from 80 to 150 grammes (Dewar n.d.). Since then, everybody believes that he or she has been cutting down on sugar, and so they have in their direct consumption. But this has been compensated for by an increasing use of sugar as an additive to, or ingredient of, other manufactured foods.[9]

The flexibility of sugar use reflects its many properties (Yudkin 1986); it has sweetness, flavour, mouth feel or body; it acts as a preservative or gelling agent; it has a range of textures, depresses freezing point, caramelises; it can be used in decoration and is fermentable. Lindley (1987: 41) points to its specific properties for baking: as a texturiser, it controls spread; it influences colour, flavour and appearance; it prolongs freshness through moisture retention; and, in yeast-leavened products, it can act as a yeast food source. As for substitutes, 'fructose can lead to excessive browning in baked goods, and the volumes of glucose and fructose cakes may be less than their sucrose counterparts' (ibid.: 44). Lindley concludes that without sucrose, life would be more complicated for manufacturers and more costly for consumers.

So much for sugar's properties in production and in satisfying taste. Considerable opposition to its displacement as an industrial ingredient reflects another side of the picture, its highly monopolised position as an established industrial sector.[10] Although it has been readily admitted that sugar is a major source of tooth decay, many obstacles have been placed in the path of publicising its role in causing more serious ailments like heart disease. Yudkin (1986) documents in great detail how he, his research and its dissemination were blocked by the sugar lobby. In this, government has not been entirely innocent. A report completed in April 1983, and only finally published in September of that year, is described by Walker and Cannon as:

> the only expert report published in Britain that incorporates modern medical and scientific thinking not just about one disease (like heart disease, for example) or one part of our diet (like fats), but about the British diet as a whole, and the effect of diet *as a whole* on health. It is, however, written in medical language.
>
> (Walker and Cannon 1985: xxxvii)

They deplore as a scandal the failure to translate its findings and recommendations into everyday language and to publicise them vigorously. These are easily grasped and involve the straightforward suggestion that on average, per capita consumption of sugar should be cut by half, salt by half, fat by a quarter, and alcohol by a third.

In this case, it might be argued that governmental inertia is prompted by the defence of the interests of particular capitalists committed to the refining, use and sale of sugar. More generally, Cannon (1987) documents that in the 1980s over a third of all Britain's MPs (250 politicians and over a half of all Conservatives) had some connection with the food industry. He also points to the 246 advisers, connected with the industry, who serve on food policy committees.

It is perhaps easier to see in retrospect when government itself, charged with responsibility for the health of its people, has caved in to political imperatives which force it to deflate the extent and significance of poor diet or nutrition for the health of its people. In 1931, a medically based survey found that:

> only half the country were living at a level of nutrition so high that on average no improvement could be effected by improved consumption, and also – because of the effect of large families on family budgets – a fifth of the country's children were chronically ill-nourished.
>
> (Mayhew 1988: 457)

Yet government sought to deny this evidence, and did nothing to remedy its causes, although a survey of 5,000 in 1938 confirmed the earlier evidence. As Mayhew concludes, 'At a time of mass unemployment, low-wage labour and fiscal retrenchment, government ministers and civil servants were desperately concerned to disprove links between malnutrition, ill-health and low income' (ibid.: 462)

Even when confronting producer interests and government inertia, the health lobby may not be successful in highlighting the most significant nutritional problems. The most sensitive and appealing issues are not necessarily the ones that have the greatest impact on diet and nutrition. O'Beirne makes the point, however validly, in extreme form:[11]

> For some time it has been apparent that the attitudes of a minority of consumers and the content of press comments on the relative risk in the diet have tended to reverse the generally accepted risk priorities. The actual order of importance of risks has been estimated to be first those due to microbiological contamination and nutritional imbalance, then (one thousandfold less) those due to environmental pollutants, contaminants and natural toxicants, then (one hundredfold less again) those due to pesticide residues and food additives. The more extreme consumer and press comments have tended to make food additives, pesticide residues, and environmental contaminants the top priorities.
>
> (O'Bierne 1987: 215–16)

Nor is the struggle for 'genuine' ingredients confined to the pursuit of healthy or healthier products. In the case of Coca-Cola, it was decided in 1986 to replace the old with a new formula for the drink which, apart from water, continues to comprise 99 per cent sugar or sweetening. In retrospect, this appears to have been a marketing ploy, an attempt to retain markets in the competitive conflict with Pepsi-Cola (which, perversely, as one of its minor rivals, Coca-Cola had the opportunity to purchase in the 1930s).[12] The two companies are now locked in a fierce battle to capture and expand the world's thirst (more soft drinks than water are now consumed in the United States).[13]

Weapons include franchising, joint ventures, acquisitions and mergers, and vertical integration whether into bottling or into fast food outlets; McDonalds, for example, sells Coke exclusively.

There is something ironic in Coca-Cola itself changing its own formula which had always been carefully shrouded in an aura of secrecy. Such secrecy can hardly have been motivated by the wish to preserve the quality of the product by denying its ingredients to other potential, possibly adulterating, competitors. It has served as a focus for the most extensive, persistent and changing of advertising campaigns, to create the image of uniqueness. New advertising campaigns and catchy slogans have been introduced, usually at least once per year.[14] Advertising expenditure by Coca-Cola has reached £30 million per annum in the UK, for example, and $160 million in media expenditure in the United States in 1990. With a similar marketing drive throughout the world, originating in its strength from the role of providing US servicemen abroad during the Second World War – 'Coke deluged the globe' (Oliver 1986: 20) – its consumption has risen to over 300 million bottles per day in 155 countries (ibid.: 13). Pepsi also serves over 140 countries with 800 bottling plants (Louis and Yazijian 1980). No wonder there is reference to Coca-Colonialism and the idea that, 'within every bottle dwelled "the essence of capitalism"' (ibid.: 76).

Note, however, that the Coke formula has not remained unchanged over the previous hundred years. Initially, from its birth in 1886, associated with the church and temperance as a selling angle, it suffered from the taint of narcotics – at least until the cocaine content was eliminated by changing to the use of spent coca leaves at the beginning of the 1900s. Moreover, the protection of its uniqueness lay less in preserving the secrecy of its ingredients than in eliminating rivals through lawsuits:[15]

> In 1916 alone, 153 impostors were struck down in the courts, including Fig Cola, Candy Cola, Cold Cola, Cay-Ola, Koca-Nola, as well as Coca and Cola. Precedent proved no deterrent to the pretenders as they kept up a barrage through the years – Caro-Cola, Coca-Kola, Kora-Nola, Kola-Nola, Ko Kola, Coke Ola, Kos Kola, Toca-Cola, Sola Cola, and King Kola. As many as seventy of the imitators on the scene in 1909 still contained cocaine, such as Kel Kola ('It has the kick') and Kaw-Kola ('Has the Kick').
>
> (Louis and Yazijian 1980: 32)

None the less, against this forgotten background, customers reacted against the replacement of what was later to be restored as classic Coke, Oliver (1986: 8/9):

> Dan drove to the San Antonio bottler and purchased 110 cases for $979.00. When Libby . . . heard the Coca-Cola Company's news, she not only rushed out and bought $700 worth of Coke, she also got angry.
>
> (Oliver 1986: 8–9)

A campaign was orchestrated by a self-appointed representative of Coke drinkers, Gay Mullins, and a song – 'Coke Was It'[16] – was played on the radio between 300,000 and 400,000 times. When the decision was made to restore the old formula alongside the new one (not an unusual ploy to sell two products to expand market share against a competitor) a proposal was submitted to employ Mullins on a $200,000 fee plus $1,000 expenses for each appearance on behalf of Coke. This plan was abandoned once Mullins had been courted by the United States Sugar Association (USSA) in its campaign against Coke. Opportunistically adopted in the wake of the pressure for the old formula, the USSA fought from 1980 onwards the contracts which allowed bottlers to substitute high-fructose corn syrup for sugar.

In short, at one extreme, naturally or socially given tastes and properties of foods are used to explain consumption; at the other, conflict over the control and display of nutritional information. Neither one nor any combination of these seems capable of explaining diet. Significantly, in exploring specific examples, such as sugar and cola, emphasis shifts away from the intrinsic and informational basis of food choice towards the issue of food availability, particularly around the imperatives of the food industry. How has this duality between the provision of food and the provision (and receipt) of knowledge been perceived?

## 2 DIGESTING INFORMATION[17]

The purpose of this section is to focus on one particular aspect of the food system – the role of information in determining food choice. What is the source of our knowledge about food and how does it give rise to the exercise of particular food choices? A review of some of the literature in this area demonstrates that this process cannot reasonably be understood except as part of the operation of the food system as a whole. The information system is, in fact, heavily integrated with, and determined by, the food system; it cannot be legitimately endowed with a life of its own as a determinant of food choice.

Possibly the most important idea influencing those writing on the informational determinants of food choice is the evolving role of what may be termed current human nutritional thinking (CHNT). Such thinking is derived from the scientific profession through research, and is perceived to filter through to the general public so that the consumer's diet may be improved through the exercise of informed conscious choice. Within this framework, there are perceived to be obstacles standing between the experts and the consumers, obstacles which have to be overcome for CHNT to trickle down and influence diet.

From this perspective, the duty of government is to disseminate appropriate knowledge about healthy eating in the most effective way. In reality, whatever it attempts to do, it has proved signally unsuccessful given the continuing rise in diet-related diseases. Nor is this simply a matter of insufficient commitment to informational campaigns. For however much a UK government, for example, campaigns against high levels of sugar consumption, it is bound to fail while it is inconsistently supporting sugar production, and hence consumption, through being a party to European Community Common Agricultural Policy. This represents a particularly blunt example of the way in which the food and informational systems interact through government policy. Oversimplifying, if the latter in the agricultural domain simply serves to sustain level of consumption (to match demand for allocated producer quotas), then healthy eating campaigns trickle down through the food system by shifting the sugar content between products and between consumers (depending upon their relative aversions to sugar), who are more or less powerless to change the overall level of sugar consumption.

This provides one example of the potential relationship between the food and informational systems in which the impact of trickle-down is heavily circumscribed. But the notion of trickle-down of information or CHNT is in itself far from acceptable. The first criticism of this approach, from which all others flow more or less directly, is its failure to recognise that CHNT is not a neutrally given body of steadily improving scientific knowledge but is itself socially constructed.[18] First, CHNT is a response to health concerns derived from the identified incidence of diet-related disease. Research is funded and undertaken where nutritional problems are perceived to arise and to require remedy. This is illustrated by the extent to which CHNT is now concerned more than before with the general diseases of affluence and longevity and less concerned with nutrition in the context of 'deviancy' associated with deficient diet.

Second, probing this a little deeper in connection with the food system rather than demography, CHNT is in part a product of changing diets because of the diseases that these create, in the way that cancer research is a product of the tobacco industry. Large increases, for example, in per capita consumption of sugar and of meat are as important influences on CHNT as the natural physiology of the human species. Consequently, the scope and delimitation of CHNT are hotly contested with, unsurprisingly, heavy involvement by scientists and those representing, and funded by, the interests of corporate capital. What scientists do, who pays them, and how the results are used, determines both the direction and the impact of CHNT.

Third, and consequently, CHNT is not a given and fixed body of knowledge but is subject to change over time and to differences of opinion between experts. This has led to a belief in what might be termed a 'pyramid of confusion' in the trickle-down of CHNT. It is argued that until clear and consistent advice is given by the experts, the consumer will be unable to respond and to adopt healthy eating habits. This is misleading in two ways. It fails to recognise how differences in opinion are positively manufactured and exploited in order to undermine or delay the consequences of conclusions unfavourable to corporate interests. And it presumes that other determinants exercise only limited influence on food choice – as if healthy diets would be adopted if all expert opinion were uniform. This is demonstrably incorrect, as the cases of tobacco and alcohol reveal.

Fourth, the relationship between CHNT and food information more generally is too simply conceived by those seeking to improve its availability and use. It certainly is recognised that CHNT becomes distorted, as it trickles down; it is confused and not properly understood in the minds of consumers. This is perceived, however, as a problem in the translation of scientific results into lay language. But the parallel that might be drawn with nuclear physics or astronomy is entirely inappropriate. For neither the atom nor the solar system is an artefact of the kitchen or the shopping bag.

The consumer is involved in different practices from the nutritionist and, consequently, applies a type of knowledge that is different from rather than inferior to the other. Thus, while the latter is concerned with the physiological effects of toxins on rats or the average impact of diet across populations, the former is involved in the purchase and preparation of specific foods, for which knowledge is both practical and derived from a variety of sources without being organised in a consistent or coherent fashion. At least partly for this reason, it is often found that even when consumers have reasonable knowledge of which foods are healthy, as they often do, and which ones are not, they do not necessarily act upon that knowledge. More generally, as the determinants of food choice themselves are known to be both varied and complex, it cannot be presumed that efforts to improve the trickle-down of CHNT will exercise a positive influence on diet.

Consider, for example, the growth of low sugar and low or polyunsaturated fat products. Over the past decade, these have been promoted as healthy products and have become a major market segment over a very short period. The message from CHNT seems to have got through. However, as Heasman (1990) reports, it is the image of healthy products that is succeeding rather than the health message itself. As the food industry presses to sustain its sales, 'lite' products are consumed in addition to, as well as substituting for, others. Consequently, energy derived from fat still remains at the unacceptably high level of 40 per cent, while the growth of artificial sweeteners in drinks has not been accompanied by a corresponding decline in sugar consumption.

This is a clear illustration of the way in which the imperatives of the food system intervene between the generation and dissemination of CHNT. How has the relationship between the food and information systems been understood when it has been addressed? Essentially, there have been two approaches. One identifies the food system, and corporate capital within it, as essentially antagonistic to healthy food. It is associated with 'food activists', who perceive the food industry as responsible for poor diets and government as complicit with this state of affairs. Profitability and the anarchy of the market rule but can be struggled against.

Whatever the analytical depth with which this position is explored, it does support the suggestion here that interaction between the food and information systems has to be carefully examined. The second approach, however, sees the food industry as a potential ally or conduit for improvement in diet. The basis for this stance has been admirably laid out by Ippolito and Mathios (1990) in a way that is representative of, but more rigorous than, other contributions. Consequently, it is carefully assessed here. A turning point in the application of current scientific thinking to advertising provided a focus for their argument. Specifically, although a link between fibre and cancer had been established as a consequence of accumulating scientific evidence before 1984, it was not until then that producers' advertising and labelling incorporated such information to promote their, possibly new, products containing fibre. In that year Kellogg, in co-operation with the National Cancer Prevention Awareness Program, began an advertising and labelling campaign which cited the National Cancer Institute's (NCI) position on the link between fibre consumption and cancer. The lead provided by Kellogg was quickly followed by other cereal manufacturers eager to capitalise on the presumed health benefits of fibre.

What happened? Before 1984, with only the limited (sources) of information provided by 'non-producers', such as government health programmes, there was no significant increase in the consumption of cereals containing fibre. After 1984, when the same information was employed in advertising campaigns for cereals, per capita consumption of fibre in cereals shot up to double their previous levels. The implication is obvious: that the effective impact of scientific information on the purchase of specifically healthier products can depend positively upon the role of producer advertising, especially where non-producer information has proved ineffective:

> In summary, public and general information sources appear to have some effect on consumers' understanding of the relationship between diet and health, though this effect was limited in the case of communicating the fiber–cancer link. Augmenting this information flow with producer advertising resulted in dramatic increases in knowledge of the fiber–cancer link and in fiber cereal consumption.
>
> (Ippolito and Mathios 1990: 418)

This is confirmed by examining the incidence of consumption of high-fibre cereals (and knowledge of its effects) across different socioeconomic groups; those who are more educated and hence more likely to rely on non-advertising sources of information, for example, knew more about such cereals and ate more of them prior to the producer advertising campaigns. Thus:

> The use of producer advertising had a significant effect on both the knowledge of fiber–cancer link and on consumption of fiber cereals. The gains in knowledge occurred for all education groups, whites and nonwhites, smokers and non-smokers, etc. In terms of consumption,

> those groups that were not well reached by government sources were the groups that showed the largest increases in consumption.
>
> (ibid.: 423)

In addition, the success of the Kellogg–NCI initiative led to the more general introduction of higher fibre content into cereals:

> Cereals introduced between 1985 and 1987 were significantly higher in fiber than the average cereal on the market in 1984. . . . Thus, the evidence on new product developments in the cereal market is consistent with the hypothesis that the ability to use health claims to advertise new products is a significant factor in stimulating the development and introduction of more nutritious products in the market.
>
> (ibid.: 424)

Drawing upon this example, Ippolito and Mathios address two broader questions; first, why should producer advertising have proved so successful in this case and not in others and, second, what is the appropriate regulatory regime for science-based claims in advertising which will best contribute to healthier eating through information dissemination? Their critical interest in these issues leads them implicitly to construct answers dependent upon an analysis of the information system, the food system, and their interaction. Whilst their examination of these is heavily influenced by their focus on the cereal case, it is posited as a more general framework and is open to assessment as such.

Their view of the information system is founded on a dual structure: on the one hand, knowledge originating from non-producers, predominantly seen as government and education; on the other hand, knowledge originating from producers, predominantly through advertising and labelling. The sharp and exhaustive division between just the two sources of information is presumably motivated by the empirical evidence under scrutiny, in which the initiation of a producer advertising campaign for fibre cereals after 1984 is readily contrasted with the earlier exclusive reliance on non-producer information.

This is, however, to absorb empirical observation directly into an analytical structure which may be of only limited use in extending our understanding of the issues involved. The sources of information on nutrition are highly diverse and are certainly not confined to formal producer and non-producer channels alone. In particular, what people are already eating provides an important source of practical knowledge, both in terms of their own immediate responses (whether they like it or not, for example) and in terms of acquired tastes and habits through whatever mechanism (cultural, familial, etc.).

In other words, there is already an informational system in place with a content over and above that provided by producers and non-producers. This is potentially of some importance in explaining why cereals are being eaten for breakfast in the first place. Whatever the role of other sources of information in determining this food choice, it is crucial that they be recognised (even if only as of limited importance or absent), since their impact has to reinforce or be overcome by the absorption of new information supporting the adoption of fibre cereals. Even if cereal consumption is determined on the informational side purely by producer and non-producer information, the strength of this relationship does not hold true for all foods; the successful promotion of fibre through advertising may be exceptional, reflecting in part the directness of the link in this case between consumption and cancer and the previously limited sources of information.

Cereal consumption has increased dramatically during the postwar period. On the basis of a casual analysis, its growth reflects the perception of the morning rush at breakfast time and a preference for self-selection and convenience. Breakfast is, after all, the meal that is most commonly skipped. This no doubt generates guilt around poor domestic provision, especially for children. Consequently, with whatever validity, nutritional claims for cereals are liable to be more than welcome to, and influential upon, consumers. It is also significant that the cereal market is one that had already been built up on the basis of advertising, both the cause and effect of intense brand competition between large-scale producers. In addition, and possibly more important, the rise of cereals as breakfast foods is of convenience to the food manufacturing system. For cereals are the least susceptible to decay as an organic product, so that producers have had an incentive to promote cereals through marketing in order to avoid wastage associated with turnover time in sale or use.

Quite apart from dependence on producers and non-producers alone as the perceived sources of information, a related but separate issue is the extent to which this is an appropriate analytical starting point. It obviously has some empirical convenience but, as the authors themselves observe, the successful campaign to introduce fibre cereals was founded on cooperation between Kellogg and the NCI. More generally, as has already been remarked, producers have a heavy influence on the creation of non-producer information through a variety of mechanisms, including the funding of scientific research. This brings into question the analytical validity of setting up, as a starting point, a fundamental opposition between the two, especially if it can be overcome as demonstrated by the Kellogg example.

The point is reinforced by reference to the second highly simplified component in the Ippolito and Mathios analysis of the information system. This is their understanding of information itself. Again they pose an apparent duality, in this instance between science and deception. While it is recognised that science is itself surrounded with doubt and subject not only to evolutionary progress but also to the rejection of earlier verities, it is, none the less, readily associated with the truth as opposed to the non-scientific claims that might be made by producers through their advertising. Not surprisingly, then, the issue of healthy nutritional information conforms to a large extent to the pyramid model outlined earlier. The goal of this model is to overcome the obstacles in the way of 'timely and effective dissemination of scientific information to consumers' and to examine 'the ability of alternative regulatory approaches to deter potential deception while not inhibiting the dissemination of truthful science-based claims' (Ippolito and Mathios 1990: 413).

For two reasons, this approach is also too simplistic. First, as observed, science is too readily associated with neutrality and objectivity, rather than being seen as socially constructed by the influences and interests that act upon it. Second, the sharp dichotomy between scientific claims or truth and deception cannot be sustained. The nature of the information or knowledge employed in different activities, in the lab as opposed to the kitchen, are very different. Nor is this a matter of truth or fiction (or to deny that the two sorts of knowledge have a connection with one another). In general, the language and content of the information is transformed even if we accept the pyramid of trickle-down as an appropriate analytical framework. 'This cereal is good for you' (or 'good for your health') may have a scientific rationale but it is not a scientific statement and it has a context and interpretation that is very different from scientific thinking and practices. Even where the language might be similar – 'Eating fibre in cereals may reduce the risk of cancer' – the meaning remains distinct according to how, for example, risk and cancer are understood.

It follows that the two dualities, between producers and non-producers and between science and deception, have a close correspondence to one another, since the producers have a predilection for deception as opposed to the non-producers who are presumed to have a single-minded commitment to truth derived from science. This double-knit analytical structure has the effect, as remarked, of excluding both alternative sources of information and a more complex understanding of information itself.

A further element needs to be added to complete the analytical structure for the information system; lines of communication between the structure as described and consumers are stronger or more effective for producers than for non-producers. In other words, while information put out by non-producers is relatively more effective with the educated consumer, producers use popular media and advertising much more extensively and these are directly associated with purchase decisions. The differential impact of these two sources is only cursorily explored. A deeper examination of the reasons for this might well have led to a more complex understanding of the information system as well as to a questioning of the presumed fundamental opposition between producers and non-producers as sources of information. None the less, the conclusion is that non-producers can only effectively reach consumers through the conduit provided by the producers, along which there is the potential to pick up deception. This creates a situation of conflict and co-operation between the two; both regulations (on labelling or advertising science-based claims) and scientific knowledge are fed to, but not necessarily through, the producers by non-producers.

For Ippolito and Mathios, producer motivation for the selective use of non-producer information is provided by the pursuit of profitability rather than by the direct provision either of healthy food or of 'true' information about these foods, whether they are healthy or not. However, they do not carry this starting point much further. It is essentially confined to a model of trade-off by individual producers between the use of science-based claims and other forms of (false) advertising according to their effectiveness on sales. At a systemic level, there is an idealised model of an 'unfolding process'. Comparable products with full information available on their nutritional content will lead to the better products competitively eliminating the worse. Those without information will be outcompeted by those with information. Thus, healthy and informative products will chase out the bad and uninformative. However, Ippolito and Mathios recognise that markets are far from perfect, so that there will be a continuing balance between truth and deception in advertising.

The limitations of this approach arise from its failure to recognise the complexity of the food system itself or its failure to examine the imperative of profitability upon it. In the case of cereals, for example, as already observed, eating habits around breakfast have been transformed, and these have been fed by a monopolistic corporate structure whose previously rapidly expanding markets have given way to relative stagnation. Consequently, the use of advertising around a new gimmick (fibre and cancer) serves both to reinvigorate the sector and represents a continuity with the past in the use of advertising as a form of competition between producers. Significantly, there is no reference to the industrial structure of the cereal manufacturing sector. Why was Kellogg in a position to form an alliance with the NCI? It is precisely because of its corporate power in general and its presence in cereals in particular.

A second limitation is the analytical collapse of the food system into the market relations between producers and consumers, although there is some reference to government in its informational and regulatory role. But cereals are produced first as crops, and are then processed; they also have to be distributed, retailed and prepared in the home (for which convenience and self-selection/service has already been noted). While, as far as cereals are concerned, it is possible that these factors have not been of importance over the period studied, they remain potentially important factors when other foods are involved. US cereals, for example, are branded goods sustained by high advertising expenditure; in the UK, for some foods, the role of large-scale retailers selling own-label products is often of greater relevance.

A third problem with the Ippolito and Mathios analysis is its lack of any identified source of innovation from within the food system. The only *source* of change is from the scientific community. Its evolving knowledge leads to differing *choices* by producers, even to new products such as those containing more fibre. But these products were, in principle, previously available. What is absent is the innovation from the production side arising from the imperative of profitability which pre-empts and sets the future agenda for non-producers. There is, for example, the use of additives to enhance the colour, flavour, consistency and life of products and there is the desire to cut input and processing costs – each of these operates independently of nutritional implications and can be exploited by advertising. To a large extent, the narrow scope allowed to producers is a reflection of the standard approach to microeconomics, in which the firm optimises on the basis of given technological choices (here the trade-off is between the relative merits of science-based and other content in advertising).

So far an attempt has been made to highlight the separation of the information system from the food system hypothesised by Ippolito and Mathios. But they are also sometimes combined. For them, co-operation/conflict in the dissemination of information is mediated by producers' pursuit of profitability. Given discrete choices over the content of advertising, non-producers have to tread cautiously over the regulations they impose on producers to forestall the exclusion of such information altogether:

> Broad disclosure requirements, especially in broadcast advertising, raise the cost of making any health claim. If the cost of making health claims is increased, firms will find it profitable to use fewer health claims and competition can be expected to move firms away from a focus on the choice of health characteristics of products to other aspects of food choice, such as taste, convenience, price, etc.
>
> (Ippolito and Mathios 1990: 425)

The incomplete information implicit in health claims thus raises a standard problem of trade-offs. If we require more complete information whenever the health issue is addressed, we may actually reduce rather than increase the flow of health information to consumers. Whether such a move would be good for consumers requires careful consideration.

In short, given the primary motivation of producers to make profit and of non-producers to promote healthy (science-based) eating, the latter have to accept that they work through the producers' profit motive, even though it is geared, in part, to deception. To do otherwise is potentially to frustrate even further the trickle-down of CHNT to the consumer.

If then, Ippolito and Mathios are to be congratulated for developing a theory that incorporates the interaction of the food and information systems, the result is open to criticism both for its limited scope and for its accommodation with the food industry. Food activists, by contrast, tend to adopt an uncompromising and more realistic stance, in relation both to corporate capital and government, seeing one as responsible for poor diet, the other as irresponsible for not taking stronger counteracting measures. Consequently, they tend to be labelled as extremists in an attempt to marginalise them and to deny them legitimacy. Their claims are dismissed on the grounds that they lack scientific certainty, just as their authors lack scientific credentials.

This quibbling draws attention away from the overwhelmingly unscientific claims by which food is already made attractive, through labelling and advertising, and from the complex processes by which food knowledge is both acquired and acted upon. In many ways, food knowledge is better seen as an enabling device than as a decisive influence. Its availability allows rather than determines food choice; it rationalises decisions which have been made for other reasons, not necessarily on a coherent nor on an entirely food-related basis. This is perhaps why food activists are frowned upon; in the realm of the media and lack of veracity of claims, their role is miniscule compared to that of the food industry. But in providing an alternative ideology for consumption, their effectivity is what is most feared in providing an alternative rationale for food choice.[19] But how has such choice been understood more generally, and at a more considered analytical level, across the social sciences?

## 3 THE ANALYTICAL MENU

The lack of a systematic relationship between food consumption and nutritional and biological determinants creates the opening for the various social sciences to address the issue of what we eat and drink and why. Here we first confront what will become a familiar refrain – the neglect of consumption as an object of study. Beardsworth and Keil observe: 'It is a surprising and rather bewildering fact that sociologists have devoted relatively little to the rich complexes of human action and experience which cluster around the production and consumption of food' (Beardsworth and Keil 1990: 139). Murcott concurs in so far as: 'Social anthropology has paid considerably more attention to the study of food and eating than has sociology. Indeed its scholarly interest in food is probably as old as the discipline itself' (Murcott 1988: 1). Yet Montgomery and Bennett (1979: 124) ask of anthropology, 'why the study of food has not become centrally located in the discipline' and suggest that it has been more prominent only in response to problems that have emerged,[20] such as poor and changing diet and the role of famine relief. For psychology, Lyman suggests that:

> The thoughts, images, ideas, feelings and even fully-fledged emotions evoked by food touch on every aspect of our conscious and unconscious mental life. It is surprising, therefore, that psychologists have paid so little attention to the development of food preferences and to the psychological effects of food and food-related activities. Of the many books published on food there is practically nothing on the psychology of food.
>
> (Lyman 1989: 7)

As has already been seen for food in particular, and for consumption more generally in earlier chapters, commodities are often interpreted across the social sciences in terms of their socially constructed attributes. This lends an added meaning and, by implication, reason, for their consumption. Perhaps most significant in this has been the work of Mary Douglas and also of Lévi-Strauss, in which food and eating take on the role of ritual and form part of a much wider social intercourse, embroiled in taboo and custom.[21] For Lévi-Strauss specifically, food must be 'good to think' – feelings about food are more important than its taste. Such themes, in different ways, have been taken up by a variety of authors. The colour of food can be crucial in its representation of purity as in the preference for white bread, for example, despite its poor nutritional qualities – although, buried in history, dark bread was tougher and of inferior quality. On the other hand, whilst white-shelled eggs are preferred in the United States and the Middle East (King 1980), brown eggs in the UK are perceived to be healthier in representing a more varied (and even free-range) diet for the hens (although brown shells are now easily produced by appropriate feed to battery hens).

On the theme of colour, Bennett (1988: 141) points to the absence of blue foods, somewhat inaccurately given certain fruits and cheeses, but more significantly sees learnt tastes as analogous to language (ibid.: 6), and in which there tends to be an extreme conservatism (ibid.: 10). Lyman more generally brings out the contextual determinants of taste, in the reaction against the notion of a dish of gravy and ice-cream (Lyman 1989: 34), and in emphasising how relatively unimportant are food's sensory qualities as indicated by our ability to dislike things before we have even tried them.

In principle, this sort of approach could be extended indefinitely across the social sciences. For once it is recognised that food performs a variety of personal and social roles, then, correspondingly, the tool-kits of sociology, anthropology and psychology can be brought to bear to reveal the emulational, encoded or emotional content of consumption.[22] The interpretation of food becomes the academic counterpart to the advertisers' attempts to sell it as homely, satisfying, manly, filling, classy, etc.

Against such interpretations, there have been two closely related critical reactions, each indicating the extent to which food consumption has been understood as a system of provision. First, those concerned with the history of food, other than documenting who ate what and when (rather than who ruled and conquered, although the two sets of issues are not independent of each other),[23] have rejected interpretative analysis as incapable of explaining changes in consumption (see especially Goody (1982) and Mennell (1985)). Thus, for Barthes, in referring to American sugar or French wine consumption, 'these institutions necessarily imply a set of images, dreams, tastes, choices and values' (Barthes 1979: 167). But they also imply a lived history involving slavery and protectionism which cultural analyses typified by Barthes tend to neglect, even at the most mundane level. For Barthes,

> When he buys an item of food, consumes it, or serves it, modern man does not manipulate a simple object in a purely transitive fashion; this

> item of food sums up and transmits a situation; it constitutes an information; it signifies.
>
> (Barthes 1979: 168)

Most likely 'it signifies' that it has been shopped, cooked and served by a woman!

As an alternative to such cultural explanations, the historical approach seeks much wider causes than the proximate meaning and role of food. Mennell (1985), for example, gives three possible reasons for the inferiority of English as compared to French cuisine first: the role of the Protestant ethic in practice; second, the effortless superiority of the English ruling class leading it to need no culinary symbols of display to distinguish itself from, and hold itself above, the lower orders; and, third, the differing evolution of the relationship between town and country, for which the organisation of English catering around (hotel) management and cost reduction is of importance. Similarly, Goody (1982: 40) points to the early death of the peasantry in England as well as to the virtual absence of the vine and the olive. He does, however, maintain a sense of proportion (and humour) in assessing the consequences of modernism for the fate of British cuisine:

> The British diet went . . . straight 'from medieval barbarity to industrial decadence'. But . . . medieval barbarity meant culinary differentiation . . . at least into systems of supply, preparation, cooking, serving and consumption of food that resolutely set aside the high from the low. And 'industrial decadence', whatever its consequences for the *haute cuisine* (larks' tongues are not promising ingredients for a mass cuisine, canned food is not always the best basis for a gourmet meal), has enormously improved, in quantity, quality and variety the diet (and usually the cuisine) of the urban working population of the western world.
>
> (Goody 1982: 154)

A second critical reaction against the cultural approach to food is to be found in the materialist school, predominantly within anthropology. Here, Harris (1985) is a leading representative, provocatively parodying Lévi-Strauss' notion of food as 'good to think' by the alternative, and apparently simplistic notion, of food as 'good to eat'. The starting point for this alternative is the rejection of the leading causal role of the symbolic or ritual. The cultural content of food is seen more as a consequence of material necessity than as a structurally determining aspect. Evidence for this is the high variability in what constitutes good to think as far as food is concerned and the lack of uniformly applicable models to explain symbolically why there are, for example, forty-two different societies in which people eat rats. One person's meat being another person's poison, ranging over meats and animals, insects and vermin, seafood and even milk, serve to demonstrate that the uneaten are designated as holy or profane because they are uneaten and not vice versa. Pets, for example, serve as such because they are inedible relative to other foods available and are otherwise useless for other practical purposes – and, consequently, become highly functional as objects of emotional attachment instead. We love the things we cannot eat.

This rejection of the culturalist explanation of food and diet puts in its place an emphasis upon material factors. Most important is the role of comparative advantage in the production of food, although this is both supplemented and defined by a range of other factors such as genetics and the role of conflict over subsistence and surplus. Thus, in the case of cannibalism, although the Aztecs were not impelled by a protein shortage:

> Captives were worth more to them dead as meat than alive as serfs and slaves. The Aztecs were unusually ill supplied with meat and other animal products; and the tribute populations were unusually unrewarding as a source of subservient labor: they could not relieve the Aztecs' meat hunger; and they themselves ate up much more of the grain surplus while carrying it to their masters. The Aztec solution was grim but cost-efficient: they treated their captives the same way Midwestern cornbelt farmers treated their hogs. They walked the grain harvest to Tenochtitlán on the hoof. . . . The scarcity of animal food among the Aztecs did not compel them to eat human flesh; it simply made the political advantages of suppressing cannibalism less compelling.
>
> (Harris 1985: 232)

For some, following George Bernard Shaw, meat eating is akin to cannibalism without the main course. For Fiddes, meat eating is perceived as symbolic of human power over nature (wild beasts). As the environment has worsened, the notion of what constitutes nature has changed the global ecology and, given the domestication and mass production of meat and poultry (if not fish, which still remain predominantly wild), then vegetarianism in its various forms is seen as a product of twentieth-century civilisation. Meat has been tamed and so does not present a challenge of nature to be symbolically overpowered by eating it.

At a less exotic level, Ross (1980) charts the decline of pork and the rise of beef in the United States over the past century. He does so by reference to the destruction of buffalo herds and the displacement and confinement of Indians to reservations; the decline of the southern slave culture, organised around pork and beans; the preferred flavour of fresh beef (as opposed to salted pork) made available through refrigeration and transport; the greater by-products available from beef; and, ultimately, the move in the 1900s from grass feed on the Great Plains to the use of corn in feed-lots.

These are undoubtedly crucial factors along with others that are mentioned, such as the role of the hamburger in allowing women to go out to work, and the availability of imports from the Third World. But as an alternative explanation of the actual composition of food consumption, these accounts remain problematic. Methodologically, they tend to substitute the necessary conditions for the existence and predominance of certain foodstuffs for the sufficient conditions for their adoption at the expense of others. The material, economic and social conditions that are emphasised do more analytically to constrain the options available than to explain choice amongst them. In historical retrospect, this easily leads to the presumption that what happened is thereby determined. But as the food choices widen, as among the wealthy of the past and more affluent contemporary populations, the problem intensifies. For as Murcott suggests, there would still be difficulties in explaining, 'learned preferences for elaborate eating among the 18th century European aristocracy, or the ingenious products of the modern food industry' Murcott 1988: 19).

Consequently, although Ross provides a trenchant critique of other food theories, his own description of the triumph of beef over pork by reference to comparative advantage and, ultimately, the rise of monopoly capitalism, is suggestive rather than conclusive. It broadens and shifts the emphasis in the explanatory factors employed but it leaves open the question of what alternative routes were open and whether they could have been adopted and adapted differently. The suspicion must arise that the approach is one informed not only by materialism but also by its anthropological origins in the study of the more primitive societies on the margins of subsistence. Insights borrowed, possibly unconsciously, from the political economy of cannibalism are not necessarily the best utensils with which to assault the rise and fall of Porkopolis (Cincinnati) and its displacement by Chicago as beef capital of the Western world. Confining the explanation of what food is eaten to the narrowest of material factors, and reducing the role of other, especially cultural, influences to dependent consequences, has much less appeal when food provision is distanced from physical survival. For, by the turn of the century, as Levenstein noted:

> Perhaps nothing more symbolises the change in American attitudes towards food between 1896 and 1928 better than the slogans of the winning presidential candidates in each of those years. William McKinley rode to victory by promising workmen 'the full dinner pail'. Herbert Hoover promised them 'a chicken in every pot'. Quality had replaced quantity as the prime consideration.
>
> (Levenstein 1988: 194)

And, more recently, as Waslieu observed: 'For the majority of the US population, income is no longer the principal limiting factor of what foods are chosen; instead, the time available for food purchases, preparation, and consumption has become of paramount importance' (Waslieu 1988: 240).

There is, then, an enormous variation in diets within as well as between countries, and despite (perhaps even because of) the monopolisation and globalisation of the food industry, it is not certain that this variation is declining, even given the more obvious examples to the contrary offered by McDonalds and Coca-Cola.[24] In other words, it is far from clear why, for modern capitalism, the determinants of food consumption should be any more based on material conditions than is the fashion system for clothes.

So far in this section, the discussion of the consumption food system has leant towards supply side explanations in a reaction against a focus on individual food choice alone. But such choice cannot be simply set aside. To bring it down to earth or, more exactly, to the hearth, consider the recently evolving literature on distribution of consumption within the family or household. Much of this takes as its justifiable starting point a rejection of the Chicago household economics associated with Becker (1976; 1981). In this, orthodox economic theory of resource allocation is applied to the family, recognising eventually the absence of market mechanisms within the household and, consequently, drawing upon transactions cost literature (Pollak 1985). In this, children, for example, are treated as part cost, part consumption good, and part insurance for old age.

A major deficiency with this approach is the failure to recognise power, conflict and control within the household. In particular, it cannot be presumed that distribution of resources within the family is subject to harmonious or, even necessarily, co-operative allocation and re-allocation. With the increasing levels of divorce and family breakdown, this would require at least a parallel for the household with a theory of bankruptcy for the household parallel with that for the firm – something with which orthodox economics is already uncomfortable. But, presumably, family breakdown is only the end (or mid) point of continuing conflict.

This can be recognised, as in the work of Pahl (1980; 1983; 1989), through positing different systems of management and control of the family budget – with differing implications for the relative benefits of men and of women. In the specific context of food, Wilson observes that there were roles for:

> Food as an expression of gender differences (first in preparation and second in consumption); food as part of a healthy life style; food as a way of meeting family preferences; and food as a marker of status. Finally . . . household income and household financial organisation cannot be ignored in any consideration of food systems.
>
> (G. Wilson 1989: 174)

The work of Charles and Kerr (1986; 1988) and Kerr and Charles (1986) brings to the fore much more sharply the conflicts involved over the food system within the family. They conclude that three separate processes are at work. Two of these lie within the family organisation itself – through the role of patriarchy and the gender division of labour – in which women do the work and men get the best food. The third major influence to which they point, the influence of class, recognises that the impact of the other two influences is not uniform across socioeconomic groups.[25]

Such analyses of the family are to be welcomed in so far as they focus upon its internal workings, something which has been neglected both for ideological reasons as well as for practical reasons concerning the availability of information. However, the method of analysis continues to reflect an affinity with the household economics with which it seeks to break – although this may have more to do with its origins in the sociology of the family. For the family is constructed as a basic unit of analysis, a multitude of islands within the ocean of society. Whilst the latter is subject to sea-changes which undoubtedly affect the internal organisation of the family, the relation between family and society is poorly developed. Indeed, the three categories of patriarchy, division of labour, and class can at best serve to describe the changes that take place rather than to explain them.[26]

There has, after all, been a long tradition of examining the gender division of food in primitive and Third World societies because, in this case, the consequences of inequalities are poor nutrition and higher chances of death through disease.[27] Exactly the same three categories of analysis could be used to uncover these inequalities, but obviously they would be entirely insensitive to the different organisation of such families and societies. In some cases, for example, women doing hard manual wage labour have the privilege of eating bought food outside the home in order to provide conveniently the necessary calories for the physical effort that they exert in earning cash for the household, still controlled by the male.[28]

What we know for contemporary advanced societies is that changing divisions of labour within (but especially outside) the home, in conjunction with the changing provision of the foods available (especially convenience foods), are intimately connected with each other (and with broader patterns of consumption, family organisation and more general socioeconomic change). Nor is there some simple relation between these factors in so far as Piachaud (1982), for example, observes that those families containing women who do more paid work do not necessarily possess more labour-saving durables.[29] Thus, it is important to study the changing organisation of the family and its division of labour, resources and power. But these can only be explained, particularly in relation to consumption, by an analysis of broader scope, encompassing systems of provision and their relation to other socioeconomic factors.

These can interact with one another in complex ways. Children, for example, tend to gain nutritional knowledge from their mothers whilst they spend time together in the kitchen during the preparation of meals. With the advent of microwaves, mothers now spend less time in the kitchen and so less time 'educating' their children.[30] On the other hand, mothers tend to feel guilty about not providing home cooking which is associated with 'good' food and may compensate by trying to serve more nutritious convenience foods, possibly learning and passing on different food knowledge and habits to their children in the shorter available time.

To conclude: even this partial survey of analyses of food choice points to a multitude and variety of influential factors, selection from which provides for an equally varied menu of theories. Every element along the food system appears to be of potential importance. Consequently, food systems as a whole must be examined in order to discover who we are by virtue of what we eat. Such a general conclusion is not so vague as to be worthless, for it is open to specific application when bringing together vertical and horizontal factors. This has already been demonstrated in the previous chapters, where adulteration and manufacturing of food were discussed. It will now be taken up in the context of advertising and retailing.

# 14

# ADVERTISING

## ADVERTISING

This chapter addresses the role of advertising in the selling of commodities. Broadly, two different approaches have dominated the subject, each corresponding to a different aspect of the commodity. The first approach to advertising, as outlined in section 1, is primarily concerned with the ideological reconstruction of the use value of commodities through advertising, which acts to give commodities new or different meanings. The use value approach corresponds to the experience of targeted consumers who must be convinced of the desirability of the commodity, the worth of its use value whether as water or diamond.

As a result, the way in which advertising is understood analytically tends to depend upon a prior theoretical stance adopted towards consumption. As seen in Chapter 2, use values for Haug contain an aesthetic illusion organised around sexuality. Accordingly, adverts would work upon this to effect a sale. However consumption is interpreted analytically, a theory of advertising lurks not far behind. And, in this context, the economic content of the commodity, the source of its exchange value, as opposed to the constructed source of its desirability, tends to be neglected. In this light, section 3 explores how advertising has been understood in a number of academic disciplines. Section 4 discusses the relationship between advertising and material culture, particularly in the context of sexism.

Before these two sections, the second broad approach to advertising is outlined in section 2. It is based on the *exchange value* of the commodity and is primarily economic in content. It seeks to locate advertising within the circulation of capital, as a lever of competition, either through the high fixed costs needed to create brand loyalty and inhibit entry by other firms or as a more general means of manipulating demand. When this economic role is interpreted within a more critical perspective, there is usually some greater recognition of the ideological function of advertising – in systemically supporting consumer society, however this might be construed, to conform with the dictates of mass production.

Section 5 gives a cursory consideration to the performance of advertising in its economic and ideological roles. This serves as a preface to section 6, which argues that both of the two approaches outlined earlier, as well as attempts to combine and synthesise them, omit the influence of capitalist production on the development of the content of the commodity and, hence, by extension, on advertising. In other words, those who see advertising as simply an attempt to enhance sale, whether from an exchange value or use value perspective, have generally taken what has been termed a *horizontal* analytical perspective which explores different commodities merely for their relation to supply and demand or to the media culture, sexism, etc. What is termed a *vertical* perspective is proposed as an alternative. This posits each commodity as the creation of an interdependent system of production, distribution, retailing and of specific cultural determinants including, where appropriate, advertising. Recognising that the origins of, and linkages between, each of these factors will be different for each commodity makes it possible to explain the changing extent and nature of advertising rather than simply interpreting it at the visible end of each of these chains. A comparative analysis of the advertising of food and clothing in Chapters 15 and 16 demonstrates the implications of this alternative approach.

## 1 ADVERTISING AND USE VALUE

As all who have studied political economy know, a commodity is both an exchange value and a use value. Adam Smith constructs the famous paradox of water with its high value in use but low value in exchange in contrast to the position held by diamonds. The use value of water is its capacity to satisfy thirst and to guarantee survival, that of diamonds primarily to demonstrate beauty and wealth (leaving aside their industrial use). However, the tidiness of this contrast has been eroded over the past two hundred years. Water, at least in its bottled form, has become a new fad, signifying a number of altered conditions, not least the ability to pay for what has been otherwise freely available from the tap. As diamonds are deemed to be 'forever', bottled water is arguably relatively more expensive as a form of conspicuous consumption – at least on the current account.

In Chapter 2, the simple separation of the commodity into a use value and an exchange value was seen as the logical starting point for a much more complex anatomy of the commodity – one which looked forward to its consumption and backwards to its origins in production. For use value, reference was made to Haug's idea that commodities were endowed with sexuality through advertising. As water has now adopted the mantle of a use value that is socially constructed, so it too becomes subject to the pressures of advertising. Adverts for water take at least two forms. One literally stresses the natural properties of bottled water, idealising the mineral content and the environment from which it is drawn. Images are employed not far removed from those that once were used to promote cigarettes – mountain streams linked with the freshness of menthol, the country within Salem, or the cowboy and open space with Marlboro. The other form of advert works on the lifestyle content of the product. To drink Perrier is to belong to a certain set, one which appreciates advertising of a particular sort that is clever rather than direct, entertaining rather than hard-hitting; sophistication, in a word, is for sale. This is exemplified by the genre of surrealism in advertising that has been pioneered recently by Benson and Hedges, and has been copied by other tobacco manufacturers in Britain, like Silk Cut. People can now buy because they appreciate the advert at least as much as the product.[1]

Clearly, to make the distinction between the different types of adverts on the basis of their realism is somewhat forced. Even if adverts were to be confined to a faithful and comprehensive listing of physical properties, they would be guilty of the utmost in commodity fetishism, stripping goods of their social content whether as fruit from South Africa or salmonella eggs from the hen battery. Accordingly, one approach to the analysis of advertising is to focus on the use value aspect of the commodity. In this, commodities are perceived to be presented as something which they are not – in order to enhance their chances of sale. This can relate to the product itself – the notion of Golden Wonder Peanuts as 'jungle' fresh is about as credible as fish untouched by water. Or it can be conveyed through the ambience of the product's setting through a depiction of the mundane events of respectability in family life, as in 'Persil Washes Whitest', or the excitements associated with seduction, in any number of adverts for drinks, perfumes, clothes, etc.

In looking at the use value side of advertising, the starting point is the gap between the physical properties of the commodity and the properties that it is presented as having. Relative to Haug's notion of aesthetic illusion which advertising creates through sexuality, Williams takes a broader view of both consumption and advertising, referring to the 'Magic System':

> Advertising, in its modern forms, then operates to preserve the consumption ideal from the criticism inexorably made of it by experience. If the consumption of individual goods leaves that whole area of human need unsatisfied, the attempt is made, by magic, to associate this consumption with human desires to which it has no real reference. You do not only buy an object: you buy social respect, discrimination, health, beauty, success, power to control your environment. The magic obscures the real sources of general satisfaction because their discovery would involve radical change in the whole common way of life.
>
> (Williams 1980: 188)

This 'magic' emerges most clearly where, in the competition between brands of what are otherwise essentially identical products, advertising serves the function of differentiating between them. For Williamson:

> There is very little real difference between brands of product within any category, such as detergents, margarine, paper towels and so on. Therefore, it is the first function of an advertisement to *create* a differentiation between one particular product and others in the same category. It does this by providing the product with an 'image'. . . . The bulk of advertising covers exactly the areas where goods are the same: cigarettes, cornflakes, beer, soap.
>
> (Williamson 1978: 24)

In quoting an advertising executive, White (1988: 117) points to this artificial differentiation as constituting advertising in its pure form: 'I like cigarette advertising. It's advertising in its purest sense – no product difference, but a perception of difference in the product.' Here the emphasis is upon the role of advertising in manufacturing a difference between one product and others. This is done by projecting the difference into an enhanced consequence of individual consumption. But the distinction between a product and how it is perceived is not solely determined by advertising, since it depends upon the social and cultural context within which consumption takes place – and is not unique to commodity-producing society. Precisely for this reason, advertising can address the physical properties of the commodity at one extreme, its illusory properties at the other, or the gap itself between the two. In the 'Persil Washes Whitest' adverts, all of these are combined. There is a statement about the physical properties of the commodity, the gap between it and other products, and an inevitable accompanying image of superior status or a life enhanced as a consequence of its use.

This role for advertising has been seen in a number of different ways. For Dunn (1986: 51), 'advertising soon became less a sales effort for specific products than an expression of lifestyle, self-esteem, and social order'. Leiss *et al.* (1986: 59) claim that, 'most consumer items today are the combinations of two types of characteristics, physical and imputed'. In the more abstract formulation of Goldman and Wilson (1983: 123), 'advertising teaches us to consume, not the product, but its sign. What it stands for is more important than what it is'.[2] Most simply for Berman (1981: 47), 'it sells the mundane, but invokes the fabulous'. At its extreme, Clark (1988: 11) argues that: 'products themselves are no longer sold by advertising – increasingly they *are* the advertising' and quotes an advertising executive dealing in beer:

> The many competitive brands are virtually identical in terms of taste, colour and alcohol delivery, and after two or three pints even an expert couldn't tell them apart. So the consumer is literally drinking the advertising, and the advertising is the brand.
>
> (Clark 1988: 24)

Marchand argues that advertising serves as a hall of distorting mirrors: 'People did not usually want ads to reflect themselves, their immediate social relationships, or their broader society exactly. They wanted not a true mirror but a *Zerrspiegel*, a distorting mirror that would enhance certain images' (Marchand 1985: xvii). Marchand's purpose is to use ads as raw materials in unravelling their distorted reflection of history, to 'work backward to the underlying social realities by correcting advertising's depiction of American society for the refractions introduced by such biases, motives, and assumptions' (ibid.: xx). Here, there is some recognition of another way in which advertising might be viewed – as creating both an illusory product and a corresponding consumer. For Lasch, 'In a simpler time, advertising merely called attention to the product and extolled its advantages. Now it manufactures a product of its own: the consumer, perpetually unsatisfied, restless, anxious, and bored' (Lasch 1979: 137).

Consumption and commodities are offered, through advertising, as the relief from these and other 'age-old discontents of loneliness, sickness, weariness, lack of sexual satisfaction'; their inability to fulfil their promise entails further self-indulgence. Featherstone describes the process whereby the mass production of images transforms cheap, imitation goods into, 'the symbolic promise of luxury, abundance, style and hedonism' (Featherstone 1983: 4). But the mechanisms for doing this become part and parcel of the consumption process; commodities 'become subjected to a continual process of symbolisation and resymbolisation . . . commodities masquerade as experiences and experiences are turned into commodities . . . to experience the image, the illusion, the spectacle' (ibid.: 6). The ad as experience is part of the product.

This extensive referencing has been cited to demonstrate the common features of the use value approach. From the same starting point, namely the commodity, as that adopted by the 'exchange value schools' (to be discussed in the next section), it moves in the opposite direction. Both begin with the notion that advertising may endow materially identical commodities with an illusory differentiation between them. But one then focuses on the implications for economic factors, such as competition, aggregate demand or efficiency, while the other is concerned with what advertising makes of the commodity as something that has already departed from the economic arena. Thus, each of the use value approaches, with a greater or lesser degree of complexity, seeks to uncover the relationship between the commodity as it is and as it is presented and consumed. In understanding the nature of advertising, it necessarily shifts attention away from the commodity's economic and productive origins. The emphasis on interpreting the created image of the product, and the focus on the individual as consumer, also fail to connect with the economic effects of advertising associated with the exchange value approach.

To some extent, this might be explained by the distance set up by advertising itself between consumption and the economy, especially production. The focus of advertising is upon the isolated individual (or household) as consumer. Williamson (1986: 229) notes the 'absence of any sense of a relationship between the spheres of production and consumption' and perceives this to be an effect of advertising.[3] It is significantly rare for an image of paid work to be employed within advertising – not only because it has unpleasant associations but also because paid work and consumption (within the home) are structurally separated from each other in capitalist society.[4]

The use value approach to advertising tends to autonomise consumption as a self-contained activity which gives it creative licence in determining the 'content' of the commodity, a process which dovetails with the increasing focus by cultural theory on consumption at the expense of production (see Williams 1980: 45–6). Baudrillard's use value approach is perhaps the most extreme example of the separation between consumption and production. He emphasises a separation, not simply between consumption as it is and as it is depicted and understood, but also a separation between the commodity and its deeper origins in material conditions. For him, there is created a 'symbolic exchange value' which tends to take on a life of its own, so that what the product is or represents becomes independent of its physical properties. This viewpoint has drawn criticism from some quarters, such as Goldman (1987: 692): 'Instead of specifying the actual mode of production and form of social labour which gird the production of sign values, Baudrillard moves to the clouds.' And, more explicitly, Gardner and Sheppard argue:

> This is not to say that products act *only* as signs or symbols – a position which Baudrillard seems to arrive at in his later work. Obviously, objects have functional attributes, but use-value now includes these intangible, more emotional, less predictable *meanings*. While advertising and marketing can make use of this fantasy system, if you like, they can never exhaust it. Total colonisation of the psyche (another Baudrillian nightmare) is impossible.
>
> (Gardner and Sheppard 1989: 50)

The idea that the use values of commodities are more complex than they appear lies at the heart of the study of consumption as material culture. This has been emphasised most recently through the development of discourse theory and semiotics. It is also commonplace amongst those advertisers who have increasingly geared their advertising towards the setting or context within which they place their products rather than relying upon the commodity to speak for itself in terms of its physical properties. What is offered for sale is a variety of contexts or particular feelings, such as those associated with fantasy, humour or exotic surroundings. Thus, Leiss *et al.* (1986: 46) point to the informational and transformational role played by advertising with increasing emphasis on the latter, since depiction of favourable lifestyles and attitudes are targeted rather than the products themselves. This is all, however, in sharp contrast to the exchange value approach which looks to the economic impact of advertising.

## 2 ADVERTISING AND EXCHANGE VALUE

The exchange value approach to advertising emphasises its economic function and its informational role. Commodities are taken to have well-defined properties which advertising either displays or conceals. For the orthodoxy, advertising is good or bad as it tells the truth or not; or, more exactly, if it performs a useful function for consumers, even where it misleads them, by informing them of the availability of a (new) product. Its direct economic effect is to shift out the demand curve for the good concerned. It is the means by which even the smallest differences between goods can be created or enhanced, thereby giving rise to product differentiation, as revealed by Fox:

> If a client's product was identical to its competition and could not be altered to acquire USP [unique selling proposition], the public might still be told something new about it: 'This is not a uniqueness of the product, but it assumes a uniqueness, and cloaks itself in a uniqueness, as a claim'.
>
> (Fox 1984: 192)

Fox gives the examples of beer bottles washed with live steam (like all bottles) and tobacco that is roasted (like all tobacco). Theoretical underpinnings for the effects of this activity is that of the discriminating monopolist or monopolistic or imperfect competition, as derived from Chamberlin (1933) and Robinson (1933), respectively. Here, starting from the same point as the use value approach, namely the commodity, emphasis is upon distinctions between producers (and their products); distinctions between consumers and the consumed (as for the use value approach to advertising) fade into the background.

More generally, within economics, advertising has usually been slotted into a pre-existing theory. In oligopoly theory, it has been seen as a fixed cost which can serve as a barrier to entry, or as part of information theory, with search costs and asymmetries. As such, it is a response to or a source of market imperfections.[5] Advertising can also be a response to scale economies, where markets have to be created, through branding, in order to take advantage of high output with low unit costs.

But the most transparent example of economic theory colonising advertising as a subject is to be found in Kaldor (1950). He recognises that most commercial advertising is far removed from the transmission of accurate information, and so it must be judged on its indirect economic effects:

> If advertising is to be justified it must be by reference to its indirect consequences rather than to its direct benefits; it must be justified by demonstrating that improvements in productive and distributive efficiency resulting from advertising more than offset both the direct cost of advertising and the balance of further social losses caused by distortion of demand.
>
> (Kaldor 1950: 7)

In a macroeconomic context, reflecting his Keynesian orientation, advertising can perform a useful function even though it is a waste of resources:

> In an economy where the general level of production is determined by effective demand, and not by the amount of the available resources, the ordinary rules of welfare economics are, in a sense, reversed: here 'waste' is economical and economy is wasteful. In such an economy, a higher output of any particular commodity or service will not mean a lower, but usually a higher output of other things; the marginal social cost of one commodity or service, therefore, is not positive, but zero or even negative.
>
> (Kaldor 1950: 10)

Furthermore, reflecting his own Keynesian preoccupation with the different propensities to consume of different classes, advertising is seen as promoting consumption through the middle classes (to both a small and undesirable extent) and through a shift of income from profits (spent on advertising) to the wages and salaries of those employed by it.

At the microeconomic level, there is emphasis upon the potential gains from increasingly large-scale production – this corresponds to Kaldor's interest in the dynamics of productivity increase through growth. Otherwise, he points to advertising as part of a competitive battle for dominance between manufacturers and wholesalers, with his own preference for advertising by retailers in the belief that this is liable to impart information in the strict sense.

A different approach is found in Arriaga's (1984) Marxist critique of advertising. Her contribution, although far from prominent, is a useful starting point from which to pose a critical alternative. She locates advertising as an expenditure and activity within the sphere of circulation and, by reference to empirical observation, limits it further to the sale primarily of consumer goods (particularly goods of US origin or destination since roughly half of world advertising is estimated to be accounted for by the United States). First, Arriaga argues that 'advertising is restricted to the process of circulation of some consumer goods and services leaving out all Department I goods (i.e. means of production and raw materials) and consumer goods that are not advertised' (Arriaga 1984: 54). This proposition is empirically derived and is certainly not an absolute nor an analytically derived truth (where it is not a tautology). A glance at any professional or trade journal will demonstrate that all sorts of capital goods and raw materials goods are advertised. The difference between consumer goods and capital goods is that one involves large numbers of sellers buying small amounts whilst the other involves small numbers buying large amounts. This clearly has implications for the cost-effectiveness of different types of sales or promotions efforts, but it does not confine advertising to consumption goods.

A second point is that the logic of the purchaser is different in each case. Whilst the general consumer may be systemically bound to economic and social reproduction, this does not assert itself through an individualised and common imperative as simple as the coercion on capitalists to generate profitability. It would be a mistake to presume that the only influence on capitalists is the generation of profit – the choice of machines that extract surplus value and control the workforce do not, for example, exhaust the parameters of management style, ethos and design. Nevertheless, the need to be profitable does dictate that commodities purchased as constant capital should be able to function as such, thereby limiting the fantasy element and promoting the informational content of advertising for producer goods. For this reason, there may be more informational content to producer advertising, although it is infamous for its sexism, presuming a male work culture and male control of purchasing.

Arriaga's assertion that advertising has nothing to do with the actual consumption of goods is also false in so far as advertising has an effect both on the demand for goods and what it is that is perceived as being consumed. The assertion is motivated by the need to identify advertising as 'functional for capital and . . . subordinated to the general logic of capital reproduction and accumulation' (Arriaga 1984: 53). Necessarily, this leads to the location of advertising as part of merchant capital. From this a number of insights follow: that advertising has the ability to become a specialised activity, thereby reducing the costs and time of circulation for individual capitalists; that it tends to appropriate normal profit but not to generate surplus value; and that the limits to advertising are imposed by the scale of production (you cannot sell more than you have produced).[6]

This approach has certain strengths. It locates advertising structurally within a well-defined (Marxist) economic theory. But this strength is a source of weakness also. For it fails to address the specificity of advertising as an economic function within the sphere of exchange, let alone confronting the ideological and cultural significance that it has. In addition, in analysis of commercial capital, Fine (1985/6) argues that the structural differentiation between the spheres of production and exchange (and within exchange between merchant and interest-bearing capital) only exists tendentially – activities involved in moving from production to final sale may fall at different times on different sides of the divide. This is obvious in the case of transport, an issue discussed by Marx. Does it fall under the control of merchants or producers, and with what implications for whether it is an act of production or circulation?[7] As will be seen in Chapters 15 and 16, who advertises and how is of some significance, and this relates to the evolving structure of the economy, differentiated by sector. This casts some doubt on Arriaga's proposition that advertising has nothing to do with the sphere of production of any good. While advertising is not production, it certainly can have an intimate connection to the sphere of production. It has to sell its products!

So, in Arriaga's hands, advertising is a part of merchant capital with its associated capital-logic and empirically contingent areas of application – the realm of US economic hegemony and some unspecified consumer goods. From a different perspective, the same procedure of imposing a given economic theory holds true of neoclassical theory, for which advertising is reduced to a corollary of oligopoly theory. It also applies to Arriaga's main target, viz., the monopoly capital school of Baran and Sweezy (and to its more orthodox counterpart in writers such as J.K. Galbraith), for which advertising serves to manipulate and create what are perceived to be false needs. For each of these contributions, advertising is an analytical sideshow for the display of more general theoretical propositions.

In the last case, however, advertising is understood at a systemic level. For the monopoly capital school, the central proposition is the stagnationary tendency associated with low levels of demand from (monopoly) investment and wage income. Consequently, other economic and social phenomena are ordered in terms of their acting as counter-effects to the inadequacy of demand.[8] There is the paradox that increased costs and reduced profitability to the economic system as a whole tend to have a positive impact upon its functioning (as argued by Kaldor also). In particular, advertising not only expands demand but also absorbs potential surplus that would otherwise contribute to stagnation. Similarly, for Galbraith, the affluent society is one that functions partly through the mechanism of advertising, to create an upward spiral of demands that are only satisfied by being continually extended (see Galbraith 1962: 135; 1969: 46–7; 1973: 137–8).

Thus, advertising creates as well as satisfies unwanted needs. However, since it is inadequate simply to rely upon the psychological manipulation of society alone, advertising ought to be linked analytically to economic imperatives, such as those associated with large-scale capital. Instead, there tends to be a critical stance towards what is perceived to be excessive consumption, and those influences that are held responsible for encouraging it at the expense of nobler motives. As Kellner notes of the moralistic critique of advertising, there is more going on than that: 'Commodities are alluring sirens whose symbolic qualities and exchange-value seduces the consumer into purchase and consumption. There is both a manichaeism and puritanism in this perspective' (Kellner 1983: 71).

Advertising has also been systemically situated within the theory of Fordism as a central component in the creation of a mass production *and* a mass consumption society.[9] In this perspective, the historical rise of advertising as a major business within the United States is dated to correspond with the arrival of mass production and Taylorism in the 1920s. Workers were not only to be made to labour like machines; they were also to be manufactured as consumers (see especially Ewen 1976; Lasch 1979: 155–7). This is perceived to be as much a part of business strategy as the Taylorism adopted in production. It is specific both to individual products and to working-class life in general, which is perceived to have previously resisted the invasion of capitalism into its lifestyle, (Ewen 1976: 18).[10]

In the analysis of those such as Galbraith and Ewen, the focus moves away from economic factors alone, although advertising is still assigned a generalised role across commodities.[11] This might be described as a movement from critiques of the economy masquerading as critiques of advertising towards what Leiss *et al.* (1986: 30) describe as 'critiques of society masquerading as critiques of advertising'. Critiques of advertising within both the economic or social domain do tend to see it as lending specific support to a more general critique of society – just as those who support capitalism view advertising as a necessary evil.[12] The result is that the specificity of advertising has long been lost within the general (economic) logic of the analysis involved. As has been seen in the previous section, this unfortunately applies equally to the approach that focuses on use values in advertising.

From our perspective, the exchange value or economic approach to advertising fails to distinguish between one commodity and another precisely because it sets aside use value. Advertising tends to be treated like any other cost for its quantitative effect on exchange value. It may have a greater or lesser impact across different commodities, but this is not explored (there is a parallel here with economics, where the derivation of preferences for consumption goods is also left unexplained). Even where the exchange value approach takes on a critical edge, condemning the cost of creating false needs, it is little concerned with what these are, as long as they can be shown to exist. Whether it be in the commercial usurpation of working-class norms in the 1930s (as for Ewen) or the co-existence of public squalor and private affluence in the postwar United States (as for Galbraith), the general economic function performed by advertising is too broad to be analytically married successfully to an account of what is actually consumed (except by lofty critique) and how it is to be understood as such.

## 3 ADVERTISING AND SOCIAL THEORY

In contrast, in social, as opposed to economic theory, advertising is seen as addressing the perception of what is consumed. But it would be a mistake to believe that this is a novel point of departure from economic analysis, derived from recent developments in social theory. Each orthodoxy in social science has had its own theory of consumption and, with it, an implicit presumption of the intended or unintended role of advertising. Only economics has essentially ignored the social construction of use value in its focus upon the informational, competitive and utility-maximising aspects of advertising. Advertising, in this perspective, may lead you to buy something you did not want if you were misled, but this does not extend to the act of consumption itself, where the truth is revealed in the utility provided. In other words, for economics, a car is a car, and there is no room for the idea, for example, that 'You Are What You Drive' – as a 1984 advertising slogan for Renault, quoted in Leiss *et al.* (1986: 23), would have us believe.

Psychology operates with a far richer individual motivational and behavioural basis than that provided by economics. Here, the major determinants of consumption are the feelings generated by and about commodities. Accordingly, advertising is perceived to endow commodities with (positive)

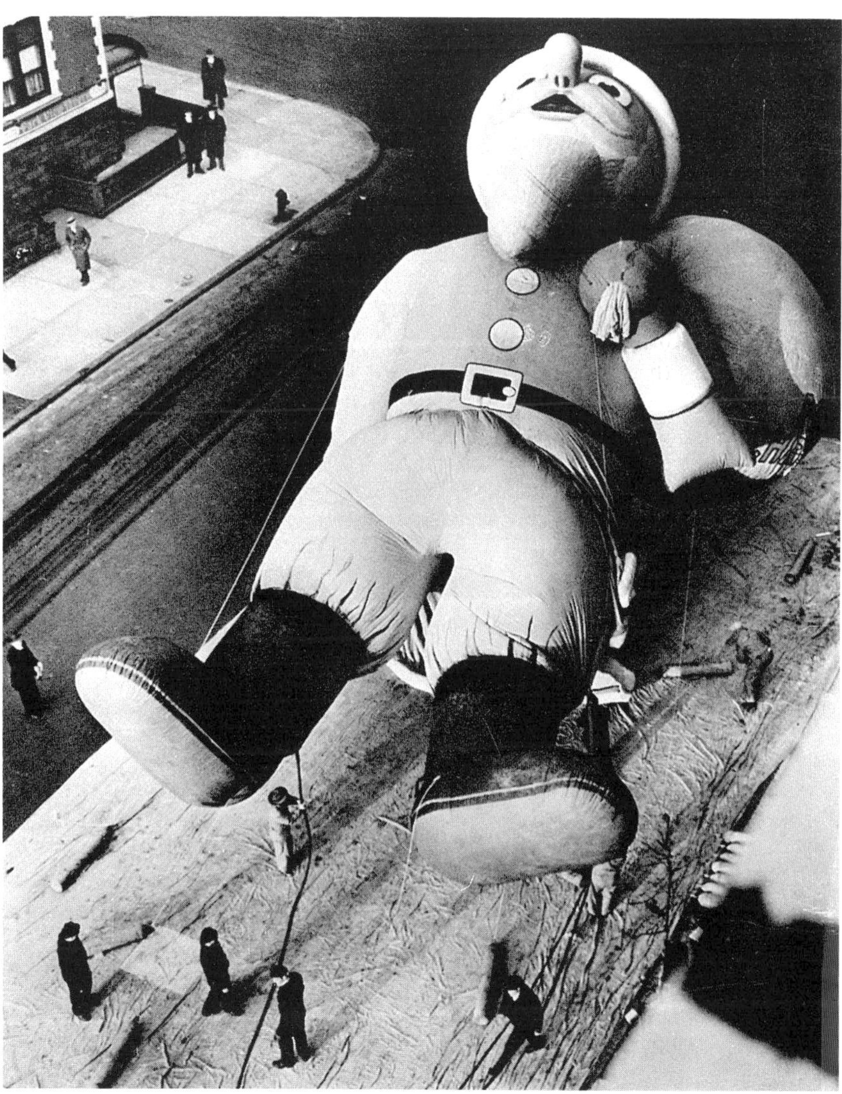

*Figure 6* Father Xmas usurps another festival: Macy's Thanksgiving Day Parade, 1962.
*Source*: Photo by Weegee

psychological properties – from which the advertiser hopes to solicit the impulse to buy, possess and consume – through the use of slogans like 'Naughty but Nice', for example, for cakes made with fresh cream. This constitutes a neat inversion of commodity fetishism, whereby things are personified rather than social relations reified! It opens up a world of selling points for the advertiser to exploit. These may not all be equally effective with every consumer; Grafton-Small and Linstead (1989) argue that each advert is open to a different individual interpretation with uncertain effects.[13]

For anthropology, consumption is perceived as a ritual. The standard reference for this anthropological view is Douglas and Isherwood (1980). The link of such ritual to the commercial world, however, is more immediately recognised in the figure of Father Christmas. Belk charts the displacement of Jesus Christ by Father Christmas as the triumph of commerce over religion:

> The similarities of the secular Santa figure to the religious Christ figure include miracles (flying reindeer, travelling to all houses of the world in one night, and, reminiscent of the loaves and fishes miracle of Christ, Santa's bottomless bag of toys), elves as Apostles, reindeer as manger animals, letters to Santa as secular prayers pledging 'good' behavior if they are granted, and offerings of cookies and milk as sacrifices placed upon a fireplace mantle altar. It is also possible to consider Santa's travels on Christmas Eve as parallel to Christ's journeys and secular Christmas carols about Santa as hymns. Just as Christ brought his gifts of love and salvation to earth and then ascended to heaven, Santa brings his gifts of toys and treats and then ascends up the chimney. Furthermore, Santa is immortal, omniscient, knows how children behave, and holds them ultimately accountable for their actions by bestowing the rewards that he alone can offer.
>
> (Belk 1989: 117)

Belk's analysis, quoted at length to highlight the point, reveals the potential use of anthropology to explain consumption, and hence advertising as a corollary, through its recognition of the transfer of ritual from one context to another. Advertising has both exploited and contributed to the re-ritualisation of Christmas, necessarily promoting its commercial potential even when drawing on religious imagery and ideals in its advertisements.

For sociology, the treatment of consumption is primarily either through status theory or through socialisation, as in emulation, although the two are not entirely separate. For the definition of status, consumption allows differentiation from those who do not possess or consume and emulation of, or uniformity with, those that do. In this and other respects, consumption is organised around the learning and reproduction of social roles. Advertising can be perceived to be addressing these aspirations and roles.

## 4 ADVERTISING AND MATERIAL CULTURE

The different approaches sampled from the social sciences can be construed as relevant to advertising through the particular way in which consumption is understood in each of them. They inevitably raise the question of the causal relation between the two – do advertisements serve and reflect or rather *create* the material culture which they incorporate? There is some evidence that advertising in the 1920s did conspire to create an ideology of consumer society to boost the demand for mass production. However, this is now of only limited continuing relevance since advertising is predominantly competitive and focused on the selling of particular products. Furthermore, the dynamics of historical change in advertising and consumption is little appreciated in the context of theory that autonomises consumption and deconstructs the imagery of commodities. This is indirectly recognised by Sinclair, who observes the limitations of much of the use value approach because of its neglect of the origins of commodities:

> We should look at the marketing moves which bring products and advertisements into being, and at the responses which they elicit from their markets or audiences. Structuralist and especially post-structuralist theories are inherently limited in both of these aspects, because for them all that matters is contained within the linguistic structures of advertisements as texts.
>
> (Sinclair 1987: 61–2)

By now, it should be apparent that advertising functions within marketing by concealing as much as it reveals (just as commodity fetishism functions in relation to production). Consequently, (consciously) interpreting adverts is highly dependent upon the sensibilities of those involved in interpretation (whether as consumers or as social scientists) because each will have a view of what is hidden or absent as well as of what is explicitly present. As Goldman observes:

> Readers' active interpretation of advertising texts may result in ratification of advertisers' 'preferred meanings' and in 'aberrant' meanings of one sort or another. Even readers who share tacit social knowledge about how ads mean, may produce disparate interpretations of what is meant. Interpretations vary by subculture and interpretive community as well as by class, gender and race.
>
> (Goldman 1987: 695)

Other commentators express similar views:

> Semiology suffers from a number of related weaknesses ... it is heavily dependent upon the skill and of the individual analyst. In the hands of someone like Roland Barthes or Judith Williamson, it is a wonderfully creative tool that allows one to reach the deeper levels of

> meaning-construction in ads. A less skilful practitioner, however, can do little more than state the obvious in a complex and often pretentious manner. As a result there is little chance to establish consistency or reliability in these types of studies, that is, sufficient level of agreement among analysts on what is found in the message.[14]
>
> (Leiss *et al.* 1986: 165)

Consider racism, for example. The days of overt racism within advertising are passing – blacks can no longer be portrayed as inferior or subordinate to whites, as was the case, for example, in the advert where a little white girl enquires of her black companion, 'Why doesn't your mamma wash you with Fairy Soap?'[15] Racism now presents itself in a more subtle way – usually through the absence of blacks altogether (an absence commonly overlooked even by the decoders of advertisements), or by their presentation in an exotic context, or through the image of harmony and equality between different ethnic groups. Where blacks are present, it often serves as an advertising ploy – either to flaunt or flout the new conventions of anti-racism. In general, however, blacks are still largely excluded from the (Western) world of advertising.[16]

The same is not true of women; sexism explicitly persists in advertising.[17] But this is more complex than the simple exploitation of women. There are two ways in which women and images of them are used in advertising (corresponding to the enhancement of use value on the one hand and of exchange value on the other). For women serve both as a means of persuasion and as a market for products (EC 1987, Annex: 17). In appealing to men in the former case, they are most likely to be employed as sex objects in order to sell 'male' products such as alcoholic drink, tobacco and motor cars:

> Sexual access to the female is the reward for buying the advertised product. Viewed singly, most adverts . . . seem acceptable [!]. However, after viewing hundreds of slides showing women's portrayal in advertising, the cumulative impact is extremely powerful.
>
> (Courtney and Whipple 1983: 11)

But most of the commodities that are most heavily advertised are purchased predominantly by women, especially those used on a regular basis in housework – such as food and cleansing materials. On TV, ads for these are directed at women both by their content and by the timing of their appearance (aired in the afternoon).[18] Moreover, these ads rely almost exclusively upon the presumed effectiveness of male voice-overs to explain to a woman why she should purchase the product in question:

> 75 percent of all advertisements using females were for products generally found in the kitchen or bathroom . . . 38 percent of women were shown inside the home, but only 14 percent of men . . . voice-overs were predominantly male: 87 percent used a male voice, 6 percent a

female voice, and 7 percent a chorus.

(Courtney and Whipple 1983: 17)

In general, women are more likely than men to be portrayed as married, less likely to be in groups or the workplace (other than in the home engaged in housework).[19] This applies equally to the socialisation of children:

> Like the adult female, the girl in commercials plays a stereotyped role. Girls are portrayed as more passive than boys. They are shown assisting their mothers in serving men and boys. They are shown learning household tasks and ways to become beautiful. They are not shown learning how to become independent and autonomous.
>
> (Courtney and Whipple 1983: 23)

Interestingly, Jay (1987) finds in nineteenth-century trade card advertising that, whilst women were frequently portrayed as dutiful wives and loving mothers, their role as explicit sex objects was notably absent – with the possible exception of ads for corsetry, primarily aimed at a female clientele.

Most recent studies of sexism within advertising tend to conclude that its imagery has lagged far behind economic and social change and attitudes (Courtney and Whipple 1983: 69), particularly given the growing participation of women in the workforce. Moreover public opinion polls, 'consistently find that the majority of consumers agree that advertising is insulting to women' (ibid.: 41). Indeed, more 'realistic' portrayal of women in ads have been found to be more effective than traditional stereotypes (EC 1987, Annex: 21). As EOC (1982) concludes:

> *The treatment which incorporated a less restricted, modern, female role-portrayal was consistently found to enhance the marketing-effectiveness* of the brands' advertising . . . not only do the better educated, more affluent and younger female consumers respond more positively to the liberated role portrayals, so do older women, and those in lower socio-economic groups. . . . Non-employed as well as working women preferred the modern role-portrayals and found them more persuasive. . . . The modern styles of advertisements are more effective than the traditional ones for two reasons: they portray women as attractive, independent, capable people in roles in and out of the home, and they do it in a manner which is realistic and natural.

In short, despite the view of advertising as culturally in the vanguard in the way in which it presents images, it seems most likely that traditionally conceived advertising has persisted in ideologically obstructing the changing role of women, by continuing to portray them as sex objects or mothers. Although advertising has begun to respond by creating new images of glamorous, wealthy and independent women,[20] this has much to do with the selling of convenience products and less to do with the direct portrayal of the more typical 'new women' who is liable to be using them – a mother returning to (part-time) work after her youngest child has begun school.

As evidenced above, advertising is not merely a particular cultural artefact; it also responds to, and is interpreted within, the context of broad economic and social change. This, together with the (changing) physical properties of the commodities to be represented, prevents advertising from being elevated, or degenerating, to the realm of pure fantasy. Its intended function is to sell. Within these broad parameters, how well does it function?

## 5 SOME EMPIRICAL PARAMETERS

Before attempting an evaluation, however, it is important to recognise that advertising is itself only a part of total selling costs. Advertising expenditure, even for those commodities where it is most important, rarely exceeds half of all sales costs. More generally, the development of sales techniques and institutions, often in conjunction with advertising, has had a profound impact on the process of retailing. The development of supermarkets, retail chains and shopping centres has arguably been far more important to sales than adverts themselves. Indeed, specialised advertising has emerged for particular stores rather than for branded products. In the long chain between production and final sale, it may be more important to persuade a store to carry a product than it is to persuade people to buy it.[21] Even the ambience surrounding the purchase of goods may be more important than the desired attributes associated with them:

> What is distinctive about consumerism is that the form of life accumulated through commodities is displayed as much through the means whereby the commodities become accessible and are acquired, as through what are held to be desirable features of particular commodities.[22]
>
> (Cheney 1983: 27)

In a catalogue of qualifications on the effectiveness of advertising, it must be acknowledged that it fails to sell most new products, even if it may be a necessary condition for success. Sinclair (1987: 12) reports that 80 per cent of new products fail in Australia and 90 per cent in the United States. Schudson (1984: 25) argues that: 'Most authorities agree . . . that advertising helps expand demand when underlying conditions encourage growth and cannot overcome weak demand when underlying conditions are unfavourable.' In other words, if advertising were highly effective, there would never be recession induced by lack of demand. On the other hand, the success of some products, like marijuana and cocaine, requires no advertising whatsoever. At the other extreme, no amount of advertising can halt the decline of some economic activities like the hat industry or male hairdressing.

Advertising also appears to fail at the immediate ideological level in so far as the vast majority of people claim not to believe what they are told. Leiss

(1986: 4) reports that 60 per cent of respondents to a survey thought that adverts were an insult to the intelligence. Fox (1984: 200) quotes Ronald Reagan as saying that, 'I don't believe there is a human being in the world who believes a motion picture ad.'[23] The failure of advertising is signified indirectly in the general contempt with which it and its practitioners are held in popular culture, although in recent times yuppie wealth associated with finance has attracted even greater scorn.[24]

Even where advertising gets its message across, it does not guarantee success in the form of sales. The possibility of a split between the ideological and economic impact of advertising is illustrated by the fate of adverts for non-alcoholic beer. While the product called Clayton failed commercially, the name became a by-word in Australia for anything that was phoney (Sinclair 1987).[25] Nor can it be presumed that the resistance to the sexist stereotyping of ads is synonymous with the resistance to purchase of the associated products, even if this is what is reported in tests, since ads are known and are intended to work unconsciously. The (negative) source of brand recognition may not be recognised at time of purchase.

Finally, it is worth viewing advertising from a historical perspective from which, over the longer term, it is easier to recognise the presence or absence of causal connections. The content and imagery of ads suggests, with some slight exaggeration, that little advance has been made over the past two hundred years, setting aside the prodigious changes in the methods of communication. As McKendrick documents for the eighteenth-century manufacturer of shaving accessories, George Packwood:[26]

> Few modern copywriters can match the battery of advertising gimmicks unleashed on the public by this single entrepreneur in the space of less than two years. For Packwood used riddles, proverbs, fables, slogans, jokes, jingles, anecdotes, facts, aphorisms, puns, poems, songs, nursery rhymes, parodies, pastiches, stories, dialogues, definitions, conundrums, letters and metaphors. He used advertisements disguised as 'sporting intelligence', 'electioneering', 'financial intelligence', 'farming intelligence', or trading information. He used advertisements disguised as law reports, as genealogies, as medical recipes . . . as miracle cures . . . or as business history (naturally the history of his own business). He used advertisements aimed at men, women, and children. The letters he published as advertisements appeared in the guise of letters to the editor, letters to himself, or letters between friends. His Dialogues were cast as conversations between Christian and Jew, between Merchant and Black Servant, between Welshman and Irishman, between English sailor and French barber, or simply between two friends. But they all resounded to the greater glory of Packwood. They all praised and promoted Packwood goods. They all underlined Packwood's special quality. They might be cast in the mould of a warning how not to misuse his goods and

> therefore blunt their distinctive qualities; they might be cast in the mould of knocking copy of rivals, or as warnings against deceptions and fakes; they might reveal the merits of his product by way of a discursive narrative, or simply draw attention to his existence by virtue of autobiographical reminiscence; they might embed the virtues of his wares in the middle of a parody of a soliloquy from *Hamlet*, or a well known nursery rhyme, or a popular song, or ex tempore verse; but whatever the approach they sought to engage the eager attention of the customer, attempted to cajole an initial trial, and once hooked they attempted to secure his lasting allegiance.
>
> (McKendrick 1982: 153)

Yet, despite this remarkable foretaste of modern techniques, many presume the features of the industry to belong distinctly to the twentieth century. For Dyer (1982: 15): 'Modern advertising is effectively no more than a hundred years old, dating from a period when the capitalist system underwent major changes.' And for Vestergaard and Schrøder:

> The social and institutional setting in which advertising exists today has thus been present since the beginning of this century: mass-produced goods, a mass market reached through mass publications whose single most important source of revenue is advertising, and a professional advertising trade handling all major advertising accounts.
>
> (Vestergaard & Shrøder 1985: 4)

Ewen (1976) puts forward modern advertising as a contemporary counterpart to Fordist production; Packard (1957) suggests that advertising comes of age with the adoption of psychological techniques associated with motivational research. Although these writers assign different dates to their hypothetical turning points, common to each is the dependence of the modern form of advertising on mass production and capitalism. For each, accordingly, the mode of production in the narrow sense has had a determining influence; for Ewen especially, advertising has been the means by which capital penetrated the US working-class home in the interwar period. If so, it can only have served to open the door for non-advertised products as well, for as Berman (1981: 22) notes: 'There are some logical difficulties with the central matter of created demand. The bulk of advertising's budget goes into household items like soap, food, and automobiles.' Further, as Sayer (1989) has indicated in his critique of post-Fordism, the notion of the all-pervading presence of mass production/consumption for the earlier hypothesised Fordist period is too readily accepted. The corresponding role for advertising is thrown in doubt by the limited extent to which Ford workers owned the cars they manufactured (in the interwar period), and by the targeting of car advertising to the wealthier middle classes, (although this was possibly designed to promote broad-based consumerism by encouraging emulation).

Apart from advertising technique and mode of commodity production, the history of advertising has also been presented in terms of the media through which it has been expressed, with its passage from newspapers to magazines, to radio and to television, and in terms of the cultural context of the increasing consumerist and individualistic ethic of modern capitalism. For Leiss (1983), for example, advertising has gone through three phases: reinforcing existing female roles between 1900 and 1930; reorienting them towards making purchases for consumption rather than use in the home between 1930 and 1960, and broadening their horizons from 1960 onwards. A more empirically oriented and catholic interpretation of the 'sizzle' content of print advertising decade by decade from 1900 is provided by Pollay (1985), with emphasis moving, for example, from playing on fears in the 1930s to consumer values in the modern period.

In an attempted synthesis put forward by Leiss *et al.* (1986), advertising is presented as a social, economic and cultural construct, with primary emphasis on the increasing bond between media and advertising as a system of communication. A distinction is made between industrial society in 1900 and modern consumer society. The former emphasises class structure through which different cultures give rise to different access to a different array of goods. For contemporary consumer society, culture is seen as more homogeneous and classes give way to lifestyles and market segments. This structural change dovetails with their periodisations of other economic and social factors – for the media, for the message (running from information to lifestyle), and for style (which they see as moving from idolatry to totemism).

## 6 THE IMPACT OF PRODUCTION

The conclusion to be drawn from this cursory and partial review of the history and the impact of advertising is that, both in its origins and in its effects, it is the consequence of an extremely diverse and shifting set of determinants. The empirical and theoretical evidence suggests that the impact of advertising is far from systematic either in the commercial or in the ideological field. Leiss *et al.* (1986: 61) view the situation as one in which there has now become a 'disintegration of goods as determinate objects'. Consequently, the marketplace is a site where fragmented needs and fragmented goods are to be bound together, with advertising acting as a gel. They conclude that: 'Commodities are, therefore, a unity of what is revealed and what is concealed in the processes of production and consumption.' (Leiss *et al.* 1986: 274).

Leiss *et al.* suggest a specific mediating link in the role played by mass communications. Sinclair (1987: 11) makes an explicit attempt at synthesising the different approaches. He deplores the loss of a dialectical relationship between cultural and economic factors, even though he has primarily interpreted the latter to be synonymous with marketing activity. In the absence of an economic framework, it becomes impossible to explain why certain commodities have a much higher proportion of total costs due in marketing and why some have a much higher proportion of advertising within marketing costs. It is owing to the nature of the product and its distribution and sale as much as to its created image.

It follows from all this that *production* as such is more notable for its absence than for its presence in the analysis of advertising, even where some attempt at synthesis is made. The exchange value approach, despite its economic orientation, tends to set production aside since advertising is perceived to be an activity and cost within circulation. Within this framework, it really does not matter what has been produced and how (other than that it must embody surplus value) as long as it can be sold as soon and as cheaply as possible. While this does formally root the analysis in capitalist production, with the implied division between industrial and merchant capital and competition between individual capitals, there is no reference to the capitalist methods of production themselves – whether there is highly machine-intensive production or not, for example.

In the use value approach, the links with capitalist production are even weaker. Indeed, with the focus on the nature of the individual commodity, there need be no reference to capitalism. The analysis could equally well be concerned with simply commodity production or not with commodity production at all. For in advertising itself, there tends to be limited emphasis on the price form and on buying as such. To claim to be the cheapest, for example, always carries the risk of being associated with lower quality. More attention is paid to the context of use, so that the image portrayed rather than the product assumes the central position. Moreover, advertising is no longer concerned exclusively with commerce; it now also promotes political propaganda and privatisation, for example, as well. Although these newer applications may rely upon some of the same techniques as those used to sell commercial products, to lump them together is to overlook important differences in their economic profiles and histories, differences that help to determine the character, timing and intended role of advertising.

When cultural interpretations of advertising come to the fore, they focus narrowly on specific analytical concerns, whether they be sexism, psychology, decoding or structuralism, etc. No doubt, these are of importance in interpreting advertising at different moments but the content of advertising is potentially as diverse as the use values that are being both reconstructed and peddled. Indeed, they are more diverse. Advertising can appeal either to the product's uniformity or to its differentiation from other products, logically doubling its scope of application – appealing to the traditional or to the counter culture surrounding the object. The commodity can be presented either as it is or as it is not. In practice, its representation by attributes unconnected with its actual use value can be expanded indefinitely. As Dyer points out, even the criticism of advertising can itself provide the basis for copy, as antipathy towards advertising is parasitically reincorporated in conformity with any targeted ideology:[27] 'Advertising rebuffs criticism and validates its own existence . . . by appropriating hostile criticism and counter ideologies.' (Dyer 1982: 185). Adverts can be made that exploit anti-racism, anti-sexism and so on.

More seriously, preoccupation with the cultural interpretations of advertising leads to a consistent neglect of what is perhaps the most obvious systematic influence on advertising, namely its involvement with the creations of capital. Commodities, and not just images of them, have to be produced before they are (packaged, distributed and) sold – and they are produced and sold to make a profit. And advertising is itself concerned with the creation of a product, the ad and advertising campaigns, and has its own economic parameters in terms of costs, technologies, etc.

How, then, is a systematic link between the production and advertising of goods to be forged? After all, it is rare to find an image of work or a factory used as a means by which to glorify a product. Indeed, it would be a paradox if commodity fetishism, as understood by Marx, which conceals the underlying relations of production, were to be stripped away by the act of promoting sale.[28] One link is to be found in the way in which changing production processes and their products influence the conditions within which advertising can operate (just as mass production as such expands its potential).

In this, a crucial start has been made by Haug, as discussed in Chapter 2. As observed, his analysis is too one-sided in two different senses. First, the aesthetic illusion, the gap between the commodity as it is and as it is presented, is not filled exclusively, or even primarily, by the sexuality of commodities. Even if this were so, the use of sexism changes substantially over time and across the population in its emphasis and in its nature: the classic housewife/ mistress syndrome used to sell goods is now losing its appeal for the single and/ or independent woman.

Second, and more important for the purpose here, the gap between what is produced and what is sold does not always open up in the manner suggested by Haug. In contrast to Haug's expectations of product deterioration, machine and mass production tend to bring with them an increase in the quality and availability of goods. The history of food adulteration provides a good example, as presented in Chapter 12. Significantly, such adulteration is most closely tied in Britain to the middle of the nineteenth century, to the period *prior* to the hegemony of machine production. The emergence of mass production technologies removed the more flagrant abuses of food. Mass production is, in general, superior to hand production. The idea that it is not superior is based partly upon a nostalgia for the superiority of the past (no doubt an idea fostered by advertising) and partly on the necessity for those more costly hand-made products to be (or claim to be) of superior quality in order to survive. They are not, however, necessarily representative of what used to be produced by hand.

In short, machine production may improve upon hand production through the use of materials and production processes that previously might have been unavailable. Both offer benefits linked to the potential scale of production and to the technical capacity of machinery. True, they may also be associated with a reduction in the quality of the raw materials and in the labour employed, as well as with a quickening of the production process. But such developments do not lead unambiguously to adulteration of the product, although this can occur. It does mean, however, that advertising needs to address, even if to conceal, the changing nature of products and the production process. The rising interest in environmental issues has brought this visibly to the fore. There need be very little immediate difference between the eggs of the past and those of today, but battery production is not stamped upon the shell and would be unacceptable to many more consumers if it were made explicit. The same is true of the much earlier growth of the large-scale abattoir, a precondition for the mass consumption of beef.

The function of advertising is not, however, simply to conceal these changes. It may even highlight them. The superiority and uniformity of mass production can be a selling-point, especially when it is linked to the wonders of technological change. The Ford motor car is an obvious example. The acceptance of mass-produced housing in the United States has also been linked to an appreciation of the virtues of mass production. Wright argues that the popular acceptance of the standardised house required the beating out of the hegemony of skills supplied by the craft building worker:

> By the 1920s, the fascination with the machine rather than with the hand would produce a new romance. The expert with scientific knowledge and the modern technology at his command would rule. The anonymous industrial-design look eliminated all evidence of individual effort or skill by the workers who turned out houses or radios or any other industrial products. Modernists glorified a clean and conspicuously machine-made aesthetic. . . . The modern machine aesthetic could be accepted in American homes because, at the turn of the century, the romantic Victorian idealization of the building worker as a craftsman had been destroyed.
>
> (Wright 1980: 197–8)

Similarly, Jay (1987) has revealed how important the display of smoking factory chimneys were in the trade cards of the nineteenth century, as a means of advertising quality of product; though the same depiction of 'heaviness' of industrial plant would today fully offend our sense of high tech, clean, and environmentally-safe production.

Thus, the relationship between production and advertising cannot be set aside for a number of reasons. First, production is the source of commodities upon which advertising must work both to create and to bridge the aesthetic illusion – the difference between use values as they are and as they are presented and perceived. Second, developments in production can themselves constitute the raw materials for advertising and for the cultural meaning of commodities more generally – the ideology of production, for example, incorporating science (mass production) or craft (and differentiation by use of skilled labour). Third, commodities have to be both produced and sold before they are consumed, and these processes and their component parts are not independent of one another. These points are reinforced in the following section by linking them to an understanding of consumption in terms of systems of provision.

## 7 ADVERTISING AS A COMPONENT OF THE SYSTEM OF PROVISION

In previous chapters, for (theories of) consumption in general as well as for specific commodities such as food and clothing, it has been shown that an extraordinarily diverse range of factors are involved as explanatory and interpretative variables. Given that (commercial) advertising has sale and purchase as its goal, ultimately leading to consumption, it is hardly surprising that it too should, as has been shown, be subject to an equally wide range of analyses. At times, it merely reflects a pre-existing theory of consumption; at other times, it is enriched by incorporating some aspect of the way in which it functions (in retailing, the media or culture).

Starting from the commodity as use value and exchange value, two broad classifications of approaches to advertising can be discerned. The relationship of advertising to each of these and as a whole is, however, inadequately understood unless they are fully incorporated together. Given our own approach to consumption through systems of provision, the determinants and effects of advertising will be distinct for each such system. The justification, then, for adding the changing contours of production to the analysis of advertising is twofold. First, and most obviously, production becomes another determinant to stand alongside the factors previously considered. Acknowledging changes in the corporate structure or organisation of production over time clearly adds to, rather than detracts from, the quality of debate. In the nineteenth century, for example, before the emergence of industrial conglomerates, there was a close identification between a particular product, or group of products, and the company itself. While this persists, corporations are now more highly diversified. Consequently, advertising for the brand and/or a range of closely related products on the one hand, and advertising for the corporation on the other, are quite different. Mars, for example, is both a product and a corporation but it only tends to use its corporate identity to promote its most important product – the Mars Bar. Its other products are advertised in their own right and are not readily identified with Mars. On the other hand, Cadbury has both a series of brand images and a corporate identity which links them together, a consequence of the increasing concentration and diversification of corporate production.[29]

Second, and more significantly, the search for synthesis, including a role for production, points to a dichotomy in theoretical approaches to advertising. One approach, which might reasonably be labelled consumerist, takes a horizontal and layered view across society in which advertising is linked consecutively to factors such as culture, demand and, occasionally, production. Consequently, it presumes and seeks uniformity, but frequently finds diversity in uncovering the role of these factors. Thus, whilst different commodities, and hence different use values, are being bought and sold, the horizontal approach searches for common means by which advertising reconstructs use values to enhance the potential of any commodity for sale.

The alternative approach elaborated in this book views advertising from a vertical perspective. Each commodity is produced and, ultimately, after distribution and sale, is consumed as a consequence of the demand created for it. There is no presumption that this structure of provision, through the economic and social relations involved, is uniform across commodities. In fact, the divergence in the horizontal and current patterns of provision for each commodity and its impact on the character of advertising in each case is, by contrast, drawn out and highlighted. Both the economic structure (such as the extent of factory production and the nature of distribution and retailing) and the level of demand (which depends upon who can afford to purchase and how often) vary across the range of commodities. Running parallel with this, the associated cultural creation of demand will depend on specifically suitable types of advertising for each commodity and on other ideological determinants.

Within this framework, consistent horizontal uniformities are unlikely to be present across commodities because they are splintered by vertical forms of provision. Since production, distribution and retailing must have an impact on demand, and hence on consumption and advertising, it follows that their influence will vary from one commodity to another. More pronounced similarities will emerge between goods that share a common structure of provision.

To conclude: the introduction of production (and other economic factors along the system of provision) not only remedies neglect of an important determinant, it also reorients the understanding of advertising. It shifts away from a horizontal search for a variety of uniformities across commodities in their role as creatures of semiology or of media and cultural studies and towards a vertical specification of diversity in the role of these factors.[30] To be a little less abstract, advertising around (constructed) commodities as diverse as housing, clothing and food, owes as much, surely more, to the differences in the way they are provided as in the way that they are construed, these themselves being mutually dependent. This is illustrated more concretely in the next two chapters by reference to clothing and food.

# 15

# ADVERTISING CLOTHING

## THE MEDIA AND THEIR MESSAGES

Differences in the role played by advertising in the food and clothing industries reflect differences in their overall systems of provision, not simply differences in products and tastes. Distinct features in the productive chain, in the relative strength of suppliers, manufacturers and retailers, in the role of design, all feed into a pattern of advertising which is unique to each industry. While the discussion in this chapter (predominantly concerned with clothing) and that in the following chapter (covering food) cannot attempt to supply a comprehensive picture of advertising in either industry, it does attempt to highlight some of the distinctions causally revealed by reference to their systems of provision. We begin in this section by highlighting such differences.

First, the sharp contrast between the large-scale and stable production of standard food products and the extremely unstable and fragmented production of clothing finds a correspondence in the nature of advertising in the two industries. Many branded foods have been marketed steadily for a half a century or more and have achieved national if not international recognition (Hovis bread, Kellogg's Corn Flakes, Coca-Cola, etc.). Though the contents and the perception of these products have changed over time, they have done so within limits. This has made it possible to run national advertising campaigns which live on for years, even decades.

But while advertising at the national level helps to establish and strengthen brand recognition, advertising at the local level, where it exists, often reflects price competition between retailers. Because the goods themselves are liable to be known fixtures, local adverts do not often draw attention to their attributes (taste, nutritional value, etc.). Typically, newspaper ads for food feature crude black and white drawings of tins and turkeys surrounded by bold, large-point typeface announcing the week's special reductions. The appeal is clearly to the pocket rather than to the product as such, for which demand is already presumed to exist rather than needing to be created (or diverted).

*Figure 7* A good illustration of the constancy of food labels, a magazine advertisement, 1922.
*Source*: Campbell's Soups.

The much greater diversity to be found in advertising for clothing reflects the more highly segmented marketing characteristic of an industry that is still driven by competing technologies; the market for one-off *haute couture* outfits (still supported primarily by hand-sewing) co-exists with the market for mass-produced, cheap dresses (manufactured largely by unskilled labour and machines). The contrast between clothing advertisements in *Vogue* magazine and those in local newspapers reflects as much the contrast in systems of provision as the contrast in the consuming habits of the rich and poor.

The *Vogue* ad, in its extreme form, deliberately suppresses any association of the clothes on display with the disappointing limitations of daily life; often there is no context at all, just a wash of seamless colour behind the model. The product itself, and the publication within which it appears, suffice to suggest lifestyle and taste. Prices are rarely mentioned. At the other end of the spectrum, the newspaper ad, in its extreme form, carries no illustrations of garments which could not compete with the more glamorous high fashion ads to which readers are all now accustomed. Instead, garments are simply listed with their accompanying prices. This renders them inferior products merely by virtue of the source of their appeal, i.e., their price. The antipathy between price and quality appears to lie at the heart of clothing, reflecting not only quality of ingredients as for other goods but also recognition of distinct forms of provision which play an important role in the segmentation of markets.

In between the two extremes are many other forms of presentation including the fanciful, almost calligraphic sketches of fashion illustration that evoke the style of fashion garments without revealing much in the way of hard details. But while the various forms of advertising in the food industry are all directed to the sale of the same goods, in clothing, these different techniques and the different media that convey them to the public address different product markets and different income groups.

Advertising, in this respect, reproduces the market segmentation exemplified in women's clothing by the differentiation of goods into 'price lines', i.e., into distinct price ranges used and accepted by manufacturers and retailers alike. As discussed in Chapter 9, the adoption of price lines early in the twentieth century enabled producers to expand their markets by fragmenting the demand for dresses. Designed to exploit the competitive advantage offered by small-batch production, it would inevitably retard the move towards the mass production of standardised garments.

A more recent demonstration of the same strategy is found in the introduction by major clothing designers of what has been called a 'second line' or a 'bridge collection' in addition to the designer's main collection. The second line offers the so-called 'house' look but at more affordable prices (although still well beyond the reach of those on average incomes).[1] Like the earlier introduction of *prêt-à-porter* in the 1950s, these cheaper collections extend the range of markets into which designer labels can penetrate. Over the past few years, a dozen or so high-fashion designers have launched moderate lines to broaden their consumer bases; they are expected to account for 10–15 per cent of the $6 billion women's apparel market in the United States. This strategy is perceived as an alternative to a reduction in the price range of top quality lines. As the director of an apparel marketing agency put it, 'lowering prices would dilute a designer's cachet. A secondary line is the surest way to broaden a designer's base'.[2] Even though rejected here, the very possibility of restructuring price ranges at the top end of the market confirms the separation of price from quality, a separation which is promoted and sustained by the structure of this industry.

Fashion magazines (and, to a lesser degree, newspapers[3] and Sunday supplements) constitute the primary source of advertising for higher-income clothing. The magazines are, in fact, supported largely by advertising purchased by fashion manufacturers. The so-called 'serious' articles and editorials on fashion, with which the adverts are interleaved, strive to bestow some kind of legitimacy to fashion concerns; these are presented as exercising an independent and potentially pre-emptive influence on manufacturers. Fashion stories or 'spreads' at the very top end of the market present models in clothes and in postures that push the limits of both social convention and human anatomy in bizarre and often precarious mélanges of gold leaf, chain mail, feathers, leathers, jewels, etc. These images clearly require the expenditure of considerable hands-on labour in both the workshop and the photographer's studio and so convey a message of absolute exclusivity, denoted by astronomical price tags or by the more discrete label 'prices available upon request'. They serve to renew on a regular basis the desire for the exotic and the unattainable.

Although fashion manufacturers clearly cannot attempt to duplicate the fantasies purveyed in these pages, they can and do exploit the appeal of the exotic and the unpredictable which the fantasies stimulate. Displaying a product turnover unimaginable in the food industry, clothing manufacturers introduce advertisements for completely new outfits almost every month, reflecting their capacity to 're-tool' production over short intervals. Yet compared with the often provocative set pieces in the fashion pages, adverts appear as relatively tame, conveying the impression that there is an unbridgeable gap between the fashion ideal at any moment (the flavour of the month) and the capacity of the industry to catch up.

Paradoxically, this creates a functional tension which the manufacturers can work to their advantage, even though they appear to be incapable of satisfying requirements. For the magazines inspire and sustain the idea of a perpetually unfulfilled and unfulfillable demand, with changes in fashion driving a lethargic system of provision back along its links to the relatively unresponsive capacity of supply and manufacture. In reality, this disguises countervailing mechanisms in the system of provision, activated by pressures operating in the opposite direction. The fashion system is required both to justify and to camouflage technical constraints on productive capacity. To this end, the wide-ranging visibility and volatility of fashion demand must be constantly nurtured and replenished; the illusion of a demand-led system of provision provides the only vindication of the status quo.

While the food industry advertises to set up and sustain unvarying habits of repetitive consumption, the fashion industry is forced to promote the habit of purchasing itself, repetition for variety, rather than promoting loyalty to a particular product. A dress on the market in any one year will not, in any case, be available the next. This helps to explain why the imagery of clothing adverts rejects association with the mundane details of life in real time with its reminder of responsibilities and constraints (including constraints on purchasing power). Where food advertising for the most part disguises changes in the content of established branded products (substitution of ingredients, reduction in volume, etc.), clothing advertising positively celebrates – is in fact pushed to exaggerate – the 'newness' of this month's offerings.

The contrast in the structure of provision is reflected in the difference between the supermarket and the clothing boutique. The supermarket wins and keeps its customers by the constancy of its product range (the great majority of new food products fail within a year; those of fashion need to have succeeded, and even 'failed' again, within a year). The boutique and department stores more generally depend upon the perpetual lure of new fashions to draw customers back repeatedly.

The volatile nature of clothing advertising is symptomatic of the absence of a long-range planning perspective in production. There is a clear incompatibility between the production cycle (which is variable but generally short, from three to eight weeks) and the requirements of media buying and campaign strategies, both of which entail forward planning over a considerable period. (This is why billboards can advertise Smirnoff Vodka or *Yellow Pages* but not dresses in a Harrod's sale.) In contrast to the food industry, volume production in many branches of the clothing industry is achieved by the repeated reordering of small batches of successful styles ('runners') rather than by the continuous production of standard goods. Which styles achieve the status of 'hot numbers' cannot, however, be predicted in advance. Unlike production in packaged goods, output in fashion industries is measured not in terms of productive capacity but by the movement of inventory.

Hence the sharp contrast in the scale of marketing and promotional operations between the packaged food and apparel industries. In the former, each of 142 brands put at least $10 million into media expenditures in 1990 and eighteen of them (nine of them cereals) spent more than $25 million each.[4] In the apparel and accessories industries, just sixteen brands reached media expenditures of $10 million, with only three spending more than $25 million each (Levi's Jeans, Dockers Sportswear – also owned by Levi Strauss, Fruit of the Loom Underwear and L'Eggs Pantyhose).

Historically, most of the advertising carried out by clothing manufacturers has been directed not at the final consumer but at the retailer. Again, this has been partly for reasons of scale; retail chains have reached vast proportions with total annual sales in billions of dollars. And retailers spend a significantly higher proportion of their higher volume sales on advertising (on average 2.5 per cent against the 0.8 per cent spent by producers).[5] For the larger firms, media expenditure can exceed $50 million: Sears Roebuck, at the very top of the market, spent over $300 million on the media in 1990.

Advertising and promotional activity on the part of the garment maker is, by comparison, exceedingly modest. Much of its marketing budget in fact goes into 'co-operative' advertising in which manufacturers and retailers share the cost of ads which jointly promote the manufacturer's product(s) and the store. The remaining share of the budget has gone largely into advertisements within retail trade journals. 'All fashion advertising is aimed at the buyer: only when the budget gets up around $1,000,000 do you start to talk to consumers.'[6] Beginning in the late 1970s, some advertising budgets in the fashion world began to reach this hitherto unheard of level. This was a reflection of the transformation of one garment in particular, namely blue jeans, into a nationally marketed, mass-produced good. As the production of jeans more closely approximated that of packaged goods like food, so the pattern and scale of its advertising followed suit.

The popularity of jeans sparked the growth of brand recognition in apparel and, with it, the development of 'concept' and 'lifestyle' imagery in apparel advertising. Brand recognition of clothing arrived much later than that for most other goods (including both textiles and foods); arguably, this reflects the later arrival of mass production within the industry.

A pair of jeans was a basically simple garment that could, much like washing powders, be subjected to product differentiation through advertising. Since no one brand of jeans could offer any greater functional usefulness than any other, advertising created brand identities on the basis of their immanent allure. Memorable storyline adverts for Levi 501s emphasised the desirability of the product (in both the Soviet bloc and in the American Far West) in much the same way that Cadbury advertised adventurous knights risking life and limb to gratify the Lady's passion for Milk Tray. In other words, imagery took precedence over information.

The basic uniformity of the product coupled with the relatively modest capital requirements for entering the market opened up opportunities for old-fashioned entrepreneurial competition through advertising. Many small producers (like Jordache, Guess, Murjani) introduced minor variations on the basic Levi Strauss model and relied upon an advertising medium new to clothing (television) to parlay these garments into multi-million dollar markets.

Traditionally, television accounted for only a very small slice of the advertising budget in the apparel industry – well under 5 per cent. TV was the medium which catered most effectively to the packaged goods industry, selling frequently purchased, low-priced and largely invariant commodities (like Weetabix and Cheerios) which were universally available. These were not attributes commonly associated with clothing, which typically had a changing product and often expensive price tags. The marketing of 'designer' jeans on television beginning in the 1970s reflected the growing accommodation of at least one segment of the apparel industry with more orthodox forms of mass production. In a further manifestation of the paradox described above (in Chapter 9), the arrival of a national market for a standardised garment brought in its train a frenzy of product 'differentiation' to gain market share through advertising. The national market was large enough to sustain multiple images of exclusivity cultivated by many designer jean labels. By 1979, sales of designer jeans reached a billion dollars, close to 10 per cent of the total jeans market, despite their selling at prices three times higher than conventional jeans. Designer jeans manufacturers spent about 10 per cent of total revenue on advertising compared to just 2 per cent spent by makers of traditional jeans (Finlayson 1990: 73).

Television advertising by apparel manufacturers tripled between 1978 and 1981.[7] By 1985, television outstripped magazines as the primary medium for advertising, claiming half of all media expenditure.[8] Though this represented a substantial increase, it was still dwarfed by the sums spent by packaged goods industries. Even during the heyday of jeans advertising in 1979–81, when Levi Strauss, the clear leader in apparel advertising, spent $423 million on TV, Procter and Gamble (the soap and washing powder giant) spent close to $500 million. In the same year, the total spend of the food industry on television advertising was $1.4 billion compared with $212 million spent on clothing.

Significantly, all of these campaigns were controlled and co-ordinated not by the retailers but by manufacturers. And, of equal significance, the group of big spenders began to include designer-manufacturers like Ralph Lauren and Calvin Klein, a combination that is in many respects unique to clothing. Ralph Lauren's Polo Group spent between $15 million and $25 million on the media in 1990 and Calvin Klein Sportswear between $5 milllion and $10 million.[9] The advertising leverage of designer labels is evidenced by the reach of their licensing agreements,[10] which enable them to sell their name under contract to manufacturers of a wide variety of unrelated products in exchange for royalties. The sale of a designer's name, divorced from his or her original sphere of influence to serve as an endorsement on every conceivable product from make-up to sheets and pillowcases to eyewear, attests to the ability of advertising to facilitate the diffusion of designer fetishism. As Ralph Lauren put it: 'I don't design clothes, I design dreams.'[11]

Unlike the controlled advertising framework for other branded products that seek to establish recognition of a single stable image, the dreams of fashion are subject to their own laws. There is no apparent contradiction in the simultaneous promotion by Ralph Lauren of two distinct images for the home environment, both harking back to the European imperial heritage, but one set in Africa[12] and the other in the Scottish Highlands. As a marketing strategy, this tactic blankets two non-overlapping market niches, thereby reducing the risks associated with investing exclusively in either one. To maximise the marketing potential of each distinct 'lifestyle', Ralph Lauren and Calvin Klein exercise complete control over all aspects of their advertising campaigns, which are designed and carried out in-house under conditions of great secrecy. These most often take the form of a series of artfully photographed domestic tableaux, following one another in a sequence designed to reveal the full range of social possibilities opened up by the active pursuit of the style portrayed.

In another important departure from the food and other packaged goods industries, apparel designers have, over the past twenty years, set up independent shops carrying their own products exclusively. Because this enhances the reputation of the designer (extending his/her exposure), it is deemed to support rather than to hinder sales of the same designer's products in department stores, acting as a more concentrated form of advertising. Thus, Sloane Street can amicably boast over a dozen designer boutiques within a stone's throw of Harrod's, which carries some of the product range of most of these labels. No such independence exists for major food brands, which remain in thrall to retailers who often sell their own-brand goods in competition with, and alongside, the nationally known brands.

Although successful brand names in the food industry are also expected to help market new products, these are confined to food-related products rather than ranging freely over the world of consumer goods. The wider transfer of food brands is thwarted by one of the basic determinants of the system of provision in food. The imperative to retain freshness, to minimise the time and distance between the garden and the table, set psychological caps on the capacity to purchase as well as to consume.

Except for a few products like wine, which make a virtue of purchasing in advance of consumption, the enduring awareness of perishability inhibits prospects for hoarding or 'collecting' food in quantities incompatible with reasonable consumption. Because clothing is not constrained by any comparable limits imposed by nature, either perceived or actual, advertising has been able to sever the link between purchase and consumption. Though purchase has become more or less continuous, actual consumption of clothing (which would involve the wearing out of fabrics and trimmings over several years) hardly ever occurs. Even consumption in the more orthodox sense of use is limited by the hours of the day, by social conventions, and by a host of other practical considerations.

This potential for separation between purchase and consumption is an important factor in the treatment of clothing as fashion. If a commodity allows for the possibility of postponing consumption, then it can shed the status of a basic necessity and aspire to something higher, which assigns a greater role to the exercise of choice and selection. The increase in monetary value of goods purchased twenty years earlier but consumed sparingly if at all over the intervening period (like Rolex watches) attests to the rewards that can be reaped by either postponing or prolonging the consumption of fashion goods. In either case, the relationship is neither predictable nor determined, as it is where food is involved.

Over the past few decades a great number of humble products have made this transition, from Giorgio Armani bubble bath to Ralph Lauren sheets, a Donna Karan change purse and Hermes garden scissors. Once the designer label is attached, prices rise to a level that widens the profit margin as well as supporting advertising. Adverts then help to cement the change in status by moving the formerly lowly commodity considerably up-market, emphasising its visual appeal over its practical usefulness. Adverts for watches (now often called 'timepieces') no longer refer to attributes of sturdy reliability but borrow the language and price tags of jewellery, a luxury good.

Paradoxically, in the food and clothing industries, there appears to be an inverse relationship between the durability of the goods themselves and the duration of advertising that promotes them; the paradox runs deeper in that materially most foods are perishable and most clothes are not, but the length of life-cycle of these products in practice reverses this relationship. The food industry supports advertising campaigns which can be recycled unchanged from one year to the next to sell products that perish relatively quickly but which can be easily replaced. The clothing industry sponsors a continuous sequence of discretely packaged, short-term advertising to sell products that, in theory at least, could last for decades but which the market makes available for only a very brief period. Food advertising emphasises the stability of its markets; clothing, their volatility. In both cases, advertising helps to manufacture and sustain habits that are conducive to profitability in conformity with each system of provision.

## THE ROLE OF INTERMEDIATE SUPPLIERS

The production of clothing requires a much lengthier sequence of industrial operations than food, each contributing added value to the finished product. Textile producers, transforming fibres into yarns and weaving or knitting yarns into cloth, occupy one end of the system of provision; manufacturers who make up cloth into finished products, occupy the other. The two types of activities also represent two extremes along the spectrum of industrial production. In scale, organisation and diversification, the textile industry is a giant; the top ten mills in the US generate nearly one-third of the industry's sales and most of them are vertically integrated (processing the fibre, spinning the yarn, making and finishing the cloth).[13] Though apparel products are the single biggest user of textiles (consuming 37 per cent of output), home furnishings (carpets, curtains, etc.) claim an important share (30 per cent), as do industrial, military and medical products.

The apparel manufacturing industry, by contrast, remains dominated by specialised small-scale producers. Though some huge corporations have emerged over the past twenty years (like Jonathan Logan, Leslie Fay, Levi Strauss), concentration in the industry is much lower than in textile production; the largest eight firms are responsible for just 17 per cent of total sales;[14] the bulk of the industry remains privately owned and small. While technological innovation in textile production has increased the scale of investment needed to operate, for example, weaving mills (especially since the introduction of shuttleless looms and computers in the 1950s), the garment industry is still dominated by the individually operated sewing machine.

In this contrast of extremes, the final manufacturing of garments appears as a kind of necessary, though labour-intensive, form of packaging or assembling of textile goods which have essentially been manufactured by capital-intensive machinery incorporating state-of-the-art technology. Up to the last stage of the process, intermediate goods destined to be clothing are treated in much the same way as other mass-produced goods. But at this stage, the process breaks down and is fragmented by the dictates of sewing production and the fashion cycles with which it is enmeshed. The powerful productive capacity of the textile industry and its drive towards mass markets is interrupted and dissipated by the final stage of production.

It is this curious relationship between contributors to the finished product that distinguishes the character of advertising in the clothing industry. In more typical package goods industries, like food, each participant in the productive chain focuses advertising on its immediate customer rather than on the final user. And, to a considerable extent, this applies in the clothing industry: the converter is the fabric mill's target, the retailer is the garment producer's target. But in contrast to other industries, advertising in clothing does not simply follow the flow of goods; the intermediate producers also independently focus sales and advertising efforts on the final users.[15] This can be viewed, at least in part, as an attempt to circumvent the bottleneck and risks associated with the final design and manufacture of clothing. To protect and promote its own interests, the textile industry has used advertising to create additional components of demand influencing decisions about what to buy.

Perhaps the best example of this intervention by intermediate suppliers has been the direct promotion of generic and brand name fabrics. Beginning in the 1960s, fibre manufacturers began to advertise jointly with garment manufacturers to establish brand recognition for particular fabrics – Christian Dior jeans, for example, made of 'Qiana by Du Pont'. International trade associations like Cotton Incorporated raised their visibility through campaigns designed to promote the improved qualities of cotton (better shrinkage control, durable press) in the face of increasing competition from synthetic fibres. Advertising was directed both to final consumers and to members. In the early 1970s, the Cotton Seal logo was introduced to accompany garments produced with the new 'improved' cotton. Within a few years, the seal was considered an advantage to retailers who requested it.[16] The wool trademark has become equally popular, again achieved through direct advertising to the consumer. Bi-annual international textile trade shows are also designed to influence the consumption patterns of both intermediate and final consumers, enhancing demand from both quarters. They introduce new fabrics with improved performance features – permanent press, stain-resistance, etc. and also suggest new fashion colour combinations and textures well in advance of manufacturing.

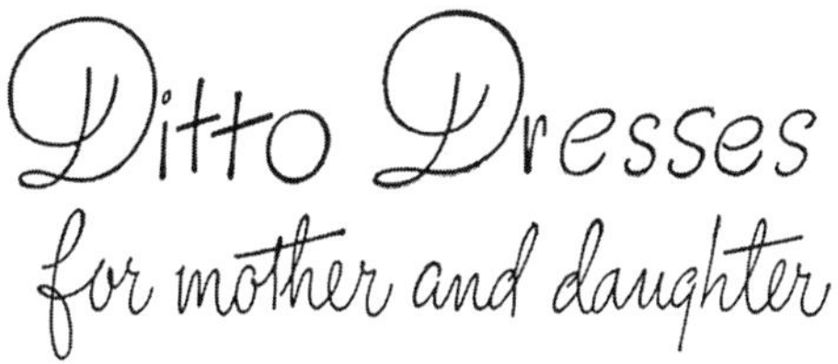

*Figure 8* Promoting the fabric rather than the finished product.
*Source*: *Parents' Magazine*, 1941.

The closest analogy in the food industry is the advertising carried out by the Milk, Cheese and Meat Marketing Boards in Britain. These promote consumption of generic products, conveyed through both print media and television to raise awareness of the variety of preparations to which each of these foods lend themselves, and to make claims about the nutritional values they offer. The fact that this type of marketing does not exist in the United States reveals differences in the organisation and control of production in the two countries. Britain's higher population density and relatively small size (1/40 of the land area of the US) facilitates the operation of national marketing in all these products. By comparison, the supply of milk in the United States is still controlled by competitive regional fiefdoms, which does not facilitate co-operative marketing strategies at the national level.

The ultimate goal of textile advertising is to influence the structure of consumer demand, elevating the choice of fabric to a role of at least equal importance as that played by style and detail in the selection of a new garment. To the extent that decisions about fabrics take precedence over other components of fashion (i.e., that a garment is selected primarily because it is linen or cotton, knitted or woven), textile producers gain more control over the planning and production of clothing at the expense of the manufacturers. The greater this control, the better able they are to bypass and hence minimise the risks associated with the fragmented nature of manufacture at the end of the chain of production.

The direct appeal of intermediate suppliers to final consumers distinguishes the pattern of advertising in clothing from that obtaining in most mass production industries, not just those with a shorter production chain like food but also those with equally substantial inputs from intermediate suppliers, like automobiles: steel manufacturers make no direct appeal to car buyers in an attempt to influence their purchasing habits. Unlike textiles, steel rarely makes an appearance in the advertising pages of publications directly targeting consumers.

The contrast in the intra-process roles of textile suppliers and garment producers (in scale of investment, productivity) helps to explain the marked difference in their advertising budgets. As mentioned above, the average expenditure by clothing manufacturers on advertising has been estimated at just 0.8 per cent of net sales, compared with 2.0 per cent in textiles. The relatively small advertising budget among manufacturers is, in part, a symptom of the continuing prevalence of small firms in the industry, producing on a modest (sometimes extremely modest) scale. The economic futures of these firms may not be secure enough to warrant the relatively long-term investment required to establish brand recognition through repeated advertising.

By contrast, the giant scale of textile operations and their need to create final markets for established and innovative lines well in advance of, and independently from, final producers encourages more generous use of advertising while at the same time providing the long lead-in time that successful ad campaigns require. Total advertising expenditure on clothing must, therefore, consider inputs from both the textile suppliers and manufacturers together.

## THE ADVERTISING OF MEN'S CLOTHING

The impact of the fashion system on the pattern of advertising is both more visible and more pronounced in women's clothing markets than in men's. Today, women's fashions account for more than three times the volume of sales achieved by men's; they are responsible for almost three-quarters of all sales in the clothing industry.[17] The striking disparity in their shares of the market and of fashion advertising is itself an indication of the inveterate differences which have shaped the twentieth-century systems of provision in the two sectors.

To see the linkages between advertising, distribution and production, one has only to take a longer view of the clothing industry, back to the first half of the nineteenth century when gender roles in the fashion industry were reversed. During this period, menswear dominated both clothing sales and public attention to fashion. Ready-to-wear markets were already sizeable. One New York retailer advertised an 'immense stock of fashionable ready made clothing . . . 1,000 coats . . . 5,000 vests . . . 5,000 pants' (Feldman 1960: 86). Emerging alongside these markets were all the now-familiar trappings of a supporting fashion industry but, at this stage, directed exclusively to the promotion of menswear. As a marketed and publicised phenomenon, women's wear did not exist.

One of the first periodicals, *Le Miroir du Beau Monde* which appeared as a weekly in 1829, included coloured plates and a promise to alert its readership to 'every change in fashion' (Feldman 1960: 72). The editor of *The Mirror of Fashion*, which followed in 1840, considered 'dress, which invests and decorates the body . . . not less one of the fine arts than architecture' (ibid.: 73). Newspapers began to include editorials on men's dress. Specialist fashion reporters (often renegade tailors) emerged on the scene to inform men of the latest changes in European dress. In short, the men's fashion industry showed all the basic features that came to be identified with and elaborated by women's wear a century later.

In its original form, the nineteenth-century fashion industry preceded the arrival of the sewing machine, developing instead in response to a system of production still based on hand-sewing, though increasingly carried out in factories. In this context, publicity and advertising could exploit the flexibility of craft production, which the rapid turnover of fashion goods would show to advantage. The same intimate connection between advertising used to promote style change and craft-based production reappeared in women's wear a century later. Though by then, basic sewing was no longer carried out by hand, the way that machines had been incorporated into production in many women's wear branches preserved much of the character of the tailoring process and its competitive advantage in the world of small-batch production. This was no longer true for most sectors of menswear production which, by the early twentieth century, had moved much closer to mass production technologies.

Looked at in this way, the relationship between advertising and production reflects a specific stage in the industrial development of clothing, one which menswear passed through considerably earlier and with much less fanfare than did women's wear. Explanations for the significant lags in the technical development of women's wear must draw upon a variety of economic and demographic changes that occurred during the intervening period. But they do not require and are not enlightened by gender-based theories of consumer behaviour.

The earlier arrival of mass production and mass marketing of men's clothing derives less from the tradition of bespoke tailoring than from the early ready-to-wear markets for cheap work clothes for those without direct or indirect access to tailoring services (sailors, slaves, indentured servants, domestic servants) and all those engaged in building the nation's infrastructure (described briefly in Chapter 9). It was price and utility that sold these basic garments, not fashion. Styles were often limited and style changes infrequent, allowing manufacturers to plan production well in advance in sufficient quantities to cover store orders and expected re-orders.

The availability of these clothes, unchanged season after season, encouraged customer loyalty and so facilitated the introduction of brand names (particularly in men's shoes, slacks and suits). Women's wear, lacking both the national markets and the reliably stable products of the menswear branch, had no incentive to introduce brands; these did not, in fact, appear in the United States until the 1950s, a half century after their emergence in menswear (Packard 1983: 156). Corresponding to this lag in the development of brands in women's apparel was a similar lag in the emergence of national advertising. Most lines of men's apparel were represented in advertisements by the turn of the century: for example, Hart, Shaffner & Marx, high-volume producers of men's tailored clothes, began promoting their name in 1890. In women's apparel, only those items (shoes, corsets, underwear) that had reached levels of mechanised production and volumes of output comparable to those achieved by menswear appeared in the advertising pages of catalogues and magazines.

The earlier introduction of brands in men's clothes encouraged market segmentation based on price rather than on fashion. Each brand was associated with an undeviating level of quality and range of product which made the promotion of brand recognition relatively straightforward and efficient. Over time, different market segments came to be associated with small-scale specialist retailers rather than with the large department stores which typically catered to a wider spread of women customers.

At a technical level, one of the distinguishing factors of men's clothing in general has been its relatively greater emphasis on fit. The tailoring of stock

*Figure 9* Brand advertising used to sell men's clothing in the 1890s, half a century before it was adopted for women's wear.
*Source*: Hart, Schnaffer & Marx.

model clothing to the unique requirements of individual bodies provided the basis for the development of large-scale, made-to-measure tailoring establishments[18] which catered exclusively to male clients. Their operations were facilitated by the compilation of standard sizes, particularly height and chest measurements, supplied first by Civil War recruits in the early 1860s. Fifty years later, there was still no comparable study of women's measurements available to dress manufacturers, who continued to supply their customers with poorly sized garments (Brew 1948: 439).

Men's clothes, on the contrary, have always been tailored with a much greater concern for a close fit to the body. Even the simplest shirts are differentiated by neck size and by sleeve length. A basic long-sleeve shirt requiring the minimum stock range of six neck sizes, four sleeve lengths and, say, three colours, produces a minimum assortment (to include all permutations of these attributes), of 72 units. Selling any one of the 72 renders it out-of-stock.

The number of units in an assortment inevitably proliferates with the addition of other measurements, as a shirtmaker writing to the *New York Times* recently explained:[19]

> In today's market, the three most popular collar styles are the button down . . . the tab collar . . . and the Prince of Wales spread collar. . . . We make each one of the three basic collar styles in four different back heights, depending on the length of a man's back and five different front heights, depending on his posture and age. . . . We also make each collar in three different point lengths, which makes 60 variations and three different widths – making 180 variations of each style.

The difficulties facing both the retailer and the manufacturer in supplying the right assortment of sizes and colours of any one style are already formidable. The more variable stock becomes, the more these difficulties will be multiplied.

It is arguable, therefore, that the complexity imposed by the tailoring requirements of men's clothes have themselves limited the penetration of fashion to those changes compatible with mechanised tailoring. While tailoring operations transferred to machinery could accommodate extensive size variations in the pieces of one style of garment, they would find it less easy to handle the complexities introduced by a multiplicity of styles or to adopt more superficial variations in design commonly associated with women's dress. In other words, the continued concern with the technical requirements of a tailored fit in menswear took precedence over, and to a great extent crowded out, the demands of fashion.

Variations in sizes of garment pieces, e.g., in neck and sleeve sizes (as well as variety in fabric colours) could be more readily introduced in the earlier, more efficient stages of production, i.e., in the more mechanised cutting and dying processes than in the later processes of sewing and finishing. On the other hand, changes dictated by fashion (other than those affecting cut and colour) often involve the substitution or the addition of a wide variety of fabrics and/ or trimmings which are typically handled in the later, less efficient stages of production by an individual machine operator working on one garment at a time. These are the kind of changes associated primarily with fashions in women's clothes, rather than in men's.

Dedicated machinery used in the production of men's shirts cannot readily accommodate the same range of fabrics that can be worked up by the mixture of hand and machine sewing common in workshops producing women's dresses. The same applies to the addition of embroidery, appliqué work, frogging, decorative ornaments, bows, the substitution of toggles for buttons, etc. These are changes that exploit the small-batch capacities of the traditional sewing shop to advantage but which lie beyond the scope of factory production geared to high-volume output of standardised products. Most of menswear falls into the latter category.

The influence of high-quality hand-tailoring, however, remains strong. The notion that a suit represents a long-term investment in top-quality materials and skills has a much older and longer pedigree in men's apparel than in women's. Factory production, when it arrived, did not undermine the expectations of longevity associated with such a purchase but exploited them in novel ways. When mechanised production simplified the manufacture of trousers (they were more vulnerable to wear and tear than jackets), it became customary to supply a suit with an extra pair of trousers in order to extend the lifespan of the outfit. The development of the 'made-to-measure' business early in the twentieth century also exploited the received wisdom linking custom-made methods of manufacture to durability. Now, although the share of output produced by traditional tailoring skills is small, their influence on the character and content of menswear advertising remains disproportionately high.

It is, paradoxically, the dominance of mass production in menswear that allows advertising to exploit the virtues of hand-crafted production. Mass production serves the needs of what has traditionally been a much narrower dress code. The persistence of male uniforms (the white shirt, the pinstriped suit, the tuxedo) has simplified production requirements and contrasts with the apparent freedom of choice available to (or forced upon) women dressing for the same occasions. Compared to women, men appear to be sartorially circumscribed, by their relative uniformity in dress and by the standardisation of their garments (according to company publicity, Arrow shirts claim to represent 25 per cent of all shirts sold in America). In this context, the availability of distinctive, high-quality, hand-tailored garments offers the occasional compensation for long-suffering compliance with the prescribed dress code stereotypes while reinforcing the models on which they are based.

The techniques of hand-sewing that appear as retrograde in the context of women's fashion (where they predominate and are, therefore, liable to be veiled) are elevated through menswear advertising to furnish a distinct fashion niche at the top of the market. Here, advertising highlights the proportion of hand-sewing involved[20] – 'One machine can do the work of 50 ordinary men. No machine can do the work of one extraordinary man'.

This is consistent with a market segmented by price rather than by fashion since it emphasises enduring (if expensive) quality that is made available at the top end of the market. It is presumed to correspond to a parallel and measurable spread in production techniques and, in fact, menswear manufacturers were traditionally rated by a number designating tailoring level which ranged from one (the lowest) to six (representing the finest needlework) (Packard 1983: 137). By contrast, in women's apparel it is sensitivity to the pulse of fashion – rather than price alone or some corresponding perception of gradations in durability – which creates the hierarchy of clothing labels. The form of advertising that grows out of this suppresses production altogether, denying the existence of any link at all between methods of manufacture and the markets they serve. The effect is to enhance the commanding role of demand, playing up, and upon, its unpredictability and its rate of change; playing down its roots in the short cycles of batch production.

Menswear advertising chooses instead to emphasise the stability of demand for its products. It is characterised more by its sedateness and its emphasis on 'classic' and 'traditional' values than by any sense of provocation or stimulation of the sort evoked by the more imaginative advertising in women's wear. Though the contrast in adverts for men's and women's clothes has begun to attenuate with the spread of men's fashion design, unisex shops, etc., men still make fewer purchases than women. The contents of a man's wardrobe are more constant and more limited in scope than those of a woman's. Although it may in aggregate represent a greater investment, on average a man's wardrobe still includes fewer fabrics, fewer styles and fewer colours than a woman's. This is clearly reflected in the contrasting forms and content of advertising that promote the two clothing sectors.

It is, in fact, an implicit comparison between a man's and woman's wardrobe that underscores the use of the term 'conservative' or 'traditional' in the promotion of menswear. In some sense then, the fashion advertising of women's wear (which dominates the advertising of clothing as it dominates sales) serves as a benchmark for menswear advertising, setting the limits of style and tone. In another sense, the subordinate role played by the menswear branch also signifies its relatively greater independence from advertising; the more stable and predictable the product range, the longer any single advertising campaign can run.

In other words, menswear occupies a middle ground between two extremes, in both its advertising and in the structure of its system of provision: at one end sits traditionally hand-crafted clothing which cloaks itself in an aura of timelessness, substituting the reliability of taste and quality for the trendiness of fashion; at the other extreme is the unchanging high-volume output of standardised, machine-made garments. To understand the contradictory dynamics at work across this spectrum and the way they filter through to advertising requires a special awareness of the tensions created by the separate structures of provision in both women's wear and menswear.

The continuing survival, alongside the menswear industry but separate from it, of women's wear branches that depend on the promotion of individuality in advertising has had two contradictory effects. First, it has forced menswear branches to adopt an almost apologetic stance towards its very long tradition of uniform dress. This may have helped to keep alive the tradition of expensive bespoke tailoring at the top end of the market, in an attempt to provide comparable access for men to the individuality that is made so continuously available to women. At another level, the need to suppress any association between uniformity in dress and uniformity in production (embedded in menswear) betokens a deeper conflict between the longer tradition of mass production (which grew from the bottom up, supplying common necessities to working people on low incomes) and the more elitist tradition of fashion (which dictates silence on the production front altogether, seeking direction from the realm of demand). The theory of the trickle-down serves here to elevate and sanctify both the presumed innate drive towards individuality in dress and the role of the upper classes as responsible for the introduction of fashion change.

The second influence of the women's wear tradition on menswear has been the increasing absorption of the latter into the fashion system. Through a variety of devices, from increasing the rate of turnover in fashion styles to extending the range of necessary accessories (like cosmetics and perfumes), men have been encouraged to adopt the consuming habits of women. Fashion advertising of products for men has increased correspondingly, beginning with the inclusion of men's fashion pages at the back end of women's fashion journals and extending to the more recent profusion of fashion magazines designed exclusively for men.

# 16

# FOOD, RETAILING AND ADVERTISING

In exploring the relation between the system of food provision and advertising, the focus is here primarily on grocery retailing in Britain. A number of recent trends have been apparent which need to be highlighted in order to locate the role of advertising. First, there has been an increasing concentration of the business into a very small number of dominant multiples, most notably led by Tesco and Sainsbury. Multiples overall accounted for 78 per cent of the food trade in 1987 compared with 57.1 per cent in 1976 (Gardner and Sheppard 1989: 155). Of this, corporate share percentages were as follows –

*Figure 10* Still the most common form of food advertising in 1993.
*Source*: Hudson Place.

Tesco 14.2, Sainsbury 14.1, Gateway 11.4, Argyll 10.2 and Asda 7.7, so that the five largest retailers accounted for well over half of all sales (ibid.: 163).

The growth in concentration has, in part, been the consequence of a rapid and extensive phase of acquisitions; in the 1980s, as much as a quarter of all multiple business in value terms had changed hands, with Argyll in the forefront trading as Presto, Lo-Cost and Safeway. But, as a second trend, a major source of expansion has been through internal growth which has taken the form of superstores or hypermarkets. These are located away from central urban sites. In numbers they have grown from 282 in 1983 (when owned by thirteen separate retailers) to 580 in 1989 (when owned by only eight separate retailers). Projections of future development estimate that there will be 825 such superstores in Britain by 1993. Their food share has risen from 17.8 per cent in 1980 to 24.5 per cent in 1988 (when they also accounted for 23.2 per cent of DIY and 24.1 per cent of clothing) (MINTEL 1989). The total number of supermarkets is actually declining as total floorspace increases in the smaller number of larger hypermarkets.[1] Noting these developments in a series of contributions, Wrigley (1987, 1989, 1991) observes the increasing use of the stock market to raise funds to finance expansion into new site hypermarkets. As Moir (1990) observes, this reflects a form of 'store-wars' in which such a store effectively becomes a local monopolist over its retail catchment area. Shaw *et al.* (1989) and McLelland (1990) question whether this is dictated by the overwhelming importance of scale economies in supermarket retailing, since unit selling costs do not appear to fall above a middle-range store.

Third, accompanying these changes, there has been a significant growth in the selling of own-label groceries in place of manufacturers' brands. This has risen from 22.5 per cent of grocery sales in 1977 to 29.9 per cent in 1988 (Gardner and Sheppard 1989: 159). In the lead has been Marks and Spencer, which has always been a purely own-label retailer under the trademark of St Michael, and which has prided itself on high quality.[2] It has been an important market leader in this respect since, traditionally, own-brand groceries have been associated with both lower prices and poorer quality.[3] With its basis in clothing, M&S's move into food has had the added effect of undermining the image of own-label as inferior, a precondition for its general acceptability (de Chernatony 1989a).

Food-based multiples were responsible in 1985 for 85 per cent of own-label produce as compared to a 65 per cent overall share (Martell 1986). Amongst the major grocery retailers stocking own-brand and other manufacturers' brands, Sainsbury has been in the lead in marketing own-label produce. This made up 57 per cent of its sales in 1984 compared with 36.3 per cent for Tesco (Hurst 1985: 395). Interestingly, though, the role of own label in Sainsbury's sales had fallen from 65.7 per cent in 1976 (as compared to 24.4 per cent for Tesco at that date). The explanation for this is that superstores have recently had to accommodate a rapid expansion of highly diversified, fast-moving and highly advertised grocery sales, as well as catering for own-label brands.

Many of these developments are thought to be the consequence of, amongst other factors, the abolition of retail price maintenance in 1964, sluggish demand, and the shifting balance of power between manufacturers and retailers.[4] However, the parallel to some extent with similar changes in the United States (Lusch 1987), and the example of the declining share of Sainsbury's own-label products, illustrate that there has been more of a shift in the way in which competition is fought rather than an unambiguous and permanent shift in favour of the large-scale retailers (except at the continuing expense of the small shopkeeper).[5] In general, despite, even because of, extreme concentration of sales by the major retailers, it has been argued by some that competition between them has become more intense. Whilst each is able to negotiate discounts on price either for a manufacturer's own brand or for its own label, this would be expected in any circumstances of bulk purchase. So this alone cannot be taken as evidence of shifting power to retailers. In addition, a manufacturer has the capacity to choose between a number of retailers in the production of own labels as well as the option of branding products as their own (and, as will be seen, circulation costs become shifted to the retailer in the form of advertising for own label).

It is worth placing this discussion in a historical context so that present-day trends are neither exaggerated nor seen as uniform across retailing as a whole.[6] At the end of the nineteenth century, retailers were not only knowledgeable about their wares but also often partially responsible for production. As Jefferys observes, apart from there being a significant layer of wholesalers between producers and retailers:[7]

> The retailers proper and the producer/retailer were for the most part craftsmen, apprenticed to the trade they served. . . . In the grocery trade, for example, the blending of tea, the mixing of herbs and spices, the curing and cutting of bacon, the cleaning and washing of dried fruit, the cutting and millgrinding of sugar, and the roasting and grinding of coffee were essential functions of the retailer, apart entirely from the tasks of weighing out and bagging.
>
> (Jefferys 1954: 2)

Of course, these functions have now been entirely removed to the realm of manufacturing whatever the degree of quality control exerted over them by powerful retailers, and Jefferys reckons that this shift of function from retailer to wholesaler or manufacturer continued in the interwar period and was associated with deskilling of the retail workforce (ibid.: 49).

The turn of the century also witnessed the emergence and growth of department stores, multiple retailing and mass production of branded goods (which were often designed through advertising to eliminate the middle stage of wholesaling). According to de Chernatony and McWilliam, manufacturers increasingly occupied the pole position:

> Thus, in an era of manufacturing dominance lasting from around 1900 to the early 1960's, a competitive tier of products historically referred to as brands (or national brands, manufacturer brands or advertised brands), dominated the majority of consumer goods.
>
> (de Chernatony and McWilliam 1988: 2)

This was all perceived to change with the growing importance of own-label groceries starting from the mid-1960s when they accounted for only 10 per cent of sales. But it is crucial to recognise that this shift, and associated trends discussed previously, have not been uniform across all consumption goods. And though they are clearly important for groceries, their influence varies from product to product. For example, Heinz Baked Beans has taken an increasing share of the market, rising from 38 per cent in 1984 to 40 per cent in 1987, whilst own-label share has also increased from 34 to 39 per cent (EIU 1989b). In the case of cigarettes, no own-label brand has emerged at all. For biscuits, own label accounted for 23 per cent of sales in 1987 compared to 36 per cent for the branded production of United Biscuits.

What emerges is a structure shifting towards the *co-existence* of high concentration in both own label *and* branded goods. The particular balance between the two varies from product to product according to brand strength and the implications of restructuring in both manufacturing and retailing. The interactions involved can be complex and may even enhance the role of branded goods, revamped department stores and smaller-volume retailing as high streets, abandoned by supermarkets, become the preserve of specialised stores:

> In the 1980s in the UK, traditional department stores suffered. A combination of out-of-town shopping for furniture, finishings and household goods grew, together with a move by grocery retailers into hypermarket trading with an enlarged consumer durable product range, and a rise in popularity of specialist clothing stores eroded the demand for the traditional department store products.
>
> (Johnson 1987: 3)

Given the trends identified here, it is hardly surprising that they have significant implications for advertising. The most notable change has been in the nature of the advertisers, with a major growth on the part of retailers. As Fulop (1986: 25) reports, in the 1970s retail expenditure on advertising was the fastest growing of all sectors, increasing seven times in money terms, compared to the trebling of that by manufacturers of other consumer goods. From 1970 to 1983, it increased at twice the rate of advertising by food manufacturers.[8] Sainsbury, for example, doubled its advertising to sales ratio to 0.2 per cent, low compared with Tesco and Asda at 0.5 per cent. Even M&S

felt compelled to embark upon its first major advertising campaign, its previous reluctance no doubt reflecting a view that to do so would impair its reputation as an own-label producer of quality.

During the 1980s, own-label advertising began to grow. This has been most notable for Sainsbury; own-label expenditure matched general advertising expenditure at £4.9 million each in 1989 (these grew from £2.2 and £3.4 million, respectively, in 1984 (EIU 1989d)). Own-label advertising is considerably less significant for the other retailers, often only just emerging during this five-year period. But it must be recognised that corporate advertising is, in substantial part, a major if indirect contribution to own-label advertising. Evidence is provided by Douglas:

> Why then are retailers such a dominant force in advertising today, to such an extent that in many countries they have been the fastest-growing spenders in the last ten years? Why do many retailers now spend more on advertising their stores, than most manufacturers spend on promoting any one of their lines? . . . Seven of the top ten 'brands' are retailers. . . . The word 'brand' is not inappropriate here. Many retailers are now using advertising and other elements of the marketing mix, to create a brand image for their companies as powerful as those of Kellogg's and Heinz. In doing so, and in selling quality goods under their own name rather than those of the established branded goods manufacturers, they are posing a major challenge to the manufacturers.[9]
>
> (Douglas 1984: 36)

This is strongly brought out by consideration of the content of the ads concerned and, to a large extent, by the media in which they are placed. Consider labelling first of all. In the case of M&S, whose shops do not hold competing products, design can be varied to maximise sales:

> Because St. Michael products do not have to compete with manufacturers' brands on the shelves, M&S can . . . afford to adopt an extremely varied approach to packaging. Not so the average supermarket trader which should aim to use packaging design as a measure of reinforcing the corporate image.
>
> (Relph-Knight 1988: 53)

Thus, brand design and corporate image become closely identified for commercial purposes:

> The pack designs also have to reflect the retailers corporate message. Consumers will not be swayed into buying own-brands more than once, unless the quality of the product is right but appropriately attractive packaging might tempt a first sale.
>
> (Relph-Knight 1988: 53)

First of all, though, the shopper has to be induced to go to the corporate store rather than to a competitor's. And, although the first preference is for the store's own brand to be purchased, the second preference is for another brand to be purchased in the same store – which is why the products of competitors are made available. This has had an effect on the content of advertising which sees close identification of the store with *groups* of own-label products. The nature of the advertising here has been more of the 'realistic' and 'informative' type, appropriately by display of products in a double-page spread in a colour magazine. Magazine share of Sainsbury's advertising rose from 4.7 per cent in 1979 to 29 per cent in 1984; for Tesco and Asda over the same period, it rose from negligible amounts to 13.8 per cent and 6.8 per cent, respectively.[10]

Although manufacturers may well have increased their absolute expenditure in order to maintain the attraction of their branded products to advertisers, there has been a clear switch in the share of advertising from manufacturers to retailers. This trend, however, has been overlooked by those pursuing use value interpretations. This is so for a number of reasons. First of all, somewhat tellingly, their focus on the *form* of the advert has deflected concern away from a discussion of its sponsors. Even the necessity of sale as the ultimate objective of advertising falls away as analysis focuses on understanding how the commodity is made desirable (rather than purchased).

Second, primary interest in interpreting the adverts requires the selection of those with the richest possible content combined with the greatest ease of presentation (inevitably a still or reproduced printed image). This tends to restrict discussion to branded goods alone. In the attempt to reveal the construction of complex meanings, the projection of these on to a particular product will be particularly helpful. Thus, selectivity in how to interpret adverts goes hand in hand with the choice of what to interpret. Whilst the commodities chosen may represent a wide selection, they are all of one type – brands. The almost exclusive preoccupation with branded goods in the interpretative literature stands in sharp contrast to other areas which investigate other attributes of adverts.[11] For example, Relph-Knight (1988) reports that Asda has 4,000 own-label products and that it has won a prize for the label series designed for its wines and spirits.[12] Histories of advertising also tend to look at commerce more widely, tracing, for example, the creation of corporate images.

Third, the focus on branded goods has the effect of exaggerating or even misreading trends in advertising. There is a general idea that these have become more sophisticated in their forms of representation and that this reflects a move away from 'realistic' or 'informative' content – partly as a consequence of changing technology and the increasing powers and scope of mass media/communications. Yet the rise of retail advertising, especially in the context of own-label goods, is associated with 'informative' and 'realistic' ads through the media of magazines, partly as supplements to newspapers, which have themselves been made possible through advertising revenues and new technology in printing.

## CONCLUDING REMARKS

Finally, this discussion needs to mention that a substantial volume of output from both the food (and clothing and other) industries is consumed without the intervention of advertising of any kind. Government procurement – of military, firefighting, police uniforms, of hospital and school foods, etc. – eliminates the need for the type of marketing and advertising that form an essential part of the chain of supply associated with exclusively private capitalist production and exchange. The systems of provision that operate in the absence of marketing and advertising are, correspondingly, distinct from those in effect when the chain encompasses them. Though this book primarily restricts itself to a discussion of economies based on market exchange (which is assumed by most of the theories of consumption addressed here), the implications of alternative institutional arrangements needs at least to be recognised. Put very briefly, the presence of markets brings out and exploits differences between the food and clothing industries that tend to be attenuated when purchasing decisions by individual consumers disappear. This is food for thought for further investigation!

Though brief and selective, the discussion of advertising in this and the previous chapter suggests that important distinctions emerge between one industry and another when advertising is refracted through the lens of a systems-of-provision approach. At the very least, the discussion should discourage the continued practice of lumping food and clothing together as largely undifferentiated goods for the purposes of horizontal analyses of consumption. Though the practice has been justified by the common attributes shared by food and clothing markets compared with, say, those of the automobile or housing markets, there is clearly much to be gained from distinguishing between them and from considering the many invisible but interconnected processes involved in bringing each set of goods to market.

# Part IV

# MARXISM AND CONSUMPTION

# 17

# THE NEW URBAN SOCIOLOGY

## INTRODUCTION

Chapter 17 examines consumption in the light of the new urban sociology; this brings to the fore the idea of the city as a site of collective (or public) as well as private consumption. Despite the varied (consumption) activities associated with urban areas, focus for analysis in the literature has been restricted to housing, particularly to forms of tenure. As a result, even housing as an item of consumption in itself has been neglected in the sense that its changing quality and standards, and its role as a site of consumption, have not been prominent. Instead, as this chapter demonstrates, consumption has been put forward as a substitute for production to serve as an explanatory category within sociology. Ironically, this has come about despite an earlier attempt to eschew the reductionism associated with exclusive dependence on class relations of production. However, though the outcome has been a reductionism to strata cleavages in consumption, it has not been a purely negative exercise. It has at least highlighted the social nature and provision of consumption in striking contrast to most analyses, which focus narrowly on the private individual or household. This necessarily places in the forefront the role of the state in influencing consumption, also a matter that has been more generally neglected, but one taken up in the concluding chapter.

## 1 ANALYTICAL CLEAVAGES

In the Introduction to a special issue of *Sociology* devoted exclusively to articles on consumption, Wardle begins with a refrain familiar across the social sciences:

> Historically, sociologists have never paid a great deal of attention to consumption. When not considered the mere reflection of production it has been treated as a derivative of distribution, a matter of the availability of resources rather than of who consumes what. When attention was devoted to actual consumption behaviour, it was most often as a branch of social pathology, concerned with social problems of insufficient

> nutritious food, excess alcohol, inadequate health care, too many cigarettes. Only rarely did the sociological classics examine consumption for its own sake.
>
> (Wardle 1990: 1)

So, with the exception of defining it as an epiphenomenon or as deviancy from an unexplored norm, sociology is perceived as having only recently come to grips with consumption. Wardle suggests a number of reasons for current interest in the matter. First, diminished support for the British Labour Party is explained by shifting commitment to a consumption-based politics ('second coming of the embourgeoisement thesis'); second is the ideology of the decreasing importance of work, especially associated with Gorz (1982); third is the post-Fordist view of the end of mass production with its concern for flexible products and market niches; fourth has been the crisis of provision within the welfare state. In response to these stimuli, Wardle identifies two newly developing approaches to consumption: one concerned with its cultural content and context, the other arising out of innovation in urban sociology. The first has been examined in earlier chapters. Discussion here takes up the second.

The origins of the new urban sociology are to be found in the work and influence of Castells. He grapples with the specific nature and dynamics of city-life. His analysis is extremely complex, drawing upon the idea of a close relationship between collective consumption and the reproduction of labour power. He takes these two features as defining the city, although this does not exclude the presence of other activities located in the urban environment:

> A concrete city . . . is not only a unit of consumption. It is, of course, made up of a very great diversity of practices and functions. It expresses, in fact, society as a whole, though through the specific historical form that it represents. Therefore, whoever wishes to study a city (or series of cities) must also study capital, production, politics, ideology, etc. Furthermore, one cannot understand the process of consumption without linking it to the accumulation of capital and to the political relations between the classes. The problem still remains of deciding the specificity of this process of reproducing labour power and the relations that exist between the collective reproduction of labour power and the urban problematic.
>
> (Castells 1977: 440)

This, for most readers, must be more or less uncontroversial, subject to language and a wide enough concept of consumption; more innovative and subject to dispute in Castells' work has been the emphasis placed upon consumption in urban movements and conflicts – his seeing it as being separate in location, content and support from those activities traditionally associated with the classic sites of working-class practices, places of employment, and carried out primarily with the central role adopted by the working class itself, constituted as workers.

Saunders (1986a), at the centre of debates in the new urban sociology, sees himself as breaking decisively with Castells' arguments. His own approach has gone through a process of evolution,[1] particularly in rejecting an earlier view, drawn from Rex and Moore (1967) of class divisions based on housing tenure. Saunders sees consumption as participating in a more general determination of social stratification. None the less, there have been some common themes throughout his work. First, there is a wish to appeal to consumption as an element in the process of creating stratification. Whilst this is generally presented as something that supplements the influence provided by production relations, the inevitable consequence of its introduction is to dispute the privileging of production and, potentially, to open the way for many other factors, such as race and gender, to enter equally into the process of stratification.

Saunders views consumption as enjoying at least a degree of autonomy from production and possibly a level of parity. He observes that Castells 'recognises linkages between production and consumption but [his] real offence [to Marxism] is to allow consumption to have independent effects' (Saunders 1986a: 225). In commenting upon Dunleavy (1986) and Preteceille (1986), Saunders (1986b) acknowledges that class (production) divisions and consumption are related, but he questions whether the former is the key factor. Although Saunders is deeply anti-Marxist, he endows Marxism with sufficient influence to have deflected appropriate attention away from consumption because of its tunnel vision in focusing on the capital–labour relation at the expense of the interests of consumers (although, paradoxically, Marxism initiated the new urban sociology despite itself). Saunders (1988) blames the 'Marxist tunnel vision of predominance of capital–labour over the interests of consumers'.

Like Castells, however, Saunders is concerned with the mode of organisation of consumption, distinguishing three forms historically in sequence; market, socialised and privatised.[2] He also sees conflicts over consumption as essentially distinct from class or production relations (Saunders 1986a: 297): 'When and if people do mobilise or align themselves around consumption questions, their class interests . . . will tend to figure less centrally than their sectoral interests.' This is verging on the tautologous and illustrates the extent to which the theoretical stance adopted by Saunders has a close correspondence with the empirical events and developments that he seeks to explain.

For Saunders, the central commodity giving rise to consumption-based effects is housing – 'the single most pertinent factor in the determination of consumption sector cleavages' (Saunders 1984: 207).[3] Consequently, criticism of his approach has also tended to focus on housing. Hamnett (1989) questions more generally the empirical and theoretical basis for Saunders' hypothesis of consumption strata. But Savage *et al.* (1990) argue that the notion of consumption strata ground out by access to housing is not stable over generations as there is considerable intergenerational mobility between different types of housing consumption from parents to children: 'housing tenure does not appear to be an axis of social closure. In this respect it differs fundamentally from social class' (ibid.: 113). This completes, at an intertemporal level, the earlier and more common critique that consumption strata based on housing are not well defined and, even to the extent that they are, will be heavily dependent upon production/class related factors, which influence both what consumption locations are available and who will fill them (see especially Sullivan 1989). Nor is the idea of generalised dissatisfaction with public housing (which is a major component of Saunders' argument) empirically sound (Forrest and Murie 1990).

Given the heavy dependence of Saunders' views on conditions prevailing in Britain and on the central role of housing, it naturally follows that the issue of owner-occupation versus council housing (there being little and decreasing levels of private rented accommodation in the UK) should be generalised into one of public (or collective) versus private (but supported) provision or consumption. However, the distinction between public and private provision is far from clear-cut, as observed by Preteceille (1986) and by Harrison (1986), who prefer the term 'organised consumption'. This is pertinent, especially when it is related to non-housing consumption such as healthcare; Busfeld (1990) points to the continuing dependence on the public sector of those with private health insurance – and the same is obviously true of transport with its mix of public and private vehicles, both sharing a common infrastructure.

The intention here is not to add to this critique of Saunders[4] – but to investigate his concept of consumption. Despite its prominent analytical role, very little of a specific theory of consumption is in fact developed. Many important contributing factors are overlooked entirely. The actual history of housing standards and design, crucial to the evolution of housing as an item of consumption, and the ways in which housing is itself consumed, facilitating or thwarting the consumption of a great many other commodities, are all neglected.[5] Other major changes in the determination of housing provision are also absent, not least the demographic factors influencing household size and composition, migration, etc.[6] The preoccupation with housing tenure on its own is a peculiarly British pastime and, unsurprisingly, comparative material by country and by time is notable for its absence.[7]

Rather than address these issues, consumption has been projected on to other social relations, in particular on to voting patterns (do owner-occupiers vote Tory?) or other forms of social protest.[8] Indeed, whether to explain voting behaviour, urban conflict or social stratification, the new urban sociology's interest in consumption has been to use it to displace more traditional explanatory factors such as class and production.

But, to a large extent, consumption in the new analysis has displaced production in name alone. In this way it offers a striking parallel with the previously discussed identity between the theories of production and consumption in neoclassical economics. The differences between the two disciplines of sociology and economics could not be greater, particularly in their respective emphases on strata on the one hand and on atomised individuals on the other. But each appears to be capable of reconstructing a theory of production as a theory of consumption.

This transformation begins with Castells. His concept of collective consumption has an analogue with the collective labourer in Marxist theory of production (whereby both a common interest and greater productive powers are ground out by the process of co-operation as it is organised within the capitalist factory). The city is to consumption what the factory is to production. And distinctions within housing could also be thought to correspond to segmented labour markets and job hierarchies – with their attendant mobilities and structures.

Further, Castells (1977: 454–5) divides the role of consumption into three parts – the appropriation of the product, the reproduction of labour power and the reproduction of social relations. But these are precisely the roles that are ascribed to the production (and circulation of surplus) value in Marxist political economy, even if the first includes both productive as well as individual consumption and the latter two are analysed at the economic level in terms of the value of labour power and the scheme of economic reproduction. With this shifting of the site of appropriation and reproduction from production to consumption, and the creation of the category of collective as opposed to individual consumption, so there is a corresponding shift of site from the industrial estate to its parallel in the urban structure, or the city, 'a concrete analysis of these processes of collective consumption must illuminate in the end, the essence of the problems usually referred to as the "urban"' (ibid.: 450). By the same token, the organisation and objects of conflict are displaced away from class and production to consumption categories and localities.

Saunders' approach is less a break with, than a modification of, these steps first taken by Castells in the new urban sociology. His major difference is to free the impact of consumption from any predetermined influence of class or production. But he sustains the consumption-as-production analogue. Most recently, Saunders and Harris (1990) set up an opposition between production and consumption, not only analytically but also as a determining conflict between agencies. Consequently, 'the crucial question, therefore, is under what conditions producers may prevail over consumers, and *vice-versa*'. Following on, the economy and society are conflated into a homogeneous exchange between producers and consumers, in which distributional conflict rules as each party attempts to extract the maximum and crudest material advantage:

> Consumers want high values at low prices; producers prefer to provide low values at high prices. This is as true of state systems as of market

> systems. It is sociologically naive to pretend, for example, that the 'profit motive' only operates in the private sector and that it is transcended in socialised systems.
>
> (Saunders and Harris 1990: 62)

There are three major problems with this. First, by counterposing production to consumption in this way, it is presumed that the only exchanges that take place are those between producers and consumers wheras, of course, productive consumption presumes an exchange between producers.[9] Second, the notion of high value and low prices or vice versa is meaningless in the absence of a theory of value and of corresponding prices. Otherwise the conflict alluded to is part of the mechanism for establishing the levels of values/prices. It is not responsible for causing them to be what they are, although the associated confusion over this tends to locate value/price at the level of consumption (as in the role played by utility in neoclassical economics) and draws attention away from the production of the values (of housing) concerned. Third, different types of economic activity, whether in the public or the private sector, are reduced to this production/consumption logic with its dynamic of distributional conflict even though the imperatives of profitability do not apply to each.[10]

Consequently, for Saunders, private property rights in consumption become such that:

> Private home ownership in Britain is exploitative for two reasons. First, it functions as a source of wealth accumulation and thus provides a means of augmenting material resources. . . . Second, because like any other form of property ownership owner occupation entails not only the right to use the dwelling . . . but also rights of control . . . and alienation (i.e. rights of sale and inheritance) which are denied to non-owners, it tends to intensify inequalities of power and to perpetuate such inequalities across the generations.
>
> (Saunders 1984: 220)

Thus, consumption (of housing) becomes both a means of exploitation and of accumulation (ibid.: 209), just as this is a central component within Marxist production theory. Similarly, as Marxist theory of the mode of production can be made to turn upon the extent and manner of access to the means of production, so the same can be applied to consumption:

> Saunders argues that just as class relations are determined by the (non)ownership of the means of production, so the main cleavage within the sphere of consumption is determined by the (non)ownership of the means to fulfil consumption requirements.
>
> (Burrows and Butler 1989: 342)

Finally, with the positing of fundamental cleavages between production and consumption and also within consumption, the methodological significance of the latter is transformed. For most analyses, and especially for economics, consumption serves as an endpoint for explanation – it is what has to be explained, whether in satisfying utility, marking class distinctions, meeting psychological needs, playing out rituals, or symbolising a social discourse. But the new urban sociology *begins* with consumption – to define different strata, for example. From this point of departure, consumption patterns are the basis for explaining further factors such as voting behaviour, social conflict and differing ideologies. Again, relative to Marxist theory, the analytical displacement of production by consumption is striking.

To conclude, there are insuperable problems in constructing an opposition between production and consumption and then in fragmenting consumption along a variety of autonomous consumption items and/or strata of consumers (creating, interestingly, a parallel with supply and demand in orthodox economics whether for partial or general equilibrium analysis). These problems concern both theoretical coherence and empirical relevance even for the preferred terrain of housing, whilst the analysis itself can easily be seen to arise out of a sociology of production reconstructed as a sociology of consumption. But it is possible to draw out some less negative implications from the debates that have taken place.

First, production and consumption must be analysed as a unity rather than as a simple opposition, and the latter must not be perceived as a simple passive response to, or mirror image of, the former. But, as has been shown in other chapters, this does not place production and consumption in a symmetrical place relative to each other as there are systematic influences on the structure and development of production that have a profound effect on how consumption is organised, what is consumed, and who consumes.

Second, different modes of consumption do exist across different commodities and even for the same commodity, as the example of housing illustrates. These must be analysed as systems of provision, as has been fully realised in debates around housing provision which have increasingly recognised that different forms of tenure are only one (exaggerated) influence on the housing market.[11]

Third, the state has at times had a profound impact on the way in which consumption is provided and in the distribution of consumption, whether in directly acting as a source of supply, as in healthcare or council housing, or in its less direct interventions in systems of provision. Generally, in analyses of consumption during the modern period (which has witnessed an increasing role for the state) there has been an undue emphasis on privatised consumption through market purchase. At the very least, the new urban sociology has attempted to give full recognition to the social aspects of consumption, for which the role of the state is of prime significance.

# 18

# MARX'S ECONOMICS AND CONSUMPTION

## INTRODUCTION

The increasing preoccupation with consumption throughout the advanced capitalist countries has attracted the attention of the academic world. For consumption easily and positively places on the agenda those issues that have been an increasing focus of attention in the intellectual climate of post-modernist times. Consumption, *par excellence*, concerns the position and activity of the individual in capitalist society. It involves the interpretation of objects, ideologies and culture. Yet consumption is an immediate economic category. Commodities have to be designed, produced, distributed and marketed before they are sold, bought and, ultimately, consumed.

Interest in consumption, however, faces certain obstacles in entering the academic arena. It has become a common complaint, heard especially in history and sociology, that the analysis of consumption has been sorely neglected. For Miller:[1]

> Important is a series of academic trends which have led to an overwhelming concentration on the area of production as the key generative arena for the emergence of the dominant social relations in contemporary societies, and a comparative neglect of consumption.
>
> (Miller 1987: 3)

Within economic history, for example, this has been reflected in a degree of technical determinism – that production and supply make the world what it is over the long term. For a perspective grounded in the orthodoxy of neo-classical economics, this is justified by the assumption that the market can be assumed to work perfectly in the long run, so that supply rather than demand becomes the determining factor. Paradoxically, this goes hand in hand with a view of the consumer as sovereign in determining the composition of what is produced (and how much is saved rather than consumed), even if the level of output overall depends upon the dry statistics of the growth in inputs and total factor productivity.[2]

The growing dissatisfaction with methodologies that have given priority to production has led to attempts to redress the balance by focusing on consumption independently of production. The result has been the failure to develop, and a hostility towards, theoretical structures that unite production and consumption. This is understandable in the case of neoclassical economics. For whilst consumption through utility maximisation is the ultimate economic determinant, understanding of consumption is severely impoverished. It is confined to demand analysis, which has remained essentially unchanged over the century or more since the marginalist revolution. It depends upon assumptions that are false and limited, which have the effect of narrowing the scope of enquiry – viz., that 'rational' consumers should maximise utility subject to price and income constraints on the basis of unchanging and innate preferences.[3] It does not, therefore, provide much of a target for those academics dissatisfied with the traditional emphasis on supply. Marxism has proved a more substantive target, given its greater presence within many social sciences besides economics. With its heavy reliance upon the determining role of production, Marxism is well suited to be the scapegoat for the neglect of consumption in the non-economic social sciences.[4]

And academia abhors a discovered vacuum. So the attempt has been made to fill the theoretical void surrounding consumption. The apparent lack of a weighty tradition in the area has not proved an insurmountable obstacle. Previously, the ground has been occupied by the intellectual savages of the commercial world – advertisers, marketers, packagers and the media – whose anthropological artefacts are now dug up or, more likely, viewed on a video, and unscrupulously stripped of their hidden meanings and significance. Consumption and its individual and social context are con-, decon- and reconstructed in the light of recent developments in social theory.

For the analytical terrain on which consumption is being discovered is one devoted to the 'post-' rather than to the past. This is the period of post-Marxism, postmodernism, post-Fordism, in which discourse and semiotics play a vital role, one tending to autonomise consumption.[5] At the extreme, consumption is presumed to have separate, independent and ambiguous effects and content, distinct from other constituent economic (especially production) and social relations. This emerges particularly with the linking of consumption to, or its being enclosed within, the field of cultural studies.

To some extent, there must be some doubts about the originality of these concerns if not the form in which they are posed and the attitude adopted to them. After all, the 1960s witnessed considerable angst about the morality and stability of consumer society, perceived to be one in which manipulated demand for unnecessary goods reflected the combination of the power of advertising and of the individual's psychological need to aspire, conform and surpass. For Galbraith (1962: 135):[6] 'As a society becomes increasingly affluent, wants are increasingly created by the process by which they are satisfied.'

This was the golden age for recognising and spotlighting the role of monopolies and their influence over what is consumed. It was also the period of unprecedented growth of the advanced capitalist economies. Consumers were consuming as never before. How ironic that the current period, of faltering expansion in living standards, especially amongst the worst-off, should witness a critical analysis of consumption of a rather more circumspect variety, based more on understanding as interpretation than as critically hostile and suspicious. Even this posture has a long pedigree. In the history of that most immediate item of consumption, food, Brillat-Savarin could hardly have imagined how popular his idiom would later become amongst the historians, sociologists and nutritionists:[7] his 'Tell me what you eat and I will tell you what you are' has been taken up in the twentieth century and simplified to 'You are what you eat.'[8] Our modern theorists merely have to interrogate what it is that is being eaten. There is more than a plum and a proof to be found in the eating of the pudding, for identity and meaning themselves appear to reside there.

This chapter sets some of these interpretations of consumption in perspective by examining the role played by use value in Marx. As consumption depends upon the use value of commodities, the presumption that Marx neglected use value, together with his assigning priority to production, is often thought to explain why there is no theory of consumption in Marx. Section 1 demonstrates the inadequacy of this view. The conclusion concerning the absence of use value in Marx is shown to be erroneous. Marx's economic analysis treats consumption as contingent upon, if not determined by, the production, distribution and circulation of value. This holds true even in the absence of analysis of the social construction of the meaning of particular commodities. Consequently, such an absence does not justify the rejection of Marx's value theory as deficient in understanding consumption, nor for its being incapable of, and incompatible with, construing the significance of use value. Section 2 demonstrates that, on the contrary, Marx's political economy has much to contribute to the issue of consumption, although this has more to do with its structural location than with concern over particular consumption goods.

## 1 THE USE VALUE OF MARX

The notion that Marx had very little to say about consumption is based on two closely related, but separate, propositions; first, that Marx was unconcerned about use values as such except in so far as they were a necessary condition for a product to be an exchange value; and, second, that this resulted in a neglect of the activity of consumption itself, except in so far as it was determined by the causally prior act of production.

Both of these propositions contain an element of truth but each is fundamentally misleading. To demonstrate this requires quite a detailed knowledge of Marx's political economy which may be beyond the general reader who may find some of the following discussion both esoteric and heavy-going. Marx's treatment of use value has to be teased out of his works but, as Rosdolsky (1977) has persuasively argued, Marx is far from silent on the matter.[9] Marx's analysis of specific use values emerges when they have been shown to have a social significance rather than a specific useful property. In *Capital*, this occurs first of all in the case of money, which is shown, as a consequence of its property as general equivalent, to acquire a number of functions which, of course, lead it to be desired by individuals, as a symbol of wealth and status, quite apart from its social functions as means of payment, store of value, etc. Later in Volume III of *Capital*, the use value of money is elevated to a higher level since money can function as capital. It becomes a commodity *sui generis* and commands an 'irrational' price for its ability to initiate a circuit of capital and appropriate surplus value. The rate of interest is a special price signifying the specific use value of interest-bearing capital.[10] Thus, for both of the commodities, money and money capital, Marx's analysis of use value is extremely highly developed (although the matter is not usually seen in this way – he is more thought of as having a sophisticated theory of money and money capital as such).

A precondition for this use value analysis, however, is the availability of the commodity labour power that has the use value, not only of producing use values, but also of producing (surplus) value. The use value of labour power is one of the main focuses of Volume I of *Capital*. It is the key to the analytical discovery of capitalist exploitation. This is so in two closely related, but different, senses. It is a relation between the two classes of capital and labour, in which one class buys the other's labour power and coerces surplus labour over and above what is required to produce working-class levels of consumption. And, in the greatest of detail in Volume I of *Capital*, Marx analyses the use value of labour power in the narrow sense of how labour is used; that is, addressing the way production and the labour process develop under capitalism – from domestic industry to the factory system.

In Volume I, money as a use value allows the general formula for capital, M–C–M', to be revealed in contrast to simple commodity circulation, C–M–C, and the use value of the commodity labour power is needed to derive the source of the difference between M and M', which makes up profit.[11] Subsequently, other use values are specified by Marx in terms of his analysis as it unfolds. The notion of relative surplus value, for example, which roughly corresponds to increased profitability through raising productivity, is impossible without conceptualising the division between constant capital and variable capital; the former corresponds to the use value of the raw materials in production (and to dead rather than living labour), and the latter to the money capital laid out to employ wage, or living, labour. Subsequently, in Volume II of *Capital*, the distinct use value of fixed capital emerges in the analysis of the turnover of capital, and does so in terms of its productive use outlasting a single circuit of capital.[12] A distinction is also made, in the context of the famous reproduction schema, between the use values of Departments I and II, respectively means of production and consumption, in order to bring out their different significance for the circulation of commodities as a whole. In Volume III of *Capital*, Marx's theory of agricultural rent depends upon analysis of the use value of land (not treated as a commodity as such, since it is not produced by labour) in its position as part of the social relations of production.[13]

## 2 PRODUCTIVE AND FINAL CONSUMPTION

The first proposition, discussed in the previous section, that Marx overlooks specific use values, is undoubtedly false. Marx does, even if implicitly, substantively analyse the position of a number of specific use values in uncovering the laws of motion of capitalism. But this 'defence' of Marx is liable to call forth the charge of unfairness or 'inadequacy'. Marx does not examine the role of particular commodities, other than in the broad ways specified. Moreover, those that he does examine are specifically linked to the (expanded) reproduction of the economy as capital rather than as an engine of consumption which, consequently, is confined to a passive or determined moment.

This is to move to the second charge against Marx, i.e., neglect of consumption. First, consider the standard rejection of Marxist, and classical, political economy by the neoclassical orthodoxy. Lumping a variety of its targets together as cost of production theory, it suggests that they neglect the importance of demand. Accordingly, it sees itself as remedying this and providing a more general theory through its demand analysis, based on utility maximisation and the potential substitution between different goods (use values). Whatever the merits of this alternative, its claim to provide a theory of demand (and associated consumption) has in a major sense been too readily and too uncritically accepted. For the theory itself fundamentally makes no contribution to the understanding of consumption; it is entirely indifferent as to the specific use values that are included in the analysis. This is transparent in mathematical presentation and in the concepts employed, such as the marginal utility of the unspecified things, A relative to B.[14] In the neoclassical world, what individuals consume is not specified.[15] Paradoxically, this is not so in classical political economy, for which the labouring class, in particular, is strongly identified with the consumption of corn, whose declining productivity in the hands of Ricardo, for example, leads to falling profitability and a stationary state.

Analytically, the poverty of neoclassical theory of consumption arises out of two factors. First, as Jevons made clear, his break with the economics of Ricardo was to reject the labour theory of value as applied to industry and, in its place, to apply his own marginal theory of rent to the economy as a whole. All production becomes agriculture-like, although it is called industry.

Second, the distinction between production and consumption is itself extinguished as the latter takes on the mode of achieving a given level of output (called utility) at a minimum cost (called income). The chain of activity from initial factor inputs to final utility makes little conceptual distinction along the way, since all those involved are optimising by setting relative marginal productivities/utilities equal to relative prices.[16]

This failure effectively to distinguish production from consumption is a charge that cannot be brought against Marx. There is, for example, the capitalist structure of the economy, distinguishing (or separating) between production and exchange, with final consumption itself lying outside the realm of the circulation of value, and no longer participating directly within it. The structured isolation of consumption from production is not necessarily characteristic of other modes of production, and this offers one way of interpreting Marx's well-known but tortuous analysis of the unity of production, distribution and consumption in the *Grundrisse*.[17] It is not simply a matter of the nature of the relations between these three economic moments, in both structure and causation, but also the very definition of what constitutes each of them that is open to variation between one mode of production and another.

This can be illustrated by comparing consumption under slavery and under capitalism, an example used by Marx. Under slavery, workers' consumption is indistinguishable from other inputs to production, comparable to the feed for beasts of burden. As far as the slave-owner is concerned, there is a total outlay of corn; feeding workers differs little from feeding the fields with seed. By contrast, one of the civilising effects of capitalism is to sharpen the distinction between human consumption and consumption for production, thereby removing the consumption attached to the production process away from the consumption attached to the worker:[18]

> The worker's productive consumption and his individual consumption are therefore totally distinct. . . . In the latter, he belongs to himself, and performs his necessary vital functions outside the production process. . . . The fact that the worker performs acts of individual consumption in his own interest, and not to please the capitalist, is something entirely irrelevant to the matter (of social reproduction of labour power) . . . *the capitalist may safely leave this to the worker's drive for self-preservation and propagation.*
>
> (Marx 1976: 711, emphasis added)

Thus, the position of (workers') consumption is very different between modes of production. On the other hand, this passage, and others like it, can be viewed as confirming the passive role of consumption within Marx's analysis – it seems, as in the emphasised passage, almost to imply that the social reproduction of labour power becomes automatic under capitalism, not only left off the capitalist's agenda but also disappearing off the theoretical agenda. This interpretation is, however, misleading. For the passage is merely locating the act of consumption of the working class relative to the economy. Just as the economic reproduction schemata of Volume II of *Capital* show how values and use values are reproduced through the circulation of capital, without thereby precluding the possibility of economic crisis, so Marx's analytical siting of consumption does not condemn the working class to the role of an unresisting agent for capital in effecting its own reproduction. Otherwise working-class consumption under capitalism would be treated as comparable to that obtaining under slavery, where reproduction of the workforce includes the raising of children for sale. Indeed, whilst Marx does draw the analogy between capitalism and slavery in this context, it is only in so far as labour's consumption is functional for capital in the reproduction of labour power. Slaves know only too well what will happen to their children as a continuing means of production to their current owners, or as a potential source of exchange value if sold; wage labour can have other aspirations, both in the economic as well as in the civil arena.

In short, this abstract discussion around production, consumption and reproduction reveals that each is made up and structured differently between modes of production – even if there are inevitable parallels in the role of consumption in the reproduction of the workforce (which must consume both to work and to breed). But this commentary does not shed light only upon workers' consumption, which under capitalism is isolated from work. *Consumption* of raw materials and other means of production, which are in the monopoly possession of the capitalist class, remains within the economy to form what has already been termed productive, as opposed to final, consumption. Such elements of consumption are, in general, produced and exchanged as commodities under capitalism. They too, like final consumption, are use values whose character is in part defined by their relation to the capitalist economy.[19] This has already been mentioned in section 1 in the specific context of constant and fixed capital. As use values in exchange, however, the buying and selling of means of production tend to dominate the process of circulation quantitatively, even if overall a majority of *net* income is consumed through wages. For very little final consumption involves smoking factory chimneys and the use of sheet steel. The weight of *final* consumption, i.e., the removal of use values from the process of circulation, is proportionately limited, the more so if, as Marx argues, capital accumulation is associated with the expulsion of living labour from the production process so that an increasing share of the value of commodities is taken up by constant capital which is exchanged between capitals.

To raise the distinction between final and productive consumption – something structurally specific to capitalism – is to highlight the point that whilst final consumption is driven by the market, it is not uniquely defined as such from an economic point of view. For exactly the same applies to the items of *productive* consumption that are also exchanged as commodities even if they do not, as items of consumption, thereby make their way out of the circuits of capital. To base a theory of final consumption on an economic content derived purely from the dependence on the purchase of commodities would unwittingly fail to distinguish between productive and final consumption, as both have these characteristics in common. But exchange as such is often perceived to be sufficient to specify the economic content of final consumption. And it is much rarer to find analyses of the culture of consumption surrounding those exchanges associated with productive, as opposed to final, consumption, despite considerable attention to the labour process and the culture of production.[20] This will prove significant in the following chapter. There it will be shown that analyses of consumption draw propositions from the exchange value of the commodity in general rather than from capitalist (commodity) production and final consumption in particular. This is a major deficiency which allows consumption to be more easily analytically autonomised, since it is presumed to be characterised in its economic content purely by virtue of exchange alone. In the often referenced Simmel, for example, exchange value and value are linked to final consumption at the expense of the role of productive consumption. He concludes: 'This is the basis and source of that valuation which finds its expression in economic life and whose consequences represent the meaning of money' (Simmel 1978: 78).

This has the effect of distancing both final consumption and the role of money from their *capitalist* foundations, as is observed by Bottomore and Frisby in their introduction to Simmel. Treating consumption as a relationship between economic agents, commodities and money is to strip each of them of their dependence on capitalist production and its associated relations. It is as though consumption, through its origins in exchange via money, were constituted on a foundation of simple commodity production alone. To put it in another way, it is consumption not only without capital but also without wage labour. If money is the root of all consumption (evil or otherwise), it is a very shallow root analytically speaking. Whilst final and productive consumption are structured differently within the capitalist economy, they are effectively treated as identical if consumption is only examined as derived from its commodity origins through the expenditure of money. Barthes, however, makes the point well in distinguishing between the different rationalities surrounding productive and final consumption in the context of the planned obsolescence of clothing through fashion: 'Calculating, industrial society is obliged to form consumers who don't calculate; if clothing's producers and consumers had the same consciousness, clothing would be bought (and produced) only at the very slow rate of its dilapidation' (Barthes 1985: xi). Thus, different economic imperatives inform productive and final consumption, and they must be identified in their capitalist origins over and beyond the commodity form taken by use values, and exchanged for money, which is common to both.

Consequently, as the culture and significance of productive and final consumption are quite different because of their different locations *vis-à-vis* the economy, then the relationship between final consumption and the economy has to be established as something more than the provision of use values in the form of commodities. In other words, commodity production as the dominant form taken by final consumption must be recognised to be influenced as *capitalist* commodity production. Otherwise, no distinction is made between capitalism's consumption and that derived, possibly ideally, from a system of simple commodity production.

So there are differences in commodities (as means of production and as means of consumption) and in the way they are consumed according to their relative position in the economy. But there are quantitative differences too. These have already been referred to implicitly in the schemata of economic reproduction. Productive consumption and final consumption goods circulate quite differently as values and also have definite quantitative relations to each other in simple and expanded reproduction.

More significantly, because final consumption involves the exit of its value from continuing circulation, its role is no longer defined by the internal logic of capital and its laws. Instead, it has a simple and undifferentiated relation to economic agents as purchasers. It no longer matters what their economic position is – with one proviso – they must have money to pay. As Marx observes:

> [As] *worker* . . . as consumer and possessor of exchange values, and that in the form of the *possessor of money*, in the form of money he becomes a simple entry of circulation – one of its infinitely many entries, in which his specificity as worker is extinguished.
>
> (Marx 1969b: 420–1)

In other words, exchange of final consumption goods knows no well-defined class boundaries. Of course, this is only true in so far as no account is taken of the different spending power of the different classes. Here, Marx observes how much this affects the pattern of final consumption. For example, Marx (1969b: 565): 'A large part of the consumption of workers enters into that of capitalists and landlords but not vice-versa.' The latter, as consumers, 'give rise to very considerable modifications in the economy' (ibid.: 493) and for them, a 'reduction in the value of labour power through machinery allows the scope of luxuries to be extended' (ibid.: 572).

In short, and surely uncontroversially, the structure and dynamics of the capitalist economy does not readily determine the nature and composition of final consumption. The relationship between consumers and the economy, with the former merely as possessors of money, entails that there is no guarantee of stereotypical patterns of consumption. And, even if there were, the distribution of income across consuming groups has first to be determined, before the 'moral and historical' elements that make up workers' consumption can be analysed in terms of socially constructed use values. The qualitative and quantitative elements involved in Marx's value analysis does not preclude the more general social construction of particular commodities and is, indeed, a necessary basis for it – as has been shown in previous chapters exploring and justifying the approach based on systems of provision which is inspired by a Marxist methodology that weds but does not subordinate consumption to production.

# 19

# MARXISM AND THE RECONSTRUCTION OF USE VALUE

## INTRODUCTION

In the previous chapter, reference has been made to cultural theories of consumption that concentrate on the meaning of use values to the final consumer. Such concern with the interpretation of the objects of consumption often locates the origins of consumption in exchange since, in contemporary capitalist society, a major part of consumption is derived more or less directly from the purchase of commodities. Indeed, the ideological construction of the use value of a commodity, as in advertising and brand image, often explicitly addresses its market origins either to establish a claim to quality – a product is 'the best money can buy' – or to deny its commercial origins altogether when presented 'as good as home-made'.

The recognition of the relation between commodities and their exchange value aspect does not suffice to root their interpretation adequately within *capitalist* society. Further, such origins also tend to be set aside in the ideological construction of the commodity's use values. There is an even stronger tendency for the capitalist origins of use values to be obscured and analytically set aside than is the case for their origins in exchange. Companies, for example, project themselves, not their products, as profitable. To do otherwise might suggest over pricing or poor quality. While some of the factors underlying profitability might be incorporated into the meaning of the commodity – for example, the skill or high technology with which it has been manufactured – it is hardly conceivable that 'the best at making a profit' could displace 'the best money can buy' as a favourable attribute of a commodity.

But in practice, even if these attributes of commodities bound for final consumption are ideologically denied, the social construction of commodities as use values, the meaning endowed to them for and by consumers, takes place in the context of both *capitalist* commodity exchange and capitalist commodity *production* (and distribution). This is important in assessing the attempts that have been made to rectify Marx's presumed neglect of use value and of consumption. However, the false charge of neglect is a very different proposition from the one that is often used to criticise Marx; viz., that his political economy essentially *precludes* the possibility of opening up the analysis of use value and consumption. As shown in section 1 of this chapter, this is the position adopted in the work of Baudrillard. It leads to emphasis upon the social construction of use value from a (false) starting point critical of Marx for having neglected such considerations. It proceeds, however, very little further beyond the confines of interpreting use value as culturally determined by the marriage of final consumption (how the commodity is received) with simple purchase (how it has been obtained). It is an analytical stance guilty of the neglect of the determining influence of capital in production and distribution (as well as through exchange and cultural factors, even if these are more direct influences upon the consumer as such).

By this means, the determination of use value tends to become freed from its material foundations in an even more dramatic fashion. When use values are freed from their capitalist origins, the meaning of consumption is construed as a relation between consumer and consumed. Even though this does not have to be interpreted individualistically and subjectively, there is a tendency to neglect the material content of the commodity itself, that is, what its physical properties are. Even if culturally determined through society, the meaning of commodities in consumption becomes sufficiently flexible that they are what they mean. They *are* now home-made or the best money can buy since that is what they are believed to be and that is what these expressions themselves come to mean.

In this way, there is a curious inversion of the logic to be found in Marx's treatment of use value (if it is recognised rather than presumed to be absent and/or precluded). For Marx, the use value of commodities, both materially and culturally, is founded on, if not reducible to, the social relations by which they are produced, distributed and exchanged. These relations involve, for example, various aspects of the exercise of power, for which there are symbolic counterparts in the world of consumption, whether it be in bigger cars, or richer clothes. But neither the nature, nor the source, nor the role of these symbols in representing and reproducing power can be defined by reference to their consumption alone. For if consumption represents power (or some other attribute), from where does that power come and why does it (or why does conflict over it) not exercise an influence over how it is represented? Failure to address such questions is the inversion of Marx's logic, for which social relations have to be identified before they can be represented (although this does not allow the reduction of representation to insignificance). Otherwise, power and other material relations are taken as given, as external referents, purely employed for the purpose of providing consumers with the targets on which to project their interpretation of what they consume.

In section 2, a second inversion of Marx's logic is presented. Focus on use value implies that the commodity is stripped of its quantitative dimension; it no longer matters that it is associated with the production of a definite amount of (surplus) labour. This has the further consequence that the dynamics of the capitalist economy associated with the law of value, however interpreted, are not of relevance. Tendencies and structures within the economy tend to shed no light on the social construction of commodities (as they are not distinguishable through exchange alone, even less through the variable meaning assigned to use values). Interpretation of the use value as it is tends to displace any analysis of why it is there and how it has changed.

It might be thought, possibly with some justification, that this chapter is unnecessarily abstruse; that it deals with propositions and positions so blatantly false that these might be better set aside altogether; and that the route through which such analysis has been obtained, via a critique of Marxism, is essentially irrelevant to the final destination. However, just as the commodity journeys along its system of provision, often leaving behind little immediately observable trace of its origins in the imperatives of production, so the theoretical understanding of that system of provision, and its significance for the nature and meaning of consumption, can lose all trace of its analytical origins. By examining fanciful theories of the cultural determination of consumption, it is possible to add positively to the role played by the meaning and interpretation of (exchange-derived) use values, whilst integrating this with, and restoring to, the analysis those underlying determinants in the system of provision that have been stripped away.

## 1 CONSUMPTION AS THE INVERSION OF THE LOGIC OF VALUE

Irrespective of the meaning of use values to the (final) consumer, what actually constitutes consumption and how it is structured in the economy and society more generally are specific to particular modes of production. A qualitative, as well as a quantitative, grasp of the relations governing consumption is a precondition for examining who gets to consume what, and this will in turn influence how such consumption is construed over and above the role of other cultural determinants. Marx's theory of commodity fetishism makes the criticism that exchange relations are presented purely as relations between use values – x of commodity X exchanges for y of commodity Y – whereas they also embody (and conceal) the underlying determinants associated with the exploitative relations between producers. X and Y are the consequence of the exercise of human labour organised under definite conditions geared towards production of the market. But Baudrillard (1981: 92) understands (or 'reads') Marx as having fetishised the role of commodity fetishism in his critique of the reification of social relations of production. Marx may have revealed production relations but only at the expense of assigning the significance of use value itself to the realm of ideology and superstructure where it can be quietly neglected.[1] Commodities must be seen as created in two senses; they are produced as physical objects but they are also created culturally according to how they are interpreted – as items of consumption, for example.

However, Baudrillard does at least connect the (erroneous) view that Marx neglects use value to a more constructive analysis by correctly recognising, emphasising and exploring the social construction of use value, rather than treating it as a purely physical or natural property (of which Marx is not guilty):

> The whole discourse on consumption, whether learned or lay, is articulated on the mythological sequence of the fable: a man, 'endowed' with needs which 'direct' him towards objects that 'give' him satisfaction. Since man is never really satisfied (for which, by the way, he is reproached), the same history is repeated indefinitely since the time of the ancient fables.
>
> (Baudrillard 1988: 35)

In place of this mythology, Baudrillard (1981: 30) suggests: 'The fundamental conceptual hypothesis for a sociological analysis of 'consumption' is *not* use value, the relation to needs, but *symbolic exchange value*, the value of prestation, of rivalry and, at the limit, of class discriminants.' Haug employs the term aesthetic illusion to make the same point: 'In all commodity production a double reality is produced: first the use value; second, *and more importantly*, the *appearance* of use value. . . . Appearance becomes just as important and practically more so – than the commodity's being itself' (Haug 1986: 16–17, first emphasis added).

This qualitative conclusion defines the social construction of the meaning of use value in consumption. What is the relationship between the consumer and the consumed in terms of the way in which the latter presents itself to the former, not now, as in commodity fetishism as a relationship between things, but as a mongrel relationship between the human and the non-human? Not surprisingly, the human partner in the relationship may be endowed with the more active determining role, as in subjective preference theory. More generally, the consumer may be constituted through socially determined cultural relations concerning power, gender, happiness or whatever. But, in either case, this would itself be indicative of commodity fetishism, of setting aside the underlying social (and human) relations that bring the use value to the point of being consumed. These have a quantitative component, comprising the complex determinants of the levels and patterns of what is consumed (usually thought of as economic factors, however broadly defined). These, however, must also influence what is produced and how it is interpreted in consumption.

However, for Baudrillard, symbolic exchange tends to take on a life of its own, especially in its independence from production.[2] This bias is, however, veiled to some extent by his use of terms such as class, power and productive forces to describe the foundations of consumption. Such determinants do then enter into his analysis. But, crucially, they only do so as external referents, as the given material factors which will be symbolised in consumption. They do not enter as determinants of what is consumed or how it is interpreted, only of what is interpreted. Thus, the classic elements of Marxist (or other materialist analysis) are rarely tied to the formal abstract theory around the logic of symbolic exchange, and inevitably act more as the symbolic content of meaning. This represents something of an inversion of Marx's logic, for the layered analysis of use value and exchange is now projected on to productive forces, power and class, rather than these acting as determinants of consumption and its meaning.

It follows that the elements of symbolic exchange are insecure within the analysis. Other symbols are equally possible as externally given referents, as potentially variable as the myriad of (meanings of) available use values. Take power, for example. Whilst Baudrillard argues that consumption distinctions (i.e., who gets to consume what and how)[3] signify, for example, power relations, this is less a logical stance than a lingering influence from his analytical origins from within (and, in breaking with) Marxism. Paradoxically, such power relations, which enable differentiated consumption relations to exist between different classes, might otherwise themselves have no determining influence as far as the social construction of use values is concerned. Power serves to symbolise, not to create, the meanings of consumption.

Baudrillard (1988: 42) does, however, make reference to the determining role of production and power relations: 'The truth is not that 'needs are the fruits of production' but *the system of needs* is *the product of the system of production*.' And, historically, 'to socialise the masses (that is to control them) into a force of consumption' is seen as the twentieth-century product of the nineteenth-century's rationalisation of production (ibid.: 50). But these assertions do not move analytically beyond their own level of rhetoric. From here, it is but a short logical step either to excise power relations from what is symbolised or to reinterpret power relations by reference to their meaning within consumption. From a position in which power has been commonly understood as derived from capital and of importance as a symbolic reference, it is liable to evaporate away altogether.

Thus, it can be argued that the connection between the consumption of use values and social relations is inverted. Consumption does act as a class discriminant, but such discrimination has a prior role in making consumption available in the first place. Moreover, the long route to consumption from class relations itself plays a major role in the construction of use values, even if – as revealed by the theory of commodity fetishism – it is more by way of concealment. No one wants to be reminded of the world of work and commerce when contemplating consumption, not even Baudrillard.

In fact, more prominent as symbols in Baudrillard's work than standard categories of Marxist analysis are those of orthodox sociology, dealing with stratification, mobility and aspirations (Baudrillard 1988: 381), and the unusual concept of prestation is understood as a mechanism of discrimination and prestige. Thus, 'it seems that the norm of consumption attitudes is simultaneously distinction and conformity' (ibid.: 36). Again this represents an inversion of the relations between use values and their interpretation, as will be shown in what follows. For uniformity and distinction in consumption do not arise spontaneously as sources of social stratification, although they are undoubtedly exploited for that purpose in capitalist as well as other societies.[4] The nature and content of uniformity and distinction arise out of the particular societies in which they occur and not exclusively, nor necessarily primarily, from the culturally constructed meaning of use values.

For capitalism, the logical origins of such stratification lie in the system of commodity production itself. Particular class relations induce the forms in which stratification occurs, both in consumption as well as in other arenas; these forms of stratification then constrain the more detailed processes and symbols involved. Such abstract considerations can most easily be brought down to earth, as is experienced on a daily basis by that most common form of human species, the consumer. Whilst often treated as an interest or socioeconomic group, even though all belong, stratification and distinction are heavily influenced by the availability of income. In practice, we all know that those who live by wage revenue (or social security) have different consumption standards than those who live by profit or other unearned income.

Crucially, however, this is not logically so. The newspapers love a story in which a common worker is exposed to be living a life of luxury, the better to be able to rationalise a cut in wages for those who are not. But distinctions in the sources of revenue do not determine their levels, so that a worker could live like a king and vice versa. But a worker cannot be a king, nor consume like a king, in a society other than capitalism, in which the monarchy holds a ruling position. For, then, consumption and its symbolic role (including distinction and conformity) have entirely different roots and meanings.

In this context what, within capitalism, differentiates the content of the diode, distinction and conformity, is the dependence of consumption on its derivation through exchange. As discussed in the previous chapter, the emergence of money in a system of general commodity production gives *all* the right to consume *everything* – at least in principle. Hence, the basis exists for the process of emulation through consumption – although the detailed paths that it takes other than through the market is not determined. By contrast such emulation cannot occur in non-commodity-producing societies (the peasant cannot buy a way into being a lord).[5] The ideology associated with the potential for uniformity is revealed by Haug:

> In the sphere of circulation, only the money in customers' pockets is important to capital irrespective of the customers' class position, and it is precisely in response to this in commodity aesthetics there dominates

> the illusion through which a particular class culture tends to integrate the workers – the capitalist distortion of a classless culture.
>
> (Haug 1986: 104)

By the same token, the commodity form of consumption implies that *each* (involved in exchange) has the ability to consume *something* in particular. Hence, differentiation in consumption is a necessary product of the commodity form of consumption. Commodity production, entailing a particular form of access to consumption, is the basis for distinction/conformity under capitalism. As such, it appears prior to capitalism, as excessive conspicuous consumption, and early on in capitalism as the elite display of consumption.[6] As Marx argues:

> When a certain stage of development has been reached, a conventional degree of prodigality, which is also an exhibition of wealth, and consequently a source of credit, becomes a business 'necessity' to the 'unfortunate' capitalist. Luxury enters into capital's expenses of representation.
>
> (Marx 1976: 741)

Before commodity production is generalised, the form taken by such conspicuous consumption is necessarily confined to a narrower range of items and may even be focused on one item alone, even the body of the individual to signify wealth, literally, in the capacity to consume. Where the symbol of wealth is accumulated money, as in the cliché of the miser, the capacity to consume is represented by its opposite, the formation of hoards and abstinence from consumption. These casually constructed examples illustrate how material relations govern symbolic exchange value rather than merely serving as its representatives.

## 2 BAUDRILLARD IS TO USE VALUE AS SRAFFA IS TO EXCHANGE VALUE?

A second aspect of the reversal of the logic of value is to be found in the treatment of value itself. Traditionally, within economics, Marx's value theory has been criticised and rejected – by Sraffians, especially – for its presumed quantitative inadequacies as a theory of price.[7] This has been done without reference to the qualitative side of value, and Marx's value theory has been defended on the basis of its understanding of the form of value.[8] In the case of Baudrillard, the critique is rather different. There is a total absence of the quantitative dimension of value – does it matter for him that commodities are even the product of labour? – and the focus is upon form analysis alone; that Marx's theory of commodity fetishism, etc. is inadequate and account needs to be taken of the social form taken by *use values*.

Whilst the Sraffian and the use value critique of Marx are polar opposites, they do have something in common in their respective one-sided interpretations of value. In each case the analysis tends to be static. The use value critique does not move beyond the opening chapters of *Capital* in its focus upon the (use) value form. Similarly, the Sraffian critique, which is based upon the comparative statics of equilibrium analysis with unchanging technology and scale of production, happily leaps between Volume I of *Capital* and Volume III to unite the definition of value (in their terms as embodied labour) with the transformation problem, interpreted as the derivation of equilibrium prices.[9] The dynamics of production, and even of circulation despite the concern with consumption, are simply set aside.

One consequence of this is that the use value approach has little place even for the most abstract of historical content, unless it is derived from outside the economy. In particular, the laws of development of capitalism and its dynamics are neglected. Even the impact of the simplest, and generally uncontroversial, distinction between *laissez-faire* and *monopoly capitalism* need have no perceptible effect. Haug (1986: 107) points to the difference between a gun used in an imperialist war and one used in a war of freedom. It is the difference between an instrument used to free rather than to oppress. But, 'one cannot tell from the gun itself. . . . Its detached and reproduced sensual impression does not reveal the essential difference but serves to disguise it'. Much the same is true of whether an item of clothing has been produced under conditions of monopoly capital, creating relative surplus value through the use of advanced machinery, or whether it has its origins in the backstreet sweatshop dependent upon absolute surplus value.[10]

These breaks, or inversions, of Marx's analysis have profound implications. For the nature of explanation and causation is itself transformed. Marx is usually perceived as employing a simple determinism from production to consumption by which his method is degraded by neglecting, first, the role of contradictory tendencies or laws and, second, the dialectics for which the concrete and the complex are derived from the abstract and simple as the product of many determinants. For Miller:

> The abiding influence of Durkheim and Marx has created a tendency towards a highly objectivist emphasis in much contemporary anthropology. A characteristic feature of much of this tradition is that society is always prior to culture; it is social relations and classifications which are given form in cultural classifications.
>
> (Miller 1987: 64)

Further, the use value approach itself requires explanatory variables that are arbitrarily embraced as external referents – as has been previously recorded in the case of class and power, etc. – although this might be done through the use of abstract categories and theoretical schemata. Sexuality, for example, is extremely prominent (as in its role in advertising), so that gender relations are seen as represented by particular patterns of consumption and their meaning.

The content of the analysis depends upon the judicious choice of what is perceived to be most significant in the fetishism of use value. But, for the reasons already outlined, it is inadequate merely to read off changes in the social content of consumption without being able to explain fully why they have occurred. For example, gender representations in advertising do not simply mirror but are determined by changing gender relations, as new products come to be advertised, such as the microwave (to combine work with domestic chores) and video (to combine domestic chores with home entertainment, especially for children) or as old products come to be advertised in new ways to represent the new, independent (usually childless) woman. Further, unless the meaning of consumption is rooted in what is consumed and how it comes to be consumed, the division between the physical and the symbolic content of use values tends to become open to infinitely elastic interpretation – in which case it hardly seems to matter what is consumed, as fantasy can be (better than) the real thing. Coke is a drink, but it is represented as any-(real)-thing.

There are strong parallels here with the limited explanatory content of the longer-standing orthodox approaches to consumption to be found in sociology, psychology and anthropology and which are treated as matters of status, symbol and ritual. Goody (1982) begins by questioning the extent to which so much of significance is hidden in the use values of consumption – after all, advertisers, market researchers, academics and, it might be added, consumers are all too aware of what is going on in their different ways. He puts rather neatly two distinct ways of understanding the hidden meaning of consumption, the one as a purely symbolic fetish which cannot be so, the other as a code of what is so but hidden: 'Do social relations and social structures stand in the same relationship to the bread and wine as the body and blood of Christ, or as a naval cipher does to open speech?' (Goody 1982: 30). It seems that it is only as consumers that we have the wool pulled over our eyes. But when we buy a pullover, what exactly do we know and not know about what it is, and how important is this? Whatever the answer, Goody sees the question as inhibiting the analysis of change:[11] 'The concentration on "meaning" in a specific cultural context . . . has tended to push aside studies of long term change' (ibid.: 37). Similarly, Mennell observes:

> The great virtue of the structuralist approach is that it clearly recognises that 'taste' is culturally shaped and socially controlled. Its weakness is that it tends to be static, and has little to say about how tastes change and develop in society over time.
>
> (Mennell 1985: 6)

Ultimately, the result is that little more emerges than the idea that people eat what they like – as presented within an organised framework determined by the academic discipline concerned (ibid.: 13).

In summary, building on from section 1, it is crucial to acknowledge that use values are socially constructed, both as products themselves, with material and social origins, and as products with meaning to those that use them. As items of consumption under capitalism, such use values have complex roots in the economy which reach beyond their simply being acquired as commodities in exchange, with their social construction otherwise being a consequence of non-economic factors. These matters are more positively explored by use of analysis based on systems of provision, since these are the way in which commodities are socially constructed both materially and culturally. Although previous chapters have primarily been concerned with the material content of commodities, the analysis has been extended from time to time to their cultural content as items of consumption, most notably in the analyses of advertising. In the context of food and clothing, in particular, the meaning of consumption, as created through advertising, was indeed shown to be dependent on the system of provision as a whole.

# 20

# RELOCATING RETAIL CAPITAL

## INTRODUCTION

Whether shopping at the local corner shop, the high street department store or the superstores located in the urban hinterlands, retailing presents itself as a pervasive and tangible part of economic life. It has perhaps been subject to neglect as a specific economic category, symptomatic of the neglect of consumption across the social sciences and the preference for the role of production as the primary causal factor. But what exactly is the significance of retailing and how is it to be located theoretically? Few have attempted to answer this question in anything other than a superficially descriptive account.

In a recent paper, however, Ducatel and Blomley (1990) have made a valuable theoretical contribution to the understanding of what they term 'retail capital'. Their contribution is far from being well known and might not appear to justify the close attention that is devoted to it here. But, unlike much of the literature, it specifically seeks to construct a notion of retail capital within a well-defined theoretical, rather than empirical or descriptive, framework. As such, its analytical importance is much greater than its academic prominence. Essentially, these authors adopt the view that retail capital can be constructed as an abstract category, so that the diverse forms and sectors in which selling takes place can be set aside to give rise to a homogeneous portion of commercial capital. The virtue of their paper is to pose this proposition, backed up by strong and detailed arguments. This allows alternative views to be sharply drawn and contrasted with their own.

This chapter seeks to clarify and develop the arguments put forward by Ducatel and Blomley. But, in doing so, apparently minor points of theoretical difference lead to diametrically opposite conclusions. Retail capital does *not* emerge as an appropriate abstract category to develop within Marxist theory and, by implication, within other theoretical frameworks. Rather than being viewed as a separate part of aggregate (commercial) capital, and therefore internally undifferentiated, retailing arguably should be located at the very least in an analysis sensitive to the differences *between* sectors of the economy to which it is attached. In terms previously outlined, whilst retail capital is a horizontal aspect operating across the economy, it is more appropriately treated analytically as falling within separate, vertically interconnected systems of commodity provision.

In other words, retail capital is not considered here to be a homogeneous category operating in exchange; it is heterogeneous to the extent that its separate components are linked to particular sectors of the economy. To pose this concretely, retail capital in housing is very different from retail capital in food. Indeed, this is so much so that we do not conventionally think of the selling of housing as retailing. More generally, if less sharply, differences between sectors of the economy and the structure of production in relation to exchange give rise to differences in the nature of the retail capital that serves them. Whilst it might be argued that different sectors of the economy give rise to productive capital that is of a single genus – industrial capital – despite the different use values that each creates, here the intention is to deny that capitals involved in retailing can be seen legitimately as forming a similar abstract category (except at the most immediate empirical level, where they are identified by their involvement in the business of buying and selling goods for profit). In the first section, the discussion addresses the question of whether Ducatel and Blomley have provided either a coherent or a distinct definition of retail capital and whether this is possible beyond its proximate, empirical identification with sale and purchase for final consumption. The second section seeks less to resolve these problems of precise definition than to question the validity of an abstract concept of retail capital. This is followed by a brief look at some empirical illustrations of the more theoretical analysis. Finally, the previously derived conclusions are pulled together to affirm the dependency of retail capital on the separate systems of provision that exist across the different sectors of the economy.

In a coda at the end of this chapter, Ducatel and Blomley's methodology is subjected to critical scrutiny. This serves the purpose of reaffirming the problems of constructing retail capital as a separate category. It also suggests a broader conclusion in line with the systems-of-provision approach. The Marxist methodology of assigning casual priority to production does not entail an analytical structure in which all production is constituted separately from all circulation and exchange (of which retailing is a part) at all levels of analysis. Rather, causal priority to production across commodities is compatible with what has been termed vertically differentiated relations between production, distribution, sale and purchase, and final consumption. In this sense, the analysis of retailing suggested here is similar in methodology to that for advertising in Chapter 14, although the substance of these two horizontal factors is necessarily substantively different. For each, its specificity has to be located by reference to its connection to particular commodities and not to production, or some other horizontal factor, in general. These two examples, then, suggest a more general methodology for analysing horizontal factors in consumption and in critically assessing other theories that have generalised across such factors.

## 1 THE SPECIFICITY OF RETAIL CAPITAL

Ducatel and Blomley's stated objective is to locate theoretically the specificity of retail capital. No doubt this is inspired by the increasing prominence and apparent diversity of contemporary retailing activity. Their strategy for doing so is to set aside diversity and approach it from the more, if not the most, abstract and general of categories. Their starting point is the circulation of capital as a whole, the total movement of the economy between production, exchange and final consumption; within this, commercial capital is identified as that lying within the sphere of exchange and retail capital is that part of commercial capital which handles 'final exchange of commodities' (Ducatel and Blomley 1990: 213). In the context of this broad analytical strategy, how well is retail capital uniquely characterised? Because of its particular intentions, a close analysis of Ducatel and Blomley provides an opportunity to bring out the distinctiveness of retail capital – although the conclusions it leads to here differ radically from those reached by them.

First, Ducatel and Blomley present a number of general characteristics of commercial capital – essentially cost reduction in its operations of buying and selling through the division of labour and specialisation (within it as well as between it and production) and through decreased turnover time (ibid.: 211). Second, commercial capital is seen to be mutually dependent on, and in conflict with, productive capital. This dependence/conflict is true of all capitals of whatever ilk to some degree. So its significance has to be carefully constructed. On the one hand, for Marx, all commercial (and hence retail) capital, like industrial capital, is perceived to be subject to the tendency of the rate of profit to equalise (as accepted by Ducatel and Blomley 1990: 211, 217). This is a consequence of the mobility of capital between sectors. Thus, if Ducatel and Blomley perceive retail capital to be distinguished by a competitive conflict with other capitals, this does not suffice.

On the other hand, if there is a barrier to mobility of capital – if retail capital has some monopolistic position – then the rate of profit of commercial capital may be sustained above the general rate. Ducatel and Blomley do hint at this, as will be seen. Its impact, however, would be contingent upon what makes such barriers to entry into retailing both operative *and* permanent. It seems implausible theoretically to suggest that they both exist and are of even strength across sectors. Indeed, if there are some structural barriers to the free flow of capital between industrial and retail sectors, this would appear to suggest the heterogeneity, not the homogeneity, of retail capital, according to the source of strength of these barriers, sector by sector.

Thus, if subject to a tendency to equal profitability, with variations as within industrial capital according to the rhythm of competition, then this does not set retail capital apart as a distinct category, any more than it does cars, steel or oil within industrial capital – even though these may experience monopolistic conditions. Yet, in discussing empirically the presumed increasing dominance of retail over productive capital, Ducatel and Blomley (1990: 221) argue that: 'This has given retailers a better position in bargaining for a greater share of surplus value.' Retail capital not only occupies a structural location and, consequently, a logically distinct position *vis-à-vis* other capital by Ducatel and Blomley's account, it also does so on some sort of monopolistic basis, presumably able thereby to obtain a higher appropriation of surplus value (which implies non-equalisation of the rate of profit).

Thus, the operation of capital in the sphere of exchange is logically either subject to a tendency to equalise profitability or, alternatively, it must be seen as setting itself apart structurally from capital-in-general and to appropriate surplus value in the absence of this tendency. Marx does allow for a category of capital in exchange, structurally separate in its sphere of operation from all other capitals and which is not subject to the tendency for equalised profitability. For profit of enterprise, conflict between fractions of capital takes the form of competition over individual profitability and is subject to equalisation; but, for the rate of interest, Marx argues that surplus value is divided off from profit of enterprise. There is no question of interest being equalised to profit by competitive tendencies. To identify interest as the reward for a specifically distinct fraction of capital, Marx in Volume III of *Capital* develops the category of interest-bearing capital, and it yields the rate of interest as opposed to profit of enterprise. The latter is equalised for both industrial and commercial capital.[1]

The problem for Ducatel and Blomley is that if they treat retail as part of commercial capital, as they do, then it does not appear to have a structurally separate existence as a specific form of (commercial) capital any more than do separate sectors of industrial capital. On the other hand, if it is structurally separated, and able to obtain non-equalised profitability, at which they hint, then it no longer forms a part of commercial capital – as it undoubtedly must in view of its function in buying and selling. So at this abstract level, there is either confusion or an inability to specify retail capital distinctly. If it is part of commercial capital, it cannot be structurally distinct with superior profitability; if not, its logic of serving final sale does not set it apart from commerce, in general.

Third, what appears to distinguish retail capital is that it leads directly to final consumption. Ducatel and Blomley acknowledge this by reference to the logic of exchange as against the logic of final use, as the seller is concerned with the exchange value and the buyer with the use value of the commodity. This is loosely linked by Ducatel and Blomley to the ideology of people before profits (ibid.: 214) by citing temples of consumption bursting with commodities and co-existing with unemployment and hunger (but not, it should be noted, with acknowledgement of excess productive capacity). The fact that capitalism generates gluts and commercial display alongside poverty and degradation is deplorable but not a rationale for a distinct analytical category of retail capital. The analytical status of observing capitalism's wastefulness and paradoxes is dubious, moral imperatives aside, and once again it is not specific as such to retail capital. The growth of wealth and productive power, as well as of retail capital, is equally represented in the mountains of goods for sale and unsold. Nor is reference to retail capital as dependent on a logic of exchange specific to final consumption. The logic of exchange applies equally to productive consumption (and, it must be added, nobody went to market to buy without an attention to the value, or price, that had to be paid).

Fourth, although, or precisely because, retail capital is homogeneous in dealing in buying and selling for final consumption, its location within total circulation of capital and commodities is complex and diverse. All classes participate in consumption: hence the apparent legitimacy of consumers as an economic or political interest group – even though this group comprises everybody. But the sources of revenue to purchase differ between classes. Some commodities will depend for their demand to a greater extent on wage revenue, others on profits. Because the scope of retail capital is limited by the extent of what is produced for final consumption and by what can be purchased out of revenue, it can too easily be tied analytically to problems of deficient demand. For Ducatel and Blomley, there is a series of undercon-sumptionist references, chaotically linked to the availability of money (capital) (and no indication is given that this is anything other than a fixed or independent magnitude, with no reference made either to Marx's theory of money's quantitative dependence on the mass of commodities to be circulated or to the role of the credit system). Thus:

> Any decline in the stock of money capital in the hands of consumers will endanger the very basis of commercial profits, given the need for the conversion of commodity capital into money capital. . . .
>
> Shopping is a social act, having meaning within the realm of privatized reproduction in and of itself. Certainly, it is an act of exchange; that is, it is essential to the realization of value in commodity production. The ultimate quantitative limit to this exchange is determined by the level of wages.
>
> (Ducatel and Blomley 1990: 215)

Whilst retailing here has been confined to purchases out of wages (and the ultimate quantitative limit is given by the value produced, not by the wage revenue with which to circulate it), it is extended later on to include consumption out of surplus value:

> Competition between retailers can be understood, at one level, as a struggle for a share of consumer expenditure, which at any one time is

> fixed by the total money capital attributable to wage labour and the bourgeoisie's consumption (which is extracted from surplus value).
>
> (ibid.: 217)

Here, wage revenue is mistaken for a portion of money capital and consumption out of surplus value as an extraction, rather than an expenditure, of it. Once again, though:

> For retail capitals, accumulation is constrained on the one hand by the surplus value already within production, and on the other, by the spending power of the mass of wage labourers and their families, which at any one time is fixed by the production process.
>
> (ibid.: 219)

The confusion between consumer revenue and money capital is repeated in arguing that, 'retailers compete for the finite amount of money capital' (ibid.: 224). Whilst these confusions are specific to Ducatel and Blomley, they arise out of the wish to homogenise retail capital, even though its structured dependence varies according to whose consumption revenue it circulates.

Fifth, the difference in dynamics between retail and other capital is not brought out. Ducatel and Blomley do point to the advantages of scale and the consequences of this in eliminating small-scale capital. But this is general to the capitalist factory and is not specific to its retail equivalent, namely the superstore:

> Retail capital has penetrated and restructured this sphere, driving out independent retailers through strategies such as direct price and quality competition, and through the ability to develop large stores in prime sites which operate a high turnover and require a larger staff than small-scale, owner-operator retailers can support.
>
> (ibid.: 219)

Nor does retailing's distinctiveness derive from the drive to reduce costs. Whilst reduction in retail costs does reduce individual price, it has no aggregate effect (other than to raise general profitability). This is a difference for all commercial, rather than specifically retail capital. Thus Ducatel and Blomley are correct to argue that: 'Given that the circulation costs incurred in capital do not contribute to the production of value, we should expect retail capitalists to reduce them as far as possible' (ibid.: 222). But we also expect productive capital to reduce costs as far as possible even though they *do* contribute to the production of value (through variable capital, v) and the preservation of value (through constant capital, c).

In short, in ranging over possible ways of distinguishing retail capital, it seems to rest on what Ducatel and Blomley call 'final exchange of commodities' (ibid.: 213). Here their intended definition is crystal clear – where capitalists specialise in selling consumption goods to be taken away for personal/final consumption outside the circuits of capital. The 'final exchange' is, however, a poor expression since all commodities are finally exchanged prior to consumption, even if the consumption is not final as in the sale of constant capital (to be subsequently consumed as means of production).

What is significant about this definition is that it is unexceptionally descriptive – it is difficult to imagine any theory (or observation) that would not incorporate it. Whilst it is accompanied by a theoretical approach based on a particular version of Marxist political economy, it is itself in no way dependent upon it. Retail capital is simply capital engaged in selling consumption goods (usually to workers), just as oil capital would be engaged in manufacturing petrochemicals.

Some added distinctiveness might be added to the abstract notion of retail capital by analytically stripping away any activity that it involves which is not directly concerned with buying and selling (although, interestingly in Ducatel and Blomley, more attention theoretically is given to the dependence of retailing on *selling* to customers than on *buying* from suppliers). In particular, transport as a genuinely productive activity might be treated, following Marx, as creating value even though it may fall under the control of retailers.

This is, however, to open up a can of ill-defined worms, as has become apparent in the debate over productive and unproductive labour, especially in its application to the specification of class structure. Which workers produce surplus value as opposed to those who simply depend upon it unproductively? And when does this happen? How can we tell which transport, warehousing, etc. activities are productive and which are not – without recourse to tautology and circularity or to the ideal invention of an exchangeless economy in which only genuinely needed transport counts? In short, the definitions involved are more problematic even on this simple descriptive terrain than they would appear to be at first sight, a matter returned to in the following section. And such issues must be confronted theoretically, not empirically or descriptively. The question still remains of what constitutes retail capital if its construction as an abstract, general category is denied.

## 2 TOWARDS AN ALTERNATIVE

Marx's theory of merchant capital is more complex than is suggested by Ducatel and Blomley, who use it and the term commercial capital interchangeably. Marx divided merchant capital into two parts: commercial capital proper dealing in commodities, and money-dealing capital that accounted for the handling of money, bookkeeping, etc. In addition, capital operating in exchange also includes interest-bearing capital which is concerned with lending money as capital (to create or appropriate surplus value by industrial or merchant capital, respectively) and not with generally making credit available for purchases.

The logical derivation of merchant capital arises from two aspects; first, the general formula for capital, M–C–M', buying in order to sell dearer; second, from the nature of the commodity itself for in its simple circulation, C–M–C, an initial use value is transformed through exchange to an alternative use value. This is reproduced at a more complex level in the structures and process of the circuits of capital, once the nature of productive capital has been unravelled. Thus, merchant capital is an abstract concept which is justified analytically by reference to the tendency towards specialisation between it and productive capital and between its two components (commodity dealing and money dealing) as superimposed upon the circuits of capital. In particular, the division between commercial and money-dealing capital, which would appear erroneously to set a precedent for the division between retail and non-retail capital, has its roots in the *simpler* division between the circulation of commodities and the circulation of money (the latter is derived logically from the former). More concretely, these activities, and their division from those of productive capital, are not so clear-cut and may be all undertaken by the single industrial or commercial capitalist. This will be returned to below.

In the case of merchant capital, it does operate according to an equalised rate of profit with industrial capital. Elsewhere, it has been argued that the general rate of profit is modified in the presence of merchant capital from the well-known formula $r = S/(C + V)$.[2] If K is the commercial costs incurred (corresponding to constant and variable capital for industrial capital) and B is the money capital advanced in addition, used to turn over the buying and sale of commodities, then $r = (S - K)/(C + V + B + K)$. In words, 'real' commercial costs, K, are deducted from the surplus value, S, to be distributed as profit. They also serve as an advance of capital along with the additional money of the merchants employed in circulating commodities, B, in forming the rate of profit. It follows that individual commodities are purchased by merchants at below value, $(c + v)(1 + r)$, and are sold by them at their values, $c + v + s = (c + v)(1 + r) + br + k(1 + r)$. This allows for commercial costs and profits to be included in the selling price of commodities, where lower-case letters reflect sectoral rather than aggregate quantities.

Even leaving aside the transformation problem, this is a controversial construct for those, such as neo-Ricardians, who are committed to treating exchange-based activity as equivalent to productive activity. But the formula itself provides arguments against this by implication, once it is accepted that concern is with commodity production, with sale as a distinct and logically necessary aspect of this historically and socially specific form of production. For the effects of the accumulation of productive and commercial capital are quite different. The former can be accumulated even at a lower rate of profit and add surplus value, S, even if not in proportion to capital advanced C + V, leading to a lower individual or even general rate of profit (if value is depressed for the sector as a whole and not just for the individual capitalist). Even for overproduction, the use value of what is created may not be wasted if prices are reduced and sales boosted.

For merchant capital, however, there is a major difference in that however much merchant capital is accumulated, there is only so much (surplus) value to be sold. Above and beyond a certain point, the accumulation of commercial capital not only reduces the rate of profit through (B + K), like productive capital through (C + V), it also reduces the surplus value available for distribution by the additional expenditure of real circulation costs, K. Circulation costs are always at the expense of profits (even though they may, with accumulation, be reduced in proportion) and so the limits within which commercial capital operates are curtailed differently in aggregate than for sectors of productive capital. This has implications for the cyclical and secular rhythms of accumulation between the two forms of capital.

For these and other reasons associated in general with the motives for diversification, commercial capital in practice may not only become involved in the specialised act of retailing but may also itself incorporate productive activities such as transport, distribution and even production itself (through, for example, the putting-out system). Similarly, it may also be involved in money-dealing and credit operations which have affinities with banking (as interest-bearing capital may come to incorporate money-dealing activities). Thus, the abstraction in dealing with these different types of capital is in identifying their pure forms, and the more concrete analysis is not simply to parade their institutional and competitive structure but also to identify the boundaries of these capitals in practice.

Take transport, for example. Logically, it exhibits the possibility of a productive activity being chronologically situated within the sphere of exchange if distribution follows after sale. However, distribution and storage costs may be, for example, a consequence of speculative commercial activity in the broadest sense as far as the commodities are concerned. A retailer hiring a capitalist firm to do its transport and storage supports a productive activity even though part of its output is used for speculative purposes (just as the means of production employed by commercial capital, or the computers in the stock exchange, are the products of industrial capital).

Suppose, on the other hand, that these activities are undertaken entirely in-house as part and parcel of the functioning of retail capital. Then, by contrast, this opens up the possibility that the entire transport activity is the consequence of unproductive commercial capital, even though the same functions are performed. This is not a matter, however, of the volition of the individual merchant. If there is a competing and independent transport industry establishing a value for its activities, then even where some merchants do their own fetching and carrying, it will still constitute the operation of productive capital within the sphere of exchange (and under the auspices of commercial capital). Consequently, the boundaries of what constitutes retail capital are competitively and historically contingent – ultimately depending upon whether a certain function has become normally directly dependent upon, and integrated with, merchant capital or not.

It might be argued that where the boundaries between commercial (including retail) and productive capital lie is of little consequence. But the relevance is in the restructuring of capital which, in part, often involves a redivision between sectoral activities and in which, especially during the course of a recession, productive and commercial capital can experience differences in both the rhythm and the depth of excess capacity.

In short, whilst commercial capital can be legitimately isolated in its pure form, despite its empirically contingent boundaries with productive capital, the same does not apply to retail capital since, leaving aside the problems posed by functions such as transport, there are two potential definitions for the pure form of retail capital. Whilst Ducatel and Blomley jump between them, each will be shown to be inadequate.

One is sale for final consumption. The problem here is that, whilst there is a division between sectors I and II – means of production and consumption, respectively – this is derived from the conditions under which accumulation takes place, as simple or expanded reproduction and as discussed in Volume II of *Capital*. This is not a division based on the way in which commodities are sold, and there is no logical basis either within the commodities themselves or in the operation of commercial capital (given its tendency both to specialise within and to diversify across sectors) for a distinct category of retail capital. Indeed, many commodities are sold both as constant capital and as wage goods. A topical example is electricity in the UK where the ten distribution companies, as distinct from the generators, have served all classes of customers, although privatisation is now opening up the possibility of direct sales from generators to large-scale industrial users (and not, thereby, a different fraction of non-retail capital). Another example is provided by DIY superstores which sell to the building industry as well as to the house-improver, despite their displacing conventional builders' merchants who have always served both the professionals (with discounts) and amateurs (without).

The alternative definition of retail capital is by reference to a more exclusive dependence upon sale for final consumption to workers. Here again, as in the division between sectors I and II, there is a logical basis for the abstraction that separates workers' consumption from that by capitalists or other classes. It is not, however, derived from their class positions and from the cultural implications, through 'moral and historical' influences determining what each class consumes. This is, in any case, a matter for complex, empirical contingency, and there can be no presumption of limited overlap between the consumption goods enjoyed by the different strata and the shops (retail capital) from which they are bought. TV sets, for example, in the UK are almost universally owned and, hence, purchased by all classes.

Rather, the division between wage revenue and expenditure of surplus value as revenue (and not as money capital for accumulation) lies in their origins and not in their destinations. As Marx is at great pains to analyse in Volume II of *Capital*, wage revenue and surplus value circulate quite differently – especially since wages (as the advance of variable capital) are the precondition for capitalist production and since profits (as a form of surplus value) are its consequence. This still leaves as empirically contingent the overlap between what workers and capitalists consume and how they buy it, just as for the overlap between means of production and consumption. There is no need for some underlying, simple, abstract category of retail capital. Indeed, the mode of purchase of means of consumption by workers, with or without capitalists, as the definition of retail capital is an immediate empirical category with no deep abstraction behind it.

By way of digression, a stronger case could be made for the existence of retail capital as a consequence of the consumption out of surplus value. Once again, there is a basis in accumulation and production for a separate category for luxuries, or sector III. They do not enter into the production of relative surplus value. But nor do they enter into the consumption of the working class; according to Marx (1969: 565): 'A large part of the consumption of workers enters into that of capitalists and landlords but not vice-versa.' Presumably, this observation is empirically contingent and an analytical consequence of the greater wealth of the recipients of surplus value. Accordingly, it is arguable that the merchanting and consumption of *luxuries* (rather than the sale of mass-produced goods) will take on unique and common characteristics – an issue explored by Veblen, for example.

## 3 EMPIRICAL ISSUES

Precisely because retailing is a heterogeneous and heterogeneously organised fraction of capital, theoretical observation is readily supported by selected empirical examples, especially if caution is not taken to avoid overgeneralisation. A critical assessment of Ducatel and Blomley's empirical observations illustrates this. Each of their three areas of empirical commentary is problematic and none contributes to a unique specification of retail capital. The first concerns the concentration of retail capital. This is presented as characteristic of capital in general as part of a general logic, as well as by reference to the specific competitive elimination of (an analytically unspecified) petty bourgeois retailing. It must surely be doubted whether this is uniquely characteristic of retail capital, given the propensity of cheap mass production to eliminate small-scale producers. In addition, no account is taken of counteracting tendencies, namely the ability of mass production itself to support small-scale retailing, since it renders cheaper than production in the home the availability of locally bought commodities even with a higher mark-up on production costs than is normal for a large-scale store. This raises spatial considerations in retailing that, to be fair, Ducatel and Blomley explicitly set aside.

Ducatel and Blomley also emphasise the drive of retailing into virgin territory having asserted that:

> The extent of concentration now achieved by major retailers implies that capital has extended into the final consumption exchange relation as far as is presently possible. Given retail capital's limited ability to create value, further accumulation strategies have included both an extension of operations into new spatial areas, and diversification into the retail of relatively underdeveloped product fields, such as home improvements.
> (Ducatel and Blomley 1990: 220)

This is too sweeping a generalisation to apply across individual countries and across different commodities, let alone on a global scale. Even if it is correct, it is doubtful whether retailing is uniquely dynamic in diversifying or in promoting diversification. For retailing to invade new product markets, such as home improvements, it is first necessary that the commodities already be produced, so the origins of the impetus do not necessarily derive from within exchange. Although this is a matter for conjecture, it would appear to be unusual for retailers to develop new products themselves in order to expand the scope of retailing, though there are some obvious examples such as Marks and Spencer's move into ready-prepared and chilled foods. It is arguable that the growth of DIY retailing is the consequence rather than the cause of the demand for home improvements, reflecting the structures of both the UK housing markets and the construction industry in the UK and their consequences for poor and costly repair, maintenance and refurbishment in the context of high levels of owner-occupation.

Nor is it the tendency of capital to expand its markets without its own counteracting influences. Clearly, the growth of DIY occurs at the expense of the products and participation of the construction industry. Around the turn of the century, the growth of the mass market for foodstuffs allowed an increasing range of food to be prepared in the home, and the development of domestic sewing machines increased the market for fabrics at the potential expense of ready-to-wear and custom clothing. Consequently, the tendency to increasing reliance upon convenience foods, which relocates preparation in the factory and away from the home, will mitigate the tendency towards eating out of the home – for which restaurants are equally the 'retail capital' for food increasingly prepared off the catering premises. Most significant in this context currently is the marketing of leisure, in which the home-based reliance on TV and its accompaniments has been bought at the expense of entertainment retailing outside the home, visibly expressed in the decline of cinemas and pubs and in the rise of sales of canned beer.

The second empirical area broached is that of the 'productive-commercial interface'. It is presumed, along with much orthodox analysis, that the increasing concentration of retail capital and the rise of own-label products has strengthened the hand of retail capital against productive capital.[3] It is not quite clear what this means for, as previously remarked, retail and productive capital are mutually subject to a tendency to equalised profitability. The strength of retailers is moderated by their own competition and diminished margins (no less intense because of rivalry predominantly between Tesco and Sainsbury in the UK). Retail stores do have the power to promote or to block a new product but they are also compelled and seek to sell established branded goods alongside their own because these are fast selling and commercially profitable from the point of view of pace of turnover (and added mark-up). Moreover, even manufacturers of non-branded goods have the option of sourcing a number of outlets and make up some of the biggest and fastest-growing food manufacturers.[4]

Thus, it is important not to generalise from and misinterpret relations between large-scale retailers and a multitude of subcontracted producers (as often conveyed in discussion of flexible specialisation). Even in cases of large retailers subcontracting from many small producers, it might also be more appropriate to consider that, far from retailers dominating productive capital, they are incorporating it in all but formal ownership.

The third empirical area is the reduction of circulation costs. Important points are made by Ducatel and Blomley concerning the shifts of costs to consumers (travelling to shopping centres, self-servicing and, associated with this, the construction of shopping as a leisure activity with appropriate stores, atmosphere and lay-outs), the deskilling and dilution of the workforce (loss of knowledge by staff of goods sold, itself associated with standardisation, and substitution of female for male labour) and fewer larger stores located on out-of-town sites.

These developments are linked to the question of the power relations between consumers and retailers and the imperative of individual retailers to promote demand through stimuli to wants. These are significant factors but they are not historically confined to the most recent period – indeed, they accompany all exchange societies to one degree or another and so cannot distinctly give rise to retail capital.

## 4 CONCLUDING REMARKS

Ducatel and Blomley observe that Marx did not himself specify retail capital. They presume that to do so is a valid objective especially as (predominantly non-Marxist) others have been unsuccessful in moving towards a systematic analysis. In conclusion, it can now be argued that this is not appropriate for retail capital within Marxist theory – that it cannot be legitimately constructed as a category like merchant or interest-bearing capital. Why is this so?

First, Marx's theory of each of these exhausts the logical possibilities for capital in exchange, and the division between the two is based upon the specialised functions of circulating commodities and loaning money, respectively. Breaking down merchant capital into commercial capital and money-dealing capital is also rooted functionally in the circulation of money as opposed to the circulation of commodities. Retail capital does not occupy a comparable analytical position. It does circulate commodities destined for final consumption. Whilst there may be some distinctions between expenditure on these by workers and capitalists, that expenditure is variable capital and surplus value as revenue (wages and profits, respectively) which, when it comes to be spent, is spent in simple commodity exchange for which the money's origins become irrelevant. As Marx observes of the worker:

> As consumer and possessor of exchange values, and that in the form of the *possessor of money*, in the form of money he becomes a simple entry of circulation – one of its infinitely many entries, in which his specificity as worker is extinguished.
>
> (Marx 1973: 420–1)

Consequently, the boundaries of retail capital are not determined by the circulation of capital but by the circulation of revenue, which is at a much lower level of analysis since it depends upon distributional struggle (and the potential divergence of the value of wages from the value of labour power, etc.). Moreover, there is no necessary distinction between retailing for final consumption and retailing constant capital – as evidenced by the construction industry's dependence on DIY stores as much as home-improvers.

Second, the level of analysis at which it is possible to identify retailing as a well-defined activity is, consequently, that of the individual sector – and not even across the broad division into sectors I, II and III. If retail capital were to be defined by its dependence on wage revenue, it would have to be confined to circulating the products of sector II (means of consumption). But there is no reason why retail capital should confine itself to this sector. In addition, even then the boundaries of retail activity would be contingent upon how a chain of provision connecting production to final consumption has been historically realised. Ducatel and Blomley employ examples that tend to be clear-cut, such as supermarkets, if not DIY stores, but what about the retailing of (newly built) houses?

In short, in breaking down commercial capital into its constituent parts, the homogeneity required for a distinct section of retail capital is absent. Retail capital cannot be structured as an aggregate in relation to commercial capital in the same way as commercial capital can relative to merchant capital, nor this to interest-bearing capital. In any case, what would be the amorphous category of non-retail commercial capital?

These conclusions are reinforced by considering the necessarily selective way in which Ducatel and Blomley have structured the role of demand. This has been construed as something lying outside and confronting (retail) capital – most notably conveyed by the struggle of consumers to substitute or impose their use value logic on a more entrenched logic based on exchange value. They appeal to Bourdieu and a 'dialectic of supply and demand' around products and tastes (ibid.: 216).

Once again, however rigorously these factors are situated in relation to the logic of the circuits of capital, their causal significance for retailing (and for other points along the chain of provision) is highly variable for different sectors of the economy. Consequently, to hinge the specificity of retail capital on its complex relation to the system of demand and its determinants ends by negating, not supporting, the validity of a general category of retail capital. In short, there is no more reason for there to be a Marxist concept of retail capital than there is for there to be a Marxist concept of steelmaking or engineering (although Marxist theory need not be silent on these).

This is not to deny the importance of retailing. But in terms of both its origins in production and its destinations in final consumption, retailing is better situated in a vertical rather than a horizontal framework. Each commodity group – such as food, housing, energy, clothing, transport, etc. – is (re)structured as a system of provision and the links between the various moments of production, distribution and exchange will be historically evolved and sector-specific rather than, unlike tendencies and overall economic structure, general across all sectors.

Consequently, for each of these systems of provision, the location and role of retailing will be different (as will be the case between the same sectors in different countries). For this reason, it is important not to generalise from the operations of a few prominent sectors, such as supermarkets and DIY stores, and to presume that they (and other sectors) have common determinants and effects. Recent developments in superstore grocery trading, for example, are in major part a response to the increasingly capital-intensive mass production of uniform food commodities, whereas the DIY superstore reflects the failure to subordinate construction, and repair and maintenance, to mass factory production!

More generally then, Ducatel and Blomley develop retailing at an abstract level on a par with the analysis of commercial capital. For them, institutions and competition provide for its more detailed specification. Here it is argued that such factors are prerequisites for the very definition of retail capital as something distinct, and this must be undertaken at the sectoral level of the various systems of provision.[5]

## CODA

## PROBLEMS OF METHODOLOGY

Questions of methodology are extremely complex and often infuriatingly abstract in the absence of specific application. Whilst debate understandably surrounds methodology in disputes between rival schools of thought, it is often as intense within Marxism. It is appropriate then to address methodological issues in locating retail capital theoretically. Fortunately, Ducatel and Blomley's contribution allows this because of their attention, sometimes implicit, to a number of such issues. Drawing quotational support from

Mandel and Marx, they adopt what is apparently an orthodox methodology. There are, however, a number of problems with it. These begin with their use of the notion of contradiction, an essential aspect of Marxism in all but the most recent school of 'analytical Marxism'.

First, there is appeal to the dialectical method, which rests on unfolding the consequences of inner, underlying relations, and these are also linked to the process of change:

> The great power of Marx's analysis lies in its dynamism. Hence, we must consider the manner in which the capitalist mode of production and retailing change over time. Change, qualitative and quantitative, is inherently related to the inner contradictions of capitalism.
>
> (Ducatel and Blomley 1990: 214)

Here is the idea that there are dynamic forces underlying, and determining changes in, retailing. This might be thought to include the laws of development of capitalism and the imperatives associated with the pursuit of profitability.

Second, there is the process of abstraction which involves a theoretical movement from higher (simpler) to lower (more complex) levels. This analytical movement is certainly intended to include the relation of simpler to more complex concepts and must also have some relation to the previous aspect of dynamism. For example, capital and wage labour are simple concepts highlighting the economic relations between classes, for which exploitation and appropriation of surplus value are central. But the value relations underlying production are expressed, after exchange, in the more complex forms of wages, prices and profits. Moreover, the attempt by capital to expand the surplus produced leads to the accumulation of capital as an engine of further economic and social change of great variety.

Ducatel and Blomley employ three particular examples of the movement between higher (simpler) and lower (more complex) levels of abstraction. There is the relation between the overall circuit of all capitals and those capitals confined to the sphere of circulation or exchange:[6]

> So far we have identified a series of phases of capital which together make up the totality of capital, as well as the changes of form which take place in the overall production process. From this level of the overall circuit of capital we now move down a level of abstraction to consider the nature of capital which is specific to the sphere of circulation.
>
> (ibid.: 210)

Thus, exchange is located at a lower level of abstraction than production.

Movement to the more complex level is also associated with the institutionalisation of retail capital (ibid.: 216): 'We now intend to move down a step, and consider the institutional appearance of retail firms, and the internal consequences of this specific manifestation.' In some respects, this might be considered to be equivalent to the relation between industrial capital as a general category and its more complex occurrence in the form of the factory system or even as particular factories. By analogy, there is the more complex existence of the retail system or particular shops.

Third, even with an abstract identification of capital and its fractions, such as those engaged in retailing, there is also the use of contradiction as the complex consequences of competition between capitals and, equally, between individual retailers: 'Retail capital manifests itself as a number of competing retail firms. Accordingly, individual retail capitals are the more complex development, after considering competition, of retail capital as a whole' (ibid.: 217).

Apart from inner, underlying relations and levels of abstraction, a third way in which contradiction can be understood is as the co-existence of conflict with dependence. Wage labour, for example, is both supported by capital and in conflict with it. But such relations of conflict/dependence are endemic to society. They can exist within the family, for example. They are also closely related to competition, for example between retail and productive capital as well as within each of these fractions of capital. For Ducatel and Blomley: 'Whilst retail capital and productive capital are dependent upon each other for their existence, the point of contact between these forms will be a potentially abrasive one in which retail capital will be inevitably implicated' (ibid.: 214). Conflict between consumers and retailers is also highlighted:

> When consumer and retailer meet, they do so for profoundly different reasons. The former seeks use value, the latter seeks to maximize exchange value. This indicates the potential for conflict and the negotiation of that conflict between retail capital and consumers is general.
>
> (ibid.: 214)

A fourth aspect of contradiction is to draw the distinction between form, function and logic. The logic of capital, for example, is to produce surplus value through exploitation. This is a function of the production/labour process, whereby labourers are coerced to work beyond the time required to create their subsistence. The form this takes is an apparent *equality* in exchange, whereby buying and selling occurs without direct coercion at prevailing wages and prices. For Ducatel and Blomley, a similar method is to be employed in specifying retail capital:

> By *form*, we mean the specific expression which capital adopts as it moves from one phase of its circuit to another. By *function*, we mean the specific role which each form effects in the overall movement of capital. Each form of capital has its own *logic*, which is not reducible to its function. This logic is the internal rationale for the chronic application of investment capital in a specific form of capital. In moving

> from form through function to logic, we proceed from the abstract towards the specific.[7]
>
> (ibid.: 208)

Fifth, contradiction might be seen as a problem of co-ordination between different activities. To be realised, for example, surplus value (in commodities) has to be sold and this cannot be presumed:

> Volume II of *Capital* addresses this issue, notably the disjunctures that can occur in the process of the circulation of capital . . . and thus the reproduction of the relations of production is, therefore, not an unproblematic procedure, but one potentially riven with contradictions and tensions.
>
> (ibid.: 210)

Here contradiction is perceived as the potential disjuncture between separate economic processes.

Finally, the notion of contradiction can be attached to the formation of economic and social structures. Because of their organisational reliance upon the circuits of capital, Ducatel and Blomley divide production from exchange, with each encompassing distinct spheres of activity. This allows the corollary distinction to be drawn between industrial and commercial/merchant capital (and, subsequently, a further substructure subsuming retail capital). In addition, the distinction of the circuits of capital from the sphere of final consumption which lies outside these circuits, is subsumed within the structures of private, as a part of social, reproduction:

> The implication of this is that there are at least two quite different types of consumption. One of these is undertaken solely to further the accumulation of capital. In such transactions the purpose of the exchange is not to consume the commodity in itself but as part of the process of production. Retail capital, however, relates to the other type of consumption, that being consumption necessary to the maintenance of the private sphere of reproduction.
>
> (ibid.: 213)

Clearly then, these six elements point to a rich methodology with affinities to classical Marxism, although this is always subject to controversial interpretation. The details of such debates are not of direct concern here. Rather, the presence of these methodological elements also implies that the conceptualisation of retail capital (and other categories of political economy) requires a complicated treatment of inner relations, higher and lower levels of analysis, conflict and dependence, form, function and logic, and co-ordination between and within the structurally separated spheres of economic and social reproduction. However, whatever the validity individually of each methodological element and their mutual compatibility and coherence, there are severe problems in their specific application to retail capital.

First, there is a problem of consistency of application of these methodological elements. In general, the methodology is one based on simple concepts, such as value, capital and labour, from which the contradictory (economic) totality can be reproduced at a series of more complex levels – in analysing the accumulation of capital in its various aspects. To what extent, however, can contradictions be identified at lower (or more complex) levels of abstraction without necessarily relating them to the simpler concepts? There do appear to be precedents for this in Marx's own work. He sees the commodity as embodying a contradiction between its use value and its exchange value aspects. In *Capital*, this is presented prior to consideration of capital and exploitation. Does this justify treating the problems of sale or realisation as being contradictory in and of themselves? This is the view, for example, of Ducatel and Blomley: 'Marx also isolates contradictions that are rooted less in production and more in circulation and consumption, specifically the problem of the realization of the value bound up in commodities' (ibid.: 215). If contradictions can be *rooted* more superficially in the lower levels of abstraction, i.e., within circulation and consumption alone, then there is some support for the category of retail capital, for it can be seen as the mediating link between circulation and consumption, addressing the general problem of sale as contradictory irrespective of the role of production.

This is, however, dubious since there is a total neglect of other influences on the problems of sale; those derived indirectly from the imperatives of production (such as how much is produced and with what level of potential profitability) as well as those more direct influences such as levels and distribution of income, the availability of credit, etc. Inevitably, basing retail capital on the contradiction between circulation and consumption leads to an underconsumptionist stance, one that essentially depends on the relationship between retailing and the level of demand. This is more or less equivalent to a Keynesian analysis for which the other aspects of Marx's method, outlined above, can be allowed to fall away. Possibly aware of this, Ducatel and Blomley immediately claim the contradiction between circulation and consumption is due to contradictions between production and consumption and not a matter of overproduction or underconsumption: 'The issue is not one of "overproduction", or of "underconsumption", but reflects the dialectical relation of the two spheres of consumption and production.' Yet the definition of retail capital is not rooted in this more fundamental contradiction in production, and their analysis that follows is essentially one of too little demand for too much production, although this is shrouded in discussions of the uncertainty and manipulation of demand. As will be seen in other examples as they occur, this is symptomatic of the methodology being applied piecemeal rather than fully and consistently throughout.

In short, even if a case can be made for lower-level contradictions, as between circulation and sale, this can only be done by setting aside underlying determinants, such as production, so that the lower-level contradictions can be autonomised. This raises a second problem which has only been implicit so far – the relationship between methodology and causal analysis. It might be thought that the descent to lower levels is both explanatory and causal. Indeed, there are potentially three conceptual structures – from the simple to the complex, from the essence/content to the form/appearance, and from the determining to the determined. These cannot coincide in general in so far as the simplest concepts such as use value, exchange value and the commodity – from which Marxist abstraction begins – precede the basic causal categories of capital and surplus value production. This perhaps explains Marx's reference to contradiction within the use value and exchange value of the commodity. It allows the building up expositionally of more complex categories, such as capital itself, and their associated contradictions. But this does not mean causally that the contradiction within the commodity can be projected at the lower level of circulation and consumption alone when dealing with capitalist circulation.

This is possibly the source of Ducatel and Blomley's confusion. For, as relatively orthodox Marxists, they seek to target production as determinant but, in specifying retail capital as a general, lower-level category of Marxist analysis, they need to autonomise it from production. By way of illustrative digression, it is worth dwelling on where this leads them. For, whilst positing a conceptual structure, Ducatel and Blomley have only a limited causal analysis which is predominantly assertive in terms of the significant but presumably lower status of retail as opposed to productive capital. This, as will be seen, leads to some questionable specifications of retail capital itself, but has the added disadvantage of leaving other theory uncriticised except by counterposing an alternative within the Marxist tradition.

Specifically, the orthodox economic approach to retailing has been to treat it as akin to any other (productive) economic activity, like steelmaking or carpentry. It has its own conditions of supply and demand and industrial structure, etc. Such an approach is most notable within the neo-Ricardian tradition of Marxism, in which such commerce is seen as indistinguishable analytically from the operation of productive capital – it exploits wage labour and buys and sells commodities after performing labour upon them. Now, in the rejection of the distinction between productive and unproductive labour, neo-Ricardians do not accept the view that only productive labour is the source of value since they essentially collapse the structure of the economy into a set of otherwise undifferentiated activities. Similarly, neo-Ricardians would reject the view that retail capital appropriates profits at the expense of productive capital. They argue instead that retail capital is an equal participant in its creation and distribution through its use of surplus, exploited labour – just as they argue that all exploited labour contributes to profitability, even in social reproduction, such as domestic labour or welfare state employees.[8]

Ducatel and Blomley note orthodox theory's lack of a specific analysis of retail capital as their opening gambit. Their paper, 'derives from a dissatisfaction with the wholly inadequate analysis of retailing and retail change. . . . Traditional accounts . . . appear to lack a systematic theoretical account of retail capital' (ibid.: 207).[9] But they do not account for this lacuna nor appear to recognise that it is theoretically plausible to reject the need for a specific theory of retail capital – leaving it to be determined by general principles at an empirically contingent level of analysis, as a portion of commercial capital similar to the separate sectors of industrial capital. To argue convincingly otherwise, it is necessary not only to pose an alternative conceptual structure, as Ducatel and Blomley do, but also to bring out its causal implications (from which a differing empirical understanding will arise). This does depend upon rooting retailing's contradictions within production (rather than sale alone), for which homogeneity across different sectors cannot be presumed. Otherwise, some variant of Keynesianism results according to the supply and demand effects of retailing.

A third methodological problem is the complexity of the relation between simple abstract concepts and the more complex concepts at lower levels. Between the factory and final consumption there are many intermediate steps, of which retailing is but one. How is it to be linked, not only to production and consumption, but also to distribution, wholesaling, financing, etc.? It cannot simply be presumed that retailing is integrated with these in a way that preserves its homogeneity. Ducatel and Blomley's avoidance of this difficulty is reflected in their limited number of levels of abstraction moving from the simpler to the more complex. Indeed, the staircase of descent employed by Ducatel and Blomley's abstraction has very few steps and quite a few leaps. Given their intent to construct an abstract notion of retail capital, it necessarily occurs at a high level of abstraction. So, as it were, approaching from above, retail capital is fixed by a simple division of commercial capital into two parts: retail and, presumably, an unspecified 'non-retail' or everything else. Carrying on down appears to require a huge step in the dark from the form, function and logic of retail capital to the most immediate empirical form – through the simple expedient of institutionalisation even to the level of the firm. At one level:

> By way of definition, the form of retail capital is that part of total social capital which is located between productive capital and the final consumer. From this statement of form, it follows that the distinctive function of retail capital . . . is the final exchange of commodities. . . . For the purposes of this introductory paper, we assume that the logic of retail capital is the same as that of commercial capital. . . . However, we would argue that the dominant logic of retail capital is that of exchange.[10]
>
> (ibid.: 213)

Apart from the extent to which this distinguishes form, function and logic (each seems to be concerned with sale for final consumption), it is, repeating a quotation from above, followed by a single step to an unmediated subsequent determination of the concrete form of retail capital (ibid.: 216): 'We now intend to move down a step, and consider the institutional appearance of retail firms.'

Finally, there is methodologically the problem of the Marxist notion of tendency or law. It can in part be considered as inner contradiction, in part as the dynamism associated with accumulation, and also as giving rise to empirical trends. But tendency or law within Marxist theory is an abstract category drawing upon the notion of underlying forces with counteracting influences whose interaction gives rise to contingent, complex outcomes. This is most clear for the law of the tendency of the rate of profit to fall (and its counteracting influences).[11] Less closely observed and debated, laws or tendencies apply equally to the categories of political economy themselves. Value, as socially necessary labour time, for example, depends upon the tendencies of individual capitals both to better and to fall behind the socially established norm.

Similarly, as will be seen, the category of retail capital is the product of a number of processes. It is formed in practice through conflicting tendencies, not neatly as a matter of analytical logic that attempts to appropriate (some of) those processes in thought. To put it crudely, the car sector may or may not include component manufacture, depending upon the degree of vertical-integration of the two industrial activities. Similarly, the processes, i.e., specific activities, that make up retailing may belong to a greater or lesser extent to the sector defining itself as retailing. It cannot be presumed that retail capital is clearly defined at a high level of abstraction and that these more complex processes are simply the way in which such capital reveals its form. Retail capital has to be formed, not simply to have a form; and its ingredients or content may vary across the economy as different tendencies interact heterogeneously sector by sector.

# Part V

# CONCLUDING PERSPECTIVES

# 21

# THE SHIFTING BOUNDARIES OF CONSUMPTION

Although the neglect of consumption as a subject of academic investigation is being rapidly eroded, approaches to it have been fragmented and insulated from one another. The variety of both the methodologies employed and the explanatory factors with which they engage have generated widely different interpretations. This book has attempted to explain why consumer theory has developed in this way. The location of consumption within different systems of provision has helped to expose the complexity and heterogeneity of its underlying causes, role and character. It is in part the very multiplicity of explanatory factors that has generated such a variegated diet of theories, with each tending to generalise from its own specific focus, whether inspired by a particular consumption good or by a particular variable deemed to be of decisive importance.

The conclusion offered here is that the rifts and voids between different theories of consumption can best be bridged by a synthesis premised upon an interdisciplinary stance – a goal that has proved elusive given the non-overlapping segmentation of the analyses. In addition, a level of generality must be sacrificed to allow contributions from the various social sciences to be brought together under the rubric of a particular system of provision. Some theories will be compromised by this approach; others may be more accommodating if not enriched. Hopefully, the advantages to be derived, demonstrated by the critical assessments and empirical studies presented in this book, will far outweigh any sacrifices involved, especially since these are often associated with overgeneralisation.

There is another important perspective on the analysis of consumption which needs to be acknowledged. Throughout this book, there has been an implicit presumption in favour of private aspects of consumption and their contribution to the evolution of private systems of provision. Typical of the bias of most recent academic work in the area, it reflects, to some extent, the ultimate concern of many academic disciplines with individual acts, whether motivated by behavioural or other imperatives. But it does not sufficiently recognise the radical changes that have taken place in the concept of consumption itself, changes which have overhauled former definitions of, and distinctions between, public and private provision.

Until the mid-1970s, the services made available through public sector systems of provision (in education, healthcare, housing, transport, etc.) were accepted as attributes of civil society. Public provision through the British welfare state signalled a commitment to collective rather than individual interests; social and political objectives took precedence over narrowly economic concerns. As long as the consensus underpinning these objectives held together, state expenditure used to finance public systems of provision was subject to its own terms of reference and its own performance criteria, independently applied and evaluated. It has only been in the past fifteen years, with policies ideologically designated as dismantling the welfare state, that both the theoretical and, in some respects, the practical independence of public provision have been undermined. One of the earliest and sharpest indices of this conceptual invasion of the public by the private sector is found in the notion of the 'social wage', as if workers could be paid either in cash or equivalently in public services. Paradoxically, it is in the work of Marxists such as O'Connor (1973) and Gough (1979) that more general categories derived from the private sector have been imposed upon the public sector, with insufficient sensitivity being displayed to the differences in systems of provision that each sector entails.

From a totally different perspective, the rise to dominance of aggressive, free market economics has brought in its wake new forms of calculation with the same analytical effect; it seeks to sweep aside all the political and social objectives that distinguish public from private provision in order to subject all economic activity across the board to the same ironclad rules of the market. Stripped of its special features, public provision is treated simply as an alternative to private sector provision. Since the latter is theoretically dominated by the twin pillars of consumption and investment, it is not surprising that these concepts have infected the portrayal of public systems of provision. In a convergence within the world of economics of both terminology and practice, the degradation of public services has been achieved as much by the privatisation of language as by the actual privatisation of goods and services. Atomised individuals are now cast as 'consumers' of healthcare, housing or education, i.e., making rational choices about where to 'invest' their tax contributions. Public services are reduced to commodities like beer and soap, subject to the same constraints of utility and income. Individuals appear to be burdened with massive decision-making responsibilities as their participation in consumption mushrooms.

In other words, the concept of consumption has been crudely expanded to accommodate the expansion in commitment to market economics. This distorts the nature of the relationship between individuals and a variety of social services and activities they are now thought to 'consume'. Moreover, at the macroeconomic level, if considerations of consumption and investment alone govern decision-making across the economy as a whole, then the choice between one sector and another is no longer a choice between ideologies but simply one based on cost-benefit calculations prescribed by market economics.

Yet even within this framework, the dividing line between aspects of consumption that are strictly private (individual) and those that are social (public or collective) is rarely clear cut. However powerful the reductive tendencies of neoclassical economics, they cannot suppress the dynamic relationship between public and private provision. The nature of this relationship at any one time must be viewed, in part, as reflecting the current balance in the interaction of systems of provision active in the economy.

The distinction between private and social and between collective and individual are much more readily recognised in production. Work is social, the worker deemed to be private when out or outside of work. The factory as a site of production is a collective form of organisation, but its products are presumed to be individually consumed by purchase. In addition, less attention is paid to the world of work as an arena of constructed experience – at least compared with consumption. Surely, production and work offer considerable scope as a terrain for ideological manipulation, exemplified in notions of the manager's right to manage, a fair day's work for a fair day's pay, and in the gendering of work to define masculinity and femininity. But it is rare to find work so readily and substantially transformed as consumption; the consumer may be king (or queen) but the worker cannot be boss – although modern capitalism is such that the boss, especially as a non-owning managerial functionary, can be perceived as a worker.

In contrast to production, consumption cannot be so readily self-contained. A few small examples illustrate both the clear lack of boundaries between one form of consumption and another and their mutual interdependence.

Many of the new domestic appliances that have enlarged the scope of consumption within the home are spin-offs from technologies developed for, and sponsored by, the state for purposes of defence. In this context, technology transfer constitutes a shift from public to private consumption, accompanied by a shift in the mode of provision from the public supply of unmarketed goods and services (unproductive and unprofitable) to the individual purchase of goods through the market. They often enter the market as luxuries whose development costs have been borne more by the public purse than by private investment.

It is worth noting that the means by which public provision has stimulated private consumption in the case of technology transfer have been very different from those which stimulated the earlier development of consumer industries. In the nineteenth century, development of mass production in both the food and clothing industries was spurred by government procurement policies. Guaranteed demand in the form of large-scale orders for military uniforms and packaged foods encouraged technical innovation. But, for the most part, these innovations arose in the factory, without any direct public investment in the process of production. The state supplied the market rather than the technology. But the ultimate consumer was an individual soldier, of the same size and shape and with the same appetite in civilian as in military life. In this sense, government involvement in the chain of provision contributed to the creation of postwar consumer demand. In the twentieth century, much defence contract work remains unmarketed and reaches no ultimate 'consumer'.

In some areas of twentieth-century technology transfer, the state supplies the rationale for consumption as well as the technology. Perhaps not surprisingly, sale of some spin-off goods often depends upon the substitution of defence of the household for defence of the nation. High-power rifles, domestic alarm systems that simulate regular occupancy when owners are away, radar systems for automobiles that allow the driver to exceed the legal speed limit with impunity, telephone answering machines that allow listeners to screen calls before choosing to answer, all add a darker tinge to the aura of private consumption. Purchase of these goods, however, tends to privatise household rather than individual consumption. Except in households composed of a single individual, the increasing mediation of contacts with the outside world will necessarily alter the social relations of those inside. It will also alter perceptions of responsibilities traditionally shared by the larger community.

At the same time that the new generation of gadgetry has facilitated the defensive isolation of the household, it has also increased that household's dependence on the technical experts who maintain, repair and alter those gadgets. The private character of consumption is surely compromised by this dependence. While some of these transactions can be carried out on the telephone (adding an extra cable channel or learning how to salvage lost computers files), some, like repairing a dysfunctional microwave or replacing a faulty hard drive, require the intervention of personal expertise. The recent mushrooming of services pandering to these needs illustrates a growing dependence on a new kind of technical 'handyman', one who is less likely to come to your house. The miniaturisation of electronics housed in new lightweight materials also makes many new appliances more portable – and more easily replaceable. Their higher turnover and the faster rate of technological obsolescence involve the consumer in more frequent trips to showrooms.

Equally important, the fast pace of technological change requires the serious investment of time to create an 'informed consumer' capable of negotiating intelligently with the army of specialist salespersons. (Some energy must also be reserved for mastering the instructions after purchase!) The private consumption of new gadgets, then, may require as a precondition, a much longer and more complex exposure to the social process of exchange before purchase as well as a more extended vulnerability to maintenance and service assistance after it. Again, this will differ significantly between commodities and may help to explain the phenomenal rise in mail order businesses (and, in the US, television shopping) for those commodities whose selling attributes can be more simply and visually conveyed (like clothing and accessories). Even the food industry has cashed in on this trend, demonstrating its continuing efforts to overcome the basic constraint of perishability that has so influenced the history of this system of provision.

A different form of 'private' consumption is typified by the DIY (home build) industry, which displaces a great deal of assembly and light manufacturing work from the factory to the home. In the case of extensive self-building activity, where the consumer purchases unfinished or semi-finished goods which require skills to complete, it is hard to draw the line between private consumption and private production. DIY firms capitalise on this blurring of the distinction between work and leisure activities.

The risks of ignorance arising from the layperson's helplessness in the face of inaccessible technology may increase dependence on what has now become 'fallback' technology, like the conventional oven or the typewriter whose 'user friendliness' is at least visible. The total displacement of one generation of technology by another (with the ultimate disappearance of the earlier one) must, therefore, vary from one commodity to another. Marketing and advertising strategies for domestic appliances will vary accordingly, each reflecting a different balance in the conflict between generations of machinery. Some, like the telephone and the radio, represent entirely new inventions rather than improvements on earlier models. For them, the marketing challenge is not to overcome ingrained habits but rather to overcome a 'natural', possibly induced, failure of imagination – or fear of the unknown.

The rise of the home entertainment/video/microwave culture is another trend that is thought to lend weight to the increasing privatisation of consumption. But the effects are no more clear-cut or unilateral in this arena. First, the rise of domestic consumption implies a restructuring of the systems of provision which supply the necessary goods and services. Second, innovations designed for private consumption have sometimes enhanced collective consumption as well; the availability of the microwave and other innovations in convenience foods have bolstered the rise in 'eating out' just as the popularity of home videos has at times breathed new life into the cinema. Third, the nature, causes and implications of the video–microwave culture are also intimately bound up with the increased participation of women in the workforce in a variety of ways, so that they become more socialised as consumption becomes apparently more privatised.

These few examples have been cited to demonstrate that discussion of the private versus social (or individual versus collective) nature of consumption must be as sensitive to differences in the way that objects are produced, distributed, consumed and interpreted as discussion that sets supply against demand. To create a false opposition for the sake of theoretical tidiness (or ideological simplicity) is to sacrifice the potential richness of understanding that may be opened up by the systems-of-provision approach. The failure to adopt a more open-ended and inclusive alternative often leads to a false ideological emphasis on one form of consumption or another. Either the market becomes the primary determinant (demand divinely sufficing through exchange to order all else) or this role is assigned to bureaucratised forms of state provision (supply similarly suffices through planning). Recent upheavals in Eastern Europe and elsewhere point to the inadequacy of this opposition.

By analogy, many of the theories criticised in this book sacrifice explanatory power for simplicity. Set against this, an understanding of consumption built upon arguments that recognise systems of provision may well lack the neatness and certainty offered by other, less inclusive, theoretical frameworks. But it will substitute a more revealing dynamism that stretches the capacity to confront issues of great complexity, a power increasingly necessary to generate innovative work in the field of consumption.

# NOTES

## 2 CONSUMPTION THROUGH SYSTEMS OF PROVISION

1 In Marx's striking image, commodities are in love with money – but the course of true love never did run smooth.
2 Of course, at times, the sexuality itself takes on a commodity form as in prostitution – but also more generally in pornography.
3 For the relation between advertising and women as sex objects, see Williamson (1978) and also Chapter 14; for the media and commodification, see Dunn (1986); for the state, there is some discussion in Miller (1987); and for the family, this is a favoured ground for marketing and the sociology of socialisation.
4 See also Lefebvre on:

> Obsolescence . . . experts are well acquainted with the life-expectancy of objects . . . such statistics are part of the demography of objects and are correlated to the cost of production and profit. . . . To this familiar theory we add two observations; first, the *obsolescence of needs* . . . secondly . . . an extreme *fluidity* of existence.
>
> (Lefebvre 1971: 81–2)

5 In Marx's terms, labour is only formally subordinated to capital in the production process which has yet to seize the methods of production that it inherits and transform them to the specifically capitalist method of production or real subordination, see Appendix to Marx (1976).
6 This might be termed Accam's Razor after the nineteenth-century chemist concerned to expose and obliterate adulteration of foods (by which genuine ingredients were confined to a minimum), and by analogy with Occum's Razor which seeks to eliminate any step in an argument that is not strictly required! See Chapter 12.
7 More generally, for the selling of the UK heritage, see Samuel (1989).
8 These issues are discussed in Fine (1992).
9 For biscuits, see Corley (1976) and, for canned products, see Johnston (1976).
10 In foods, sugar is even combined with fat, a source of heart and circulation disease, in a ratio of roughly one to one by weight since this raises the 'go-away' factor, the illusion in taste that food has left the mouth (and teeth!). See Cantor and Cantor (197

## 3 CRISIS IN THE THEORY OF CONSUMER BEHAVIOUR

1 See Arndt (1986) and Clayton (1986).
2 Jacoby refers to definitions of brand loyalty. See also Westbrook and Oliver (1981)

who note that measures of consumer satisfaction have run to eighty different items. For Anderson and Golden:

> Perhaps the most noteworthy observation is the preponderance of references purporting to be lifestyle research which provide no explicit definition of lifestyle at all. What few definitions are provided, range from the ridiculous to the sublime, from the tautological . . . to the logically inconsistent . . . from the simple . . . to the complex . . . the almost total absence of any theoretical anchorage for lifestyle research.
>
> (Anderson and Golden 1984: 406)

3 Physiology should also be added to the list, especially in so far as its influence is felt indirectly through psychology.
4 In fact, they suggest that the other disciplines have not contributed enormously to a tradition of consumer behaviour theory, a matter taken up later.
5 Sheth *et al.* (1988) suggest and discuss the relative merits of twelve different schools in marketing; Arndt (1983) finds a more modest six.
6 Thus, the discipline of history has been divided into a number of separate components – social, political, labour, economic, oral and econometric – each employing different techniques, methods and areas of investigation.
7 See, for example, Holbrook (1987), Calder and Tybout (1987) and Holbrook and O'Shaughnessy (1988). See also Cooper (1987), Hudson and O'Zanne (1988), Anderson (1986), Siegel (1988) and P. Anderson (1988a, 1988b). See also the special issue of the *Journal of Marketing*, vol. 47, no. 4, Fall, 1983.
8 See the special double issue of *International Journal of Research in Marketing*, vol. 4, nos 2 and 3, 1988. For an early contribution, see E. Hirschman (1982). It should come as no surprise that theory that focuses on symbolism should be readily taken up and applied in the theory of consumer behaviour, whether with or without the presence of advertising.
9 See Spiggle and Goodwin (1988) for a survey of the content of presidential addresses to the organisation of consumer researchers and the identification of a preoccupation both with consumer behaviour as a separate discipline and with its interdisciplinary nature.
10 Foxall (1987: 111) confirms the primary role played by psychology in consumer research: 'As even brief perusal of current texts and journals confirms, the present tendency of cognitive psychology to provide the normal science of consumer research is beyond dispute.' For an exception, see Moschis (1987), for example, who is a strong advocate of sociology in consumer research, particularly in a life-cycle perspective.
11 See also Kassarjian (1982a: 22) and (1982b: 621) and Buss and Shaninger (1983: 439), for example.
12 Merton cites Marx, Parsons and Sorokin as sources of grand theory.
13 See Baron and Bielby (1980) and Tolbert (1982) and, for a critique, Fine (1987).

## 4 ECONOMIC AND CONSUMER BEHAVIOUR

1 For a critique of which, see Godelier (1973) and Hollis and Nell (1975).
2 More generally, income is not simply taken as given but can be earned through the disutility of engaging in work.
3 See Deaton and Muellbauer (1980) and Blundell (1988).
4 Endogenous behaviour is most damaging to general equilibrium theory since it tends to yield multiple and indeterminate equilibria.
5 It is not intended here to enter into debate over the distinction between rational,

irrational and non-rational – only to observe that use of the terms tends to act illegitimately to support the arguments in which they are employed.

6 In standard treatments of work and leisure by economists, the two are seen as mutually exclusive and adding up to the twenty-four hours of the day. Each is reduced to an effect on the level of utility, negative and positive, respectively. Saving is also extremely simply treated – as a guarantee of future consumption (commanding rate of interest as reward). For a critique of this, see Green (1990).

7 See Stigler (1954: 95) and Brown and Deaton (1972: 1155), the latter reporting that, 'nor has recent research discovered more enduring or more complex "universal-laws" relating to income elasticities than those put forward by Engel and Schwabe more than a century ago'. Schwabe's Law suggests that the income elasticity of housing is usually less than one.

8 In practice, Blundell presents estimates on individual households grouped according to their type – with or without children, by level of income, etc. This involves an implicit assumption that certain types of households behave in the same way and that others do not. This is never justified nor explained; it is simply taken for granted just as previously it was assumed that all households determined consumption independently of each other.

9 This remains true of the Lancaster (1966) model of characteristics even though in principle it breaks down items of consumption into their constituent properties.

10 See Deaton and Muellbauer (1980: 65).

11 See Fine (1982). Note that in its formal general equilibrium models, the distinction between supply and demand is explicitly obliterated in so far as excess demand functions, or the algebraic differences between supply and demand, suffice for analytical purposes.

12 In the orthodoxy, the merging of consumption and production takes place explicitly in the analysis of the household – which becomes both a site of consumption and of production. Deaton and Muellbauer (1980: 245), state that for example: 'Household production theory is an integration of theory of the consumer with that of the firm.' This tends to conceal, however, that the theory of the firm and the theory of the consumer are already almost identical.

13 See Mohun (1977).

14 For a survey of recent developments in industrial economics, see Schmalansee (1988).

15 Interestingly, Dickson and Sawyer (1984) suggest that analysis of consumer behaviour might be taken up by analogy with the economics of oligopoly by exploring why consumers enter and exit the market.

16 This is discussed in depth in Chapter 14.

17 See Malhotra (1988).

18 For a survey of the role of information in consumer behaviour, see Calfee and Ford (1988).

19 Of course, the most pervasive recent development in information theory in economics is the rational expectations revolution in macroeconomics, with its new classical result of powerlessness of government in view of optimal use of information by individual agents. But there has been a long-standing corresponding result in the economics of advertising – that only truthful and cost-effective advertising will ultimately persist, since consumers will learn of false and/or expensive claims, and the associated products and producers will be eliminated.

20 See Akerlof (1970). This is a case, like money, of the bad goods driving the good ones out of circulation.

21 Thus, for E. Hirschman (1982b), symbolism is itself innovative in consumption when the same product is perceived differently.

22 Thus, S. Roberts *et al.*. (1988) discuss those producers who are lucky enough to

view their work as consumption; Deshpande and Webster (1989) seek a parallel between management and marketing culture; Grafton-Small (1987) discusses the relation between job satisfaction and product quality in workers who make mince pies for Christmas; and Kotler (1986) considers the prosumer movement (concern with how the production process affects the product).

23 As an extreme, Belk (1986b) suggests that forms of artistic criticism and appreciation should provide a basis for insights into consumer behaviour. See also Stern (1989), who views literary criticism as a potential approach to consumer research.

## 5 CONSUMER BEHAVIOUR AND PSYCHOLOGY

1 See, for example, Peterson *et al.* (1986).

2 See Derbaix and Vanden Abeale (1985) for a discussion of rationality of consumer behaviour in the context of cognitive psychology.

3 See also Poiesz and von Grumbleow (1988: 580), for whom, 'Consumer satisfaction is the ultimate goal of aggregate marketing activity'. Friedman (1988) provides a survey of consumer behaviour from the perspective of economic psychology.

4 There is also a swamping by large numbers of incomparable empirical exercises around similar topics, giving rise to articles on meta-analysis, concerned with how they can all be integrated. See, for example, Ryan and Barclay (1983), Houston *et al.* (1983), and Reilly and Conover (1983)

## 6 WHAT IS CONSUMER SOCIETY?

1 Consumerism in the United States has come to mean (the movement) to represent the interests of consumers.

2 See also Featherstone (1983: 4) who, in referring to McKendrick *et al.*, suggests that: 'Although the term "consumer society" is normally applied to post-war western societies, we should remember that may of the central features of the consumer way of life are by no means new' (Featherstone 1983: 4).

3 For the transition to mass production, see Hounshell (1984). Piore and Sabel (1984) argue that there was no necessity for fragmented production to have given way to mass production if institutional arrangements had evolved to support flexible, small-scale production.

4 See Leach (1984), Rosalind Williams (1982) and Miller (1981). Cheney (1983: 28) points to the salience of women in the culture of consumerism and hence to the role of department stores (for whom women act both as employees and as customers).

5 See also Lasch:

> In the early days of industrial capitalism, employers saw the working man as no more than a beast of burden. . . . Only a handful of employers at this time understood that the worker might be useful to the capitalist as a consumer; that he needed to be imbued with a taste for higher things; that an economy based on mass production required not only the capitalistic organisation of production but the organisation of consumption and leisure as well. . . . In a simpler time, advertising merely called attention to the product and extolled its advantages. Now it manufactures a product of its own: the consumer, perpetually unsatisfied, restless, anxious, and bored. Advertising serves not so much to advertise products as to promote consumption as a way of life.
>
> (Lasch 1979: 135–7)

6 See also A. Hirschman (1982), Riesman (1964) and the British Council of Churches (1978), for whom:

> In summary, our study has indicated that along with the undoubted benefits of the consumer goods society there are major problems. There is the danger that men and women may be valued not for who they are but for what they possess. Some producers stimulate conspicuous consumption by advertising that emphasises status and social esteem and they encourage the desire for goods by playing on people's greed, envy or insecurity. There is a threat to minority tastes from the spread of mass-production. There is a danger that the really poor in our society may be overlooked amidst the general affluence and finally there is a weak sense of interdependence at a world level. A primary Christian duty is neglected. 'If anyone has the world's goods and sees his brother in need, yet closes his heart against him, how does God's love abide in him?'

7 Even physical subsistence is socially determined, as demonstrated by the preference for starvation over food relief with unfamiliar staples, not only in undeveloped communities but, for example, in the case of American POWs in the Korean War.
8 This notion of relative deprivation was most recently initiated by Sen (1983).
9 See also Gardner and Sheppard (1989: 46–7) for whom domestic consumption, as the female agenda, is now in the ascendancy following a retail revolution, although this has also witnessed a breakdown of the previous cultural divisions between male production and female consumption, now taken as inseparable. Fox and Lears (1983), however, see consumer culture as having been founded on the culture of a dominant white male elite for turn-of-the-century America. See also, however, Gordon and McArthur (1985).
10 For a critical assessment of trickle-down effects, see especially Chapter 10.
11 For a critical assessment of post-Fordism, see Sayer (1989). For Leiss *et al.* (1986: 49), consumer society becomes an enormous assortment of goods also subject to rapid change.
12 For a more favourable but questioning assessment of postmodernism, see Harvey (1989). See also Callinicos (1989).

## 7 CONSUMPTION AND GROWTH

1 Even though, inconsistently, slower rates of growth may be explained, for example, by higher levels of unemployment. See Nicholas (1982) and Fine (1980 Chapter 5) for a critique.
2 For a critique from a Keynesian standpoint, see Davies (1985), and, from a more radical perspective, Fine and Harris (1987).
3 For an empirical critique of netting out long-term growth trends, see Stock and Watson (1988). To some extent, the dependence of long-run growth on the short run is now accommodated within recent macroeconomic models by use of hysteresis (see Blanchard and Summers 1986).
4 See, for example, Breen (1986), Jones (1973) and Weatherill (1988).
5 See Mokyr (1977) and McCloskey (1981).
6 See Fine and Murfin (1984, Chapters 4 and 5).
7 See Sawyer (1985), Cowling (1982) and, in the same tradition, Baran and Sweezy (1968). For a critique, see Fine and Murfin (1984).
8 It must be emphasised that the demand-led and the consumer-led explanations for growth are not the same since the latter focuses entirely upon final consumption to

the neglect of other sources of demand. In this, consumption is presumed to drag investment demand and, even more neglected, intermediate inputs, behind it. This raises problems in the context of innovation since, as in energy conservation and efficiency, for example, this will lead to lower demand for inputs and a contraction of the market!

9 See Gilboy (1932), Mokyr (1977 and 1984), Ben-Shachar (1984), McCloskey (1981) and Musson (1972), for example. It is also the source of a monocausal explanation. See Gaski (1982), Inkster (1983) and Bruland (1985) for a critique.

10 See also Weatherill (1986b: 40).

11 See Flinn (1984), Nef (1932), Smith (1961), Dietz (1986) and Pollard (1983) for some discussion of the complexities in the marketing and distribution of coal.

12 As in Cole (1981).

13 See Fine (1982, Chapter 5). See also Rosenberg (1968) for the importance in Smith of shifting tastes and income between different classes as a source of a growing market.

14 Interestingly, both support the progressive role of the market, but their differences over the role of landlords reflect the extent to which they are perceived to spend on commodities or not. For Malthus, in particular, perceives 'embourgeoisement' as a political and economic goal for the mass of society, so that the working class elevates itself out of its population/poverty trap. This has strong affinities with the trickle-down theory, even if it is only in the consumption of goods that emulation takes place. For a discussion of the role of demand in Malthus, see especially Vatter (1959), Sowell (1963) and Rashid (1977). Note there is a dispute about whether his theory of gluts applies to the long run or to the short run.

15 An alternative is provided by Levine (1987). He argues, in the lead up to the Industrial Revolution, that a peasant demography model of reproduction, based on cottage economy and limited access to land, gave way to a proletarian demography model, economically based on wage labour in the absence of land and for which children became potential wage-earners. Each 'model' is firmly embedded in a specification of the economic and social structure whose tensions inevitably give rise to changes but whose timing and form are contingent. The period of transition between the two models is based upon various forms of proto-industrialisation. The details of this analysis need not detain us. What is important is that it contains an explanatory content that can be disputed on substantive empirical *and* theoretical grounds.

## 8 INTRODUCTION TO AN ALTERNATIVE FRAMEWORK

1 Of course, security also plays a role in the provision of clothing sales assistants since the loss of a single garment is more costly to the clothing retailer than the loss of a single orange or tin of soup to the food retailer.

## 9 THE MANUFACTURE OF THE FASHION SYSTEM

1 See, for example, the many volumes of the Cunningtons (C.W. and P.), e.g., *The History of Underclothes* (1981), *Handbook of English Costume in the Eighteenth Century* (1972); see also Laver (1964), Taylor (1983), Ribeiro (1984) and de Marly (1986).

2 Among others, Barthes (1985) and Konig (1973). For a comprehensive critical review of these theories as well as a demonstration of her own, see Wilson (1985). Wilson seeks to liberate the potential for self-expression in fashion while

recognising the ambiguities of a fashion system operating within the framework of capitalism.

3 See Wilson (1985: 60, 92).

4 See HMSO (1947: 12).

5 Mukerji (1983: 245–54) acknowledges the conflict between demand and supply side explanations but opts for a variation of the former, arguing for a greater recognition of the role played by the growth of material culture (of international patterns of taste generating international consumerism) as a spur to economic innovation.

6 The classic text is Landes (1969). See also Rostow (1975).

7 See Nystrom (1928: 442).

8 See Shilliam (1991).

9 See Scheiber *et al.* (1976: 243).

10 See Dykstra (1968: 110, 249). Even at their peak in the 1860s and 1870s, the cattle towns at the end of the cowboy's journey (like Wichita and Dodge City) were too small and too seasonal to sustain much manufacturing activity. A town with 900 men over the age of 20 in 1875, Wichita boasted only four manufacturing concerns, employing just 21 workers. Except for a speciality trade in Texan boots, all made-up clothing had to be imported from larger towns.

11 See Robertson and Walton (1979: 307).

12 Ibid.: 256.

13 See American Social History Project (1989: 458).

14 Quoted in Levine (1924: 382).

15 As early as 1825 in Boston, Thomas Whitmarsh was advertising stock of 'from 5,000 to 10,000 fashionable ready-made garments' (Cobrin 1970: 20). Levi Strauss set up business to market ready-made jeans in San Francisco just thirty years later.

16 See Helfgott (1959: 54). The idea that the 1920s witnessed 'the birth of the idea of clothing obsolescence' is also put forward in Kidwell and Christman (1974). Though the history of dressmaking in the UK closely parallels the American experience in most important respects, the US was the source of most technical innovation that occurred during this period. Factory production of dresses in Britain lagged behind its US counterpart, dating from about 1930 (Wray 1957: 41).

17 See Baron and Clepp (1984: 37). See also Forty (1986).

18 From *Household Economics*, (New York: G. P. Putnam and Sons, 1897: 242), quoted in Brew (1948: 424).

19 See Adburgham (1981: 118).

20 See Gartman (1979: 192).

21 See Myers (1937: 43). Subsequent slackening of demand and further productivity gains *did* push out large numbers of mostly male workers from the industry.

22 See Schoeffler and Gale (1973: 512). Button-holing machines were not, however, in general use until the First World War when much improved machines, first used in the boot and shoe trade, spread to the clothing industry (Thomas 1955: 39).

23 The earliest sewing machines could sew 800 to 900 stitches per minute. The application of electric power increased their speeds to between 2,000 and 4,000 stitches per minute (Helfgott 1959: 38).

24 See Kidwell and Christman (1974: 81).

25 As late as 1950, just 1 per cent of workers and less than 1 per cent of shops in the women's dress, coat and suit industry in Manhattan worked on a 'section' work basis (Belfer 1954: 192).

26 See Meiklejohn (1938: 316).

27 See Piore and Sabel (1984: 29), referring to clothing workers in Italy.

28 In the early 1980s, Hart, Shaffner & Marx owned more than 250 stores throughout the United States and Phillip Van Heusen (giant shirt makers) owned 96 stores in

six different states. Typically, these stores do not have names that would identify them with the manufacturer that owns them (Jarnow *et al.* 1981: 184–5).

29 *Business Week*, 16 February, 1957, p. 72.

30 See Yu (1978: 95). Even in the 1960s, the sewing machine was used to carry out just 2–3 per cent of the work in high fashion houses; it still took at least four workers 65–90 hours to make a simple dress or suit (Roshco 1963: 179).

31 Roshco (1963: 153). The phrase 'line-for-line' is attributed to Macy's department store in New York City.

32 A reflection of the closeness between them was the development, patented in the 1930s, of a sewing machine designed to imitate hand stitching (Cooper 1968: 63). This retrograde application of machinery was inconceivable in other industries.

33 See *The Committee on Elimination of Waste in Industry of the Federated American Engineering Societies, Waste in Industry*, Washington, 1921: 96.

34 Ibid.: 96.

35 Special order firms or special order departments within retailing outlets persisted well into the second half of the twentieth century. The English firm of Montague Burton specialised in made-to-measure men's suits on a massive scale. Set up in Sheffield in 1900 as retail clothiers, at their peak in 1950, they were responsible for providing employment for more than 100,000 people (Hudson 1983: 68). The Bergdorf Goodman store in New York City did not abandon its custom operations until 1969, after 70 years of continuous operation (Jarnow *et al.* 1981: 279).

36 *The Committee . . .*, op. cit.: 101.

37 See Waldinger (1985: 103). Fifteen years later, in 1954, it was still possible to start up a dress or blouse firm in New York City for as little as $15,000 in capital (Helfgott 1959: 30).

38 The distribution by price range of a sample of 1,370 firms undertaken by the National Credit Office is given below:

| *Price line* | *Number of firms* |
|---|---|
| up to $3.74 | 286 |
| $3.75–6.74 | 335 |
| $6.75–10.74 | 308 |
| $10.75–16.74 | 253 |
| $16.75–22.49 | 67 |
| $22.50 and over | 121 |
| Total | 1,370 |

*Source*: National Credit Office cited in Meiklejohn (1938: 333).

39 See Blanchard (1953: 60).

40 Market Planning Service, National Credit Office, Inc. (1952: 12).

41 *The Committee . . .*, op. cit.: 240.

42 In the early 1970s, the House of Dior attributed only 4.5 per cent of its total sales revenue to couture apparel, with the balance coming from a wide range of American and European licensing arrangements (Dryansky 1973).

## 10 CLOTHING: INDUSTRIAL OR CONSUMER REVOLUTION?

1 As quoted in Hartwell (1965: 164).

2 In Dickens' *Dombey and Son*, the husband of Paul Dombey's former wet nurse wore a black armband to mark his condolences for the boy's death.

3 The durability of the basic fashion fabric is illustrated in Lemire (1984: 22), which features a dress altered almost yearly from 1781 to 1788, with the addition of steel buckles, a new gauze handkerchief and a new apron, all applied to the original dress to bring it – and keep it – up to date with the latest fashion craze.
4 In contrast, say, to the distaste for consumption shown in the works of Veblen, Galbraith, etc. A startling example of the presumed affinity between eighteenth-century pottery and twentieth-century consumerism is provided by Breen (1986: 496), as previously discussed in Chapter 6: 'Without too much exaggeration, Staffordshire pottery might be seen as the Coca-Cola of the eighteenth century.'
5 Some of the inevitable biases that have crept into a historical tradition long dominated by men have been pointed out by, amongst others, Thirsk (1978: 22–3): 'The criteria by which some [projects] have been judged more important and others less have been laid down by our menfolk. Starch, needles . . . vinegar, stockings do not appear on their shopping lists, but they regularly appear on mine.' The presentation of women as the primary consumers of impractical and often absurd luxury fashions which render them immobilised and incapable of serving any function other than adornment reinforces an image of female dependency which is completely at odds with McKendrick's earlier emphasis on women's active participation in the workforce and contribution to home demand.
6 Cannadine (1984) has reviewed the historiography of the Industrial Revolution over the past century by reference to the changing perceptions of Britain's problems over that period. For some commentary on the limitations of such an organising principle, see Fine and Leopold (1990).

## 11 TRICKLE-DOWN THEORIES

1 This is the premise of many of the essays, (McKendrick *et al.* 1982). For a more extended critique of the ideological underpinning of this view and of McKendrick's use of it in particular, see Fine and Leopold (1990) and Chapters 7 and 10 of this volume.
2 See p. 129 for a description of the rise of the frock coat.
3 See Barber and Lobel (1952). See also Fallers (1961), who considers the motivation for trickle-down through the corporate rather than the social pyramid, arguing that status-enhancing consumption is a form of compensation for those facing restricted occupational advancement through the corporate system.
4 See also Field (1970), who cites the penetration of aspects of black, youth and working-class culture (jazz, jeans, guitars) into middle-aged mainstream culture as evidence of the upward diffusion of fashion.
5 This is a point made in another context by Lang and Lang (1961).
6 Gilder (1981: 20), quoted in Rousseas (1982) which provides a helpful evaluation of competing strands of Reaganomics.
7 Gilder (1981: 34), quoted in Rousseas (1982).
8 Greider (1981: 46–7).

## 12 THE FOOD SYSTEM

1 By the end of the nineteenth century, over 8,000 growing varieties of apples were still listed by the United States Department of Agriculture. Today the only apple that most Americans eat is the (tasteless) 'Delicious'. See Hess and Hess (1989: 43).
2 Sen (1984) has examined famines in the context of exchange entitlements for which, in part, geographical locations or socioeconomic strata with higher levels of income

may attract available (not necessarily short) food supplies away from those with low levels of income. Here, there is evidence of a mirror image problem on the supply side, in which the crop varieties available within systems of food provision flow dysfunctionally in the opposite direction, from rich to poor, just as the crops themselves return to the rich.

3 Plumb's (1982) analysis of consumerism in the eighteenth century emphasises the role of cross-fertilisation of crops from the New World.

4 All figures calculated from Marks (1989: 34).

5 Filby is writing for the UK. For the US, there was little by way of preventative legislation on adulteration until 1906. According to Lewis:

> At that time, it was relatively common for floor sweepings to be added to pepper, ash leaves to tea, copper and lead salts to cheese and candy, copper salts to pickles and peas, prussic acid to wine, alum to bread, acorns to coffee, and brick dust to cocoa.
>
> (Lewis 1989: 3)

See also Chase and Schlink (1933).

6 For some history of the margarine industry on these points, see Van Alphen (1969), Hoffman (1969) and Townley (1969).

7 For water added to ham and to frozen prawns (as much as 67 per cent), see London Food Commission (1988: 179–84, 163–4).

8 See Clark and Laing (1990) for an account of the changing role of milk formula-feeding in the UK and its relation to changing governmental reviews.

9 For further discussion, using the example of sugar as an additive, see Chapter 13.

10 See London Food Commission (1989), EEC (1988), Jordans (1987), Bowers (1985) and Newby (1983). For an account of the US food industry, see Marion (1986), Connor *et al.* (1985) and McCorkle (ed.) (1988). Concentration of capital engaged in the food system can also be characteristic of retailing (Chapter 16) and wholesaling. For the latter, see especially Morgan (1980) on the transoceanic grain trade.

11 See Jordans (1985).

12 See Fellows (1988).

13 See Staff Report (1989). The other two innovations in the top ten were the microwave oven and food fortification. Meriting mention were polyunsaturated corn oil margarine, fat hydrogenation, high-fructose corn syrup, aspartame and extruded food technology.

14 Lewis (1989) provides a glossary of food additives; including different names for the same substance, this runs to 90 pages with 140 entries per page.

15 The consumption of 'trail mixes' (i.e. packets of nuts, seeds, etc.) extends habits of eating to those 'on the go', in any place or posture not traditionally associated with eating a meal.

16 As Davis (1987: 193) suggests: 'From biblical times efforts have been made to make food more convenient from the point of preserving, preparing, cooking and storing.' Driver (1983) reproduces a list of some 500 or so canned foods that were available in the UK prior to the Second World War. Canned foods have suffered from the rise of frozen foods and the resurgence of fresh fruit and vegetables, but in the United States in 1985 they still accounted for 44 per cent of consumption (with 47 per cent for fresh and 9 per cent for frozen) (Pearl 1990: 102). Of this canned consumption, however, 70 per cent was taken up by tomatoes or tomato products. According to Woodrof (1990: 94): 'During the past 50 years, more improvements were made in the freezing of fruits and vegetables than in any other processing method.'

17 Between 1984 and 1987 alone, fish and chips as a source of take-away food has

declined from 38 per cent share of value to 15 per cent. There has been considerable growth in sandwiches (from 22 to 36 per cent, probably indicating its substituting for a set meal at lunchtime) and rises from 3 to 10 per cent for pizza and pasta and from 11 to 16 per cent for hamburgers. Chinese together with Indian have just maintained their share, whilst chicken has declined from 10 to 4 per cent. McDonalds, first appearing in the UK in 1974, had 263 outlets in the UK in 1987 (and 10,000 worldwide) but these numbers had accelerated from 3 per cent per annum between 1974 and 1976 to over 10 per cent per annum between 1977 and 1980, and doubling every three years between 1981 and 1988 (see Key Note 1989a; Jordans 1988).

18 See Jerome (1981).

## 13 FOOD FOR THOUGHT

1 Lyman (1989: 20) cites the following as 'representative variables associated with long-term food preferences' along with corresponding case studies: food characteristics, body weight, age, sex or race, self-concept, socioeconomic status, peer or other models, parental attitudes, family relations, nutrition knowledge, television viewing, familiarity, context, geography, culture and food meanings. Wilson (1973; 1979) provides an annotated bibliography on the subject of food customs and nurture. For Krondl and Lau (1982: 141), food selection is determined by a triad with nutrients at its centre: perception (comprising knowledge, belief, convenience, price, prestige, familiarity, taste, tolerance and satiety); endogenous determinants (activity, age, sex and heredity); and exogenous determinants (culture, society and economy).

2 See May (1974).

3 There are many studies that seek to explain the consumption of earth or clay in terms of the nutritional requirements for trace elements. See those cited in Wilson (1973; 1979).

4 Whilst it might be argued that the potato came to serve as a staple in the UK because of its ability to feed a growing population, a favourable climate around Lancashire where it was first adopted, its being easy to store, and the ground easy to prepare (as suggested in McKenzie 1964), none the less, for Salaman (1949: 459): 'The potato was only adopted by the working class in the greater part of England, as a result of want, which overtook them towards the end of the [eighteenth] century.' Currently, in Scotland, boys and girls of the 'lower' classes continue to eat as much as two or three times as many chips as those of the 'higher' classes (Department of Health 1989).

5 See Fiddes (1991).

6 Nor are doctors necessarily useful sources of nutritional knowledge (see McCluney 1988).

7 See also Freckleton (1985). In the United States, the health lobby has also insisted on the inclusion of the number of calories derived from fat as a percentage of the total number of calories.

8 Dufty observes that:

> At the time of its introduction into Britain, sugar was prohibitively expensive, a courtly luxury in a price class with the most expensive drugs on the market. At $25 a pound it was the equivalent of a year's salary for a working man.
>
> (Dufty 1975: 21)

With its more general consumption from the middle of the nineteenth century, sugar lost to some extent its role as a symbol of social distinction and hedonism: 'In most Western societies sweetness, in much the same way as sex, has raised the question of whether the pursuit of pleasure per se is socially and ethically acceptable' (Fischler 1987: 83).

See also Mintz (1982) for a discussion of the changing meaning of sweetness. He questions Sombart's association of it with female dominance, a matter confirmed by the notion of a sugar-daddy. From meanings associated with affection, love and sex, sugar has been used to denote money and, ultimately, drugs. For a history of the cane industry, see also Galloway (1989).

9 Dewar also reports that fat consumption over the same period has risen from 80 grams to 150 grams. The strikingly similar figures to those for sugar may be explained, particularly in the later years, by the 'go-away' factor, whereby a 1:1 ratio of fat to sugar in manufactured foods tends to leave no after-taste (see Cantor and Cantor 1977).

10 For an analysis of the sugar industry with particular focus on Britain, see Monopolies and Mergers Commission (1981; 1989). For a broader account, see Abbott (1990).

11 See also Farrer (1987: 94–5).

12 See Oliver (1986: 20).

13 Tap water is seen as the 'corporate enemy' (Clairmonte and Cavanagh 1988: 27).

14 See Palazzini (1988). It is reckoned, for example, that Coca-Cola's campaign featuring Father Xmas from the 1930s to the 1950s had a major impact in enhancing the role of Xmas as a festival in the United States (Louis and Yazijian 1980).

15 See also Watters (1978: 102).

16 'Coke Is It' was the advertising slogan of 1982.

17 This section depends heavily on Fine and Wright (1991).

18 See Gormley (1987) for an account of the sources of, and influences on, scientific knowledge around the consumption of food.

19 For a fuller discussion of food activists in this context, see Fine and Wright (1991).

20 Murcott suggests that sociology:

> has barely recognised the study of eating habits. . . . It is as if sociologists, like the populations whose societies they study, could take a more than adequate supply of food for granted. When sociologists do occasionally consider food it is in precisely those arenas of industrialised society where adequate eating cannot be assumed; during wartime, associated with poverty, where pathological eating behaviour develops, 'unorthodox' dietary styles or, most recently in Britain, in the wake of debates about the development of a nationwide food policy.
>
> (Murcott 1988: 2)

See also Messer (1984) for the emphasis there has been in the study of diet in the context of deviancy.

21 Or, what was not explicitly on the menu:

> The social significance of transforming a banal activity such as eating for bodily sustenance into the elaborate symbol system. . . . In the practice of dining out, a lower order of being, namely, the nourishment of the human body, has been intertwined with a higher order of experience, namely, that of taking pleasure.
>
> (Finkelstein 1989: 27)

22 See Murcott (1988) for a useful assessment of the works of Lévi-Strauss, Douglas, Harris, Mintz, Goody and Mennell. See also Gofton (1989) discussing the work of Bourdieu (1984), who has been influential in positing (food) consumption as an index of class stratification.

23 For histories of food, see especially Burnett (1989) but also Tannahill (1988), Johnston (1977), Oddy and Miller (1976), Lewis (1976), Barker *et al.* (1966), and Drummond (1957).
24 See King (1983), who argues that there are distinct breaks in the uniformity of consumption trends in the UK from 1970 onwards.
25 The main conclusions reached by Charles and Kerr are that men eat most prestige foods and that children eat a different diet, with women's consumption lying somewhere in between; that women do the preparation of food and gain most satisfaction through the enjoyed consumption of others rather than their own consumption; and that a proper meal requires the presence of the male head of household and usually comprises meat and two veg.
26 See Fine (1992).
27 See the references in Wilson (1973; 1979) and also Sen (1984) in the context of entitlements.
28 Harris (1985: 241) points to the labouring women of Trivandrum.
29 This, however, might be explained by the fact that working women have less time to make use of labour-saving durables and, therefore, do not consider them to be worth buying.
30 As International Business Intelligence (1989: 312) reports, ownership of microwaves in France, United Kingdom and United States is, respectively, 12 per cent, 35 per cent and 75 per cent whereas time spent cooking is 180 minutes, 75 minutes and 20 minutes.

## 14 ADVERTISING

1 Ironically, in 1990 Perrier was temporarily withdrawn worldwide as a consequence of its polluted bottling.
2 See also Goldman (1987).
3 Williamson (1978: 70) concludes that, 'our lives become our own creation, through *buying*'. See also Alt (1976: 80): 'The transition to monopoly capitalist society tends to shift the source of social relations, culture and ideology from a class culture of work to a mass culture of consumption.'
4 Marchand's commentary on the interwar period has some wider relevance:

> One has to search diligently in the ads of the 1920s and 1930s to find even a fleeting glimpse of such common scenes as religious services, factory workers on the job, sports fans enjoying a boxing match or baseball game, or working class families at home.
>
> (Marchand 1985: xvii)

See also Vestergaard and Schrøder (1985: 146), 'One of the most striking ideological aspects about the world portrayed in adverts is the almost total absence of work'. For Winship (1980: 217), 'by concealing the production process, advertising similarly covers up class distinctions between people, through a form of fetishism'. Consider Cadbury's advertising campaign at the turn of the century, extolling the quality of the labour it employed. Newspaper exposure of its dependence on slave labour in São Tomé to produce cocoa beans led to a libel action for which 1/4d token damages were awarded (Wagner 1987). Benson quotes Helen Woodward:

> If you are advertising any product, never see the factory in which it was made. . . . Don't watch people at work. . . . Because, you see, when you know

the truth about anything, the real, inner truth – it is very hard to write the surface fluff which sells it.

(Benson 1986: 35)

5 For some standard accounts of the economic theory of advertising, see Boynton and Schwendiman (1980), Comanor and Wilson (1979) and Reekie (1981). Albion and Farris (1981) look to the structure–conduct–performance approach of industrial economics; Albion (1983) links economic theory to retailing and branding models; Ekelund and Saurman (1988) supplement economic theory with the notion of advertising as making up the supply of, and demand for, fraud; Fulop (1981) emphasises the dynamic role of advertising; Mather and Tucker (1980) point to what might be termed product stripping – following a merger or acquisition, some products are discarded whilst others are vigorously promoted; Bluestone *et al.* (1981) point to the retail revolution as the industrialisation of department stores in which advertising is seen as a substitute for a sales workforce.

6 See also Sinclair (1987), where there is a discussion of the significance of branded goods in stimulating advertising.

7 The designation of economic activity to the sphere of production or to the sphere of exchange is often discussed in the context of productive and unproductive labour in Marxist theory. See also Chapter 20 where analogous theoretical issues arise in specifying retail capital.

8 See Fine and Murfin (1984) for a critical assessment in these terms of the propositions of the monopoly capital school.

9 For further discussion of this and for much of what follows in the context of consumer society, see Chapter 6.

10 For an excellent summary of Ewen's arguments, see Leiss (1988: xii).

11 Thus for Berman (1981: 22), Galbraith and Marcuse are seen as the two great sources of criticisms of advertising because of the social commentary that they promote: 'Nearly all succeeding writers combine the two arguments that productivity is an economic evil and consumption, a psychological evil.'

12 For Berman, criticism of advertising is not only a veiled attack on the affluent society, the latter is what makes it possible: 'in some fundamental ways the criticism of advertising is about the nature of industrial life. . . . Whatever promotes the system is morally suspect. . . . The success of our own economy allows us to reject at least the idea of affluence' (Berman 1981: 19–20). See also Hirschmann (1982a) for the idea that economic development has asceticism as its natural offspring.

13 Hence the problem of making advertising effective when each 'customer' is potentially different. Grafton-Small and Linstead (1989) suggest that each ad is open to individual, contextual interpretation. Illustrative of this is the finding of Mueller (1991) that thirty-one variables affect whether an advertising campaign is transferred between countries. Presumably, at least as many factors are operative within a country. More generally, on the internationalisation of advertising, see Perry (1990).

14 Is there a hint of irony in this praise of the expert interpreters? Are they not, after all, transforming the use value into something else, the more so the greater their skill? The other two limitations for Leiss *et al.* are the lack of quantitative analysis and the self-serving choice of the ads for analytical interpretation.

15 As in a US trade card (Jay 1987: 73). Jay also reveals use of different stereotypes for racial groups: the negro as jovial, feckless and simple; the American Indian as the noble savage; the Chinese as undesirable and targeted for repatriation (through closure of their laundries, unable to compete with washing products and household goods); and yet the Japanese as culturally sophisticated.

16 In the United States, however, black women are often portrayed in ads as domestic servants. In a different vein, for the advertising of Marlboro in Nigeria, a black cowboy was felt to be necessary.

17 For a recent review of sex-stereotyping in TV adverts, see Communications Research Group (1990).

18 In the EC (1987) sample of TV ads, over two-thirds were for food and drink (40.3 per cent) and cleaning, hygiene and beauty products (27.0 per cent). For the latter, there has been a commercial colonisation of the body (see Bauman 1983; Vestergaard and Schrøder 1985), particularly for women but increasingly for men. Men's perfumes, etc. must be presented as after-shave, body lotion or whatever in order to avoid the implication of effeminacy or homosexuality. Selling of such items has been associated with the use of 'scare' in advertising, the most frequently cited being the reinvention of halitosis for bad breath.

19 Brown (1981: 54) concludes that: '[in] the "three pillars" of family roles – economic provision, household task performance, and child-care – the changes do not suggest any dramatic shift towards a more egalitarian family role structure.' See Goffman (1979) for consideration of the gender content of ads: men shown in the role of superior rank, for example; and when not in the former role, as childlike or incompetent. See also Millum (1975).

20 For Winship studying the launch of the new magazine *Options*:

> She is an entirely new breed of consumer. She sees herself as the kind of woman who should have a calculator in her handbag, a stereo in her car, a note recorder in her office. She is the generation for whom video and telecom were made. Busy women with open minds who will take advantage of every technical advantage to make work more efficient and play more fun. The first generation of women for whom freezers, dishwashers and microwave ovens are not luxuries but essentials.
>
> (Winship 1983: 47)

Gardner and Sheppard (1989: 46–7) go so far as to argue that the previous division in cultural identity between male production and female consumption has broken down and the two are inseparable, with domestic consumption as the female agenda in the ascendancy.

21 The *New York Times*, 3 October, 1989, reports that stores may ask manufacturers for fees to stock a product – a charge known as a 'slotting allowance'.

22 On the other hand, you can have your cake and eat it by combining godliness and acquisition at adventure parks organised at Disneylands for believers. See the discussion of the synthesis of worship and shopping at Heritage Village in O'Guinn and Belk (1989).

23 See Crane (1991) for a report of Canadian attitudes to advertising.

24 The negative ideology surrounding the advertising industry from the mid-1950s is well summed up in the titles of Vance Packard's books, *The Status Seekers*, *The Hidden Persuaders*, and *The Waste Makers*. The conflict between commerce and principle is a favoured theme of the arts – and of jokes. The student, seeking a course in 'Business Ethics' is impatiently told to make up his (her?) mind, ' Do you want a course in Business or a course in Ethics?' Seguela, Mitterand's presidential campaign organiser, wrote his first book with the title, *Don't Tell My Mother I'm in Advertising – She Thinks I'm a Pianist in a Brothel*, quoted in Douglas (1984: 13). Clark (1988: 29) quotes Raymond Chandler to the effect that: 'Chess is about as elaborate a waste of human intelligence as you could find anywhere outside of an advertising agency.'

25 Ernest Dichter, the main target of Vance Packard's attack on motivation research

in the *Hidden Persuaders*, became a celebrity and more successful advertiser as a result (Clark 1988: 73).

26 See Chapters 7 and 10 for a critique of McKendrick.

27 Lefebvre (1971: 81) illustrates the voracious appetite of the advertising industry for the images of the past in order to give its commodities ever new use values: 'The destruction of the past by the massive consumption of works of art, styles and culture . . . [are] the devices inherent to this consumption.' (Lefebvre 1971: 81).

28 Goldman (1987: 692) surely displays a misinterpretation of commodity fetishism when he suggests that, 'advertisements conceal the nature and relations of production. . . . In producing commodity signs, the origin of surplus value lies in the structure of the communicative exchange set up by advertisements'. In contrast, the origins of surplus value is to be found in the sphere of production and this is hidden by commodity fetishism in the total absence of advertisements – as a consequence of human (production) relations being expressed as a relation between things (commodities as use values, even if these are, in turn, further fetishised).

29 Mars spent £27.9 million on advertising in 1988, £4.8 million of it on Mars Bars alone. Cadbury spent £23.5 million, £4.5 million of it on Cadbury Milk Chocolate (EIU 1989a).

30 Leiss *et al.* (1986) do provide a sort of synthesis between horizontal and vertical factors through a matrix of causal variables. In the terms presented here, however, this is more by way of an organisation of the simultaneity of a set of horizontal variables.

## 15 ADVERTISING CLOTHING

1 *Lear's*, December 1991, p. 77.

2 Ibid., quoting Dudley McIlhenny, Director of New York's Apparel Marketing Resources Inc.

3 At the top end of the market, newspaper advertising is highly selective; in the mid-1980s, twenty-one of the top thirty spending brands of apparel in the United States did most of their newspaper spending in the *New York Times*. The top three brands (Lauren Apparel, Leslie Fay Clothes and Ultra Suede Apparel) did *all* their newspaper advertising in the *New York Times* (*Inside Print*, July 1986, p. 24).

4 'Superbrands 1991', supplement to *Adweek's Marketing Week*, Parade Publications Inc., pp. 136, 146–8.

5 See Packard (1983: 235).

6 *Advertising Age*, 9 September 1981, pp. 5–8.

7 *Daily News Record*, 20 April 1984, p. 4.

8 *Inside Print*, July 1986, p. 24.

9 'Superbrands 1991', op. cit., p. 136.

10 According to Taylor and Wilson (1989: 174), Coco Chanel introduced the practice of licensing in the 1920s by introducing her own perfume. By the 1940s, the practice had become widespread.

11 *New York Times*, 19 April 1986, p. 52.

12 'Safari by Ralph Lauren. A world without boundaries. A personal adventure and a way of life' (non-committal and non-specific copy from an ad in *Mirabella*, December 1991).

13 See de Paola and Mueller (1986: 138).

14 De Paola and Mueller (1986: 160).

15 See Greenwood and Murphy (1978: 179).

16 See *Advertising Age*, 5 September 1983, Special Supplement, p. M-29.

17 In 1990, the women's segment of the clothing industry accounted for 73 per cent of

total industry sales; men's clothes represented 21 per cent of the total, and children's 6 per cent – as reported in *Chain Store Age Executive*, August 1991, p. 29A.

18 Hart, Shaffner and Marx in 1900 employed 6,000 people in its factory in Chicago (Kidwell and Christman 1974: 97).

19 Mortimer Levitt, founder and owner of the Custom Shop Shirtmakers, writing to the *New York Times*, 12 April 1990.

20 Copy from an advert for Saint Laurie Merchant Tailors, *New York Times*, 1990.

## 16 FOOD, RETAILING AND ADVERTISING

1 See Lewis *et al.* (1985) for an analysis of the effect of hypermarkets in London, and the marginalisation of those who depend on local access to shopping – even where this previously meant a supermarket. Doyle and Cook (1979) recognised that successful retailers in stagnant markets had to go for increased volume and increased productivity.

2 For an account of Marks and Spencer, see Tse (1985). Its reputation for own-label quality allowed it to pioneer and dominate the chilled food market, taking 90 per cent in 1980. This had fallen to 75 per cent by 1989, with other own-label taking 15 per cent (EIU 1989c).

3 Of course, the reputation of own-label groceries for low quality is not necessarily well founded. Uncles and Ellis (1989) find no difference in coffee quality in the United States.

4 See Segal-Horn (1987), Grant (1987) and Fulop (1986).

5 Gardner and Sheppard (1989: 16–17) support the idea of a shift in power in terms of who has to bear the burdens of adjustment to market demand. This is not necessarily at the expense of producers.

6 The theory of institutional change in retailing is dominated by the idea of a turning wheel (of fortune or of re-invention?) in which new entrants begin with low quality and low price, trade up and diversify, then ossify before being born anew. See Brown (1987) and, for a debate, Brown (1988a, 1988b) and Savitt (1988). Brown (1990) provides a brief review of theories (wheel, accordion and life-cycle) to examine the rise of the retail warehouse.

7 For a history of retailing, see also Winstanley (1983), Alexander (1970), Mui and Mui (1989) and Adburgham (1981).

8 Yet, advertising expenditure has grown faster in non-food retailing (Fulop 1986: 32). The fifteen retailers in the top 100 advertisers in 1984 were MFI, ASDA, Coop Retail, Tesco, Woolworth, Harris Queensway, Dixons, Allied Carpets, Comet, Texas, House of Fraser, Currys, Boots, W.H. Smith and Sainsbury.

9 Gardner and Sheppard (1989) include a section entitled, 'The Supermarket as Brand'.

10 In a whole series of papers (McWilliam and de Chernatony 1989; de Chernatony 1989a, 1989b; de Chernatony and McWilliam 1988, 1989a, 1989b), the confusion between branded goods, generics and own label has been deplored. Significantly, the analytical point to be made is whether advertising is representational (symbolic) or functional (physical characteristics), whatever the name employed for the commodities.

11 Williamson (1978), for example, relies exclusively upon branded goods.

12 This is not to suggest that those offering awards escape from being selective and unrepresentative. Looking over the three volumes of commended adverts (Broadbent 1981, 1983; Channon 1985), women as sexual objects have generally been avoided – the exceptions being relatively mild, for Cadbury's Flake, Turkish Delight, Campari and Pretty Polly (lovely legs vs jeans). These awards include

Shakers Cocktail, a commendation for a new consumer good, which in O'Kelly (1989) is picked out as a failure in practice. This, together with the advert for British Coal which won a prize during the miners' strike of 1984–5 when it could not be shown, demonstrates how ads can become cultural artefacts separate from their commercial function. As Vestergaard and Schrøder (1985: 9) suggest: 'Not only does advertising help make the products appear as aesthetically pleasing as possible, the advert becomes an aesthetic object in itself . . . in fact not just the product but also the consumer that becomes aestheticized.'

## 17 THE NEW URBAN SOCIOLOGY

1 In Saunders' recent book, the desire for owner-occupation has become an innate human characteristic: 'A widespread desire for owner-occupation is likely to be fuelled by certain natural dispositions as well as by economic and cultural factors', (Saunders 1990: 83).

2 Socialised consumption refers to state provision through the welfare state, whereas market and privatised provision differ in that there is substantial state support for the latter.

3 In an earlier period, especially in the context of consumer society in the United States, the assertion of the importance of consumption is associated with the automobile and its culture (see Moorhouse 1988).

4 For some contributions relevant to the debate not otherwise mentioned, see Mingione (1981), Harloe (1984), Duke and Edgell (1984), Dunleavy (1986), Pratt (1986) and Harris and Pratt (1987).

5 Saunders (1990) does examine consumption and housing more extensively.

6 See Forrest and Murie (1990), for example.

7 Daunton's (1983) interest in the different architectural forms of working-class housing leads him to appeal 'to escape from the limits of single countries considered in isolation' (Daunton 1983: 28).

8 For a critique of the supposed relationship between forms of housing tenure and voting patterns and political ideology, see Ball (1985).

9 See Chapter 18.

10 Similarly, O'Connor (1973) has constructed a theory of the fiscal crisis of the state by imposing the Marxist value categories (C, V and S) on its expenditures. This has also been adopted by Gough (1975, 1979), for a critique of which see Fine and Harris (1976, 1979). See also Featherstone, who seeks a parallel between production theory (as 'capital logic') and consumption theory in a different way through: '"consumption logic" which points to the socially structured ways in which goods are used to demarcate social relationships' (Featherstone 1990: 8).

11 See especially Ball (1983).

## 18 MARX'S ECONOMICS AND CONSUMPTION

1 See also Williamson (1986: 229), who points to the neglect in forging an analytical unity between production and circulation. This coincides with the priority of production. For Preteceille and Terrail:

> A proper insistence on the determining character of the social relations of production has overshadowed not only the necessary analysis of the specific modes of consumption, but also an analysis of the relation between the two spheres, which has been reduced to a single, mechanistic determination.
>
> (Preteceille and Terrail 1985: 4)

2 See Chapter 7.
3 Thus, Duesenberry's (1967) relative income hypothesis found only a temporary and uneasy home within the theory of the consumption function, presumably because of its use of interdependent and irreversible preferences. Its attraction was its ability to explain empirically the divergence between short-run and long-run saving propensities.
4 Sahlins (1976) suggests that there is an affinity between neoclassical and Marxist economics in their mutual neglect of the social meaning of objects as opposed to their physical properties. In the context of a cultural account of production, this has immediate application to the sphere of consumption.
5 It may be slightly inappropriate to include post-Fordism within an approach that autonomises consumption in that it is heavily technologically determinist, with the availability of production through flexible specialisation proving decisive in economic and social organisation. However, it does tend to take as axiomatic, and unexplored historically and analytically, the simplistic proposition that there has been satiation in the consumption of mass-produced commodities.
6 See also Galbraith (1969: 46; 1973: 134–8), Packard (1960) and Marris (1968, Ch. 4). These ideas have their intellectual origins in Veblen's *The Theory of the Leisure Class* (Veblen 1924), although there the forces at work are confined to a specific 'class' rather than generalised to the population as a whole.
7 *La Physiologie du gout*, Paris, 1825, as quoted in Burnett (1968: 98).
8 See also Johnston (1977: 19), Burgoyne and Clarke (1983) and Goody (1982: 115) quoting Prakash (1961). The expression is particularly compelling in German; 'man ist was er isst'. Of course, the dictum is intended metaphorically. Yet, in Mintz's outstanding study of the relationship between sugar and power, the phrase is modified into: 'We are *made* more and more into what we eat' (Mintz 1985: 211). And for Barthel (1989: 431), noting the ideological association between sweetness and women: 'Self-identified 'chocoholics' are overwhelmingly female. For them chocolate provides the primary identity: *quite literally*, they are what they eat; they have a relationship with food.'
9 For a full treatment of these issues, see also Keen (1991).
10 See Fine (1985/6) for a discussion of Marx's theory of interest-bearing capital.
11 For an elementary elaboration of these ideas, see Fine (1989).
12 For a discussion of fixed capital in Marx, see Weeks (1981).
13 See especially the debate between Fine (1979, 1980) and Ball (1980), reproduced in Fine (1986).
14 For greater detail of this critique, see Chapter 4.
15 This is not exactly correct, since for parameter restrictions in econometrics, the theory distinguishes different types of commodities for the purposes of investigating additive separability.
16 For a more detailed discussion of these issues, see Fine (1982).
17 See Soper (1981) for further discussion.
18 See Preteceille and Terrail (1985: 6), for whom the representation of consumption as a specific autonomous practice gained precision with the historical development of capitalism.
19 As Marx (1969a: 298) observes by way of a different sort of production, drinking champagne is not productive consumption even if it produces a hangover.
20 Of course, the same point is made by referring to the distinction between wholesale and retail trade. Each is concerned with the buying and selling of use values but they are surrounded by different cultures due, in part, to their different economic locations.

## 19 MARXISM AND THE RECONSTRUCTION OF USE VALUE

1 See Baudrillard (1981: 89). Reference to the work of Baudrillard is to early work where the connection of his analysis both with Marx and with the economy is at its strongest. Consequently, the points made here are even more pertinent to his later work.
2 Symptomatic of this is the discussion of exchange in terms of a self-confessedly, formalistic, unarticulated division into the four logics of use value, exchange value, symbolic exchange and sign value.
3 The classic reference for the analysis of consumption distinctions is Bourdieu (1984) who, however, confines himself to a narrower and legitimate task of demonstrating that the criteria of superiority in consumption reflect hierarchy in socioeconomic class.
4 For Ewen:

> The relationship between style and social power is not a creation of the twentieth century consumer culture in particular. This alliance has a long history. Before the rise of a mass market in style, style was already a viable embodiment of power relations.
>
> (Ewen 1990: 47)

5 And when the opportunity does initially arise for income to overcome social distinctions through consumption, then sumptuary laws are enacted.
6 The treatment of emulation and discrimination as motive forces independent of production leans on the conservative side in so far as the behaviour of the rich is inevitably seen as the prime mover. See Braudel (1974) and especially Sombart (1967) for the idea that luxury consumption is an engine of history.
7 For the debate with Sraffians over the status of Marx's value theory, see Steedman *et al.* (1981), Elson (1979) and Fine (1986).
8 In extreme form, by the followers of Rubin (1973).
9 Similarly, the Sraffian rejection of the law of the tendency of the rate of profit to fall depends upon a leap between Volumes I and III of *Capital*. See Fine (1982).
10 See Taussig (1980) for commodity fetishism in the context of non-capitalist commodity production, for which the devil functions to bridge the gap between production and alienation of the product.
11 See also Miller (1987: 157).

## 20 RELOCATING RETAIL CAPITAL

1 For an exposition of Marx's theory, see Fine (1985/6). See also the debate with Panico (Panico 1988; Fine 1988).
2 See Fine (1985/6, 1989).
3 On the significance of own-label products see de Chernatony and McWilliam (1989a, 1989b), for example.
4 See Insight Research (1988).
5 Interestingly, in his thesis on teleshopping, Ducatel seems more acutely aware of the heterogeneous nature of retail capital: 'It is a hybrid of both productive and commercial capital' (Ducatel 1987: 119). This impurity is linked to an unstable component of productive capital as determined by the outcome of horizontal competition (to obtain geographical spread) and of vertical competition to forge links with the productive branch that creates the surplus value.
6 In Marxist terminology the term 'circulation' is used ambiguously. It can either

refer to the total movement of the economy through production, distribution and exchange, or it can mean movement in the sphere of exchange alone. Meaning should be clear here in context.

7 Ducatel and Blomley's movement, however, from form through function to logic, appears to be in the opposite direction to that of Marx's method.

8 For a critical review of these debates over productive and unproductive labour, see Fine and Harris (1979).

9 Ducatel and Blomley tend to exaggerate the poverty of theory in orthodox accounts of retailing, however unsatisfactory it might be. See also Ducatel (1987).

10 Ducatel and Blomley abstract from the ambiguity of transport in defining retail capital. As discussed later, this is not merely a simplifying assumption but raises pertinent theoretical issues.

11 For a discussion of the law of the tendency of the rate of profit to fall in these terms, see Fine and Harris (1979) and Fine (1989).

# REFERENCES


Abbott, G. (1990) *Sugar*, London: Routledge.

Adburgham, A. (1981) *Shops and Shopping, 1800–1914*, London: George Allen and Unwin.

Aglietta, M. (1979) *A Theory of Capitalist Regulation: The US Experience*, London: New Left Books.

Akerlof, G. (1970) 'The Market for 'Lemons': Quality Uncertainty and the Market Mechanism', *Quarterly Journal of Economics*, vol. 84, pp. 488–500.

Albion, M. (1983) *Advertising's Hidden Effects: Manufacturers' Advertising and Retail Pricing*, Boston: Auburn House.

Albion, M. and P. Farris (1981) *The Advertising Controversy: Evidence on the Economic Effects of Advertising*, Boston: Auburn House.

Alderfer, E. and H. Michl (1957) *Economics of American Industry*, New York: McGraw-Hill.

Alexander, D. (1970) *Retailing in England During the Industrial Revolution*, London: Athlone Press.

Alt, J. (1976) 'Beyond Class: The Decline of Industrial Labor and Leisure', *Telos*, no. 28, Summer, pp. 55–80.

American Social History Project (1989) *Who Built America?* , New York: Pantheon Books.

Anderson, A. *et al.* (1988) 'Nutrition Knowledge Assessed by a Structured Questionnaire in a Group of Medical In-Patients', *Journal of Human Nutrition and Dietetics*, vol. 1, pp. 39–46.

Anderson, P. (1986) 'On Method in Consumer Research: A Critical Relative Perspective', *Journal of Consumer Research*, vol. 13, no. 3, Sept., pp. 155–73.

Anderson, P. (1988a) 'Relative to What – That is the Question: A Reply to Siegel', *Journal of Consumer Research*, vol. 15, no. 2, June, pp. 133–7.

Anderson, P. (1988b) 'Relativism Revidivus: In Defense of Critical Relativism', *Journal of Consumer Research*, vol. 15, no. 3, Dec., pp. 403–6.

Anderson, W. and L. Golden (1984) 'Lifestyle and Psychographics', *Advances in Consumer Research*, vol. 11, pp. 405–11.

Arndt, J. (1983) 'The Political Economy Paradigm: Foundations for Theory Building in Marketing', *Journal of Marketing*, vol. 47, Fall, pp. 44–54.

Arndt, J. (1986) 'Paradigms in Consumer Research: a Review of Perspectives and Approaches', *European Journal of Marketing*, vol. 20, no. 8, pp. 23–40.

Arriaga, P. (1984) 'On Advertising: A Marxist Critique', *Media, Culture and Society*, vol. 6, pp. 53–64.

Aston, P. and C. Philpin (eds) (1985) *The Brenner Debate*, Cambridge: Cambridge University Press.

Attfield, J. and P. Kirkham (eds) (1989) *A View from the Interior: Feminism, Women and Design*, London: The Women's Press.

Bagozzi, R. (1975) 'Marketing as Exchange', *Journal of Marketing*, vol. 39, Oct., pp. 32–9.

Bagozzi, R. (1984) 'A Prospectus for Theory Construction in Marketing', *Journal of Marketing*, vol. 48, Winter, pp. 11–29.

Ball, M. (1980) 'On Marx's Theory of Agricultural Rent: a Reply to Ben Fine', *Economy and Society*, vol. 9, no. 3, pp. 304–26, reproduced in Fine (ed.) (1986).

Ball, M. (1983) *Housing Policy and Economic Power: The Political Economy of Owner Occupation*, London: Methuen.

Ball, M. (1985) 'Coming to Terms with Owner Occupation', *Capital and Class*, no. 24, Winter, pp. 15–44.

Ball, M. (1988) *Rebuilding Construction: Economic Change in the British Construction Industry*, London: Routledge.

Ball, R. and J. Lilly (1982) 'The Menace of Margarine: The Rise and Fall of a Social Problem', *Social Problems*, vol. 29, no. 5, June, pp. 488–98.

Baran, L. (1937) 'The Dress Manufacturing Industry: Its Problems and the Fashion Originators Guild of America', Harvard University, undergraduate thesis.

Baran, P. and P. Sweezy (1968) *Monopoly Capital*, Harmondsworth: Penguin.

Barber, B. and L. Lobel (1952) '"Fashion" in Women's Clothes and the American Social System', *Social Forces*, vol. XXXI, pp. 124–131, reprinted in Bendix and Lipset (eds) (1953).

Barker, L. (ed.) (1982) *The Psychobiology of Human Food Selection*, Westport: AVI Publishing Co.

Barker, T. *et al.* (1966) *Our Changing Fare: Two Hundred Years of British Food Habits*, London: MacGibbon and Kee.

Baron, A. and S. Clepp (1984) 'If I Didn't Have My Sewing-Machine ... Women and Sewing-Machine Technology', in Jensen and Davidson (eds) (1984).

Baron, J. and W. Bielby (1980) 'Bringing the Firms Back in: Stratification, Segmentation, and the Organisation of Work', *American Sociological Review*, vol. 45, pp. 737–65.

Barrau, J. (1989) 'The Possible Contribution of Ethnobotany to the Search for New Crops for Food and Industry', in Wickens *et al.* (eds) (1989).

Barthel, D. (1989) 'Modernism and Marketing: The Chocolate Box Revisited', *Theory, Culture and Society*, vol. 6, August, pp. 429–38.

Barthes, R. (1979) 'Towards a Psychosociology of Contemporary Food Consumption', in Forster, R. and O. Ranum (eds) *Food and Drink in History*, Baltimore: Johns Hopkins University Press.

Barthes, R. (1985) *The Fashion System*, London: Jonathan Cape.

Baudrillard, J. (1981) *For a Critique of the Political Economy of the Sign*, St Louis: Telos Press.

Baudrillard, J. (1988) *Selected Writings*, London: Polity.

Bauman, Z. (1983) 'Industrialism, Consumerism and Power', *Theory, Culture and Society*, vol. 1, no. 3, pp. 32–43.

Beardsworth, A. and T. Keil (1990) 'Putting the Menu on the Agenda', *Sociology*, vol. 24, no. 1, Feb., pp. 139–51.

Beazley, A. (1973) 'The "Heavy" and "Light" Clothing Industries 1850–1920', *Costume*, vol. VII, pp. 55–60.

Becker, G. (1976) *The Economic Approach to Human Behavior*, Chicago: Chicago Press.

Becker, G. (1981) *A Treatise on the Family*, Cambridge, Mass.: Harvard University Press.

Belfer, N. (1954) 'Section Work in the Women's Garment Industry', *Southern Economic Journal*, vol. XXI, no. 2, Oct., pp. 188–200.

Belk, R. (1986a) 'What Should ACR Want To Be When It Grows Up?', *Advances in Consumer Research*, vol. XIII, pp. 423–4.

Belk, R. (1986b) 'Art Versus Science as Ways of Generating Knowledge about Materialism', in Brindberg and Lutz (eds) (1986).

Belk, R. (1987) 'A Modest Proposal for Creating Verisimilitude in Consumer–Information–Processing Models and Some Suggestions for Establishing a Discipline to Study Consumer Behavior', in Firat *et al.* (eds) (1987).

Belk, R. (1989) 'Materialism and the Modern Christmas', *Interpretive Consumer Research*, for the Association for Consumer Research, pp. 115–35.

Belk, R. and R. Pollay (1985) 'Images of Ourselves: the Good Life in Twentieth Century Advertising', *Journal of Consumer Research*, vol. 12, Dec., pp. 265–80.

Bell, Q. (1976) *On Human Finery*, London: Hogarth Press.

Ben-Shachar, A. (1984) 'Demand versus Supply in the Industrial Revolution: A Comment', *Journal of Economic History*, vol. 44, no. 3, Sept., pp. 801–5.

Bendix, R. and S. Lipset (eds) (1953) *Class, Status and Power*, Glencoe, Illinois: Free Press.

Bennett, G. (1988) *Eating Matters: Why We Eat What We Eat*, Kingswood: Heinemann.

Benson, S. (1986) *Counter Cultures: Saleswomen, Managers, and Customers in American Department Stores, 1890–1940*, Chicago: University of Illinois Press.

Berman, R. (1981) *Advertising and Social Change*, London: Sage.

Bernanke, B. (1985) 'Adjustment Costs, Durables and Aggregate Consumption', *Journal of Monetary Economics*, vol. 15, June, pp. 41–68.

Bernard, K. (1988) 'Consumer Demand or Consumer Satisfaction', *European Journal of Marketing*, vol. 22, no. 3, pp. 61–72.

Blanchard, F. (1953) 'Revolution in Clothes', *Harper's Monthly*, March, pp. 59–65.

Blanchard, O. and L. Summers (1986) 'Hysteresis and the European Unemployment Problem', *NBER Macroeconomic Annual*, vol. 1 pp. 15–77.

Blanchflower, D. and A. Oswald (1987) 'Profit Sharing – Can It Work?', *Oxford Economic Papers*, vol. 39, no. 1, pp. 1–19.

Bluestone, B. *et al.* (1981) *The Retail Revolution: Market Transformation, Investment and Labor in the Modern Department Store*, Boston: Auburn House.

Blumberg, P. (1974) 'Decline and Fall of the Status Symbol', *Social Problems*, vol. 21, pp. 480–98.

Blundell, R. (1988) 'Consumer Behaviour: Theory and Empirical Evidence – a Survey', *Economic Journal*, vol. 98, March, pp. 16–65.

BNF, DHSS, HEC (1977) *Nutrition Education: Report of a Working Party*, London: HMSO.

Boorstin, D. (1973) *The Americans: The Democratic Experience*, New York: Random House.

Bourdieu, P. (1984) *Distinction: A Social Critique of the Judgement of Taste*, London: Routledge and Kegan Paul.

Bowers, J. (1985) 'The Economics of Agribusiness', in Healey and Ilbery (eds) (1985).

Boynton, R. and L. Schwendiman (1980) 'Theoretical Approaches to the Economics of Advertising', in Connor and Ward (eds) (1980).

Braudel, H. (1974) *Capitalism and Material Life 1400–1800*, New York: Harper and Row.

Breen, T. (1986) 'An Empire of Goods: The Anglicization of Colonial America, 1690–1776', *Journal of British Studies*, vol. 25, Oct., pp. 467–99.

Breen, T. (1988) '"Baubles of Britain": The American and Consumer Revolutions of the Eighteenth Century', *Past and Present*, no. 119, May, pp. 73–104.

Brenner, R. and M. Glick (1991) 'The Regulation School and the West's Economic Impasse', *New Left Review*, no. 188, July/Aug., pp. 45–119.

Brew, M. (1948) *American Clothing Consumption 1879–1909*, University of Chicago, PhD thesis.
Brewer, J. (1982) The 'Commercialization of Politics', in McKendrick *et al.* (1982).
Briggs, A. (1958) *Friends of the People: The Centenary History of Lewis's*, London: Batsford.
Brindberg, D. and R. Lutz (eds) (1986) *Perspectives on Methodology in Consumer Research*, New York: Springer-Verlag.
British Council of Churches (1978) *The Consumer Goods Society*, London.
Broadbent, S. (ed.) (1981) *Advertising Works, 1*, London: Holt, Rinehart and Winston.
Broadbent, S. (ed.) (1983) *Advertising Works, 2*, London: Holt, Rinehart and Winston.
Brown, A. and A. Deaton (1972) 'Surveys in Applied Economics: Models of Consumer Behaviour', *Economic Journal*, vol. 82, Dec., pp. 1145–1236.
Brown, B. (1981) *Images of Family Life in Magazine Advertising, 1920–1978*, New York: Praeger.
Brown, C. (1987) 'Consumption Norms, Work Roles, and Economic Growth, 1918–80', in Brown and Pechman (eds) (1987).
Brown, C. and J. Pechman (eds) (1987) *Gender in the Workplace*, Washington DC: Brookings.
Brown, S. (1987) 'Institutional Change in Retailing: A Review and Synthesis', *European Journal of Marketing*, vol. 21, no. 6, pp. 5–36.
Brown, S. (1988a) 'The Wheel of the Wheel of Retailing', *International Journal of Retailing*, vol. 3, no. 1, pp. 16–37.
Brown, S. (1988b) 'The Wheel of the Wheel of Retailing: A Rejoinder to Ron Savitt', *International Journal of Retailing*, vol. 3, no. 1, pp. 70–1.
Brown, S. (1990) 'Innovation and Evolution in UK Retailing: The Retail Warehouse', *European Journal of Marketing*, vol. 24, no. 9, pp. 39–54.
Bruland, K. (1985) 'Say's Law and the Single-Factor Explanation of British Industrialization: A Comment', *Journal of European Economic History*, vol. 14, no. 1, pp. 187–91.
Bryant, W. (1988) 'Durables and Wives' Employment Yet Again', *Journal of Consumer Research*, vol. 15, no. 1, June, pp. 37–47.
Budd, J. and R. McCron (1982) *The Role of the Mass Media in Health Education*, University of Leicester: Centre for Mass Communication Research.
Burgoyne, J. and D. Clarke (1983) 'You Are What You Eat: Food and Family Reconstitution', in Murcott (ed.) (1983).
Burnett, J. (1968) *Plenty and Want: A Social History of Diet in England from 1815 to the Present Day*, Harmondsworth: Pelican.
Burnett, J. (1989) *Plenty and Want: A Social History of Food in England from 1815 to the Present Day*, third edition, London: Routledge.
Burns, J. *et al.* (eds) *The Food Industry: Economics and Politics*, London: Heinemann.
Burrows, R. and T. Butler (1989) 'Review Article: Middle Mass and the Pit: A Critical Review of Peter Saunders's Sociology of Consumption', *Sociological Review*, vol. 37, no. 2, pp. 338–64.
Busfeld, J. (1990) 'Sectoral Divisions in Consumption: The Case of Medical Care', *Sociology*, vol. 24, no. 1, Feb., pp. 77–96.
Busfield, D. (1985) '"Tailoring the Millions": The Women Workers of the Leeds Clothing Industry, 1880–1914', *Textile History*, vol. 16, no. 1, Spring, pp. 69–92.
Buss, W. and C. Shaninger (1983) 'The Influence of Sex Roles on Family Decision Processes and Outcomes', *Advances in Consumer Research*, vol. X, pp. 439–44.
Cain, L. and P. Uselding (eds) (1973) *Business Enterprise and Economic Change: Essays in Honour of Harold F. Williamson*, Kent, Ohio: Kent State University Press.
Calder, B. and A. Tybout (1987), 'What Consumer Research Is', *Journal of Consumer Research*, vol. 14, no. 2, June, pp. 136–40.

Calfee, J. and G. Ford (1988) 'Economics, Information and Consumer Behavior', *Advances in Consumer Research*, vol. XV, pp. 234–8.

Callinicos, A. (1989) *Against Postmodernism: A Marxist Critique*, Cambridge: Polity Press.

Campbell, C. (1987) *The Romantic Ethic and the Spirit of Modern Consumerism*, Oxford: Blackwell.

Campbell, T. and T. O'Connor (1988) 'Scientific Evidence and Explicit Health Claims in Food Advertisements', *Journal of Nutrition Education*, vol. 20, no. 2, April, pp. 87–92.

Camporesi, P. (1989) *Bread of Dreams: Food and Fantasy in Early Modern Europe*, London: Polity Press.

Cannadine, D. (1984) 'The Present and the Past in the English Industrial Revolution 1880–1980', *Past and Present*, no. 103, pp. 131–72.

Cannon, G. (1987) *The Politics of Food*, London: Hutchinson.

Cantor, S. and B. Cantor (1977) 'Socioeconomic Factors in Fat and Sugar Consumption', in Kare and Maller (eds) (1977).

Castells, M. (1977) *The Urban Question: A Marxist Approach*, London: Edward Arnold, second edition.

Cecchini, P. (1988) *The European Challenge, 1992: The Benefits of a Single Market*, Aldershot: Wildwood House.

Chamberlin, E. (1933) *The Theory of Monopolistic Competition*, Cambridge, Mass.: Harvard University Press.

Channon, C. (ed.) (1985) *Advertising Works, 3*, London: Holt, Rinehart and Winston.

Chapman, S. (1972) 'The Genesis of the British Hosiery Industry, 1600–1750', *Textile History*, vol. 3, pp. 7–50.

Chapman, S. (1974) 'Enterprise and Innovation in the British Hosiery Industry, 1750–1850', *Textile History*, vol. 5, pp. 14–37.

Charalambous, G. (ed.) (1986) *The Shelf Life of Foods and Beverages*, Amsterdam: Elsevier.

Charles, N. and M. Kerr (1986) 'Eating Properly, the Family and State Benefit', *Sociology*, vol. 20, no. 3, August, pp. 412–29.

Charles, N. and M. Kerr (1988) *Women, Food and Families*, Manchester: Manchester University Press.

Chase, S. and F. Link (1933) *Your Money's Worth: A Study in the Waste of the Consumer's Dollar*, New York: Macmillan.

Cheney, D. (1983) 'The Department Store as a Cultural Form', *Theory, Culture and Society*, vol. 1, no. 3, pp. 10–21.

Chetley, A. (1986) *The Politics of Baby Food: Successful Challenges to an International Marketing Strategy*, London: Frances Pinter.

Clairmonte, F. and J. Cavanagh (1988) *Merchants of Drink: Transnational Control of World Beverages*, Penang: Third World Network.

Clark, B. and S. Laing (1990) 'Infant Feeding: A Review of Breast- and Formula-Feeding Practices', *Journal of Human Nutrition and Dietetics*, no. 3, pp. 1–9.

Clark, E. (1988) *The Want Makers*, London: Hodder and Stoughton.

Clayton, A. (1986) 'Research as a Voyage of Discovery', *Advances in Consumer Research*, vol. XIII, pp. 425–6.

Cobrin, H. (1970) *The Men's Clothing Industry*, New York: Fairchild Publishers.

Cohn, J. (1979) *The Palace or the Poorhouse: The American House as a Cultural Symbol*, East Lansing: The Michigan State University Press.

Cole-Hamilton, I. *et al.* (1986) 'A Study Among Dietitians and Adult Members of Their Households of the Practicalities and Implications of Following Proposed Dietary Guidelines for the UK', *Human Nutrition: Applied Nutrition*, vol. 40A, pp. 365–89.

Cole, W. (1981) 'Factors in Demand', in Floud and McCloskey (eds) (1981).

COMA (1984) *Report of Advisory Panel on Diet in Relation to Cardiovascular Disease*, Committee on Medical Aspects of Food Policy, London: HMSO.

Comanor, W. and T. Wilson (1979) 'The Effect of Advertising on Competition: A Survey', *Journal of Economic Literature*, vol. 17, June, pp. 453–76.

Communications Research Group (1990) *Television Advertising and Sex Role Advertising: A Content Analysis*, London: Broadcasting Standards Council.

Connor, J. (1988) *Food Processing: An Industrial Powerhouse in Transition*, Lexington, Mass.: Lexington Books.

Connor, J. and R. Ward (eds) (1980) *Advertising and the Food System*, North Centre Regional Research Project, NC 117, Monograph no. 14.

Connor, J. et al (1985) *The Food Manufacturing Industries*, Lexington, Mass.: Lexington Books.

Cooper, G. (1968) *The Invention of the Sewing Machine*, Washington DC: Smithsonian Institute.

Cooper, L. (1987) 'Do We Need Critical Relativism? Comments on "On Method in Consumer Research"', *Journal of Consumer Research*, vol. 14, no. 2, June, pp. 126–7.

Corley, T. (1976) 'Nutrition, Technology and the Growth of the British Biscuit Industry, 1820–1900', in Oddy and Miller (eds) (1976).

Courtney, A. and T. Whipple (1983) *Sex Stereotyping in Advertising*, Lexington, Mass.: Lexington Books.

Cowan, R. (1982) 'The "Industrial Revolution" in the Home: Household Technology and Social Change in the Twentieth Century', in Schlereth (ed.) (1982) reproduced from *Technology and Culture*, vol. 17, Jan. 1976, pp. 1–23.

Cowling, K. (1982) *Monopoly Capitalism*, London: Macmillan.

Crafts, N. (1981) 'The Eighteenth Century: A Survey', in Floud and McCloskey (eds) (1981).

Crafts, N. (1983) 'British Economic Growth 1700–1831: A Review of the Evidence', *Economic History Review*, vol. XXXVI, no. 2, pp. 177–99.

Crafts, N. (1987) 'Cliometrics, 1971–1986: A Survey', *Journal of Applied Econometrics*, vol. 2, no. 3, July, pp. 171–92.

Crane, F. (1991) 'Consumers' Attitudes Towards Advertising: A Canadian Perspective', *International Journal of Advertising*, vol. 10, no. 2, pp. 111–16.

Crompton, R. (1991) 'Three Varieties of Class Analysis: Comment on R.E. Pahl', *International Journal of Urban and Regional Research*, vol. 15, no. 1, pp. 108–13.

CTO (1988) *Designing Foods: Animal Product Options in the Marketplace*, Committee on Technological Options to Improve the Nutritional Attributes of Animal Products, Washington: National Academy Press.

Cunnington, C. and P. Cunnington (1972) *Handbook of English Costume in the Eighteenth Century* Boston: Plays Inc.

Cunnington, C. and P. Cunnington (1981) *The History of Underclothes*, London: Faber and Faber.

Daly, L. (1990) 'Nutrition and Health: Introduction', *British Food Journal*, vol. 92, no. 8, pp. 3–4.

Daunton, M. (1983) *House and Home in the Victorian City – Working Class Housing, 1850–1914*, London: Edward Arnold.

Davidson, J. *et al.* (1978) 'Econometric Modelling of the Aggregate Time-Series Relationship between Consumers' Expenditure and Income in the UK', *Economic Journal*, vol. 88, Dec. 1978, pp. 661–92.

Davies, G. (1985) *Governments Can Affect Employment*, London: Employment Institute.

Davis, B. (1987) *Food Commodities*, London: Heinemann.

Davis, M. (1985) 'Urban Renaissance and the Spirit of Postmodernism', *New Left Review*, 151, May/June, pp. 106–13.

De Chernatony, L. (1989a) 'Branding in an Era of Retailer Dominance', *International Journal of Advertising*, vol. 8, no. 3, pp. 245–60.

De Chernatony, L. (1989b) 'Marketers' and Consumers' Changing Perceptions of Market Structure', *European Journal of Marketing*, vol. 23, no. 1, pp. 7–16.

De Chernatony, L. and G. McWilliam (1988) 'Clarifying the Difference between Manufacturers' Brands and Distributors' Brands', *Quarterly Review of Marketing*, Summer, vol. 13, no. 4, pp. 1–5.

De Chernatony, L. and G. McWilliam (1989a) 'The Varying Nature of Brands as Assets: Theory and Practice Compared', *International Journal of Advertising*, vol. 8, no. 4, pp. 339–49.

De Chernatony, L. and G. McWilliam (1989b) 'The Strategic Implications of How Marketers Interpret Brands', *Journal of Marketing Management*, vol. 5, no. 2, Winter, pp. 153–72.

De Marly, D. (1986) *Working Dress: A History of Occupational Clothing*, London: Batsford.

De Paola, H. and C. Mueller (1986) *Marketing Today's Fashion*, New Jersey: Prentice Hall.

Deaton, A. and J. Muellbauer (1980) *Economics and Consumer Behaviour*, Cambridge: Cambridge University Press.

Deem, R. and G. Salaman (1985) (eds) *Work, Culture and Society*, Milton Keynes: Open University Press.

Degler, C. (1977) *The Age of the Economic Revolution 1876–1900*, Glenview, Illinois: Scott Foresman, second edition.

Department of Health (1989) *The Diets of British Schoolchildren*, London: HMSO.

Derbaix, C. and P. Vanden Abeale (1985) 'Consumer Inferences and Consumer Preferences: The Status of Cognition and Consciousness in Consumer Behaviour Theory' *International Journal of Research in Marketing*, vol. 2, no. 3, pp. 157–74.

Deshpande, R. and F. Webster (1989) 'Organizational Culture and Marketing: Defining the Research Agenda', *Journal of Marketing*, vol. 53, no. 1, Jan., pp. 3–15.

Dewar, H. (n.d.) 'The NACNE and COMA Reports – A Comment, the Implications for Agriculture and Methods of Implementation', in Dewar *et al.* (n.d.).

Dewar, H. *et al.* (n.d.) 'Three Essays on Economic Implications of Current Nutritional Thinking', mimeo.

Dholakia, N. (1982) 'Some Underpinnings for a Radical Theory of Consumption', *Advances in Consumer Research*, vol. IX, pp. 296–301.

Dickson, P. and A. Sawyer (1984) 'Entry/Exit Demand Analysis', *Advances in Consumer Research*, vol. XI, pp. 617–22.

Dickson, P. and W. Wilkie (1978) *The Consumption of Household Durables: A Behavioral Review*, Washington.

Dietz, B. (1986) 'The North-East Coal Trade, 1550–1750: Measures, Markets and the Metropolis', *Northern History*, vol. 22, pp. 280–94.

Dobbing, J. (ed.) (1987) *Sweetness*, London: Springer-Verlag.

Douglas, M. and Baron Isherwood (1980) *The World of Goods*, London: Penguin.

Douglas, T. (1984) *The Complete Guide to Advertising*, London: Macmillan.

Downey, G. (1987) 'Review and Assessment of Food and Nutrition Policies', in Gormley *et al.* (1987).

Doyle, P. and D. Cook (1979) 'Marketing Strategies, Financial Structure and Innovation in UK Retailing', *Management Decision*, vol. 17, no. 2, pp. 168–71.

Drake, L. and C. Glasser (1942) *Trends in the New York Clothing Industry, A Study Undertaken for the Mayor's Business Advisory Committee and the Committee of Fifteen*, New York: Institute of Public Administration.

Driver, C. (1983) *The British at Table, 1940–1980*, London: Chatto and Windus.

Drummond, J. (1957) *The Englishman's Food: A History of Five Centuries of English*

*Diet*, revised edition of 1939 original, with a new chapter by D. Hollingsworth, London: Jonathan Cape.

Dryansky, G. (1973) 'The Couture: Not What It Was But Still a Power', *Women's Wear Daily*, 26 January.

Ducatel, K. (1987) *Teleshopping and Retail Change: A Marxist Perspective*, unpublished PhD thesis, Department of Geography, University of Bristol.

Ducatel, K. and N. Blomley (1990) 'Rethinking Retail Capital', *International Journal of Urban and Regional Research*, vol. 14, no. 2, pp. 206–27.

Duesenberry, J. (1967) *Income, Saving and the Theory of Consumer Behaviour*, Cambridge, Mass.: Harvard University Press.

Dufty, W. (1975) *Sugar Blues*, Radnor: Chilton Book Co.

Duke, V. and S. Edgell (1984) 'The Political Economy of Cuts in Britain and Consumption Sectoral Cleavages', *International Journal of Urban and Regional Research*, vol. 10, pp. 177–201.

Dukes, D. (1990) 'European Developments in the Foodstuffs Sector', *British Food Journal*, vol. 93, no. 4, pp. 3–10.

Dunleavy, P. (1986) 'The Growth of Sectoral Cleavages and the Stabilisation of State Expenditures', *Environment and Planning D*, vol. 4, pp. 129–44.

Dunn, R. (1986) 'Television, Consumption and the Commodity Form', *Theory, Culture and Society*, vol. 3, no. 1, pp. 49–64.

Dyer, G. (1982) *Advertising as Communication*, London: Methuen.

Dykstra, R. (1968) *The Cattle Towns*, New York: Athenaeum.

Earl, P. (1990) 'Economics and Psychology: A Survey', *Economic Journal*, vol. 100, Sept., pp. 718–55.

EC (1987) *How Women are Represented in Television Programmes in the EEC, Part I: Images of Women in News, Advertising, and Series and Serials*, Luxemburg: European Commission.

EEC (1988) *Research on the 'Cost of Non-Europe' in the Foodstuffs Industry: Basic Findings*, vol. 12, Brussels: European Commission.

EIU (1989a) 'Chocolate Confectionery', *Retail Business*, no. 375, May.

EIU (1989b) 'Baked Beans', *Retail Business*, no. 374, April.

EIU (1989c) 'Chilled Foods', *Retail Business*, no. 382, Dec.

EIU (1989d) 'Grocers and Supermarkets', *Retail Business Quarterly Trade Reviews*, no. 12, Dec.

Ekelund, R. and D. Saurman (1988) *Advertising and the Market Process: A Modern Economic View*, San Francisco: Pacific Research Institute for Public Policy.

Elson, D. (ed.) (1979) *Value: The Representation of Labour in Capitalism*, London: CSE Books.

Engel, J. (1981) 'The Discipline of Consumer Research: Permanent Adolescence or Maturity?', *Advances in Consumer Research*, vol. VIII, pp. 12–4.

Engel, J. *et al.* (1968) *Consumer Behavior*, New York: Holt, Rinehart and Winston.

EOC (1982) *Adman and Eve*, Manchester: Equal Opportunities Commission.

Evans, C. and M. Thornton (1989) *Women and Fashion: A New Look*, London: Quartet Books.

Eversley, D. (1967) 'The Home Market and Economic Growth in England, 1750–1780', in Jones and Mingay (eds) (1967).

Ewen, S. (1976) *Captains of Consciousness: Advertising and the Social Roots of the Consumer Culture*, New York: McGraw-Hill.

Ewen, S. (1990) 'Marketing Dreams: The Political Elements of Style', in Tomlinson (ed.) (1990).

Ewing, E. (1986) *History of Twentieth Century Fashion*, London: Batsford.

Fallers, L. (1961) 'A Note on the 'Trickle Effect'', in Lipset and Smelser (eds) (1961).

Fallows, S. (1990) *The Food Sector*, London: Routledge.

Fallows, S. and H. Gosden (1985) *Does the Consumer Really Care?*, University of Bradford: Food Policy Research Unit.
Farrer, P. (1987) *A Guide to Food Additives and Contaminants*, Carnforth: Parthenon Publishing Group.
Featherstone, M. (1983) 'Consumer Culture: An Introduction', *Theory, Culture and Society*, vol. 3, no. 1, pp. 4–9.
Featherstone, M. (1990) 'Perspectives on Consumer Culture', *Sociology*, vol. 24, no. 1, Feb., pp. 5–22.
Feldman, E. (1960) *Fit for Men: A Study of New York's Clothing Trade*, Washington, DC: Public Affairs Press.
Fellows, P. (1988) *Food Processing Technology: Principles and Practices*, Chichester: Ellis Horwood.
Fenton, A. and T. Owen (eds) (1981) *Food in Perspective*, Edinburgh: John Donald.
Fern, E. and J. Brown (1984) 'The Industrial/Consumer Marketing Dichotomy: A Case of Insufficient Justification', *Journal of Marketing*, vol. 48, Spring, pp. 68–77.
Fiddes, N. (1991) *Meat: A Natural Symbol*, London: Routledge.
Field, G. (1970) 'The Status Float Phenomenon: The Upward Diffusion of Innovation', *Business Horizons*, vol. 13, Aug., pp. 45–52.
Filby, F. (1934) *A History of Food Adulteration and Analysis*, London: Unwin.
Fine, B. (1979) 'On Marx's Theory of Agricultural Rent', *Economy and Society*, vol. 8, no. 3, pp. 241–78, reproduced in Fine (ed.) (1986).
Fine, B. (1980) 'On Marx's Theory of Agricultural Rent – A Rejoinder', *Economy and Society*, vol. 9, no. 3, Aug., pp. 327–31.
Fine, B. (1980) *Economic Theory and Ideology*, London: Edward Arnold.
Fine, B. (1982) *Theories of the Capitalist Economy*, London: Edward Arnold.
Fine, B. (1985/6) 'Banking Capital and the Theory of Interest', *Science and Society*, vol. XLIX, no. 4, pp. 387–413.
Fine, B. (ed.) (1986) *The Value Dimension: Marx versus Ricardo and Sraffa*, London: Routledge and Kegan Paul.
Fine, B. (1987) 'Segmented Labour Market Theory: A Critical Assessment', *Birkbeck Discussion Paper in Economics*, no. 87/12.
Fine, B. (1988) 'From Capital in Production to Capital in Exchange', *Science and Society*, vol. 52, no. 3, Fall, pp. 326–37.
Fine, B. (1989) *Marx's 'Capital'*, London: Macmillan, third edition.
Fine, B. (1990) 'Segmented Labour Market Theory: A Critical Assessment', Thames Papers in Political Economy, Spring.
Fine, B. (1992) *Women's Employment and the Capitalist Family*, London: Routledge.
Fine, B. and L. Harris (1976) 'State Expenditure in Advanced Capitalism: A Critique', *New Left Review*, no. 98, July/Aug., pp. 97–112.
Fine, B. and L. Harris (1979) *Rereading 'Capital'*, London: Macmillan.
Fine, B. and L. Harris (1985) *The Peculiarities of the British Economy*, London: Lawrence and Wishart.
Fine, B. and L. Harris (1987) 'Ideology and Markets: Economic Theory and the "New Right"', in R. Miliband *et al.* (eds), *Socialist Register*, London: Merlin Press.
Fine, B. and E. Leopold (1990) 'Consumerism and the Industrial Revolution', *Social History*, vol. 15, no. 2, May, pp. 151–79.
Fine, B. and A. Murfin (1984) *Macroeconomics and Monopoly Capitalism*, Brighton: Wheatsheaf.
Fine, B. and J. Wright (1991) 'Digesting the Food and Information Systems', *Birkbeck Discussion Paper*, no. 7/91, Dec.
Finkelstein, J. (1989) *Dining Out: A Sociology of Modern Manners*, London: Polity Press.
Finlayson, I. (1990) *Denim: An American Legend*, New York: Simon and Schuster.

Firat, A. *et al.* (eds) (1987) *Philosophical and Radical Thought in Marketing*, Lexington: Lexington Books.
Fischler, C. 'Attitudes Towards Sugar and Sweetness in Historical and Social Perspective', in Dobbing (ed.) (1987).
Fite, E. (1910) *Social and Industrial Conditions in the North during the Civil War*, New York: Macmillan.
Flinn, M. (1984) *The History of the British Coal Industry, vol. 2, 1700–1830: The Industrial Revolution*, with the assistance of D. Stoker, Oxford: Clarendon Press.
Floud, R. and D. McCloskey (eds) (1981) *The Economic History of Britain since 1700, vol. 1, 1700–1860*, Cambridge: Cambridge University Press.
Flugel, J. (1940) *The Psychology of Clothes*, London: Hogarth Press.
Forrest, R. and A. Murie (1988) *Selling the Welfare State: The Privatisation of Public Housing*, London: Routledge.
Forrest, R. and A. Murie (1990) 'A Dissatisfied State? Consumer Preferences and Council Housing in Britain', *Urban Studies*, vol. 27, no. 5, Oct., pp. 617–35.
Forrest, R. *et al.* (1990) *Home Ownership: Differentiation and Fragmentation*, London: Unwin Hyman.
Forty, A. (1986) *Objects of Desire: Design and Society from Wedgwood to IBM*, London: Thames and Hudson.
Foster, H. (ed.) (1985) *Postmodern Culture*, London: Pluto.
Fox, M. (1978) 'Use of Microwaves for Reheating of Military Rations', in Paulus (ed.) (1978).
Fox, R. and T. Lears (eds) (1983) *The Culture of Consumption: Critical Essays in American History, 1880–1980*, New York: Pantheon.
Fox, S. (1984) *The Mirror Maker: A History of American Advertising and its Creators*, New York: William Morris and Co.
Foxall, G. (1986) 'Consumer Choice in Behavioral Perspective', *European Journal of Marketing*, vol. 20, no. 3/4, pp. 7–18.
Foxall, G. (1987) 'Radical Behaviouralism and Consumer Research: Theoretical Problems and Empirical Problems", *International Journal of Research in Marketing*, vol. 4, no. 2, pp. 111–29.
Frank, B. (1948) *The Progressive Sewing Room*, New York: Fairchild Publications.
Fraser, W. (1981) *The Coming of the Mass Market, 1850–1914*, London: Macmillan.
Freckleton, A. (1985) 'Who is Shaping the Label: A Report on Activities of Government, Manufacturers, Retailers and Consumers', Food Policy Research, University of Bradford.
Friedland, W. *et al.* (1981) *Manufacturing Green Gold: Capital, Labor and Technology in the Lettuce Industry*, Cambridge: Cambridge University Press.
Friedman, M. (1988) 'Models of Consumer Choice Behaviour', in van Raaij *et al.* (eds) (1988).
Frisby, D. (1984) *Georg Simmel*, Chichester: E. Horwood.
Fulop, C. (1981) *Advertising, Competition and Consumer Behaviour*, London: Holt, Rinehart and Wilson.
Fulop, C. (1986) *Retailer Advertising and Retail Competition in the UK*, London: Advertising Association.
Furnham, A. and A. Lewis (1986) *The Economic Mind: The Social Psychology of Economic Behaviour*, Brighton: Wheatsheaf.
Galbraith, J. (1962) *The Affluent Society*, Harmondsworth: Penguin.
Galbraith, J. (1969) *The New Industrial Estate*, Boston: Houghton Mifflin Co.
Galbraith, J. (1973) *Economics and the Public Purpose*, New York: Basic Books.
Galbraith, J. (1985) *The Affluent Society*, London: Deutsch, fourth edition.
Galloway, J. (1989) *The Sugar Cane Industry: An Historical Geography from Its Origins to 1914*, Cambridge: Cambridge University Press.

Gardner, C. and J. Sheppard (1989) *Consuming Passion: The Rise of Retail Culture*, London: Unwin Hyman.
Garrow, J. (1980) 'Energy Balance and Obesity in Man', in Turner (ed.) (1980).
Gartman, D. (1979) 'Origins of the Assembly Line and Capitalist Control of Work at Ford', in Zimbalist (ed.) (1979).
Gaski, J. (1982) 'The Causes of the Industrial Revolution: A Brief, "Single Factor" Argument', *Journal of European Economic History*, vol. 11, no. 1, pp. 227–33.
Geary, F. (1984) 'The Cause of the Industrial Revolution and "Single Factor" Arguments: An Assessment', *Journal of European Economic History*, vol. 13, no. 1, pp. 167–73.
Gershuny, J. (1983) *Social Innovation and the Division of Labour*, Oxford: Oxford University Press.
Gershuny, J. and I. Miles (1983) *The New Service Economy: The Transformation of Employment in Industrial Societies*, London: Frances Pinter.
Gibney, M. (1990) 'Dietary Guidelines: A Critical Appraisal', *Journal of Human Nutrition and Dietetics*, vol. 49, no. 3, pp. 245–54.
Gibson, L. et al (1990) 'Evaluation Methodologies for Food Health Policies', *Journal of Human Nutrition and Dietetics*, vol. 3, pp. 55–59.
Gilbert, S. (1986) *Pathology of Eating: Psychology and Treatment*, London: Routledge and Kegan Paul.
Gilboy, E. (1932) 'Demand as a Factor in the Industrial Revolution', in A. Cole (1932), *Facts and Figures in Economic History: Articles by Former Students of Edwin Francis Gay*, Cambridge, Mass.: Harvard University Press, reproduced in Hartwell (ed.) (1967).
Gilder, G. (1981) *Wealth and Poverty*, New York: Basic Books.
Godelier, M. (1973) *Rationality and Irrationality in Economics*, New York: Monthly Review Press.
Goffman, E. (1979) *Gender Advertisements*, London: Macmillan.
Gofton, L. (1989) 'Sociology and Food Consumption', *British Food Journal*, vol. 19, no. 1, pp. 25–31.
Goldman, R. (1987) 'Marketing Fragrances: Advertising and the Production of Commodity Signs', *Theory, Culture and Society*, vol. 4, pp. 691–725.
Goldman, R. and J. Wilson (1983) 'Appearance and Essence: The Commodity Form Revealed in Perfume Advertisements', in McNall (ed.) (1983).
Goldschmidt, W. (ed.) (1979) *The Uses of Anthropology*, Washington: American Anthropological Association.
Goodman, D. and M. Redclift (1991) *Refashioning Nature: Food, Ecology and Culture*, London: Routledge.
Goodman, D. *et al.* (1987) *From Farming to Biotechnology: A Theory of Agro-Industrial Development*, Oxford: Blackwell.
Goody, J. (1982) *Cooking, Cuisine and Class: A Study in Comparative Sociology*, Cambridge: Cambridge University Press.
Gordon, J. and J. McArthur (1985) 'American Women and Domestic Consumption, 1800–1920: Four Interpretive Themes', *Journal of American Culture*, vol. 18, no. 3, Fall, pp. 35–46.
Gormley T. (1987) 'Review and Assessment of Key Nutritional Issues and of the Criteria Currently Applied for Determining the Effects of Food of Plant, Animal and Marine Origin on Human Health', in Gormley *et al.* (1987).
Gormley, T. *et al.* (1987) *Food, Health and the Consumer*, London: Elsevier.
Gorz, A. (1982) *Farewell to the Working Class: An Essay in Post-Industrial Socialism*, London: Pluto.
Gough, I. (1975) 'State Expenditure in Advanced Capitalism', *New Left Review*, no. 92, pp. 53–92.

Gough, I. (1979) *The Political Economy of the Welfare State*, London: Macmillan.
Grafton-Small, R. (1987) 'Marketing, or the Anthropology of Consumption', *European Journal of Marketing*, vol. 21, no. 9, pp. 66–71.
Grafton-Small, R. and S. Linstead (1989) 'Advertisements as Artefacts: Everyday Understanding and the Creative Consumer', *International Journal of Advertising*, vol. 8, no. 3, pp. 205–14.
Grant, R. (1987) 'Manufacturer–Retailer Relations: The Shifting Balance of Power', in Johnson (ed.) (1987).
Green, F. (1990) 'Institutional and Other Unconventional Theories of Saving', *Discussion Paper*, University of Leicester.
Green, F. and P. Nore (eds) (1977) *Economics: An Anti-Text*, London: Macmillan.
Greenwood, K. and M. Murphy (1978) *Fashion Innovation and Marketing*, London: Macmillan.
Greider, W. (1981) 'The Education of David Stockman', *The Atlantic Monthly*, vol. 248, no. 6, Dec., pp. 46–7.
Greyser S. (ed.) (1964) *Toward Scientific Marketing*, Chicago: American Marketing Association.
Gutcho, M. (1973) *Prepared Snack Foods*, Park Ridge: Noyes Data Corp.
Guthrie, H. (1978) 'Is Education Not Enough?', *Journal of Nutrition Education*, vol. 10, no. 2, April/June, pp. 57–8.
Hall, M. (ed.) (1959) *Made in New York: Case Studies in Metropolitan Manufacturing*, Cambridge, Mass.: Harvard University Press.
Hall, S. *et al.* (eds) (1980) *Culture, Media, Language: Working Papers in Cultural Studies, 1972–9*, London: Hutchinson.
Hamilton, W. (ed.) (1938) *Price and Price Policies*, New York: McGraw-Hill.
Hamnett, C. (1989) 'Consumption and Class in Contemporary Britain', in Hamnett et al (eds) (1989).
Hamnett, C. *et al.* (eds) (1989) *Restructuring Britain: The Changing Social Structure*, London: Sage.
Hardyment, C. (1988) *From Mangle to Microwave: The Mechanisation of Household Work*, London: Polity Press.
Harloe, M. (1984) 'Sector and Class', *International Journal of Urban and Regional Research*, vol. 8, pp. 228–37.
Harper, A. (1989) 'Scientific Substantiation of Health Claims: How Much is Enough?', *Nutrition Today*, March/April, pp. 17–21.
Harrington, M. (1962) *The Other America*, New York: Macmillan.
Harris, M. (1985) *Good to Eat: Riddles of Food and Culture*, London: Allen and Unwin.
Harris, R. and G. Pratt (1987) 'Housing Tenure and Social Class: Introduction', in Harris and Pratt (eds) (1987).
Harris, R. and G. Pratt (eds) (1987) *Housing Tenure and Social Class*, Stockholm: Almquist and Wiksell.
Harrison, M. (1986) 'Consumption and Urban Theory: An Alternative Approach Based on the Social Division of Welfare', *International Journal of Urban and Regional Research*, vol. 10, pp. 232–42.
Hartwell, R. (1965) 'The Causes of the Industrial Revolution: An Essay in Methodology', *Economic History Review*, vol. XVIII, no. 1, pp. 164–82, reproduced in Hartwell (ed.) (1967).
Hartwell, R. (ed.) (1967) *The Causes of the Industrial Revolution*, London: Methuen.
Harvey, D. (1989) *The Condition of Post-Modernity: An Enquiry into the Origins of Cultural Change*, Oxford: Blackwell.
Hatcher, J. (forthcoming) *The History of the British Coal Industry, vol. 1, Before 1700*, Oxford: Clarendon Press.

Haug, W. (1986) *Critique of Commodity Aesthetics: Appearance, Sexuality and Advertising in Capitalist Society*, London: Polity Press.
Hausmann, W. (1980) 'A Model of the London Coal Trade in the Eighteenth Century', *Quarterly Journal of Economics*, vol. XCIV, February, no. 1, pp. 1–14.
Hausmann, W. (1984a) 'Cheap Coals or Limitation of the Vend? The London Coal Trade, 1770–1845', *Journal of Economic History*, vol. XLIV, no. 2, June, pp. 321–28.
Hausmann, W. (1984b) 'Market Power in the London Coal Trade: The Limitations of the Vend, 1770–1845', *Explorations in Economic History*, vol. 21, pp. 383–405.
Hayden, D. (1982) *The Grand Domestic Revolution: A History of Feminist Designs for American Homes, Neighborhoods, and Cities*, Cambridge: Cambridge University Press.
HEA (1989) *Diet, Nutrition and Healthy Eating in Low Income Groups*, London: Health Education Authority.
Healey, M. and B. Ilbery (eds) (1985) *The Industrialisation of the Countryside*, Norwich: Short Run Press.
Heasman, M. (1987) 'One Lump or Two: Current Issues and Challenges Facing Sugar in the United Kingdom', Food Policy Research, University of Bradford.
Heasman, M. (1990) 'Nutrition and Technology: The Development of the Market for "Lite" Products', *British Food Journal*, vol. 92, no. 2, pp. 5–13.
Heaton, M. (1933) 'Industrial Revolution', *Encyclopaedia of the Social Sciences*, vol. VIII, reproduced in Hartwell (ed.) (1967).
Hecht, J. (1956) *The Domestic Servant Class in Eighteenth-Century England*, London: Routledge and Kegan Paul.
Helfgott, R. (1959) 'Women's and Children's Apparel' in Hall (ed.) (1959).
Hess, J. and K. Hess (1989) *The Taste of America*, New York: Grossman/Viking.
Higgs, E. (1986) 'Domestic Service and Household Production', in John (ed.) (1986).
Hirschman, A. (1982) *Private Interest and Public Action*, Oxford: Martin Robertson.
Hirschman, E. (1982) 'Symbolism and Technology as Sources for the Generation of Innovation', *Advances in Consumer Research*, vol. IX, pp. 537–41.
Hirschman, E. (1987) 'People as Products: Analysis of a Complex Marketing Exchange', *Journal of Marketing*, vol. 51, no. 1, Jan., pp. 98–108.
Hirschman, E. (1989) 'Consumer Behavior Theories as Heroic Quest', *Advances in Consumer Research*, vol. 16, pp. 639–46.
HMSO (1947) *Working Party Report on the Light Clothing Industry*, London: HMSO.
Hoffman, W. (1969) '100 Years of the Margarine Industry', in Van Stuyvenberg (ed.) (1969).
Holbrook, M. (1985) 'Why Business is Bad for Consumer Research: The Three Bears Revisited', *Advances in Consumer Research*, vol. 12, pp. 145–56.
Holbrook, M. (1987) 'What is Consumer Research?', *Journal of Consumer Research*, vol. 14, no. 2, June, pp. 128–32.
Holbrook, M. and J. O'Shaughnessy (1988) 'On the Scientific Status of Consumer Research and the Need for an Interpretive Approach for Studying Consumption Behaviour', *Journal of Consumer Research*, vol. 15, no. 4, Dec., pp. 398–402.
Hollis, M. and E. Nell (1975) *Rational Economic Man: A Philosophical Critique of Neoclassical Economics*, Cambridge: Cambridge University Press.
Holmes, A. (1988) 'Developments in the Food Industry over the Last 150 Years', *Journal of the Royal Society for Agriculture of England*, vol. 149, pp. 58–70.
Hoppit, J. (1990) 'Counting the Industrial Revolution', *Economic History Review*, vol. XLIII, no. 2, pp. 173–93.
Horowitz, D. (1985) *The Morality of Spending: Attitudes to the Consumer Society in America, 1875–1940*, London: Johns Hopkins University Press.
Hounshell, D. (1984) *From the American System to Mass Production, 1800–1932: The*

*Development of Manufacturing Technology in the United States*, Baltimore: the Johns Hopkins University Press.

Houston, F. and J. Gassenheimer (1987) 'Marketing and Exchange', *Journal of Marketing*, vol. 51, no. 4, pp. 3–18.

Houston, M. *et al.* (1983) 'The Role of Meta-Analysis in Consumer Research', *Advances in Consumer Research*, vol. X, pp. 497–502.

Howard, J. and J. Sheth (1969) *The Theory of Buyer Behaviour*, New York: John Wiley and Son.

Hudson, K. (1983) *The Archaeology of the Consumer Society: The Second Industrial Revolution in Britain*, London: Heinemann.

Hudson, L. and J. O'Zanne (1988) 'Alternative Ways of Seeking Knowledge in Consumer Research', *Journal of Consumer Research*, vol. 14, no. 1, March, pp. 508–21.

Hunter, J. (ed.) (1974) *The Geography of Health and Disease*, Chapel Hill: University of North Carolina Press.

Hurst, S. (1985) 'The Effect on Branded Groceries of Retail Trade Concentration', *Admap*, July/August, pp. 395–6.

Inkster, I. (1983) 'Technology as the Cause of the Industrial Revolution, Some Comments', *Journal of European Economic History*, vol. 12, no. 3, pp. 651–8.

Insight Research (1988) *New Frontiers in the Food Industry: An Analysis of Trend and Change*, London: Insight Research.

International Business Intelligence (1989) *1992 – Planning for the Food Industry*, London: Butterworth.

Ippolito, P. and A. Mathios (1990) 'The Regulation of Science-Based Claims in Advertising', *Journal of Consumer Policy*, vol. 13, Dec., pp. 413–45.

Jacoby, J. (1978) 'Consumer Research: A State of the Art Review', *Journal of Marketing*, vol. 42, no. 2, April, pp. 87–96.

Jameson, F. (1984) 'Postmodernism, or the Cultural Logic of Late Capitalism', *New Left Review*, no. 146, pp. 53–92.

Jameson, F. (1985) 'Postmodernism and Consumer Society', in Foster (ed.) (1985).

James, P. *et al.* (1980) 'Is Food Intake under Physiological Control in Man?', in Turner (ed.) (1980).

Jarnow, J. *et al.* (1981) *Inside the Fashion Business Texts and Readings*, New York: John Wiley and Son.

Jay, R. (1987) *The Trade Card in Nineteenth-Century America*, Columbia: University of Missouri Press.

Jefferys, J. (1954) *Retail Trading in Britain, 1850–1950*, Cambridge: Cambridge University Press.

Jensen, J. and S. Davidson (eds) (1984) *A Needle, a Bobbin, a Strike: Women Needleworkers in America*, Philadelphia: Temple University Press.

Jerome, N. (1981) 'Frozen (TV) Dinners – The Staple Emergency Meals of a Changing Modern Society', in Fenton and Owen (eds) (1981).

John, A. (ed.) (1986) *Unequal Opportunities: Women's Employment in England*, Oxford: Blackwell.

Johnson, B. (1987) *Barbara Johnson's Album of Fashions and Fabrics*, London: Thames and Hudson.

Johnson, G. (ed.) (1987) *Business Strategy and Retailing*, Chichester: John Wiley and Sons.

Johnston, J. (1976) 'The Development of the Food-Canning Industry in Britain during the Inter-War Period', in Oddy and Miller (eds) (1976).

Johnston, J. (1977) *A Hundred Years of Eating: Food, Drink and the Daily Diet in Britain since the Late Nineteenth Century*, Dublin: Gill and Macmillan.

Jones, E. (1973) 'The Fashion Manipulators: Consumer Tastes and British Industries; 1660–1800', in Cain and Uselding (eds) (1973).

Jones, E. and G. Mingay (eds) (1967) *Land, Labour and Population in the Industrial Revolution: Essays Presented to J.D. Chambers*, London: Edward Arnold.

Jordans (1985) *The British Food Processing Industry*, London.

Jordans (1987) *Food Processors – Major*, London, fourteenth edition.

Jordans (1988) *Britain's Fast Food Industry*, London.

Kagel, J. (1981) 'Demand Curves of Animal Consumers', *Quarterly Journal of Economics*, vol. XCVI, no. 1, Feb., pp. 1–15.

Kaldor, N. (1950) 'The Economic Aspects of Advertising', *Review of Economic Studies*, vol. 18, pp. 1–27.

Kare, M. and O. Maller (eds) (1977) *The Chemical Senses and Nutrition*, New York: Academic Press.

Kassarjian, H. (1982a) 'The Development of Consumer Behavior Theory', *Advances in Consumer Research*, vol. IX, pp. 20–22.

Kassarjian, H. (1982b) 'Consumer Psychology', *Annual Review of Psychology*, vol. 33, pp. 619–49.

Kassarjian, H. (1986) 'Consumer Research: Some Recollections and a Commentary', *Advances in Consumer Research*, vol. XIII, pp. 6–8.

Katona, G. (1964) *The Mass Consumption Society*, New York: McGraw-Hill.

Keen, S. (1991) 'Paul Sweezy and the Misinterpretation of Marx', *School of Economics Discussion Paper*, no. 91/1, Jan., University of New South Wales.

Kellner, D. (1983) 'Critical Theory, Commodities and the Consumer Society', *Theory, Culture and Society*, vol. 3, no. 1, pp. 66–83.

Kerr, M. and N. Charles (1986) 'Servers and Providers: The Distribution of Food within the Family', *Sociological Review*, vol. 34, pp. 115–57.

Key Note (1987) *Retail Food Markets in Europe*, London.

Key Note (1988) *Frozen Foods: An Industry Sector Overview*, London, eighth edition.

Key Note (1989a) *Fast Food Outlets*, London, sixth edition.

Key Note (1989b) *Snack Foods*, London, fifth edition.

Key Note (1989c) *Food Flavourings and Ingredients*, London, third edition.

Kidwell, C. and M. Christman (1974), *Suiting Everyone: The Democratization of Clothing in America*, Washington: Smithsonian Institute.

King, C. (1964) 'Fashion Adoption: A Rebuttal to the 'Trickle Down' Theory', in Greyser (ed.) (1964).

King, S. (1980) 'Presentation and the Choice of Food', in Turner (ed.) (1980).

King, S. (1983) 'Trends in Meal Planning and Eating Habits', in Turner (ed.) (1983).

Kirk, T. (1991) 'Collaboration between the Dietetic Profession and the Food Industry in Health Education – a Discussion Paper', *Journal of Human Nutrition and Dietetics*, vol. 4, pp. 197–207.

Kirk, T. and U. Arens (1988) 'Legislation and Codes of Practice: Nutrition Information in Food Marketing', *British Food Journal*, vol. 90, no. 6, pp. 268–72.

Kittler, P. and K. Sucher (1989) *Food and Culture in America: A Nutrition Handbook*, New York: Van Nostrand Reinhold.

Konig, R. (1973) *The Restless Image*, London: Allen and Unwin.

Kotler, P. (1986) 'The Prosumer Movement: A New Challenge for Marketeers', *Advances in Consumer Research*, vol. XIII, pp. 510–13.

Krondl, M. and D. Lau (1982) 'Social Determinants in Human Food Selection', in Barker (ed.) (1982).

Kryk, H. (1923) *A Theory of Consumption*, Cambridge: Riverside Press, reprinted in 1976, New York: Arnos Press.

Lamphere, L. (1979) 'Fighting the Piece-Rate System', in Zimbalist (ed.) (1979).

Lancaster, K. (1966) 'A New Approach to Consumer Theory', *Journal of Political Economy*, vol. 74, pp. 132–57.
Landes, D. (1969) *The Unbound Prometheus: Technological Change and Industrial Development in Western Europe from 1750 to the Present*, Cambridge: Cambridge University Press.
Lang, K. and G. Lang (1961) 'Fashion and Fashion Leadership', *Collective Leadership*, New York: Thomas Y. Crowell Co, pp. 465–87.
Lang, T. and P. Wiggins (1985) 'The Industrialisation of the UK Food System: From Production to Consumption', in Healey and Ilbery (eds) (1985).
Lang, T. (1986/7) 'The New Food Policies', *Critical Social Policy*, vol. 18, Winter, pp. 32–47.
Lasch, C. (1979) *The Culture of Narcissism: American Life in an Age of Diminishing Expectations*, New York: Norton and Co.
Laver, J. (1964) *Women's Dress in the Jazz Age*, London: Hamish Hamilton.
Lea, S. *et al.* (1987) *The Individual in the Economy: A Survey of Economic Psychology*, Cambridge: Cambridge University Press.
Leach, W. (1984) 'Transformations in a Culture of Consumption: Women and Department Stores, 1890–1925', *Journal of American History*, vol. 71, no. 2, Sept., pp. 319–42.
Lee, R. and R. Schofield (1981) 'British Population in the Eighteenth Century', in Floud and McCloskey (eds) (1981).
Lefebvre, H. (1971) *Everyday Life in the Modern World*, London: Allen Lane.
Leiss, W. (1983) 'The Icons of the Market Place', *Theory, Culture and Society*, vol. 3, no. 1, pp. 10–21.
Leiss, W. (1988) *The Limits to Satisfaction: An Essay on the Problem of Needs and Commodities*, Kingston: McGill-Queens' University Press.
Leiss, W. *et al.* (1986) *Social Commodities in Advertising: Person, Products, and Images of Well-Being*, London: Methuen.
LeMay, B. (ed.) (1988) *Science, Ethics and Food*, Washington: Smithsonian Institute.
Lemire, B. (1984) 'Developing Consumerism and the Ready-Made Clothing Trade in Britain, 1750–1800', *Textile History*, vol. 15, no. 1, Spring, pp. 21–44.
Lemire, B. (1988) 'Consumerism in Preindustrial and Early Industrial England: The Trade in Secondhand Clothes', *Journal of British Studies*, vol. 27, Jan., pp. 1–24.
Levenstein, H. (1988) *Revolution at the Table: The Transformation of the American Diet*, Oxford: Oxford University Press.
Levine, D. (1987) *Reproducing Families: The Political Economy of English Population History*, Cambridge: Cambridge University Press.
Levine, L. (1924) *Women's Garment Workers: A History of the International Ladies Garment Workers Union*, New York: B.W. Huebsch.
Lewis, C. (1976) *Food and Drink in Britain: From the Stone Age to Recent Times*, Harmondsworth: Penguin.
Lewis, J. *et al.* (1985) *Food Retailing in London: A Pilot Study of the Three Largest Retailers and Londoners' Access to Food*, London: London Food Commission.
Lewis, R. (1989) *Food Additives Handbook*, New York: Van Nostrand Reinhold.
Lindley, M. (1987) 'Sucrose in Baked Products', *Nutrition Bulletin*, vol. 49, Jan., pp. 41–5.
Lipset, S. and N. Smelser (eds) (1961) *Sociology: The Progress of a Decade*, Englewood Cliffs, New Jersey: Prentice Hall.
Lister, A. (1988) *I Know My Own Heart: The Diaries of Anne Lister (1791–1840)*, London: Virago.
Lobstein, T. (1990) 'The Corporate Clinic', *The Food Magazine*, Oct./Dec., pp. 22–3.
London Food Commission (1988) *Food Adulteration and How to Beat It*, London: Unwin.

London Food Commission (1989) *This Food Business*, London: New Statesman and Society.

Louis, J. and H. Yazijian (1980) *The Cola Wars*, New York: Everest House.

Luba, A. (1985) *The Food Labelling Debate: A Report for the London Food Commission*, London: London Food Commission.

Lusch, R. (1987) 'A Commentary on the US Retail Environment', in Johnson (ed.) (1987).

Lyman, B. (1989) *A Psychology of Food: More a Matter of Taste*, New York: Van Nostrand Reinhold.

MAFF (1987) *The Use of the Word 'Natural' and Its Derivatives in the Labelling, Advertising and Presentation of Food: Report of a Survey by the Local Authorities Co-ordinating Body on Trading Standards*, London: HMSO.

Mahatoo, W. (1985) *The Dynamics of Consumer Behavior*, Toronto: Wiley.

Mahler, V. (1986) 'Controlling International Commodity Prices and Supplies: The Evolution of United States Sugar Policy', in Tullis and Hollist (eds) (1986).

Malhotra, N. (1988) 'Some Observations on the State of the Art in Marketing Research', *Journal of the Academy of Marketing Science*, vol. 16, no. 1, Spring, pp. 4–24.

Marchand, R. (1985) *Advertising the American Dream: Making Way for Modernity, 1920–1940*, London: University of California Press.

Marcuse, H. (1964) *One-Dimensional Man: Studies in the Ideology of Advanced Industrial Society*, Boston: Beacon Press.

Marion, B. (1986) *The Organisation and Performance of the US Food System*, Lexington, Mass.: Lexington Books.

Market Planning Service (1952) *The Apparel Manufacturing Industry*, New York: National Credit Office, Inc.

Marks, H. (1989) *A Hundred Years of British Food and Farming*, London: Taylor and Francis.

Marris, R. (1968) *The Economic Theory of 'Managerial Capitalism'*, New York: Basic Books.

Marshall, G. (1991) 'In Defence of Class Analysis: A Comment on R.E. Pahl', *International of Urban and Regional Research*, vol. 15, no. 1, pp. 114–18.

Martell, D. (1986) 'Own Labels: Problem Child or Infant Prodigy', *Quarterly Review of Marketing*, Summer, vol. 11, no. 4, pp. 7–13.

Marx, K. (1969a) *Theories of Surplus Value*, Part I, London: Lawrence and Wishart.

Marx, K. (1969b) *Theories of Surplus Value*, Part II, London: Lawrence and Wishart.

Marx, K. (1973) *Grundrisse*, Harmondsworth: Penguin.

Marx, K. (1976) *Capital*, Volume I, Harmondsworth: Penguin, original of 1867.

Mason, G. (1936) 'Native American Food: What the Indians Gave Us to Eat and How their Discoveries Influenced the Dietary Habits of the World', *Natural History*, vol. 37, pp. 309–18.

Mason, R. (1981) *Conspicuous Consumption: A Study of Exceptional Consumer Behaviour*, Farnborough: Gower.

Mason, R. (1984) 'Conspicuous Consumption: A Literature Review', *European Journal of Marketing*, vol. 18, no. 3, pp. 26–39.

Mather, L. and L. Tucker (1980) 'Conglomerate Mergers, Food Advertising, and the Cross Subsidization Hypothesis', in Connor and Ward (eds) (1980).

Mavroudeas, S. (1990) *Regulation Approach: A Critical Assessment*, PhD thesis, University of London.

Mayhew, M. (1988) 'The 1930s Nutrition Controversy', *Journal of Contemporary History*, vol. 23, pp. 445–64.

May, J. (1974) 'The Geography of Nutrition', in Hunter (ed.) (1974).

McCloskey, D. (1981) 'The Industrial Revolution 1780–1860: A Survey', in Floud and McCloskey (eds) (1981).
McCluney, J. (1988) *Answering Back: Public Views on Food and Health Information*, University of Bradford: Food Policy Research Unit.
McCorkle, C. (ed.) (1988) *Economics of Food Processing in the United States*, San Diego: Academic Press.
McCracken, G. (1985) 'The Trickle-Down Theory Rehabilitated', in Solomon (ed.) (1985).
McCracken, G. (1987) 'The History of Consumption: A Literature Review and Consumer Guide', *Journal of Consumer Policy*, vol. 10, pp. 139–66.
McCracken, G. (1988) *Culture and Consumption: New Approaches to the Symbolic Character of Consumer Goods and Activities*, Minneapolis: Indiana University Press.
McKendrick, N. (1959/60) 'Josiah Wedgwood: An Eighteenth Century Entrepreneur in Salesmanship and Marketing Techniques', *Economic History Review*, vol. 12, no. 3, pp. 408–33.
McKendrick, N. (1961) 'Josiah Wedgwood and Factory Discipline', *Historical Journal*, vol. 4, no. 1, pp. 30–55.
McKendrick, N. (1964) 'Josiah Wedgwood and Thomas Bentley: An Inventor–Entrepreneur Partnership in the Industrial Revolution', *Transactions of the Royal Historical Society*, vol. 14, pp. 1–33.
McKendrick, N. (1970) 'Josiah Wedgwood and Cost Accounting in the Industrial Revolution', *Economic History Review*, vol. XXII, no. 1, April, pp. 45–67.
McKendrick, N. (1973) 'The Role of Science in the Industrial Revolution: A Study of Josiah Wedgwood as a Scientist and Industrial Chemist', in Teich and Young (eds) (1973).
McKendrick, N. (1974) 'Home Demand and Economic Growth: A New View of the Role of Women and Children in the Industrial Revolution', in McKendrick (ed.) (1974).
McKendrick, N. (ed.) (1974) *Historical Perspectives: Studies in English Thought and Society in Honour of J. H. Plumb*, London: Europa.
McKendrick, N. (1982) 'Commercialization and the Economy', in McKendrick *et al.* (1982).
McKendrick, N. and R. Outhwaite (eds) (1986) *Business Life and Public Policy: Essays in Honour of D.C. Coleman*, Cambridge: Cambridge University Press.
McKendrick, N. *et al.* (1982) *The Birth of a Consumer Society: The Commercialization of Eighteenth Century England*, London: Europa Publications.
McKenzie, J. (1964) 'Food Trends', in Yudkin and McKenzie (eds) (1964).
McKenzie, J. (1980) 'Economic Influences on Food Choice', in Turner (ed.) (1980).
McKie, L. and R. Wood (1991) 'Dietary Beliefs and Practices: A Study of Working-Class Women in North-East England', *British Food Journal*, vol. 93, no. 4, pp. 25–8.
McLelland, G. (1990) 'Economies of Scale in British Food Retailing', in Moir and Dawson (eds) (1990).
McLoughlin, V. and J. Davies (1985) 'Conceptual Barriers to the Promotion of "Healthy Eating"', in Turner and Ingle (eds) (1985).
McManus, K. (1990) 'What Can and What Cannot be Achieved by Nutrition Education? A Challenge for the 1990s', *Proceedings of the Nutrition Society*, vol. 49, pp. 389–95.
McMichael, P. and D. Myhre (1991) 'Global Regulation vs. the Nation-State: Agro-Food Systems and the New Politics of Capital', *Capital and Class*, no. 43, Spring, pp. 83–105.
McNall, S. (ed.) (1983) *Current Perspectives in Social Theory*, vol. 4, Greenwich, Connecticut: JAI Press.

McWilliam, G. and L. de Chernatony (1989) 'The Buying of Own Labels', *European Journal of Marketing*, vol. 23, no. 3, pp. 57–70.

Meiklejohn, H. (1938) 'Dresses – the Impact of Fashion on a Business', in Hamilton (ed.) (1938).

Mennell, S. (1985) *All Manners of Food*, Oxford: Blackwell.

Merton, R. (1968) *Social Theory and Social Structure*, New York: The Free Press (first edition, 1949).

Messer, E. (1984) 'Anthropological Perspectives on Diet', *Annual Review of Anthropology*, vol. 13, pp. 205–49.

Meyer, A. (1989) 'Europe's Vanishing Breed', *Prepared Foods*, Oct., pp. 57–62.

Milkman, R. (ed.) (1985) *Women, Work and Protest: A Century of US Women's Labor History*, Boston: Routledge and Kegan Paul.

Miller, B. (1981) *The Bon Marché: Bourgeois Culture and the Department Store, 1869–1920*, Princeton: Princeton University Press.

Miller, D. (1987) *Material Culture and Mass Consumption*, Oxford: Blackwell.

Millum, T. (1975) *Images of Women: Advertising in Women's Magazines*, London: Chatto and Windus.

Mingione, E. (1981) *Social Conflict and the City*, Oxford: Blackwell.

MINTEL (1989) *Retail Intelligence*, vol. 4.

Mintz, S. (1982) 'Choice and Occasion: Sweet Moments', in L. Barker (ed.) (1982).

Mintz, S. (1985) *Sweetness and Power*, New York: Viking.

Mohun, S. (1977) 'Consumer Sovereignty', in Green and Nore (eds) (1977).

Moir, C. (1990) 'Competition in the UK Grocery Trades', in Moir and Dawson (eds) (1990).

Moir, C. and J. Dawson (eds) (1990) *Competition and Markets: Essays in Honour of Margaret Hall*, London: Macmillan.

Mokyr, J. (1977) 'Demand vs Supply in the Industrial Revolution', *Journal of Economic History*, vol. 37, pp. 981–1008.

Mokyr, J. (1984) 'Demand versus Supply in the Industrial Revolution: A Reply', *Journal of Economic History*, vol. 44, no. 3, Sept., pp. 806–9.

Monopolies and Mergers Commission (1981) *S&W Berisford Limited and British Sugar Corporation: A Report on the Proposed Merger*, HC 241, 1980–81, London: HMSO.

Monopolies and Mergers Commission (1989) *Tate and Lyle and Ferruzzi Finanziaria SpA and S&W Berisford: A Report on the Existing and Proposed Mergers*, Cmd 89, London: HMSO.

Montgomery, E. and J. Bennett (1979) 'Anthropological Studies of Food and Nutrition: the 1940s and the 1970s', in Goldschmidt (ed.) (1979).

Mooney, C. (1990) 'Cost and Availability of Healthy Food Choices in a London Health District', *Journal of Human Nutrition and Dietetics*, vol. 3, pp. 111–20.

Moorhouse, H. (1988) 'American Automobiles and Workers' Dreams', *Sociological Review*, vol. 31, pp. 403–26.

Morgan, D. (1980) *Merchants of Grain*, Harmondsworth: Penguin.

Morris, H. (1926) *The Story of Men's Clothes*, Rochester: Hickey-Freeman Co.

Morris, J. (1990) 'Fruit and Vegetable Harvest Mechanization', *Food Technology*, Feb., pp. 97–101.

Moschis, G. (1987) *Consumer Socialization: A Life-Cycle Perspective*, Lexington, Mass.: Lexington Books.

Mueller, B. (1991) 'Multinational Advertising: Factors Influencing the Standardised vs Specialised Approach', *International Marketing Review*, vol. 8, no. 1, pp. 7–18.

Mui, H. and L. Mui (1989) *Shops and Shopkeeping in Eighteenth Century England*, London: Routledge.

Mukerji, C. (1983) *From Graven Images: Patterns of Modern Materialism*, New York: Columbia University Press.

Mullins, P. (1991) 'The Identification of Social Forces in Development as a General Problem in Sociology: A Comment on Pahl's Remarks on Class and Consumption Relations as Forces in Urban and Regional Development', *International Journal of Urban and Regional Research*, vol. 15, no. 1, pp. 119–26.

Murcott, A. (ed.) (1983) *The Sociology of Food and Eating*, Aldershot: Gower.

Murcott, A. (1986) 'You Are What You Eat – Anthropological Factors Influencing Food Choice', in Ritson *et al.* (eds) (1986).

Murcott, A. (1988) 'Sociological and Social Anthropological Approaches to Food and Eating', *World Review of Nutrition and Dietetics*, vol. 55, pp. 1–40.

Musaiger, A. (1985) 'Can Nutrition Education Compete with Advertising Messages in Developing Countries?', in Turner and Ingle (eds) (1985).

Musson, A. (ed.) (1972) *Science, Technology, and Economic Growth in the Eighteenth Century*, London: Methuen.

Myers, R. (1937) 'The Economic Aspects of the Production of Men's Clothing (with Particular Reference to the Industry in Chicago)', Department of Economics, University of Chicago Libraries, Chicago.

NACNE (1983) *Proposals for Nutritional Guidelines for Health Education in Britain*, National Advisory Committee on Nutrition Education, London: Health Education Authority.

NEDO (1971) *Convenience Foods in Catering*, London: Arthur D. Little Ltd.

Nef, J. (1932) *The Rise of the British Coal Industry*, vols. I & II, London: Routledge.

Newby, H. (1983) 'Living from Hand to Mouth: The Farmworker, Food and Agribusiness', in Murcott (ed.) (1983).

Nicholas, S. (1982) 'Total Factor Productivity Growth and the Revision of post-1870 British Economic History', *Economic History Review*, vol. 35, no. 1, pp. 85–98.

Nichols, S. *et al.* (1988) 'Evaluation of the Effectiveness of a Nutritional Health Education Leaflet in Changing Public Knowledge and Attitudes about Eating and Health', *Journal of Human Nutrition and Dietetics*, vol. 1, pp. 233–8.

Nicosia, F. (1966) *Consumer Decision Processes: Marketing and Advertising Implications*, Englewood Cliffs: Prentice-Hall.

Noble, D. (1985) 'Command Performance: A Perspective on Military Enterprise and Technological Change', in Smith (ed.) (1985).

Nystrom, P. (1928) *The Economics of Fashion*, New York: The Ronalds Press.

O'Beirne, D. (1987) 'Review and Assessment of Agricultural Production and Food Processing Technologies with Respect to their Possible Impact on Human Health', in Gormley et al (1987).

O'Connor, J. (1973) *The Fiscal Crisis of the State*, New York: St Martin's.

O'Guinn, T. and R. Belk (1989) 'Heaven on Earth: Consumption at Heritage Village, USA', *Journal of Consumer Research*, vol. 16, Sept., pp. 227–38.

O'Kelly, L. (1989) 'It Seemed Like a Good Idea', in *Campaign: Twenty One Years of the Agony and the Ecstasy*, London: Campaign.

Oddy, D. and D. Miller (eds) (1976) *The Making of the Modern British Diet*, London: Croom Helm.

Oliver, T. (1986) *The Real Coke, The Real Story*, London: Elm Tree Books.

Otnes, P. (ed.) (1988) *The Sociology of Consumption: An Anthology*, New Jersey: Humanities Press International.

Packard, S. (1983) *The Fashion Business*, New York: Holt, Rinehart and Winston.

Packard, V. (1957) *The Hidden Persuaders*, London: Longmans, Green and Co Ltd.

Packard, V. (1960) *The Status Seekers: An Exploration of Class Behaviour in America*, London: Longmans.

Packard, V. (1960) *The Waste Makers*, New York: David McKay Co.

Pahl, J. (1980) 'Patterns of Money Management within Marriage', *Journal of Social Policy*, vol. 9, no. 3, pp. 313–35.
Pahl, J. (1983) 'The Allocation of Money and the Structuring of Inequality within Marriage', *Sociological Review*, vol. 31, pp. 237–62.
Pahl, J. (1989) *Money and Marriage*, London: Macmillan.
Pahl, R. (1989) 'Is the Emperor Naked? Some Questions on the Adequacy of Sociological Theory in Urban and Regional Research', *International of Urban and Regional Research*, vol. 13, no. 4, Dec., pp. 709–20.
Pahl, R. (1991) 'R.E. Pahl Replies', *International of Urban and Regional Research*, vol. 15, no. 1, pp. 127–9.
Palazzini, E. (1988) *Coca-Cola Superstar: the Drink that Became a Business Empire*, London: Columbus Books.
Panico, C. (1988) 'Marx on the Banking Sector and the Interest Rate: some Initial Notes for a Discussion', *Science and Society*, vol. 52, no. 3, Fall, pp. 310–25.
Paulus, K. (ed.) (1978) *How Ready are Ready-to-Serve Foods?*, Basel: S. Krager.
Pearl, R. (1990) 'Trends in Consumption and Processing of Fruits and Vegetables in the United States', *Food Technology*, Feb., pp. 102–4.
Perry, M. (1990) 'The Internationalisation of Advertising', *Geoforum*, vol. 21, no. 1, pp. 35–50.
Peterson, R. *et al.* (eds) (1986) *The Role of Affect in Consumer Behavior: Emerging Theories and Applications*, Lexington, Mass.: Heath and Co.
Piachaud, D. (1982) 'Patterns of Income and Expenditure within Families', *Journal of Social Policy*, vol. 11, no. 4, pp. 469–82.
Pieters, R. and W. van Raaij (1988) 'The Role of Affect in Economic Behaviour', in van Raaij et al (eds) (1988).
Piore, M. and C. Sabel (1984) *The Second Industrial Divide: Possibilities for Prosperity*, New York: Basic Books.
Plumb, J. (1964) 'The Historian's Dilemma', in Plumb (ed.) (1964).
Plumb, J. (ed.) (1964) *Crisis in the Humanities*, London: Penguin.
Plumb, J. (1982) 'Commercialization and Society', in McKendrick *et al.* (1982).
Poiesz, T. and J. von Grumbleow (1988) 'Economic Well-Being, Job Satisfaction, Income Evaluation and Consumer Satisfaction: An Integrative Attempt', in van Raaij *et al.* (eds) (1988).
Pollak, R. (1985) 'A Transaction Cost Approach to Families and Households', *Journal of Economic Literature*, vol. XXIII, June, pp. 581–608.
Pollard, S. (1983) 'Capitalism and Rationality: A Study of Measurements in British Coal Mining, ca. 1750–1850', *Explorations in Economic History*, vol. 20, pp. 110–29.
Pollay, R. (1985) 'The Subsidising Sizzle: A Descriptive History of Print Advertising, 1900–1980', *Journal of Marketing*, vol. 49, Summer, pp. 24–37.
Porter, R. (1982) *English Society in the Eighteenth Century*, London: Allen Lane.
Postan, M. and J. Hatcher (1985) 'Population and Class Relations in Feudal Society', in Aston and Philpin (1985).
Prakash, O. (1961) *Food and Drinks in Ancient India*, Delhi: Munshi Ram Manohar Lal.
Pratt, G. (1986) 'Against Reductionism: The Relations of Consumption as a Mode of Social Structuration', *International Journal of Urban and Regional Research*, vol. 10, pp. 377–400.
Pressnell, L. (ed.) (1960) *Studies in the Industrial Revolution Presented to T.S. Ashton*, London: London University Press.
Preteceille, E. (1986) 'Collective Consumption, Urban Segregation, and Social Classes', *Environment and Planning D*, vol. 4, pp. 145–54.
Preteceille, E. and J-P. Terrail (1985) *Capitalism, Consumption and Needs*, Oxford: Blackwell.

Rashid, S. (1977) 'Malthus' Model of General Gluts', *History of Political Economy*, vol. 9, Fall, pp. 366–83, reproduced in Wood (ed.) (1986).
Reekie, W. (1981) *The Economics of Advertising*, London: Macmillan.
Reilly, M. and J. Conover (1983) 'Meta-Analysis: Integrating Results from Consumer Research Studies', *Advances in Consumer Research*, vol. X, pp. 509–13.
Relph-Knight, L. (1988) 'Own-Label Now Has Designs on Labelling', *Marketing Week*, 6 May, pp. 51–5.
Rex, J. and R. Moore (1967) *Class, Community, and Conflict: A Study of Sparkbrook*, London: Oxford University Press.
Ribeiro, A. (1984) *Dress in Eighteenth-Century Europe 1715–1789*, London: Batsford.
Riesman, D. (1964) *Abundance for What: And Other Essays*, London: Chatto and Windus.
Ritson, C. *et al.* (eds) (1986) *The Food Consumer*, Chichester: Wiley.
Robbins, C. (1983) 'Implementing the NACNE Report, National Dietary Goals: A Confused Debate', *The Lancet*, 10 Dec., pp. 1351–53.
Roberts, D. (1991a) '"Natural": A Trading Standards Viewpoint', *British Food Journal*, vol. 93, no. 1, pp. 17–19.
Roberts, D. (1991b) '1992 and All That', *British Food Journal*, vol. 93, no. 1, pp. 25–6.
Roberts, S. *et al.* (1988) 'The Fortunate Few: Production as Consumption', *Advances in Consumer Research*, vol. XV, pp. 430–5.
Robertson, R. and G. Walton (1979) *History of the American Economy*, New York: Harcourt Brace Jovanovich, fourth edition.
Robertson, T. and S. Ward (1973) 'Consumer Behavior Research: Promise and Prospects', in Robertson and Ward (eds) (1973).
Robertson, T. and S. Ward (eds) (1973) *Consumer Behavior: Theoretical Sources*, Englewood Cliffs: Prentice–Hall.
Robinson, D. (1961) 'The Economics of Fashion Demand', *Quarterly Journal of Economics*, vol. 75, no. 3, pp. 376–98.
Robinson, E. (1986) 'Matthew Boulton and Josiah Wedgwood, Apostles of Fashion', *Business History*, vol. 28, no. 3, July, pp. 98–114.
Robinson, J. (1933) *The Economics of Imperfect Competition*, London: Macmillan.
Rosdolsky, R. (1977) *The Making of Marx's 'Capital'*, London: Pluto.
Rosenberg, N. (1968) 'Adam Smith, Consumer Tastes, and Economic Growth', *Journal of Political Economy*, vol. 76, no. 2, pp. 361–74, reproduced in Wood (ed.) (1983).
Rosenberg, S. (ed.) (1989) *The State and the Labor Market*, New York: Plenum Press.
Rose, M. (1981) 'Social Change and the Industrial Revolution', in Floud and McCloskey (eds) (1981).
Roshco, B. (1963) *The Rag Race: How New York and Paris Run the Breakneck Business of Dressing American Women*, New York: Funk and Wagnalls.
Ross, E. (1980) 'Patterns of Diet and Forces of Production: An Economic and Ecological History of the Ascendancy of Beef in the United States Diet', in Ross (ed.) (1980).
Ross, E. (ed.) (1980) *Beyond The Myths of Culture: Essays in Cultural Materialism*, London: Academic Press.
Rossiter, J. (1989) 'Consumer Research and Marketing Science', *Advances in Consumer Research*, vol. 16, pp. 407–13.
Rostow, W. (1967) *The Stages of Economic Growth: A Non-Communist Manifesto*, Cambridge: Cambridge University Press.
Rostow, W. (1975) *How It All Began*, New York: McGraw-Hill.
Rousseas, S. (1982) *The Political Economy of Reaganomics: A Critique*, Armonk, New York: M.E. Sharpe.
Rubin, I. (1972) *Essays on Marx's Theory of Value*, Detroit: Black and Red.

Ruf, F. (1978) 'The Market Situation for Ready-To-Serve Foods in Europe', in Paulus (ed.) (1978).
Ryan, M. and D. Barclay (1983) 'Meta-Analysis: Integrating Results from Studies', *Advances in Consumer Research*, vol. X, pp. 492–6.
Sahlins, M. (1976) *Culture and Political Reason*, Chicago: Chicago University Press.
Salaman, R. (1949) *The History and Social Influence of the Potato*, Cambridge: Cambridge University Press.
Samuel, R. (1989) *Patriotism: The Making and Unmaking of British National Identity, Vol. 1, History and Politics*, London: Routledge.
Sanderson, M. and J. Winkler (1983) 'Implementing the NACNE Report, Strategies for Implementing NACNE Recommendations', *The Lancet*, 10 Dec., pp. 1353–4.
Sanderson, S. (1986) 'The Emergence of the "World Steer": Internationalisation and Foreign Domination in Latin American Cattle Production', in Tullis and Hollist (eds) (1986).
Saunders, P. (1984) 'Beyond Housing Classes: The Sociological Significance of Private Property Rights in Means of Consumption', *International Journal of Urban and Regional Research*, vol. 8, pp. 202–25.
Saunders, P. (1986a) *Social Theory and the Urban Question*, London: Hutchinson, second edition.
Saunders, P. (1986b) 'Comment on Dunleavy and Preteceille', *Environment and Planning D*, vol. 4, pp. 155–63.
Saunders, P. (1988) 'The Sociology of Consumption: A New Research Agenda', in Otnes (ed.) (1988).
Saunders, P. (1990) *A Nation of Home Owners*, London: Unwin Hyman.
Saunders, P. and C. Harris (1990) 'Privatisation and the Consumer', *Sociology*, vol. 24, no. 1, Feb., pp. 57–75.
Savage, M. *et al.* (1990) 'The Consumption Sector Debate and Social Mobility', *Sociology*, vol. 24, no. 1, Feb., pp. 97–117.
Savitt, R. (1988) 'The Wheel of the Wheel of Retailing: Comment', *International Journal of Retailing*, vol. 3, no. 1, pp. 38–40.
Sawyer, M. (1985) *The Economics of Michal Kalecki*, London: Macmillan.
Sayer, A. (1989) 'Postfordism in Question', *International Journal of Urban and Regional Research*, vol. 13, no. 4, pp. 666–95.
Schapira, D. *et al.* (1990) 'The Value of Current Information', *Preventive Medicine*, vol. 19, pp. 45–53.
Scheiber, H. *et al.* (1976) *American Economic History*, New York: Harper and Row, ninth edition.
Schlereth, T. (ed.) (1982) *Material Studies in America*, Nashville: The American Association for State and Local History.
Schmalansee, R. (1988) 'Industrial Economics: An Overview', *Economic Journal*, vol. 98, Sept., pp. 643–81.
Schmiechen, J. (1984) *Sweated Industries and Sweated Labour: The London Clothing Trades, 1860–1914*, Beckenham: Croom Helm.
Schoeffler, O. and W. Gale (1973) *Esquire's Encyclopedia of Twentieth Century Men's Fashions*, New York: McGraw-Hill.
Schudson, M. (1984) *Advertising, the Uneasy Persuasion*, New York: Basic Books.
Scitovsky, T. (1976) *The Joyless Economy: An Inquiry into Human Satisfaction and Dissatisfaction*, New York: Oxford University Press.
Segal-Horn, S. (1987) 'The Retail Environment in the UK', in Johnson (ed.) (1987).
Sen, A. (1983) 'Poor, Relatively Speaking', *Oxford Economic Papers*, no. 35, pp. 153–69.
Sen, A. (1984) *Resources, Values and Development*, Cambridge, Mass.: Harvard University Press.

Sen, A. (1987) 'Food and Freedom', Text of the Third Sir John Crawford Memorial Lecture, Washington DC: World Bank.

Shammas, C. (1990) *The Pre-Industrial Consumer in England and America*, Oxford: Clarendon Press.

Shaw, S. *et al.* (1989) 'Economies of Scale in UK Supermarkets: Some Preliminary Findings', *International Journal of Retailing*, vol. 4, no. 5, pp. 13–26.

Sheiham, A. (1991) 'Barriers to Healthy Eating', *The Food Magazine*, April/June, pp. 18–19.

Shepherd, R. and L. Stockley (1986) 'The Role of Attitudes and Nutritional Knowledge in Fat Consumption', *Proceedings of the Nutrition Society*, vol. 45.

Sheth, J. (1985) 'Broadening the Horizons of the Association for Consumer Research and Consumer Behavior', *Advances in Consumer Research*, vol. XII, Presidential Address.

Sheth, J. *et al.* (1988) *Marketing Theory: Evolution and Evaluation*, New York: Wiley and Sons.

Shilliam, N. (1991) 'The Sartorial Autobiography: Bostonians' Private Writings about Fashionable Dress, 1760s–1860s', *Textile and Text*, vol. XIII, no. 3, pp. 5–22.

Siegel, H. (1988) 'Relativisim for Consumer Research', *Journal of Consumer Research*, vol. 15, no. 2, June, pp. 129–32.

Simmel, G. (1904) ' Fashion', *The International Quarterly*, vol. X, no. 1, Oct., pp. 130–55.

Simmel, G. (1978) *The Philosophy of Money*, London: Routledge and Kegan Paul.

Simon, H. (1984) 'Challenges and New Research in Marketing Science', *International Journal of Research in Marketing*, vol. 1, no. 4, pp. 249–62.

Sinclair, J. (1987) *Images Incorporated: Advertising as Industry and Ideology*, London: Croom Helm.

Slattery, J. (1986) *Diet Health: Food Industry Initiatives*, University of Bradford: Food Policy Research Unit.

Sloan, A. *et al.* (1986) 'Consumer Attitudes about Shelflife and Technology', in Charalambous (ed.) (1986).

Smith, M. (ed.) (1985) *Military Enterprise and Technological Change: Perspectives on the American Experience*, Cambridge: MIT Press.

Smith, R. (1961) *Sea-Coal for London*, London: Longmans.

Solomon, M. (ed.) (1985) *The Psychology of Fashion*, Lexington, Mass.: Lexington Books.

Sombart, W. (1967) *Luxury and Capitalism*, Ann Arbor: University of Michigan Press.

Soper, K. (1981) *On Human Needs*, Brighton: Harvester.

Sowell, T. (1963) 'The General Glut Controversy Reconsidered', *Oxford Economic Papers*, vol. 15, Nov., pp. 193–203, reproduced in Wood (ed.) (1986).

Spiggle, S. and C. Goodwin (1988) 'Values and Issues in the Field of Consumer Research: A Content Analysis of ACR Presidential Addresses', *Advances in Consumer Research*, pp. 5–9.

Staff Report (1989) 'Top 10 Food Science Innovations, 1939–1989', *Food Technology*, Sept., p. 308.

Stahl-Urban Company (1947) *75 Years in Work Clothes – A History of the Stahl-Urban Company 1871–1946*, Terre Haute, Indiana.

Steedman, I. *et al.* (1981) *The Value Controversy*, London: Verso.

Steele, V. (1985) *Fashion and Eroticism: Ideals of Feminine Beauty from the Victorian Era to the Jazz Age*, Oxford: Oxford University Press.

Stern, B. (1989) 'Literary Criticism and Consumer Research: Overview and Illustrative Analysis', *Journal of Consumer Research*, vol. 16, no. 3, Dec., pp. 322–34.

Steven, M. (1990) 'Strategies to Influence Nutrition Behaviour', *Journal of Human Nutrition and Dietetics*, vol. 3, pp. 183–97.

Stigler, G. (1954) 'The Early History of Empirical Studies of Consumer Behavior', *Journal of Political Economy*, vol. LXII, no. 2, April, pp. 95–113.

Stock, J. and M. Watson (1988) 'Variable Trends in Economic Time Series', *Journal of Economic Perspectives*, vol. 2, no. 3, Summer, pp. 147–74.

Stuard, S. (1985) 'Medieval Workshop: Toward a Theory of Consumption and Economic Change', *Journal of Economic History*, vol. 45, no. 2, June, pp. 447–51.

Sullivan, O. (1989) 'Housing Tenure as a Consumption-Sector Divide: A Critical Perspective', *International Journal of Urban and Regional Research*, vol. 13, no. 2, pp. 183–200.

Surprenant, C. and G. Churchill (1984) 'Can Role Playing Be Substituted for Actual Consumption?', *Advances in Consumer Research*, vol. XI, pp. 122–6.

Tannahill, R. (1988) *Food in History*, Harmondsworth: Penguin.

Taussig, M. (1980) *The Devil and Commodity Fetishism in South America*, Chapel Hill: University of North Carolina Press.

Taylor, L. (1983) *Mourning Dress: A Costume and Social History*, London: Allen and Unwin.

Taylor, T. and E. Wilson (1989) *Through the Looking Glass*, London: BBC Books.

Teich, M. and R. Young (eds) (1973) *Changing Perspectives in the History of Science: Essays in Honour of Joseph Needham*, Boston: Reidel Publishing.

Thaler, R. (1983) 'Transaction Utility Theory', *Advances in Consumer Research*, vol. X, pp. 229–32.

Thirsk, J. (1978) *Economic Policy and Projects: The Development of a Consumer Society in Early Modern England*, Oxford: Clarendon.

Thomas, J. (1955) 'A History of the Leeds Clothing Industry', *Yorkshire Bulletin of Economic and Social Research*, Occasional Paper, no. 1, January.

Thomas, J. (1979) 'The Relationship between Knowledge about Food and Nutrition and Food Choice', in Turner (ed.) (1979).

Thomas, T. (1989) 'Food, Industry and Agriculture', in Wickens *et al.* (eds) (1989).

Thorne, S. (1986) *The History of Food Preservation*, Kirkby Lonsdale: Parthenon Publishing.

Tolbert, C. (1982) 'Industrial Segmentation and Men's Career Mobility', *American Sociological Review*, vol. 47, pp. 457–77.

Tomlinson, A. (ed.) (1990) *Consumption, Identity and Style*, London: Routledge.

Towler, G. and R. Shepherd (1990) 'Development of a Nutritional Knowledge Questionnaire', *Journal of Human Nutrition and Dietetics*. vol. 3, pp. 255–64.

Townley, R. (1969) 'Marketing', in van Stuyvenberg (ed.) (1969).

Tozer, J. and S. Levitt (1983) *Fabric of Society: A Century of People and their Clothes 1770–1870*, London: Laura Ashley.

Tse, K. (1985) *Marks and Spencer: Anatomy of Britain's Most Efficiently Managed Store*, Oxford: Pergamon.

Tuck, M. (1976) *How Do We Choose?*, London: Methuen.

Tullis, F. and W. Hollist (eds) (1986) *Food, the State, and International Political Economy: Dilemmas of Developing Countries*, Lincoln: University of Nebraska Press.

Turner, M. (ed.) (1979) *Nutrition and Lifestyles*, London: BNF.

Turner, M. (ed.) (1980) *Nutrition and Lifestyles*, London: Applied Science Publishers.

Turner, M. (ed.) (1983) *Food and People*, London: John Libbey.

Turner, S. and R. Ingle (eds) (1985) *New Developments in Nutrition Education*, Paris: UNESCO.

Umiker-Sebeok, J. (ed.) (1987) *Marketing and Semiotics: New Directions in the Study of Signs for Sale*, Berlin: Morton de Gruyter.

Uncles, M. and K. Ellis (1989) 'The Buying of Own Label', *European Journal of Marketing*, vol. 23, no. 3, pp. 57–70.

Urry, J. (1990) 'The "Consumption" of Tourism', *Sociology*, vol. 24, no. 1, Feb., pp. 23–35.

Uusitalo, L. and J. Uusitalo (1981) 'Scientific Progress and Research Tradition in Consumer Research', *Advances in Consumer Research*, vol. VIII, pp. 559–63.

Van Alphen, J. (1969) 'Hippolyte Megs', in van Stuyvenberg (ed.) (1969).

Van Raaij, W. *et al.* (1988) 'Introduction to Part II: Consumer Behaviour', in van Raaij *et al.* (eds) (1988).

Van Raaij, W. *et al.* (eds) (1988) *Handbook of Economic Psychology*, Dordrecht: Kluwer Academic Publishers.

Van Stuyvenberg, J. (ed.) (1969) *Margarine: An Economic and Social History, 1869–1969*, Liverpool: Liverpool University Press.

Van Veldhoven, G. (1988) 'Dynamic Aspects of Economic Behaviour: Some Determinants', in van Raaij *et al.* (eds) (1988).

Vatter, H. (1959) 'The Malthusian Model of Income Determination and its Contemporary Relevance', *Canadian Journal of Political Science*, vol. 25, Feb., pp. 60–4, reproduced in Wood (ed.) (1986).

Veblen, T. (1924) *The Theory of the Leisure Class: An Economic Study of Institutions*, London: Allen and Unwin.

Vestergaard, T. and K. Schrøder (1985) *The Language of Advertising*, Oxford: Blackwell.

Wagner, G. (1987) *The Chocolate Conscience*, London: Chatto and Windus.

Waldinger, R. (1985) 'Another Look at the International Ladies' Garment Workers' Union: Women, Industry Structure and Collective Action', in Milkman (ed.) (1985).

Walker, C. (1983) 'Implementing the NACNE Report, the New British Diet', *The Lancet*, Dec. 10, pp. 1354–6.

Walker, C. and G. Cannon (1985) *The Food Scandal: What's Wrong with the British Diet and How to Put It Right*, London: Century.

Waller, W. (1988) 'The Concept of Habit in Economic Analysis', *Journal of Economic Issues*, vol. XXII, no. 1, March, pp. 113–26.

Walton, W. (1986) '"To Triumph Before Feminine Taste": Bourgeois Women's Consumption and Hand Methods of Production in Mid-Nineteenth-Century France', *Business History Review*, vol. 60, no. 4, Winter, pp. 541–63.

Wardle, A. (1990) 'Introduction to the Sociology of Consumption', *Sociology*, vol. 24, no. 1, Feb., pp. 1–4.

Warneryd, K. (1988) 'Economic Psychology as a Field of Study', in van Raaij *et al.* (eds) (1988).

Waslieu, C. (1988) 'Factors Influencing Food Selection in the American Diet', *Advances in Food Research*, vol. 32, pp. 239–69.

Watters, P. (1978) *Coca-Cola: An Illustrated History*, New York: Doubleday and Co.

Weatherill, L. (1986a) 'The Business of Middleman in the English Pottery Trade before 1780', *Business History*, vol. 28, no. 3, July, pp. 51–76.

Weatherill, L. (1986b) *The Growth of the Pottery Industry in England 1660–1815*, New York: Garland Publishing.

Weatherill, L. (1988) *Consumer Behaviour and Material Culture in Britain 1660–1760*, London: Routledge.

Weeks, J. (1981) *Capital and Exploitation*, London: Edward Arnold.

Westbrook, R. and R. Oliver (1981) 'Developing Better Measures of Consumer Satisfaction: Some Preliminary Results', *Advances in Consumer Research*, vol. VIII, pp. 94–9.

Westley, W. and M. Westley (1971) *The Emerging Worker: Equality and Conflict in the Mass Consumption Society*, Montreal: Queen's-McGill University Press.

Whichelow, M. (1988) 'Which Foods Contain Dietary Fibre? The Beliefs of a Random Sample of the British Population', *European Journal of Clinical Nutrition*, vol. 42, pp. 945–51.

White, L. (1988) *Merchants of Death: The American Tobacco Industry*, New York: William Morrow.

Wickens, G. *et al.* (eds) (1989) *New Crops for Food and Industry*, London: Chapman and Hall.

Wilkinson, F. (1983) 'Productive Systems', *Cambridge Journal of Economics*, vol. 7, no. 3/4, Sept., pp. 413–29.

Williamson, J. (1978) *Decoding Advertisements: Ideology and Meaning in Advertising*, London: Marion Boyars.

Williamson, J. (1986) *Consuming Passions: The Dynamics of Popular Culture*, London: Marion Boyars.

Williams, R. (1980) *Problems in Materialism and Culture*, London: New Left Books.

Williams, Rosalind (1982) *Dream Worlds: Mass Consumption in Late Nineteenth Century France*, London: University of California Press.

Williams, Rosalind (1984) 'Review of McKendrick *et al.* (1982)', *Technology and Culture*, vol. 15, pp. 337–9.

Wilson, C. (1973) 'Food Habits: A Selected Annotated Bibliography', *Journal of Nutrition Education*, vol. 5, no. 1, Supplement 1, pp. 39–73.

Wilson, C. (1979) 'Food – Custom and Nurture: An Annotated Bibliography on Sociocultural and Biocultural Aspects of Nutrition', *Journal of Nutrition Education*, vol. 11, no. 4, Supplement 1, pp. 212–263.

Wilson, E. (1985) *Adorned in Dreams*, London: Virago.

Wilson, G. (1989) 'Family Food Systems, Preventive Health and Dietary Change: A Policy to Increase the Health Divide', *Journal of Social Policy*, vol. 18, no. 2, April, pp. 167–85.

Winch, D. (1987) *Malthus*, Oxford: Oxford University Press.

Winship, J. (1980) 'Sexuality for Sale', in Hall *et al.* (eds) (1980).

Winship, J. (1983) '"Options – For the Way You Want to Live Now", Or a Magazine for Superwoman', *Theory, Culture and Society*, vol. 3, no. 1, pp. 44–65.

Winstanley, M. (1983) *The Shopkeeper's World, 1830–1914*, Manchester: Manchester University Press.

Wiseman, M. (1990) 'Government: Where Does Nutrition Policy Come From?', *Proceedings of the Nutrition Society*, vol. 49, pp. 397–401.

Wood, J. (ed.) (1983) *Adam Smith: Critical Assessments*, Beckenham: Croom Helm.

Wood, J. (ed.) (1986) *Thomas Robert Malthus: Critical Assessments*, Beckenham: Croom Helm.

Woodrof, J. (1990) '50 Years of Fruit and Vegetable Processing', *Food Technology*, Feb., pp. 92–5, 101.

Wray, M. (1957) *The Women's Outerwear Industry*, London: Wyman and Sons.

Wright, G. (1980) *Moralism and the Model Home: Domestic Architecture and Cultural Conflict in Chicago, 1873–1913*, Chicago: University of Chicago Press.

Wright, G. (1990) 'Understanding the UK Food Consumer', *Journal of Marketing Management*, vol. 6, no. 2, pp. 77–86.

Wright, L. (1989) 'Objectifying Gender: The Stiletto Heel', in Attfield and Kirkham (eds) (1989).

Wrigley, N. (1987) 'The Concentration of Capital in UK Grocery Retailing', *Environment and Planning A*, vol. 19, pp. 1283–88.

Wrigley, N. (1989) 'The Lure of the USA: Further Reflections on the Internationalisation of British Grocery Retailing Capital', *Environment and Planning A*, vol. 21, pp. 283–288.

Wrigley, N. (1991) 'Is the "Golden Age" of British Grocery Retailing at a Watershed?', *Environment and Planning A*, vol. 23, pp. 1537–44.

Yu, B. (1978) 'The Fashion Industry: A Compromised Technology', Harvard College Honors Thesis.

Yudkin, J. (1986) *Pure, White and Deadly*, London: Viking.

Yudkin, J. and J. McKenzie (eds) (1964) *Changing Food Habits*, London: MacGibbon and Kee.

Zielinski, J. and T. Robertson (1982) 'Consumer Behaviour Theory: Excesses and Limitations', *Advances in Consumer Research*, vol. IX, pp. 8–12.

Zimbalist, A. (ed.) (1979) *Case Studies on the Labor Process*, New York: Monthly Review Press.

Zukin, S. (1988) *Loft Living: Culture and Capital in Urban Change*, London: Radius.

Zukin, S. (1990) 'Socio-Spatial Prototypes of a New Organisation of Consumption: The Role of Real Cultural Capital', *Sociology*, vol. 24, no. 1, Feb., pp. 37–56.

# INDEX